FEMALE AND MALE:

Dimensions of Human Sexuality

FEMALE AND MALE:

Dimensions of Human Sexuality

Elaine C. Pierson, M.D., Ph.D.

(Mrs. Luigi Mastroianni, Jr.)
Student Health Service
University of Pennsylvania

William V. D'Antonio, Ph.D.

University of Connecticut

J. B. Lippincott Company
Philadelphia   New York   Toronto

ISBN 0-397-47294-3 (cloth)

ISBN 0-397-47293-5 (paper)

Library of Congress Catalog Card Number 73-21850

Printed in the United States of America

Library of Congress Cataloging in Publication Data

Pierson, Elaine Catherine.
   Female and male: dimensions of human sexuality.

   Bibliography: p. 329
   1. Sex instruction. 2. Sexual ethics. 3. Hygiene, Sexual.
I. D'Antonio, William V., joint author. II. Title. [DNLM:
1. Sex behavior. 2. Sex education. 3. Sex manual. HQ21
P624f 1974] HQ31.P63 612.6 73-21850
ISBN 0-397-47294-3 (cloth)
ISBN 0-397-47293-5 (pbk.)

Contents

Acknowledgments

The genesis of this book is complex, but it is substantially a reflection of our combined experience in teaching and counseling young people about marriage, the family, and the physical aspects of contraception and sexuality. We are in varying degrees responsible for each chapter, but we also bear responsibility individually for factual accuracy in our respective areas of sociology, physiology, and function.

Since much of the nontechnical material is derived from personal and professional experience, we must acknowledge the essential contributions of our students and patients. We also owe much to our associates, both personal and professional, and most especially to Dr. Michael Gordon, of the University of Connecticut, and to Dr. Luigi Mastroianni, Jr., of the University of Pennsylvania.

We wish to thank Senior Editor A. Richard Heffron and Val Rementer, of J. B. Lippincott Company, for their tactful and judicious editorial counsel. This became vital to our effort when we discovered that our long-time friendship and mutual respect did not assure full immunity to the hazards of female-male co-authoring.

We also wish to thank the following authors, artists, and publishers for giving us permission to reprint material from their publications:

From *Family Design* by Lee Rainwater, © 1964; and from *Tearoom Trade* by Laud Humphreys, © 1970. Reprinted by permission of Aldine Publishing Company.

"Homosexuality: The Contemporary and Christian Concepts," by Tom Driver. Reprinted by permission of the author and his agent, James Brown Associates, Inc. Copyright © 1973 by Tom Driver.

"Abortion and Sexual Caste," by Mary Daly. Reprinted by permission of the author.

From *The New Sexuality* by Eugene Kennedy, © 1972, and from *Looking Back: A Chronicle of Growing Up in the Sixties* by Joyce Maynard, © 1973. Reprinted by permission of Doubleday and Company, Inc.

"What Every Boy Should Know About Sex," by Louise Bates Ames and Joan Ames Chase, *Family Circle*, March 1972. Reprinted by permission of the publisher.

From *Who Shall Live, Report Prepared by the American Friends Service Committee*, © 1960, Ferrar, Straus & Giroux, Inc. 1960.

From *Sexual Latitude: For and Against,* copyright © 1971, Hart Publishing Company, Inc.

"Abortions and Embryology," by William F. Buckley, Jr., © 1973. Reprinted by permission of King Features Syndicate, Inc.

Ellen Miller for Figures 2-1, 2-2, 2-3, 2-4.

"Getting to Know Anyone," by Ralph Keyes; "I am One Man Hurt," by Albert Martin; "On Harry, and Henry and Ike and Mr. Shaw," by M. W. Lear; "Streetfighting Women," by Susan Brownmiller; all © 1973 by The New York Times Company. Reprinted by permission.

"West Point: A Question of Honor," by L. K. Truscott, 4; "The Selling of Sex: A Look through Solemn Sodom," by J. Correy; "Breast-feeding is a Public Growing Trend," by Enid Nemey; "What Code of Values can We Teach our Children Now," by William V. Shannon, all © 1972/73 by The New York Times Company. Reprinted by permission.

From "Female Sexuality: What It Is—and Isn't," by Eleanor Perry. Reprinted by permission of the author.

From *Sexual Bargaining: Power Politics in the American Marriage* © 1972, and from Herbert A. Otto, ed., *The Family in Search of a Future:* Alternate Models for Moderns, © 1970. By permission of Prentice-Hall, Inc., Englewood Cliffs, New Jersey.

"Harry the F from Philly," by Blair Sabol. Reprinted by permission of the author.

From *The Green Hills of Africa* © 1935 by Charles Scribner's Sons, and from *To Have and Have Not,* Copyright 1937, Ernest Hemingway. Reprinted by permission of Charles Scribner's Sons.

"Birth: An Impression," by Jan Seale. Reprinted by permission of the author.

Diagram of "Vulnerable Steps in the Reproductive Process, Male and Female," by Sheldon Segal from "Contraception: A Male Chauvinist Plot?" Reprinted by permission of the artist.

From *Female Sexuality: Its Nature and Conflict* © 1970. Reprinted by permission of the publisher.

Quote by Richard Burton and excerpt from "Teenage Sex: Letting the Pendulum Swing." Reprinted by permission of TIME, The Weekly News Magazine; Copyright Time, Inc.

"Letter to Dear Abby." Reprinted by permission of Abigail Van Buren.

"For a Sad Lady," by Dorothy Parker. Reprinted by permission of Viking Press, Inc.

From "Adultery." Copyright © 1966 by James Dickey. Reprinted from *Poems 1957-1967* by James Dickey, by permission of Wesleyan University Press.

William V. D'Antonio
Storrs, Connecticut

December, 1973

Elaine C. Pierson
(Mrs. Luigi Mastroianni, Jr.)
Haverford, Pennsylvania

December, 1973

"Whoa, not so fast! What happened to the colorful courtship dance?"

· · · · · · · · · Introduction · · · · · · · ·

THE UNIQUE FEATURE of *human* sexuality, its physical and emotional aspects as experienced by a single human being, is its constantly changing nature. The sexuality of an individual human being is so greatly influenced by present and past environment and real and vicarious experiences that its source and ultimate control is correctly placed in the head and not in the genital area.

Human sexuality is such a personal thing that it is difficult for any writer to bring more than her or his own personal views and experiences and, inevitably, biases to any reader. At the same time, it is evident to scientists and physicians that there are aspects of human sexuality that are common to all. We have tried to draw on both the personal and the general to help the reader expand her or his options.

We feel that what has been missing from the current literature is some reasonable source of information for late adolescents, and their parents and teachers, which gives not only some realistic information about what they can reasonably expect from their body, but also explores many of the reasons for the changing sexual scene. Thus we have attempted to avoid the extremes of a "ho-ho" comedy approach to sexuality, or a preoccupation with the minutiae of physiology on the one hand, and a vagueness about mechanics and physiology and constant reminders about morality on the other.

We have many areas of agreement, but of necessity we have written from two different sets of experiences, personal and professional—not only female and male, but also of necessity, we even have different vocabularies, sociological and biological.

Our common ground is that we both believe there is an emotional and physical "magic" involved in human sexual interaction. It is even present to some degree when that interaction has some negative aspects. We do not want to destroy or even distort this magic with too much detailed knowledge; orgasmic ability does not necessarily make a sexually whole human being, nor does it account for an intense attraction to another human being of either sex.

Neither do we wish to belittle the importance of performance; it is an essential part of the whole learning process. We are more concerned that adequate performance not become such a preoccupation that whatever else it means to be a sexual human being in relation to another is excluded, neglected, or downgraded.

Factual knowledge and a sense of responsibility are essential when the five senses begin to respond to stimuli from other human beings outside of one's immediate family. The magic of sexuality may, in fact, be a gestalt of these five senses. Sexual awareness begins with birth and the increasing awareness of the pleasures of *touch, odor, sound,* and *taste.* Early in adolescence, *visual* stimuli, alone, can begin to do pleasurably strange things to one's physiology, e.g., the aching female pelvis, the spontaneous erections in the male. When an increasing intellectual awareness of human sexual drives is combined with lack

1

of experience or information, it can thrust many young people and their parents into a state described by Toffler as "future shock"—"the dizzying disorientation resulting from being thrust in the future too soon"—though he only casually applied the term to sexual activity.

Luck has seemed to be the major factor in helping young people to cope with this "shock" when there has been very little experience and even less information readily available to them. We cannot supply luck, but would like to offer some experience and understanding in the form of sensible, useful information about some questions which have no absolute answers. Knowledge, a form of vicarious experience, does not necessarily provide answers, but it can serve to make the reader more secure in her or his own decisions. When there is a feeling of security, sexuality can evolve at its own pace—nice and easy.

Mistakes are an inevitable part of learning, but this realization does not mean that sexual learning cannot be helpful or that sex cannot be fun; nor does this awareness need to hamper the imagination, but it certainly helps to cushion the "falls" when they happen.

It is widely believed that spontaneity is the most desired state of human interaction. Young people seem to be especially sensitive to this kind of inter-action. We would only say that knowledge and competency in performance can add greatly to the spontaneity of any occasion. The pleasant surprises which spontaneity implies will come also when people find out how good sexual activity can be, different and yet the same, three or even 25 years from now. Indeed, the most pleasant surprises may occur when people discover how good sex-ual activity can continue to be long after spontaneity ceases to be a concern, which may be another way of saying that sex is more in the mind than in the genitals.

Much has been said about the new sexual morality. Some may even take exception to this book as fostering a dangerous permissiveness. We make no bones about the fact that we consider the old morality into which we were indoctrinated as quite inadequate, and less conducive to human development than we believe human beings are capable of.

We still live within the Judeo-Christian tradition, and in many ways the morality that may be discerned in our writing is conservative and traditional in nature. That is, we are indeed going back to the roots of these religious teachings and taking a new look. What we come up with is not so much a new morality as an attempt to reinterpret the moral directives to enrich human life, to assure a greater degree of development for all human beings. The directive to love one's neighbor as much as one's self must mean at a minimum that the social relationship must not be exploitative. Further, it must mean that in sexual relationships, both partners should be concerned as much for the pleasure and development of the other as for themselves. We fail to see that the pro-gression in nonmarital sexual behavior over the past 50 years from necking, to petting, to coitus constitutes a movement from more moral to less moral behavior.

Nor would we want to imply that young people are more successful at loving one another. Perhaps the most that can be said is that they are often more honest with one another. We hope to show that the process by which our sexuality becomes a part of the love relationship between human beings is just that, a *process* and only a *part*. For too long we have fostered the myth that the seat of human love lies in our sexuality.

The experience of history reveals: a) the extent to which sexual expression has always taken place outside of the marriage context, b) the extent to which sexual expression in marriage has focused more on the reduction of male tension and childbearing than on love, and c) that indeed sexuality could be an important aspect of the love relationship, in or out of marriage.

We live in an age in which the fairy tales of our youth don't seem to help us much in getting on with our adult lives. Thus, the ending, "they got married and lived happily ever after," not only doesn't correspond with the facts of modern married life in the United States—or elsewhere—but it may, in fact, be a very important reason why many young people are unable to make a go of marriage and family. There is a hidden assumption in the old fairy tale myth, that with marriage comes happiness. Marriage in this view is a steady state between a male and a female whose sexuality and sex role identification are known to each other, are unchanging, and thus bring happiness.

And then there was the student who said that he had a friend "who used to 'get more' before he got married than he is getting now." In part this book hopes to explain why he did and why he doesn't now. Or, why she did and doesn't now. We will examine the nature of female and male relationships which helped create men who think of their wives in terms of "how much they are getting" in comparison with what they got from other females in premarital days. With the questioning of traditional views on sexual prerogatives has come a gradual understanding of the fact that human beings are the only creatures on this earth whose sexual and social destiny is not predetermined for them by the mere fact of birth. Male failure to understand this fact may make it difficult, if not impossible, for them to see their wives as more than objects of their (male) sexual needs. As for women, they may be uneasy and unhappy, but also uncertain about who they are, can be, or should want to be. And what does "getting" mean for them?

But before most young people will be ready to accept the idea that they are in some significant way able to write the scripts for their life styles, they must develop a better understanding of the relationship between their own biology and human environment. In Chapter 1 we make our case. The reader may then ask, but how does it come about that we have reached the present stage of impasse, confusion, male dominance, and the rest if there is no necessary reason for it in biology? Isn't female subordination proof enough that there must be something significant to male-female differences besides the shape of the breasts and the genitalia?

A full response to the charge that nature makes destiny is not possible without at least a brief discussion of historical and cross-cultural materials. The ancient Greeks, Romans, and Hebrews shared the conviction that woman's place was below that of man's, sexually and otherwise. The Christians added a lot of new wrinkles, raising the status of women through the veneration of Mary as virgin and mother, pure and undefiled, and downgrading sexual activity and marriage through the image of Eve as the opposite of Mary. The contemporary scene owes much that is good and much that is bad to history.

A brief look at the way non-Western societies have handled the problems of sexual gratification, division of labor, and marriage will also help to refute the idea that the central concern of marriage, or of sexual activity in general, is that men "get their due."

Having covered the major issues of who we are and who we can be, we can turn our attention to sexual interaction itself for more careful and detailed analysis. It will be our purpose to show the several ways in which sexual intercourse has been and continues to be used by females and males. Central to this discussion will be an examination of the changing meaning of intercourse, and of the changing consequences for marriage and other relationships. One of the most significant consequences of sexual intercourse continues to be reproduction of the species. We will discuss in depth not only the physiology of reproduction, but also the methods of prevention of reproduction, from the pill, to abortion, to sterilization.

Adolescence is undoubtedly a greater physical and emotional change of life than menopause or, when it exists, male climacteric; this is partly because there has not been enough living experience to handle the wide variety of changes that occur. The physiological and emotional changes of the midforties and fifties are cushioned by comparative life experience. While lack of experience, naivete, and unawareness of potential problems sometimes help in difficult situations (they allow an ingenuous approach which might be just the right approach), it is also true that a little factual knowledge or simply knowledge that there are no facts can also help in understanding what is going on in adolescence.

We will examine the physical aspects of adolescence and show how social and psychological factors define how we feel and what we do about the physical. For the fact is that adolescence is not a problem in all societies. Physiological changes occur universally, but in some societies they simply mark the social change from girl to woman, boy to man. This is not so in the United States and most other Western societies. Adolescence is a problem for us precisely because we do not have clearly marked roles for these growing people to play. Rather, we have been developing roles in which we emphasize the meaning of these physiological changes; in fact, we give a variety of meanings to them. At the same time, as a result of improving nutritional standards, we have been extending this period of time because the changes begin earlier than they did 50 years ago; and in the process of attaching special cultural and social meanings to adolescence, we have lengthened it. Adult status is not fully achieved until a young woman gets married and a young man gets a job. For college youth, this may mean age 21 or 22, or even later.

In American society especially, adolescence is important as the time when young people learn about the other sex, and through dating prepare for marriage. But since this time is now so long, and since marriage has lost many of the functions which used to characterize it, premarital sexual behavior has taken on new meanings and new patterns. These we will examine in some detail.

Where does all the premarital play get one? For the most part, married! The question is not whether or not to marry, but what kind of contractual arrangement does one come to?

This raises a key question: To what extent does contemporary family structure in the United States and elsewhere contribute to the fulfillment of the sexual potential of the family members, and indeed, in an indirect way, to the fulfillment of the members of the larger society?

If the traditional institutional form of marriage is now under scrutiny, criticism, and at least some change, it must be remembered that most of those over 40 were brought up on the traditional form, and, given the limits of their education, and the strengths of the many ethnic, racial, religious, and social class ties which bind them, they may not be expected to be very enthusiastic about challenges to the type of marriage which they believe has almost sacred qualities not subject to scrutiny.

Perhaps then one of the most important factors which we must keep in mind is that there are now so many millions of families alive and intact, and representing such divergent life-styles that we may be able to do no more than point out some of the trends, while being aware that no trend is likely to become dominant. Several modes may be all that we have a right to expect, or should be concerned with in this book.

We may anticipate the paradox that we will have increasing tolerance on the one hand and continuing backlash on the other, for example, the abortion issue today. The next 30 years will be no easier in matters of sexual encounter, marriage, family, childbearing, and child rearing than they will be in other areas of human social life.

If we acknowledge that the most important commandment for our guidance remains that "we should love our neighbor as we love ourselves . . .", we may then reexamine our human social institutions to ascertain the degree to which, as presently structured, they do or do not foster this love. Have we chosen adequate means to seek this noble goal?

There would be no need for this book if there were not a widely shared belief that traditional family with its roles for women, men, and children is not adequate to the times we live in. In our own experience we find ourselves at midlife among those who were brought up on the old traditions, yet willing and, to some degree, able to see that these no longer suffice; at the same time we are not ready to throw off all the old, because we have found satisfaction in many of them, and we know many others who have also, and who freely and happily choose to retain much of the old while enjoying new options not dreamed of by their parents, to say nothing of their grandparents.

Where are we now? Premarital chastity seems clearly an alternative rather than a requirement for both female and male. The importance of chastity or lack of chastity seems to lie less in the innate drives that supposedly begin with puberty, than it does with the cultural values which undergird any society at any given time. Along with its restraints, the puritan ethic fostered the development of a strong work achievement drive in American society. As we leave that ethic with its restrictions and its individual encouragements, we would do well to assess the costs as well as the benefits to the system and to its members.

VIEWPOINT

Intimacy is a declining national resource. We don't grow up together as we once did, and we change addresses so often that really knowing another person, and being known, is nearly impossible.

Intimacy is a hard notion to pin down. Like a good orgasm, we know it when we feel it but find that feeling difficult to put into words. The best definition I know of is by C. A. Alexander, an architect and planner, who calls intimate contact "that close contact between two individuals in which they reveal themselves in all their weakness, without fear."

Such a relationship is rare to nonexistent for increasing numbers of us. We move on so readily, and guard our privacy so jealously, that sustained human contact becomes almost impossible. Yet our thirst for intimacy remains, so we seek the means to get close quickly with someone we've just met. Sex is an increasingly popular means . . . [and] is contributing to a profound shift in our sexual customs. Sex, in or out of marriage, generally has ratified an intimacy achieved elsewhere. Now the process is reversed, and the act of intercourse itself becomes a means for getting close. A psychiatrist recently defended casual intercourse by pointing out that people relate more freely once the barrier of sex is out of the way.

This seems a reasonable insight. It's certainly more difficult to keep up other masks once you've taken off your clothes. No matter how casual, sharing the act of sex builds some kind of bond between consenting parties, if only because so much trauma usually goes along with intercourse that the shared experience can be as binding as fighting a flood or surviving a war.

Except: such intimacy is handily disposable, as durable as an emptied beer can. . . . [It] can be achieved seriatim, in encounters which may be deep, but are rarely lasting.

This sexual style is consistent with our other emerging forms of intimacy. As we grow even more ingenious at seeking closeness without entrapment, handy disposable intimacy becomes the norm. A weekend's love can be found at an encounter group, on a single's cruise, or within the "family" of a rock festival. Participatory theater builds community for an evening. A joint passed along the waiting line beforehand bonds that group for minutes.

From Ralph Keyes, "Getting to Know Anyone,"
The New York Times,
4 August 1973, p. C23.

1

· · · · · · · · Female and Male: · · · · · · · ·
He Created Them

IT WAS COMMONPLACE a generation and more ago to affirm that "biology is destiny." And the meaning of the statement was clear to everyone: males were meant to be husbands, fathers, and breadwinners; females were meant to be wives, mothers, and caretakers of the house. This was the natural and proper order of things.

Males were stronger and superior, females weaker and inferior. In fact, this wisdom was supported by the belief that the proper and natural position for sexual intercourse was male on top. Those who didn't believe or practice this "commonplace of wisdom," kept quiet about their deviant behavior.

In the 1970s, it seems more accurate to say that males and females are the only creatures on this earth whose destinies are not determined by biology. Influenced by, yes, but not determined. We seem to be on the verge of a new era, but the patterns are not yet clear. Many males and females, struggle to maintain the status quo, to insist on the old aphorism that biology makes destiny. They are supported on television by Archie Bunker of "All in the Family" fame. At another extreme, many, mostly female, want to deny that biology and destiny are in any way related for the human species. Thus they argue that there are no significant differences between male and female, anybody can play any social role, and heterosexual sex may be a sign of continuing oppression of females by males.

There is also a large and increasing number of females and males who are certain only that biology, culture, and social organization are together responsible for the development of male and female roles. We don't yet know precisely how they have mixed, or can and will mix in the future, but we would prefer to keep an open mind on the subject as we examine the evidence from whatever sources. In this chapter, we will examine in particular the most recent evidence from biology, and try to explore the implications of this evidence for female and male behavior now and in the years ahead.

Catching up on Biology

The most recent research on the nature-nurture dilemma includes the following: evidence for generic predispositions is found in the fact that almost everywhere the mother is the principal caretaker of the child, and the male dominates and is aggressive. Males also act to protect females and the young. And there is evidence that babies exhibit behavioral sex differences long before they could possibly be aware of their sexual nature in any conscious sense, or know with which parent they are supposed to identify sexually.[1] At the same time, parents identify their newborn infant immediately by its sex gender, label the infant with a sex-linked name, clothe it in sex-linked clothes, and in a variety of ways so subtle most parents are not even aware of them, prepare their newborn to see herself or himself.

A more obvious example of early imposed gender identification is the father who said: "I promised myself if I ever had a son, I would start him on an exercise program right away." His 15-month-old son does five pushups and lifts a 15 lb. barbell in a regular exercise program which began the day he came home from the hospital. The family also has four older daughters.[2]

In addition to the more obvious anatomical differences, scientists have reported that: the heart of the female often beats faster than that of the male; girls develop more rapidly than do boys; there may even be sex differences in the brain, caused by different hormonal distributions. If so, such differences might lend themselves to different responses by females and males to the same stimuli. Girls respond more quickly and more strongly to the sight of faces, to touch and to pain, and perhaps more deeply to face-to-face interaction. It is still an open question whether these differences are biologically rather than culturally determined. We do know that society positively sanctions them. These differences may be real enough, but how significant are they and in what social situations?

Some people acknowledge the biological differences in genitalia, sex hormones, and childbearing and nursing capacity. But they don't see these as determining any innate male or female behaviors or role-playing abilities. Other evidence suggests that the effective presence or absence of androgen in the brain during precritical fetal life has important psychological consequences for the femaleness or maleness of the brain throughout life.[3]

More certain than the above differences are the differentials in male-female mortality rates at the conceptus-fetal stages of development. The ratio of male to female conceptions is estimated at 160 to 100. However, by the time of birth, the male-female ratio of live births is almost equal. The XY chromosome combination produces a male, but this combination also appears to weaken the human structure, thus making it more vulnerable to malfunctioning than that of the female XX combination. As a result, it is more difficult to produce and maintain a healthy male than a healthy female, and male muscular strength is offset by biological weakness.

On the other hand, males are taller, with heavier bones and muscles than females. The fact of other differences in bone and muscle structure makes it possible for males and females to behave differently. Some biologists hypothesize that natural selection has worked over time to produce males who are physically powerful, aggressive, and able and interested in being protective. At the same time, it may have favored females who are well suited to infant care, nurture, and the home. In an agricultural, nontechnological, nonindustrialized world these differences are essential for survival. But today, even if the biological differences are real, their functional utility for survival may be at an end. So we should not be afraid to recognize the differences from the past, but also to point out that they may not be significant today.

Furthermore, pure body differences mean, if nothing else, that an individual grows up in an individual body, and the physiological happenings of that body, plus how that body sees itself and others, all affect growing up and possibly behavior. But is the matter of how we feel about ourselves resolved by biological phenomena, or by how others think and feel about us? And are their thoughts and feelings determined by biology or by culture and social structure?

It would seem as unwise to try to prove female superiority by the fact that females live longer as to prove male superiority by the fact that males have stronger muscles. Indeed, increasingly, we must wonder about the use of words like inferiority and superiority to describe comparisons between males and females.

On the Matter of Origins

Until recently, the information available to us regarding the origins of female and male was limited to what we could learn and interpret from religious legends. It is interesting to note in the Judeo-Christian tradition that God made all other creatures of the world apparently without any sexual precedence. In the creation of human beings, those of our generation learned what all previous generations had learned, namely that God created Adam, and then created Eve out of one of Adam's ribs. Since God could have "managed" any way *He* wanted, there must have been a point to the story. And of course, the point was that females were supposed to be subordinate to and, in crucial ways, lesser than males.

A similar thrust is found in the ancient Sanskrit legend in which Twashtri created man and then found that *he* had no substantial elements left for the creation of woman.[4] When he finally created her out of a blend of leftovers, he gave her to man. The account also informs us that this woman was not a simple, obedient, and passive creature. She had a distinctive, if perverse, personality; and as in the case of the story of Adam and Eve, her personality was seen from a male perspective, not from her own.

The concept of male supremacy is also found deeply embedded in the mentality of the Islamic peoples who follow the Moslem religious traditions. Their holy book, the Koran, makes it clear that men are superior to women by God's choice, and that a good woman is one who is obedient to her husband or father as the case may be. The Koran carries male superiority to the point of encouraging or at least permitting males to marry two, three, or four women who seem good to them, as long as they can maintain equality among them.* The judgment of history suggests that they may have managed both plural marriage and intrasexual equality, but they have left contemporary Moslems without patterns for ready adaptation to urban, industrial life.

Tradition in the Perspective of Biology

Biology itself has not been without some responsibility in helping to foster and maintain traditional beliefs about human nature and its proper functioning. And while we can never know how many people were influenced directly or indirectly by earlier theories, it seems important to review them here, since it seems clear that their influence has been pervasive, at least among intellectuals and those treating physical and mental disorders. Until recently, it was an accepted part of biological theory that anatomical sexuality was determined at the time of conception. Thus, even though the early embryo could not be identified as male or female from external observation, the embryo was believed to be either male or female from the moment of conception. Freud developed important aspects of his psychoanalytic theory based upon this proposition of innate sexuality, which we now know is incomplete.

Because Freud has had such a profound influence on Western thought during the past 50 years, especially as related to sexuality, it is appropriate to review his theory here in the light of recent criticism.

Among his most vocal critics is Dr. Mary Jane Sherfey, a psychiatrist who has engaged in extensive biological research, and who has written a book which challenges Freudian theory and at the same time puts forth her own theory of sexuality. We will review her work here because it affords us a concise way to consider the issues surrounding human sexuality.

The key points of Freud's theory as noted by Sherfey are[5]:

1. . . . male and female structures evolve unequally with one or the other dominating. Hence everyone remains bisexual to some degree.

2. The clitoris is the homologue of the penis . . .; it becomes rudimentary and continues to function throughout infancy and childhood with a functioning precisely like that of the phallus (penis), relative to size. Like the phallus, the clitoris is readily available to stimulation during childhood; the vagina is not. Therefore, the clitoris is a small phallus which easily lends itself to participation in the total identification processes and body-image formation occurring during development and to all the prelogical thinking of which a little girl's imagination is capable. From here, Freud proceeded to his well-known

---

* In fact, the obligation of equality has narrowly limited polygyny in present-day Moslem society.

theories of female infantile sexuality, all of which follow logically, given these basic premises. In short, because the girl has a masculine homologue that is the primary source of sexual stimulation during childhood, she will necessarily have more difficulties with her innate bisexuality than the boy who has no comparable functioning feminine homologue.

3. The vagina is a singularly female possession (which) would not have even a vestigial counterpart in the male.

4. The vagina must be a second erotogenic zone supplied to females because:

a. Vaginal sensations are practically absent in childhood, while clitoral sensations are patently present. Vaginal sensations normally begin in adulthood with the first coitus, or soon thereafter, and are experienced only during the sexual act.

b. Women with vaginal orgasms unanimously report that the orgasmic sensations begin inside the vagina as the result of penile friction against the vaginal walls. At the same time clitoral eroticism seems to recede, and with some women to disappear altogether.

c. Clitoral activity and vaginal eroticism are different, the former fostering active masculinelike behavior, and satisfaction independent of a relationship with a male. Vaginal eroticism is passive and receptive and dependent on male penile activity for its expression.

d. In female homosexuals especially, vaginal orgasm is lacking, but clitoral eroticism is retained. This pattern holds generally for women with disturbed relationships with men.

These are the propositions upon which Freud built his theory of female sexuality. He concluded that the fundamental problem for woman to achieve her proper mature sexual identity was to transfer her erotogenic center from the clitoris to the vagina. Only in this way could she overcome the dual nature of her sexuality, the masculine, aggressive pleasure-seeking tendencies that were associated with the clitoral (penile) erotogenic zone, and achieve the proper passive, receptive eroticism of vaginal orgasm. As Sherfey says: "Thus it is that psychoanalytic theory has led us through a series of perfectly logical steps to a position which is in essence, anachronistic: a scientific restatement of the Eve-out-of-Adam myth."[6]

The fault lies, as Sherfey points out, not so much in psychoanalytic theory, as in the information about human sexuality supplied to psychiatry by biology. But now a new theory of sexual differentiation has evolved from recent work in comparative embryology. The data are so new that Sherfey's work itself is a pioneer effort to rethink psychosexual theory. In brief, she argues that the most fundamental fact is that the early embryo is neither undifferentiated nor innately bisexual; "(it) is a female. In the beginning, we were all created females; and if this were not so, we would not be here at all."[7] For those brought up on the Adam and Eve myth, or any of the other accounts of male dominance, this is a powerful and challenging statement indeed.[8] She explains it as follows:

1. At the moment of fertilization, genetic sex is established. But in humans the influence of the sex genes upon the embryo does not make itself felt until the fifth or sixth week of life.

2. "During those first weeks, all embryos are morphologically females."

3. "If the fetal gonads are removed (from the embryo) before differentiation occurs, the embryo will develop into a normal female, lacking only ovaries, regardless of the genetic sex."[9]*

Point No. 3 seems to be at the heart of the matter. "In the development of the embryo, nature's first choice or primal impulse is to differentiate a female. The anlagen of the sex organs when they first appear are identical for both sexes. The principle of differentiation is always that to obtain a male, something must be added. Subtract that something and the result will be a female."[10] In the case of females, even if the gonads are removed before the seventh week, thereby preventing the production of estrogen hormones, which are crucial for female development as opposed to androgens which are the male hormones, the "embryo will still develop normal female anatomy. . . . Female differentiation results from the innate, genetically determined female morphology of all mammalian embryos."[11] Consequently, in the absence of the proper product, the male hormone androgen, the human embryo will develop as a female. Sherfey puts it more boldly by stating that "male development can be considered as a deviation from the basic female pattern."[12] This so-called deviation is completed by the end of the third month of growth; thus it would seem that biology now presents us with a new myth, that of Adam-out-of-Eve.†

The most immediate conclusion regarding psychoanalytic theory is the need to rethink the clitoris-vagina propositions. Thus, in Freudian theory, and in much traditional thinking, women were thought to be suffering pathologically if they sought sexual satisfaction through stimulation of the clitoris. Since the clitoris was a leftover organ, they were striving to be like men if they sought such sexual satisfaction. But recent biological research forces us to rethink our ideas about males and females, about human sexuality, about our self-images, and about how we think of others. For example, "penis envy" is only gradually disappearing as a derogatory comment.

---

* We may question how normal it is to think of females as lacking ovaries. It is more accurate to say that the removal of the gonads during the first six weeks of life results in *something* other than a complete biological female.

† Sherfey's critics are quick to point out that she acknowledges but then ignores the fact that genetic sex is established at conception, and overstates what would or does happen if the androgen hormones are not produced during the fifth and sixth weeks of life. In fact, we may ask what it means to say the early embryo is structurally female, if the embryo containing the male chromosome cannot possibly develop into a female with ovaries. Sherfey plays on the word "normal" in saying that the embryo would develop into a normal female without the presence of the androgen hormone.

Freud's theory of "penis envy," attributed by him, his disciples and his blind followers to females in any age group, is a vastly overrated envy, if it exists at all. A mistaken diagnosis is frequently made in very young girls when they evidence the normal behavior of all young children to have something that someone else has: dolls, toys, penises. Parents often reassure their little girls by telling them that they have a "special place," or a vagina, or if they are really being accurate, a clitoris. These efforts to make up for what little girls think they lack have very little meaning, if they cannot see either the special place or the clitoris, even if described clearly as to size and location. Bigger is always better at this young age and the three-year-old penis will always win over the miniscule clitoris. Mothers' breasts probably define femaleness and growing up better than equating penises with the hidden vagina or clitoris. Penises and breasts both increase in size with growing up; these are visual realities in most homes and define adult male and female anatomy. Using this analogy, no one lacks anything but size at age two-and-one-half or three.

The mistaken diagnosis of "penis envy" in older females has always been associated with any evidence of success or ambition beyond home and family. It may seem unbelievable, but its greatest effect during the thirties, forties, and fifties was the limitation it put on bright, capable women who did not feel secure enough to direct their energies to success in other fields and risk the "behind the back" comments. These women were left behind and are only now emerging in their late thirties and forties. It had little effect on those who wanted to stay out of home and family for a while, though it was sometimes difficult to muster amusement when presented with "penis envy" on a slip of paper in a game of charades (the game of the forties and fifties). Marya Mannes suggests that not all girls suffered this envy:

> One thing was sure, after this revelation (her slightly older brother showed her his penis and scrotum in an educational session when she was eleven so that she would know what boys were like) I had absolutely no desire, no desire at all, to have something like that swinging between my legs. It was much neater without it.[13]

The Masters and Johnson Findings

The theory of the vaginal orgasm as the only proper form of sexual response in women first came under question through the research findings of Kinsey who concluded that the vaginal orgasm as an independent sexual phenomenon was an impossibility.[14] But it has been left to the more recent research of Masters and Johnson to clarify and explain the relationship between clitoral and vaginal eroticism.

In simplest terms, it appears that:

    a. The lower third of the vagina becomes an erotogenic zone during intercourse;

b. No part of the vagina itself produces the orgasm that a woman may have;

c. The actual sensation of vaginal orgasm occurs through the contractions of muscles that are outside of the vagina and which act upon the vaginal membranes;

d. The erotogenic zone of the lower third of the vagina is not separate from but an integral part of a single structural erotic unit with its primary base in the clitoris.

e. There is simply no evidence that vaginal orgasm can be achieved by vaginal stimulation alone.

f. Much more research is needed before we can fully understand the adult functioning of vaginal eroticism.[15]

On the Comparative Capacity for Orgasm

Among the myths being dispelled by recent research is the one which suggests that males have a greater natural capacity for orgasm than females, and that those females who exhibit an inordinate interest in sexual activity are somehow abnormal. The works of Masters and Johnson and their predecessors have led to the gradual recognition that multiple orgasms for women may well be the norm and that a woman so desiring can readily achieve from three to five orgasms in a normal period of sexual activity. In fact, it seems theoretically possible for her to achieve from 20 to 50, depending on the point at which sheer physical exhaustion may be reached, within a given short time period. It is *not even possible* for males to think in these terms for themselves. But the theoretically possible does not mean that such is necessary for females to achieve satisfaction in their sexual lives. In order to avoid an overemphasis on the purely biological potential, we must not isolate it from sociocultural realities. It is on this point that Sherfey seems most clearly to have extended her theories well beyond science toward the ideology of biology makes destiny, for she writes about the potential for multiple orgasms in females as if this was a biologically determined necessity of the good, normal life.

But in fact, all Masters and Johnson demonstrated was that women were capable of many orgasms, not that they needed them to be happy, or to be fulfilled. In fact, we have on more than one occasion listened to Masters and Johnson discuss the importance of the relational or love aspect in human female sexual response. In addition, the research done by McDermott in Great Britain cited later in this chapter, as well as that of Fisher, shows that at least at the conscious level many women are satisfied by a single orgasm. Given the still very limited state of our knowledge of the interrelationship of biology and sociocultural factors, we would do well to avoid new biologisms even as we try to free ourselves from the old ones.

Very few people today suggest that women seek to maximize their fecundity. Yet we know that women are capable of bearing 10 to 25 children in their procreative years. Rather, we consider socio-economic-cultural factors of such overriding importance that we are currently embarked on a population control campaign which minimizes the procreative potential of most women. And the evidence to date suggests that women feel fulfilled or not depending on socio-economic-cultural factors, and not simply on biology.

The Meaning of Biology: A Summary

Recent biological research has provided the basis for the restructuring of our ideas about males and females, their sexual and their social nature. First, the evidence calls into question traditional beliefs about male dominance deriving from the creation of the male first and the female out of the male. We now have evidence that human embryos at conception are anatomically female for the first six weeks of life, regardless of their actual genetic composition. That is, whether they are destined to be female or male, they begin structurally as female. And only through the action of specific hormones does the male embryo eventually develop between the sixth and twelfth weeks.

Second, and of greater importance, is the discovery that the focal point of female sexual pleasure lies in a single structural unit formed by the clitoris, the skin folds known as the labia, and the lower third of the vagina; thus, the vagina itself is not a separate erotogenic area.

Third, while women are generally slower to sexual arousal than men, and can be "turned off" more readily than men at any point in sexual activity, their capacity for orgasm is at least as great as that of any man, and probably greater.

Males achieve sexual maturity in their late teens and early twenties, while females achieve their sexual maturity in their late twenties and early thirties.

But what does all this mean for the roles which males and females are able to, desirous of, and willing to play in contemporary society? And what does it mean in terms of the ways that males and females can and should or must or should not relate to each other? To achieve what kind of society? To achieve what kind of personal goals? And what does it mean for the average young female and male who simply want to get on in this world without major conflicts, and who couldn't care less about the fact that all early embryos are anatomically female? Let us examine the question from both the personal and social points of view.

Personal Considerations: Female

Throughout most of the world, including the United States, the images which women have of themselves are pretty much derived from traditional beliefs and a smattering of Freudian theory. These beliefs have portrayed the ideal woman as passive, submissive, and obedient to males who are her natural superiors in all things sexual, social, and individual. Her proper function has been seen to be that of mother and housewife, doing her duty to insure the survival and development of the species. This way of life was said to be ordained by God as set down in religious precepts, and seemed to be supported by commonsense observations of the biological differences between males and females.

But now we know differently! Religious and related traditional beliefs are in a state of flux; biblical scholars have been reinterpreting the ancient books of the Bible and are offering new interpretations which do not lend themselves to literal belief in the Adam and Eve story. And physical scientists have now shown us how erroneous our earlier commonsense observations were. Freudian theory must be restructured not only in the light of the findings of biology, but also in the light of findings from the social sciences. There are two levels of consideration here—one theoretical and one purely practical.

The theoretical issue affects most directly the work of science and of disciplines which purport to develop theories about human behavior. Psychiatrists trying to comprehend female behavioral disorders can no longer proceed on the assumption that the problem is somehow focused on a misplaced fixation on the clitoris. Nor can they assert that deriving from that fixation, a woman to be herself must learn to be a passive receiver of male sexuality, to be properly rewarded for her submissiveness with a vaginal orgasm. Perhaps of greater importance is the recognition that female or male behavioral disorders may tell us little about what ought to be the normal state of things with males and females. The data from biology, only briefly sketched here, strongly urge that we go back to the drawing board in our attempt to develop a theory of male and female sexuality.

Religious scholars of all faiths must now confront not only their own new findings and understandings of what the early scriptures might mean, but also the fact that they can ignore only at their own peril the findings of biology as they redefine their own theories of human sexuality.

Meanwhile, an increasing number of people are becoming more and more curious about their sexual selves and trying to relate their daily life experiences to what the scholars and novelists claim to know. Thus, you the reader may ask, what are the implications of all this for me? This brings us to practical considerations. Let us consider some of the more obvious ones:

1. There seems now no basis whatsoever for the stigma of "inferiority" which has long been attached to the status of being female.

2. For those who so desire, the data lend full support to a female self-image of a fully-sexed person capable of great sexual responsiveness.

3. There is available now a large amount of basic information about sexual arousal, sexual responsiveness, and the erotogenic zones to help females to achieve their human sexual potential.

4. Rather than limiting and restricting female sexual responsiveness, pregnancy, childbirth, and infant care may in fact enhance and enrich it, as women become comfortable with their physical selves.

5. Female sexual responsiveness is potentially greater than that of the male; the question may even be raised as to how females are to insure that they will be allowed an adequate expression of their sexuality. Given the higher rates of male mortality and the fact that currently in the United States there are between 5 and 10 million more females than males, how will females insure adequate sexual expression for themselves? If it is not good for man to be alone, it is no better for woman. Will bisexuality become a more widely accepted option for women who cannot find adequate sexual expression otherwise? Suffice to say here that the practical implications for women involve practical implications for men as well.

Personal Considerations: Male

The practical implications of new findings in biology, of the challenge to traditional beliefs in religion and all other social spheres, promise to reshape human male behavior no less completely than that of females. For those who dare to acknowledge the findings, the more obvious implications include the following:

1. The most powerful implication is the challenge to the idea of male supremacy. In what way, now, is the male superior? How is his more aggressive behavior to be understood in contemporary society? How is the apparent or real male dominance of the economy to be understood? How has the division of labor been used as a means to strengthen the old theories? Is it not increasingly evident that economic exploitations must cease with a new sexuality?

2. The data reveal that the male is both weaker and stronger than the female. He is physically stronger, but this fact is less and less significant in a technological, computerized world. And he is weaker in that he is more subject to disease and early death, a problem which manifests itself in a surplus of some 5 to 10 million women in the United States.

3. The male rather than being the great lover, now seems threatened by the knowledge that not he, but the female has the greater sexual erotic potential. Will he be able to satisfy a female partner? Will he be prepared to redefine his sexuality vis-à-vis females?

4. Males have traditionally become sexually aroused more easily than females, and have reached orgasm more quickly. But if they are to become satisfactory sexual partners to females who have an increasing awareness of their sexual potential, they will have to change their behavior patterns rather drastically.

5. It seems fair to say that throughout most of human history males have been able to gratify themselves without being concerned about whether their partners were having fun. They cannot count on doing so much longer. Sex for recreation has become a real possibility for females also, now that sex and procreation can be separate events.

At the same time, males who are becoming secure, who are sensitive to the needs of their female partners, can find much comfort in this new information. They can look forward to an enriched sex life, their male sexuality enhanced by mutual consideration. And they can look forward to a new divison of labor, which may liberate them as well as it may liberate females. We shall give more attention to these possibilities in later chapters.

Social Considerations

Socialization

We know ourselves through the eyes of others by means of the process called socialization. The evidence from biology urges that we must rethink this process. More important, at the practical level we can see that we are rethinking what it means to be female or male. The long-hair revolution among males and the broad scale adoption of the blue jeans costume among the young of both sexes reflect and influence how females and males are changing their images. The evidence from biology has much larger implications about the roles we can and will play in society.

Social Structure: Marriage Forms

Recent evidence from biology also forces us to reconsider the meaning of such marriage forms as polyandry and polygyny. Certainly polygyny cannot be understood in terms of the simple maxim that biology is destiny. Polyandry, that is, a wife having more than one husband at the same time, seems more probable in simple biological terms. But in both cases, it seems clear that female sexuality is being ignored, and perhaps male sexuality in a direct biological sense.

In a polygynous marriage, a male may take more than one wife, over a period of considerable time. In most polygynous societies males are permitted to have more than one wife only when they have sufficient wealth to be able to support them, or to possess other desired valuables of the society in such amount as to merit the reward of another wife. The payoff for the female is that she has a husband who is a man of some means. While all of this also implies that the male has sexual prowess, it does not necessarily mean that he has to manifest or prove it. In point of biological fact, of course, males are most able to satisfy themselves with more than one female when they are younger, between the ages of 17 and 25; but they usually don't have wealth and power until they are much older.* Thus it seems that legal polygyny rather than answering any biological urges, is a response to a long-standing sociocultural pattern.

The same is true of polyandry. Those societies which have been known to

---

* We know little about the sexual satisfaction achieved by these females. We would have to assume that they know what is expected of them and behave accordingly.

practice this form of plural marriage have not granted power to the female. On the contrary, the female may or may not enjoy the pleasures of a different husband every night. That seems beside the point, which is that she is meant to serve the needs and pleasures of the male. Polyandry was practiced in societies which were very poor, where living conditions were extremely rigorous. Polyandry may even have been accompanied by female infanticide in order to insure a slow rate of population growth or no growth at all. It certainly insured low birth rates. But it did not focus on female sexuality as a desirable or necessary expression of the human condition. Again, socioeconomic factors rather than biological ones determined the destiny of women in these societies.

Changing Cultural Patterns

We know that values, beliefs, and norms for human behavior vary both within and between societies. It is also commonplace that norms are changing in our own as well as in other societies. While it is an interesting theoretical question whether behavioral changes precede and trigger cultural changes, we may accept the proposition that cultural changes do bring about changes in individual behavior, and more important perhaps, changes in behavior between generations of people.

Thus attitudes about masturbation provide an example of cultural change. The traditional view has been that masturbation was a serious wrongdoing. Even medical doctors supported that norm. The norm is now changing. An increasing number of religious and medical leaders acknowledge that there may be no harm in masturbation, and in fact, that the practice may be helpful or simply pleasurable. If we refrained from the practice before in conformity with the norm and occasionally engage in it now, our behavior may have changed on two levels: 1) we no longer feel guilty about breaking a rule, and 2) we now engage in an activity which we formerly avoided.

On a broader social level, the change may be manifested in the following way. Our generation was trained to see masturbation as wrong and evil; as the norm changes, we may cling to the old belief and norm, but our children may be unaware of the old norm, or given a choice, opt for the new normative orientation. The change occurred because many in our generation challenged it; the children simply accept the new orientation. Thus their actions serve to establish the new norm.

Other norms now changing include those dealing with the double standard and with the expectation that a female should be a virgin at the time of marriage. The male was expected to have had sexual experience before marriage, but with prostitutes since no self-respecting female would become so involved; thus Western culture patterns taught that male sexuality and female sexuality were somehow different.* It was important for a male but not for a female to

---

* The old norm implied that a prostitute was something less than a human being.

have had sexual experience before marriage. These norms and the belief systems that have sustained them have reached their extreme expression in Latin America and the Latin countries of Europe where it was commonplace for the male to engage in extramarital sexual relations. The argument in defense of this pattern was that it was in the nature of the male to be promiscuous. Clearly, this was not so with the female. In a classic argument, a Latin American lawyer asserted that male infidelity carried on discretely outside the home was of no consequence to society, and allowed the male full expression of his sexual being. On the other hand, an unfaithful female threatened the sanctity of the home, and by that fact the very fabric of society. At the same time she was revealing an unnatural proclivity for sexual activity.[16] The same drive which was presumed to be natural in the male revealed an unnatural inclination in the female. We will see how this image is perpetuated, even in current scholarly literature.

What forces buttressed these norms, made them possible in the first place? We can only surmise that their development had something to do with survival value. Given the high mortality rates at all age levels, but especially infant and maternal mortality, and given the constant threats from plagues and famines, woman's biological role as mother became dominant. To survive, the human race needed at least a basic level of male sexual gratification, namely ejaculation in intercourse. Female orgasm was unnecessary. All that was needed from females was their willingness to play the mother role. Over time, religious, political, and economic norms tended to buttress these patterns and give them meaning, value, and sanction. As we will see throughout this book, norms governing female and male sexual behavior before, during, and outside of marriage are changing rapidly. Shifts in belief and attitude are clearly taking place; how great the behavioral changes are is not yet so obvious.

What, then, of the future of monogamous marriage? We used to wonder if males were not by nature polygamous, and many condoned the activities of males on these grounds. Writers are now beginning to ask if perhaps females are not by nature polygamous, or if both males and females are. The reader is cautioned to avoid going from one extreme to another in trying to comprehend the new evidence from biology and changing beliefs, values, and norms, as well as economic changes. We are trying to show that man-made (the words are purposely chosen) sociocultural patterns are responsible for past and current definitions of female and male sexuality, and to suggest that female and male together may remake the patterns in the years ahead.*

---

* We include the economic factor here within the phrase "sociocultural." We believe the division of labor between females and males, early tied so closely to procreation, to be central in the current struggle. Indeed, women may be accorded sexual freedom before their struggle for economic liberation has been achieved. We will explore the interrelation of these two factors at other points in the book.

What is the Depth of the Problem?

We are too often led into wishfully thinking that problems will go away if we ignore them or if we begin to understand them. This is certainly true of the way many people react to the problem of sexuality as well as to more mundane problems. The problem is not yet fully grasped by scholars in the field, to say nothing of the public and its government representatives. The struggle of females at both the Democratic and Republican conventions of 1972 to establish strong platform planks for women was suggestive of its depths. The abortion law repeal debate was even more suggestive. We may say with some degree of assurance that it will be a while yet before laws against prostitution, homosexuality, and abortion are repealed across the country.* Indeed, these are some of the interesting paradoxes among developed countries. In Sweden and Yugoslavia for example, "abortion is legal but vasectomy is not, and in Japan Pills and IUDS are illegal."[17] (The Japanese equivalent of our Food and Drug Administration is still uneasy about the possible side effects of these methods; however both are being used as "research" methods and there is a growing movement among the women for release of the pill for unrestricted use. The side effects of their relatively unrestricted abortion procedures are not in their province.) In some ways China has proceeded further in revising its traditional norms on male and female sexuality than any other major nation of the world.

Sociology Texts

A recent review of contemporary, leading sociology texts on marriage and the family led to the discovery of continued stereotyping of females in four broad categories: "sexual attitudes and behavior; sex roles and socialization; mate selection, marriage and divorce; and the economics of being female."[18] A brief review of some of the main points will help to reveal how deeply our current perceptions of male and female sexuality are rooted in the past.

Sexual attitudes. Text writers continue to rely on outmoded biological information, and to draw heavily on Freudian interpretations of sexuality.

In addition, almost all illustrations are taken from a male rather than from a female or both points of view. Cultural factors are not only acknowledged, but also defended. Thus it is asserted that it may be vital to the continuation of the monogamous system of marriage that some degree of female sexual maladjustment must exist; presumably this may be a satisfactory price to pay for the societal results achieved, that is, maintenance of monogamous marriage.

There is a tendency not merely to repeat that females have a lower interest in sexual matters as reported in studies by Kinsey relating to females vis-à-vis males, but to suggest that the differences are not crucial for the female.

---

* Clearly, the attempt of several states to write new abortion laws shows that the Supreme Court decision of January 1973 on abortion has not settled the issue.

Among the stereotypes sustained in these texts are the following: male and female differences in sex interest, sex drive, capacity for arousal, and capacity for orgasm are biologically linked, with the female clearly less interested and with lesser capacities; sexually aggressive females are somehow deviates, abnormal, and undesirable as marriage partners; and because so many females apparently acquiesce in it, there may be some sound basis for the double standard. Even when authors present evidence which might counter the old myths, they are not consistent. For example, when illustrating sexual maladjustments, they view the problems from male perspectives only. They never refer to the deprived female, only to the deprived male. And they worry that making the cultural changes that would be required to bring about equality in matters of sexuality in monogamous marriage may be too high for the gains. Thus they suggest that if we wish to maintain familial-societal values, females may have to accept some degree of maladjustment as the necessary price.[19]

Sex roles and socialization.   Authors acknowledge the traditional teaching of sex roles to children, and defend them to varying degrees. Ehrlich summarizes their standard arguments in the following words: "1) It [the traditional division of labor] apparently reflects biological differences (to bear and rear children, the woman must stay home; the male is physically stronger); 2) this division of labor in marriage is 'biologically logical and practical'; 3) it is efficient and responsible; 4) it is a primary source of harmony in the marital relation; and 5) therefore directly beneficial to survival and order in the society."[20]

Female capacity to handle jobs traditionally held by males, and male capacity to do housework in an acceptable manner is not denied. What the authors fail to do is to affirm the possibility of changes in sex roles and socialization. Rather subtle bias continues to be shown. For example, one of the text writers acknowledges that many women are as strong, clever, and intelligent as their husbands. But Ehrlich asks how would we receive the reverse statement, "Few fairminded people would question the fact that many men are as strong, intelligent, clever and ambitious as their wives."[21]

Mate selection.   Among the more important images sustained is that males select females. The concern here is not merely that this has been the custom in the past, but it continues to seem the right and proper order of things. Some authors stress the trend toward egalitarian marriage, but worry about the threat to marriage posed by female emancipation and the fact that females are no longer adequately prepared to be housewives. Little is said about the possible need to rethink the whole structure of mate selection and marriage.

Working wives.   The two themes most consistently found are that most females continue to choose the role of housewife over that of worker outside the home, and that to choose to work outside is to threaten the stability of the home. In almost all cases, it is assumed that the female must make all the adjustments, and that marital failure can be attributed to her inability to cope with the demands of both roles. At least one author suggested that a woman's femininity would be in question if she were to reject entirely the mother role for that of a career.

It is interesting to note that some writers pointed out the continuing wage differentials between males and females while others seemed to suggest that all discrimination against females had passed into history.

In summary, a review of six leading sociology texts on marriage and family reveals that much mythology about and stereotyping of female, and by inference male, sex roles and sexual identity continue, even in the face of the changes which have been occurring in the past 15 years.

Popular Magazines

Space will not permit us to review here the ways in which popular magazines are participating in the sexual revolution of our time. We can find traditional stereotyping in advertisements in most popular magazines juxtaposed with articles which attempt to probe seriously the sexual revolution. Magazines continue to advertise automobiles as sex objects, together with females as obvious symbols. And magazines like *Playboy* and *Penthouse* offer at best ambiguous statements about sexuality to modern young people. At their worst, they contribute to the view that the female is the sex object for the male, to be used at his whim, and put aside when more important matters are at hand. There are also many magazines which attempt to tell the story of the new sexual revolution on more or less equal terms.

The Semi-scholarly Work

Another way to illustrate the depth of the problem is to examine the literature which may rightly be called semi-scholarly. That is, the author has done research which has yielded rich data, which he or she then uses in a popular fashion to reach a broad audience. One such example explores the sex lives of some 250 British women through depth interviews.[22] The author tried to obtain answers to the question: What have been your sexual experiences, and how do you evaluate them? For the most part, the respondents focused on their heterosexual behavior; nevertheless, evidence developed of considerable homosexual activity. In their responses, the women gave scant attention to motherhood as part of their significant sexual experience. A number of readily recognizable patterns appear to emerge from this study:

1. Female satisfaction in heterosexual encounter is directly related to the male's sensitivity to female sexual needs.
2. Male orgasm is normally assured in heterosexual acts, but female orgasm is not.
3. A large percentage of males are either insensitive or in fact indifferent to female sexual needs.
4. Even when males care, they may not always be able to help their female partners achieve orgasm.

5. Females were almost unanimous in asserting that they could get satisfaction from sexual acts even if they didn't achieve orgasm—if they loved or felt great affection for or warmth toward their partners.

6. A large but undetermined percentage of the respondents had had a variety of sexual experiences in and out of marriage.

7. A smaller percentage definitely experienced multiple orgasms, with most reporting that three such orgasms were the high point of satisfaction achieved.

8. There was no evidence that females who achieved only a single orgasm in a particular sexual encounter were left unsatisfied. Multiple orgasms were not high on anyone's list of sexual priorities. Satisfaction with one's partner entailed much more than orgasmic response.

9. On the evidence presented, sex with love seemed to produce a higher level of satisfaction than sex without love.

10. But there was no doubt that sex as pleasure *per se* apart from stable relationships and the idea of love, was a reality for many females.

11. Extramarital sexual activity seems to be emerging as an option for those who desire it, as well as continuing as a pattern for the traditional-minded male. Judging by the evidence a small percentage of couples cooperatively engage in extramarital activity, apparently with little long-term effect on their marriages. If jointly agreed upon, it may even present some short-term gains.

12. The vast majority of these females had little or no effective sex education in their youth. Many entered adolescence with negative ideas about sex derived from their parents. Yet most seemed to have made moderately decent adjustments in their sex lives, and to be satisfied.

13. The majority of the females saw sexual sharing as right and natural. That is, they recognized themselves as fully sexed persons, and wanted the joys of sexual activity. At the same time, they seemed less interested in changes in division of labor-sex roles, and in other ways of sharing equally with males in social activity.

14. Premature ejaculation seems to be a characteristic of many males, which makes it difficult if not impossible for females to achieve orgasm.*

We have taken the time to summarize the major findings of McDermott because they are consistent with other studies, with psychiatric reports, personal accounts in popular magazines, and data presented earlier in this chapter and elsewhere in this book. Premature ejaculation as a problem of males is but one topic we will explore in more detail in subsequent chapters.

Summary

We are in the midst of a new era in human sexuality. While we may expect that millions of adults will cling tenaciously to traditional views of females and

---

* There was no evidence that male partners made any attempt to stimulate their women to orgasm by other means.

males, and that millions of their children will be inculcated with these views, the evidence from all sides is that the new era means new ideas about who we are as females and males, who we can be, and how we will relate to each other sexually. The more we learn from biology, the more we come to realize that biology is not destiny. In the ensuing chapters we will attempt to present a clear picture of the physiological, anatomical, biological side of sexuality, and of the sociocultural factors which are providing the new framework for the realization of our sexuality.

VIEWPOINT

Perhaps the subtlest myth of the present time is that which says we are truly a sophisticated and sexually liberated people who have at last walked away from the religious and ethnic scruples about sexuality and into the brightly lit and comfortable fields of sexual freedomland. The core error in this myth is that man's basic problem, his failure to integrate sex into the context of his personality and human relationships—the fact, in other words, that he is plagued by sex without personal meaning and personal referents—cannot be cured by additional amounts of nonintegrated and depersonalized sex, no matter how ecstatically its phrases are sung or its therapeutic effects asserted. There may be some situations in life in which one can apply the idea that you fight fire with fire, or in the language of the man suffering a hangover, to take as a cure an additional dose of the liquor that has made him ill. It does not work that way with sexuality. It is not helped by more sexuality that has been stripped of its interpersonal settings and its profound human values. This myth is inflated when it is made the only concern, or even the most important of many concerns, in a person's life. This many-layered myth, however, is large enough to bear the weight of all the other new distortions. The myth that genital sex equals human sexuality is probably the father of all the myths of the age. Both this and the multiple myths which it tends to support must be inspected more carefully.

From Eugene C. Kennedy,
The New Sexuality (New York: Doubleday and Co., 1972), pp. 27-28.

References

1. For a more detailed discussion of these and related points, see "Male and Female: Differences Between Them," *Time*, 20 March 1972, pp. 43-47.

2. *Philadelphia Evening Bulletin*, 2 April 1973, p. 2.

3. Warren J. Gadpaille, M.D., "Biological Fallacies of Women's Lib," *Hospital Physician* 7 (1971): 36 ff.

4. Stuart A. Queen and Robert W. Habenstein, *The Family in Various Cultures* (Philadelphia: J. B. Lippincott Company, 1967), pp. 1-2.

5. Mary Jane Sherfey, *The Nature and Evolution of Female Sexuality* (New York: Random House, 1972), pp. 30 ff.

6. *Ibid.*, p. 34.

7. *Ibid.*, p. 38.

8. For another detailed statement of this embryological theory see John Money and Anke A. Ehrhardt, *Man and Woman, Boy and Girl: Differentiation and Dimorphism of Gender Identity* (Baltimore and London: Johns Hopkins University Press, 1972).

9. Sherfey, *Nature and Evolution of Female Sexuality*, p. 39.

10. John Money, "Sexual Dimorphism and Homosexual Gender Identity," NIMH Task Force on Homosexuality, Final Report and Background Papers #1724-0244 (Washington, D. C.: U. S. Government Printing Office, 1972), p. 44.

11. Sherfey, *Nature and Evolution of Female Sexuality*, p. 39.

12. *Ibid.*, p. 46.

13. Marya Mannes, *Out of My Time* (Garden City, New York: Doubleday and Company, 1971).

14. See Alfred C. Kinsey, et al., *Sexual Behavior in the Human Female* (Philadelphia: W. B. Saunders Company, 1953).

15. See William H. Masters and Virginia Johnson, *Human Sexual Response,* (Boston: Little, Brown and Co., 1966). The authors have also participated in conferences with Masters and Johnson and discussed these ideas personally with them.

16. See William V. D'Antonio, "The Problem of Population Growth in Latin America," in F. B. Pike, ed., *Latin American History: Select Problems* (New York: Harcourt, Brace Javanovich, 1969), pp. 440-482.

17. *IPPF Medical Bulletin* 6, 3 (June 1972):1.

18. Carol Ehrlich, "The Male Sociologist's Burden: The Place of Women in Marriage and Family Texts," *Journal of Marriage and the Family* (August 1971): 421-430.

19. *Ibid.*, p. 423.

20. *Ibid.*, p. 426.

21. *Ibid.*, p. 426.

22. See Sandra McDermott, *Female Sexuality* (New York: Simon & Schuster, Inc., 1971).

2

Anatomy and Physiology,
Function and Dysfunction

When the time comes that diagrams and descriptions of the normal function of these universal organs are as generally accessible and as much taken for granted as are pictures of other life processes, we shall doubtless wonder at our artificially fostered mystifications and many of our elaborately manufactured attitudes of shame, and yet not lose our feeling that privacy for intimacy is good taste as well as enhanced delight.

R. L. Dickenson, 1933

TO BE ABSOLUTELY ACCURATE, we should include the anatomy of the entire human body in any discussion of the anatomy of intercourse, because the body of the male becomes totally involved and the body of the female *can* become totally involved, if she allows it to and everything goes well. Therein lies the basic difference between males and females in intercourse: females can be passive *acceptors* or actively taking *receptors*, or any variation of the two. This has certain advantages. Males, even if so tired that they can only be seduced into activity, still have to be performing for a part of the time involved. However, under optimal conditions, when intercourse is a fully cooperative adventure, the similarities between male and female physiological and emotional responses are remarkable.

Here we will deal only with the external and internal anatomy of the pelvic area and the breasts, in order to establish a vocabulary for further discussion. However, always remember that there have been uncounted hours of pleasure and uncounted numbers of babies conceived by humans who have had no expert vocabulary and no mental picture of their internal anatomy; you, the reader, might be one of those babies, even though you were "wanted." There are still nonliterate societies that are unaware that intercourse makes babies, but are very aware that sexual intercourse is a pleasure-producing act. This latter point only serves to emphasize the basic physiological nature of its pleasurable aspects in humans, and there is much evidence in anthropological literature that it is mutually appreciated as pleasure-producing by both males and females in some, if not all, societies.

Since 1933, Dickenson, Kinsey, and Masters and Johnson have contributed commonsense, accurate, scientific knowledge about sexual behavior and physiology to the general public. They all admit the limitations of their studies, either because of the size or selection of their sample. Dickenson's *Human Sex Anatomy* was on the restricted shelves of libraries for a long time, but the life-sized diagrams of the range of normal anatomy, the written observations of the genitalia and the physiological responses of the body, pre- and postcoitus, plus his personal philosophy would make him appear a pioneer if he were writing today. Kinsey's work with a large population of males and females summarizes variations of sexual behavior and attitudes both qualitatively and quantitatively. In a smaller, basically volunteer population, Masters and Johnson have added microscopes, electronics, and additional psychological insight into sexual behavior and attitudes and their origin. Perhaps most important are their efforts to define and provide therapy for several types of sexual dysfunction. Rereading Kinsey 20 years later, we are even more impressed with the amount of valuable attitudinal material that is there, material which has only recently been used in popular magazines.

It eventually becomes relatively easy for most gynecologists and urologists to deal with an individual patient's sexual questions and concerns in an uninvolved, objective manner. But they, like most of us today, were brought up with the same "fig leaf"* mentality and taboos, and even they are not effective physicians without real knowledge of the wide variations of the normal, or when they speak only from their own emotional and physical experience. This is equally true for each individual who is communicating at a personal sexual level with another; if our experience is limited to our own feelings and thoughts, with no knowledge of the wide variation of sexual behavior and response in our own, as well as the other sex, this will be a very restricting bias. To restrict a physical act occurring in the majority of readers, in one form or another, perhaps a minimum of 2500 times in a lifetime (once a week for 50 years to use *very* round numbers) is to make something very special, very "assembly line."

There is good sexual information all around us, though sorting the good from the bad is sometimes difficult, and some people do not want to subject themselves to this. But even if all they learn is that people have been concerned for hundreds of years about the presence or absence of orgasm in the female and premature ejaculation in the male, they may feel a little more comfortable. Even these small pieces of information have only become public knowledge during the past 25 years.

One problem which has arisen since 1966 and the new scientific approach is

---

* From reading recent anthropology, we suspect that the origin of the association of the fig leaf with the genitals has more to do with hiding a pleasure-producing organ from evil spirits who might snatch it away than with shame or modesty.

that much of the writing and lecturing about sexuality and sexual behavior has been preoccupied with what we call "the beads of sweat" approach, that is, a concern with the minutiae of physiology. Example: the woman who finds herself, postdelivery, unable to *have* an orgasm. She reads the book, any sex book, and decides that her husband's penis does not pull down on the hood of the clitoris as it used to, probably because the "introitus was stretched too much at the time of delivery." In her preoccupation with mechanics, she may forget that she and her husband are both somewhat different people, postdelivery, with a baby in the house.

We will avoid this approach here, but we have included material on this subject in our bibliography for those who wish more details. For our purposes, a general knowledge and an awareness of the normal progression of events in intercourse will be sufficient and will avoid, "If I could only see the beads of

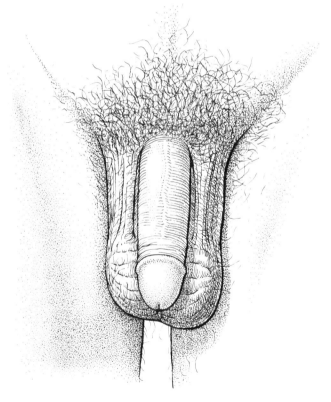

Figure 2-1. Average adult circumcised male. Note asymmetry of scrotum, some indication of the spermatic cord. The length of the nonerect penis will vary as will the size of scrotum, from one individual to the next. The exaggerated length of the dependent penis in male pornographic magazines is often due to a state of semi-erection and the camera angle.

sweat, I'd know whether she was ready," or "turn on the lights, let's check for the rash and areolar flush." This happens to be our bias, and perhaps we, too, are restricted by it.

External Anatomy

Figure 2-1 is a frontal view of the average, normal circumcised adult male. Many women do not know if their partner is circumcised or not; if they have only seen one penis, they really have no way of knowing, especially when almost every textbook picture and diagram includes the foreskin (prepuce). Variations in the amount of foreskin removed at the time of circumcision may often leave some males in doubt about themselves.

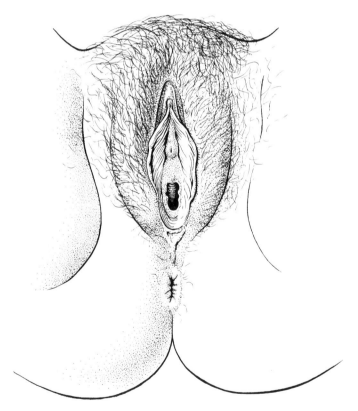

Figure 2-2. Female perineum, nonvirginal. Labia majora and minora are shown separated. Normally, even with legs spread apart, the labia remain in the midline and the introitus appears closed. The labia minora vary in size, and the relation of the urethral opening to the vagina also varies from one individual to the next. Only the end of the clitoris is ever exposed.

Figure 2-2 is a frontal view of the average, normal female. It is modified from the normal only because the clitoris, urethra, and introitus (hymeneal opening) are usually hidden by the labia majora (large lips), except in an older woman who has less fatty tissue in the labia, or a woman who has had one or two children, though this is not always true.

Pubic hair may be straight or curly, depending on the kind of hair on the head. A tendency to curl is enhanced by tight pants and a moist environment and the fact that pubic hair is shorter than the hair on most heads. Color is related to the *natural* color of the hair on the rest of the body, though pubic hair is usually darker in color. Distribution of the pubic hair on the lower abdominal wall is described as *male* if it extends toward the umbilicus, and *female* if it does not. However, females with a genetic tendency toward side-burns and hairy arms and legs will often have a masculine distribution of pubic hair. Hair distribution is important only if there is a change after the male or female pattern has been established; this change is usually associated with other hormonal disturbances.

Some women in Middle Eastern cultures shave all pubic hair routinely because of their husband's preference. Shaving is necessary with bikinis and some ballet costumes. Electrolysis, or semi-permanent removal, is possible, but expensive and temporarily uncomfortable. The pubic hair grows back completely five or six weeks after shaving. Males are shaved for hernia repairs and abdominal surgery. Clipping is recommended in both sexes if crab lice are a problem (p. 121), or if females have excessive vaginal discharge.

The Male

The penis. The normal range in length of the nonerect, flaccid penis is from $3\frac{1}{2}$ to slightly more than 4 inches. Erection may double the length of the smaller penis, but generally has less effect on the longer penis. "The size of the penis has less constant relation to general physical development than that of any other organ in the body."[1] For reasons obvious to most males, measurements of either the erect or the nonerect penis are extremely difficult. Concerns about penile size are very real. Parents look anxiously at their male babies and often question their pediatricians about "normal." Even the lower limits of the normal-sized adult penis function very well reproductively and sexually, and gross discrepancies between penile size and vaginal size are rare.

At birth, the glans, or end of the penis, is covered with a fold of skin (the foreskin) which is an extension of the skin of the penis (see Fig. 2-3). Removal of this foreskin is done immediately after birth, on the third day, or, in ritual circumcisions, on the eighth day. This is recommended in most hospitals, and since 95 percent of all deliveries in the United States are in hospitals, most males today are circumcised. Circumcision offers several advantages to the individual and to his mother. It makes unnecessary the almost daily maternal and child

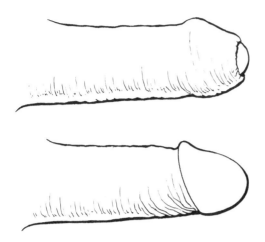

Figure 2-3. *Above,* uncircumcised penis, *below,* circumcised penis. With erection, the foreskin may retract to give the appearance of circumcision. With penetration, the foreskin normally retracts.

preoccupation with foreskin retraction and cleansing. Boys do not use soap voluntarily until age 13 or 14. If the foreskin remains, it should be retracted almost daily during the first two to three years and cleansed of secretions and cellular debris which collect underneath at the base of the glans. Failure to do this may lead to minor or severe degrees of phimosis (the foreskin is adherent to the glans) restricting retraction in intercourse and decreasing sensation; spontaneous erections can also be painful. In the adult male, phimosis is almost the only reason for circumcision.

The scrotum and its contents. The smooth muscle layer in the scrotal sac responds to decreased temperature and sexual stimulation by contracting, which raises or shortens it $1\frac{1}{2}$ to 2 inches. The testes are located in the scrotal sac, one testis on each side separated by connective tissue in the midline; they are normally mobile within the sac, and one is usually higher than the other. The scrotum is not bilaterally symmetrical.* The testes are about 2 inches long and 1 to $1\frac{1}{2}$ inches wide, each the size, shape, and consistency of a small, shelled, hardboiled egg.

The epididymis is a soft, irregular structure that can be felt on the upper, inner surface of each testis. It is occasionally the site of inflammation and discomfort (epididymitis).

The vas deferens, which carries the sperm to the base of the urethra, can be felt (palpated) as a firm cordlike structure running from the testis to the upper border of the pubic bone (see Fig. 2-1). Here, it enters the abdominal cavity at a point called the external abdominal ring (a firm edge of connective tissue) which is also the location of some hernial bulges, when and if they

---

* We are told that before cutting the pattern or the material, good tailors ask their customers on which side of their trousers they usually place their genitals.

occur. Hernias do not interfere with sperm transport (p. 38); the vas deferens does not compress easily. Blood vessels, nerves, and some fine muscle strands also run along with the vas. These structures make up the spermatic cord, whose outline is visible externally in Figure 2-1.

The Female

The external, or visible, anatomy of the female genital area is often only the outer surface of the labia majora. This is also true in most positions used in intercourse. Even on the infamous gynecology examining table, it is usually necessary to separate the labia majora to examine the clitoris, urethra, and introitus. Figure 2-2 illustrates the clitoris well.* Its visible portion is usually ¼ inch wide and partially or completely covered with a fold of move-able mucosa, a thin tissue which is not typical skin, called the hood, or the prepuce. The same secretions that collect under the male foreskin also collect here with some of the same problems, though these problems are less frequent in the female. The clitoris has the same embryological origin as the penis, the same or greater sensitivity, and, though less visible, basically the same anatomy. Actually, the cervix, which is discussed later, looks almost exactly like the glans of the penis in size, shape, and external anatomy, and this can give rise to some misconceptions about common origin or function. Girls can see their clitoris directly, if their abdomen is not too large, and they are often surprised at its minute size and the secretions found there. This area requires more than a casual washcloth to cleanse properly.

The urethral opening appears as a flattened slit and is difficult to see even in direct examination (see Fig. 2-2). Its position between the clitoris and the vaginal opening is variable; occasionally it is located almost on, or on, the anterior wall of the lower end of the vagina which makes this individual more vulnerable to problems with traumatic urethritis.

Posterior (in back of or behind) to the urethra is the introitus (opening to the vagina); in medicine, this word is often used interchangeably with hymen. Strictly speaking, the introitus is the opening, and the hymen is the tissue surrounding the opening, a membranous structure of varying degrees of thickness. Only rarely is the hymen *imperforate* (without an opening), and this is usually discovered in midpuberty when there has been no menstruation (see p. 128).

The opening varies in size and is usually capable of being dilated or stretched, if this is done slowly and repeatedly. Some of the variations are noted in Figure 2-4. The septate hymen usually presents no problems in inter-course if the septum is stretchy, but it does hamper *removal* of tampons,

---

*A young woman who answers the telephone at a local, independent counseling service said that she receives two or three calls a week from males asking how to find the clitoris—perhaps a variation of the obscene phone call, but we doubt it.

because "something seems to catch." The septum disappears, surgically, at the time of childbirth, if there has been no reason for removing it before this time. Occasionally the hymeneal ring is so firm that dilatation is impossible and surgery is necessary at some time, even for tampon insertion. In the medical sense, the "virginal" hymen, is one that will not stretch to accommodate an erect penis with ease. However, many hymeneal rings are so minimal that they function in a nonvirginal manner; that is, they offer no resistance even to the first penile penetration (see Tampons and Petting).

There are many misconceptions about the structure, the location, and even the function of the hymen. It really has no function. It is simply a remnant of embryological development. The function attributed to it is purely psychological and sociological. For example, a 22-year-old, recently married woman requested that we "break her hymen" because she wanted to have children. She had been having intercourse for the previous three or four months without contraception since, "I never felt any pain from the breaking of the hymen so I assume it is still intact." Or, a mother of a 12½-year-old asked us about her daughter using tampons and what to tell her about where to put them. Neither she nor her husband knew where the hymen was or whether it would interfere with tampons in this age group. Both women felt that it was somewhere near the cervix, at the upper end of the vagina.

The labia majora and minora become slightly engorged during sexual stimulation and enlarge, though not markedly. The labia minora are usually asymmetrical (i.e., not equal in size or shape) and may vary markedly in

Figure 2-4. Variations of the hymen. From left to right: virginal, nondilated; septate, septum may or may not stretch; cribriform; parous, at least one full-term delivery.

size from one individual to the next. Some nonliterate cultures include calculated manipulation of the labia minora as part of preliminary sexual stimulation, and hypertrophy, or enlargement, apparently occurs under these circumstances. Note in Figure 2-2 that the anterior edge of the labia minora is continuous with the fold of mucosa over the clitoris; manipulation of the labia can automatically stimulate the clitoris. A patient asked us if her labia minora (her words) were abnormal because "my boyfriend told me they were larger than normal." We reassured her and suggested that maybe this was his indirect way of asking her if she masturbated, assuming that he, too, had read some anthropology. We also suggested that sometime when she was feeling quite secure, she might ask him how many he had seen, that he was able to make this judgment.

The anus (opening of the rectum to the outside) is usually hidden between the buttocks during intercourse in almost any position. The circular muscle (sphinctor) which surrounds the opening can be tightened voluntarily or expanded by simply pushing down, with a deep breath against the diaphragm as with a bowel movement. Anal intercourse in the female or male requires cooperation and an equal amount of lubrication (see p. 119). It is a relatively uncommon variation of intercourse, though obviously a good contraceptive method, and probably occupies the fantasies of more bored people than are actually willing to practice it. Most people usually associate this form of intercourse with male homosexual activity, though some authorities feel that it is no more prevalent in this group than it is in the heterosexual population. It is slightly more prevalent in European countries than in the United States (see p. 83).

The female and male breasts are sexual organs, visually and physiologically. Direct stimulation of the male breast is more often a part of male homosexual activity but certainly need not be limited to this group, either qualitatively or connotatively. The nipple and the pigmented area (the areola) are, or can become, extremely sensitive to the touch of the hand, or the mouth of a suckling child or lover, and they also respond indirectly, in appearance and sensation, to sexual stimulation in other areas of the body (see Orgasm).

The nonpregnant breast in the female has a small amount of glandular tissue; the remainder is fat and connective tissue. There are *no* muscles except very small ones in the nipple and areolar area. To some extent the size of the breasts is determined genetically; large-breasted mothers tend to have large-breasted daughters. Deposition of fat in other areas of the body in overweight women has very little to do with increased size of breasts, though starvation will decrease fat all over the body. Marked starvation also disturbs the entire hormonal balance as well, for example, the nonovulating and nonmenstruating starving women in the concentration camps and cities of Europe during World War II. In the otherwise normal, obese male, fat tends to deposit over the entire chest wall with what often appears as an excess in the breast region. Chronic liver disease in males causes local enlargement of breast tissue, which is due to a specific hormonal imbalance. There are isolated, rare reports of lactating males, but the normal male breast has only a small amount of nonfunctioning glandular tissue and very little fat.

In lower mammals, both sexes have a bilateral row of breasts or nipples, called the milk line. The human female may have extra glandular tissue, or extra nipples, or just a pigmented area along similar lines which run from the underarm (the axilla) to the pubic bone. The glandular tissue responds in a cyclic fashion just like the breasts and can become extremely uncomfortable if located in the axilla or under the tight band of a bra. Surgical removal of extra nipples and glandular tissue is relatively simple and solves all of the aesthetic and emotional problems, as well as the discomfort.

Going braless can be a good, free, and even cool feeling on hot days, but remember that there are no muscles, only stretchy, nonelastic connective tissue, supporting the breasts. Surgery to decrease the size of the breasts is becoming more acceptable than injections or implants to increase the size of the breasts. There are many girls with chronic backaches from the weight of their breasts, who are unable to run or even walk quickly without discomfort. There are also girls who have to give up the pill as a contraceptive because of its effect on their breasts.* Bras and jock straps keep mobile body appendages from uncomfortable bouncing during strenuous activity and serve a very useful function quite aside from whatever sexual connotations either might have for the wearer or the observer.

Internal Anatomy

The Male

The unique shape, internal structure, and function of the penis is clearly designed for reproduction; there is no need for a long urethra in the male. This could almost make one doubt that Adam came first; the male was obviously designed for a preexisting female.

The testes are internal pelvic organs until the eighth month of fetal life, when differential growth and hormones assist them into the scrotal sac where cooler temperatures are more conducive to sperm development.† Testes that do not make it to the outside, or get only part of the way, are usually sterile if left behind longer than four to five years; these are also more subject to

* The pill tends to enlarge breasts, though unpredictably, and also may increase their sensitivity to movement or touch, often uncomfortably so.

† Routine wearing of tight jockey shorts of synthetic materials may have the same effect on sperm production—the testes are almost constantly against the perineum and close to body temperature.

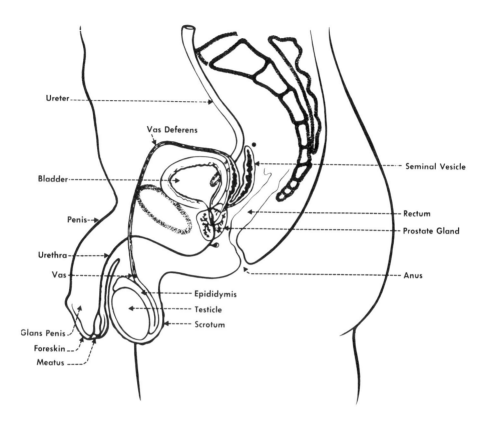

Figure 2-5. Median section of the male pelvis.

malignant disease for reasons not yet will understood.

The erectile tissue of the penis (the corpora cavernosa, or cavernous bodies) is composed of many small interconnected blood spaces which become engorged with *more* arterial blood during erection. Valves which prevent backflow of blood and maintain erection have been described by anatomists as well as muscles around the blood vessels, but the actual mechanism of engorgement, erection, and its maintenance is not yet clear. The ability of some individuals with paralysed lower extremities to have erections and ejaculations indicates that part of this mechanism is outside, or independent of, the control of the brain. And, as any male knows, erections may occur spontaneously without any apparent sexual stimulus, even when carrying heavy furniture. However, erections and loss of erections need not be accompanied by ejaculation.

There are, grossly, three cavernous bodies in the penis, two interconnecting on the upper surface, and one surrounding the urethra and continuous with the glans. Erection does not close off the urethra, even though it runs the entire length of the urethral cavernous body.

Spermatozoa are produced at a fairly constant rate (see Infertility) in the testes and travel the 12-inch path through the epididymis to the vas deferens on each side to the base of the urethra in the pelvic cavity (see Fig. 2-5). In the pelvis, they pass to each side of the urinary bladder where they join with ducts from the seminal vesicles and prostate and empty into the urethra as it leaves the bladder. As this point, these structures are more or less surrounded by the prostate gland, located under the bladder.* The prostate can be felt, or examined, through the anterior wall of the rectum. Prostatic massage, a procedure for pressing prostatic fluid into the urethra and out, for microscopic examination, is done through the anterior rectal wall. The seminal vesicles may be involved in disease and can be palpated in the same way.

The Female

The clitoris has been rediscovered, or discovered, recently and in minute anatomical detail, for public enlightenment. This has been a very successful crusade which has justified what most women have probably known for centuries: the clitoris is the central sexual focus for females. Giving it this function should not be construed to deny the intensely pleasurable aspects of sexual activity which can be derived from stimulation of any one of a number of other areas of the human body, which vary from individual to individual, or even to deny the possibility of true orgasmic pleasure and release without direct stimulation of the clitoris. But the public discussions about stimulation of the shaft of the clitoris, clitoral erection, and clitoral movement create impressions of a rather active organ which, even when it is most active, does not move more than a few millimeters.

Very simply, the clitoris does have erectile tissue similar to the penis. Its cavernous bodies are deep, and extend from the midline laterally and out under the arch of the pubic bone. These sinuses engorge during stimulation, but there is little visible, or palpable, change other than darkening, due to increased blood supply; the same is true of the remainder of the genital area in the female and the male. How the area feels with direct manual stimulation or with total body stimulation is another matter.

The enlarged clitoris of sexual mythology that resembles a small penis is usually associated with some hormonal or genetic abnormality. Hypertrophy due to long-term masturbation has been documented, but the range of normal, even with hypertrophy of this origin, is never seen in the frightening proportions often described.

Solitary masturbation or the mutual masturbation of intercourse is usually

---

*Anatomists may object to this description but it is adequate, and these structures are all very crowded in the pelvis.

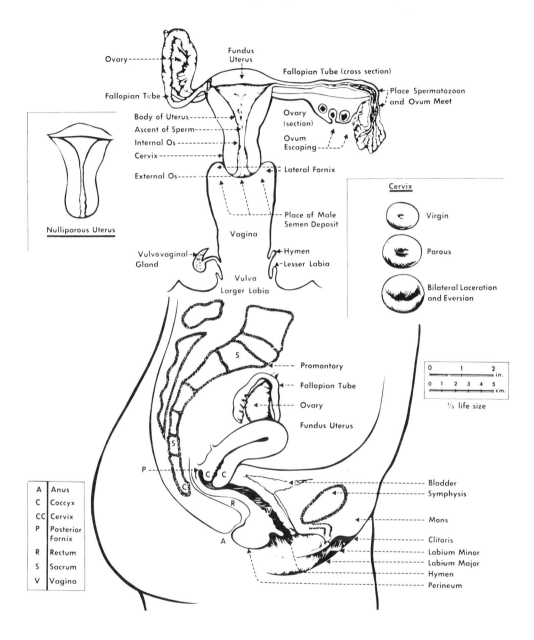

Figure 2-6. Diagrams of female reproductive organs. Upper: Frontal view with uterus, right ovary, and tube elevated to vertical position. Lower: Median view with left ovary and tube elevated. Nulliparous uterus and virgin cervix: No previous intrauterine pregnancy.

confined to the lateral aspects of the clitoris, thus stimulating the deep erectile tissue of the clitoris. The glans of the clitoris is, or may become, exquisitely and painfully sensitive to a much greater degree than the glans of the penis. Many males do not appreciate this fact, but, if they have had the experience, they should remember the exquisite tenderness and sometimes pain that can occur with excessive stimulation of the male glans. Women should also be aware of the latter fact.

Bartholin's glands are noted here because they occasionally become infected and swell to golf ball or larger size, and their location at the base of the labia minora and the entrance to the vagina can create problems, if they become infected (see Venereal Disease).

The vagina is not a hollow tube as it is pictured in most texts, but a potential space capable of accommodating itself relatively rapidly to any size object, up to and including a baby's head, with very little if any discomfort. Discomfort related to the vagina is usually due to either the nondistensibility of the lower end, the hymeneal area, or the slow dilatation of the cervical opening at the upper end during childbirth; the cervix is the vaginal portion of the uterus, and not a part of the vagina.

The outer, lower third of the vagina is more sensitive to touch and painful stimuli than the upper, or inner, two-thirds, which is said to be devoid of nerve endings. On the latter point, many women claim awareness of *movement* as well as size and shape of the *moving object* in the entire vagina, though a *resting* tampon or penis is not perceived as such. Women can also perceive a sense of fullness with an erect penis in the vagina, but this may be related to stretch receptors in the adjacent rectum. (Before surgical repair of the fallen womb, or uterus, was common, women were fitted with a doughnut-sized object, a pessary, which rested semi-permanently against the pubic bone inside the vagina and held the uterus in position. This limited penetration during intercourse, but women were not aware of it, if it was well fitted.)

There is no circular vaginal sphinctor muscle at the introitus, but the voluntary muscles, which run from the pubic bone in front, back around the anus, can be contracted and act like sphinctors to tighten the introitus. These are the same muscles which can be contracted to stop urination, since they also surround the urethra on both sides.

The basic length of the vagina is about 4½ inches, but it is so variable with position and so capable of distention by any object that exact measurements are difficult. The most important fact is that its size and shape bear little or no relation to body size and shape, as is also true of the penis. Since the pelvis is quite crowded and the internal body organs are normally fairly mobile, its shape depends to some degree on the fullness of the rectum, the bladder, and the pressure of abdominal contents. For example, it is quite easy for a female to reach her cervix when she is in a sitting position, but very difficult when she is lying down or when her hips are elevated because the abdominal, and to a certain extent the pelvic, contents tend to fall away. When the female is in the knees-to-chest position, the abdominal contents also fall away, because of gravity, to such an extent that the vagina may even balloon slightly at its upper end. This position is sometimes preferred or used as a variation in intercourse, and it is also used for some surgical procedures in the pelvis (see Diaphragm Usage).

There are soft transverse folds in the vaginal wall which allow this expansion, but these remain as more or less constant folds near the opening of the vagina where the surrounding muscle layer is quite firm. This is not always true in women who have had numerous children without adequate repair of the introitus, or who have had them without an episiotomy (see p. 178).

Rarely, the vagina is absent or represented by a thin strand of tissue in the appropriate location. Surgical construction of "artificial" vaginas is relatively easy for those who are experienced in this type of surgery, and *magically* the lining of the artificial vagina looks and functions like the normal vagina— even the beads of sweat appear—within two or three months postsurgery. Some gynecologists use skin grafts from the thigh which become indistinguishable from normal vaginal lining. Others use nothing but skilled dissection of an appropriate-sized space, and glass or plastic dilators to maintain the shape while it heals and becomes a vagina.* This operation can also be done in transsexual "males" who wish a vagina. Supplementary hormones are used in the latter case.

The uterus, or womb, is almost two separate, though continuous, muscular organs: the fundus, or body, and the cervix (see Fig. 2-6). The fundus is pear-shaped, with a small, flattened, triangular cavity. Normally it is mobile and directed anteriorly, almost at right angles, to the vagina and to the cervix. The "tipped" uterus may be vertical, or any angulation toward the back, up to 130 degrees or more. This presents few problems in pregnancy or intercourse unless the fundus is not mobile, or is fixed in position by fibrous strands. Deep penetration during intercourse can be uncomfortable if the uterus is fixed, and the pregnant, enlarging uterus which is fixed in the pelvic cavity may abort its contents.

The cervix is visible during vaginal examinations. It is a firm, muscular organ, feeling and looking like the glans of the erect penis. The cervical opening, the os, even looks like the urethral opening in the male glans, especially if there has been a term pregnancy (see Fig. 2-6). There are mucus secreting glands in the canal of the cervix which is continuous with the uterine cavity, but they contribute very little to secretions during sexual excitement. However, they do have a cyclic pattern of secretion related to ovulation.

Pap tests are often referred to as uterine cancer control (see p. 320).

---

*Another surgical procedure brings "down" the smooth lining of the abdominal cavity (the peritoneum) into the appropriate location.

Although the cervix is part of the uterus, cancer of the cervix and cancer of the fundus are quite different and carry different statistics in terms of frequency, type of cancer, diagnosis, and age groups of women affected by either. Cancer of the cervix is the most frequent and the most available for control, if detected at an early stage. Pap tests are used for diagnosis of cervical cancer.

The Fallopian tubes are firm muscular structures with a small lumen (see Fig. 2-6). They are slightly larger and softer than the vas deferens. They lead from the cavity of the uterus to the ovary, a distance of about 4 inches, ending in a fringe (the fimbriae) whose ends normally lie near the surface of the ovary. Fertilization of the egg occurs in the tube and maintaining the structure of the fimbriae and their relation to the ovary are important to reproduction and fertility (see Gonorrhea and Infertility). Any disease process which blocks the tube or distorts the relations of the tubes to the ovaries will often prevent conception until corrected surgically.

The ovaries, one on each side, are normally the size and shape of almonds with shells, though there is some variation in the normal size, shape, and position. Only part of one ovary and one intact tube are necessary for reproduction and adequate hormonal maintenance. Squeezing the ovaries during pelvic examination may give the same kind of feeling in the pit of the stomach that squeezing the testes, even gently, does in the male. A slightly enlarged ovary, with a temporary ovarian cyst, is often tender, and if located near the upper end of the vagina (but in the pelvic cavity) can cause moderate to severe discomfort with deep penetration during intercourse.

Physiology, Function and Dysfunctions

We turn now to the mechanics of physical intercourse (coitus). We have included very little love and affection in this discussion, though the reader will find some evidence of the positive effects of caring. This is not because love and affection are unnecessary, but because acts of intercourse, not necessarily the pleasures, are so natural a part of animal and human behavior that they can be performed with or without love and affection.

Males, in particular, are programmed by their hormones, their anatomy, and society to be able to function in this way, that is, to be able to release sexual tension, heterosexually or homosexually, without involvement; but, women can also do this.

Intercourse requires only an erect penis and a moderate amount of vaginal lubrication. These requisites are usually the initial response to sexual stimulation of any sort—visual, mental, direct, or indirect (nongenital) physical contact.

Under normal circumstances, the vagina is always lubricated to some degree, but lubrication increases markedly with sexual stimulation. In addition, as in the male, there is a pelvic congestion which may be felt only as an aching pelvic awareness, or throbbing in the clitoral region, or a rhythmic aching, or even shooting, spasmodic, dull pains in the vagina, labia, and rectum. This can be very surprising and disturbing to a young or inexperienced girl involved in something more than a quick, goodnight kiss, or to almost any female upon her first prolonged exposure to pornographic material or explicit sexual literature. "My *heart* aches for you" is inaccurate; the heart may pound, but it is the pelvis that aches.

We would like the reader to consider the following as more than a suggestion: The improvement in their sexual lives which many people claim to have experienced reading Reuben, or "J," and similar literature often has more to do with the direct physiological effects of reading "legitimate," explicit sexual material than with the specific "how to" instructions on techniques. This is especially true if this type of reading is done at bedtime with a friend or spouse nearby. Indirectly, such literature also tends to relieve concerns about appropriateness of behavior or about fantasies.

Touching

Touching is the physical basis for all sexual stimulation. The effect of touch depends almost entirely on the mental state of the toucher and the touched; it can be threatening, friendly, sexual, or impersonal and businesslike, and can be interpreted differently by each participant. There are several sexual and asexual ways to light another person's cigarette; the firmer the handshake or an accidental jostling on the street or in elevators, the less threatening it is from a stranger because there are fewer sexual connotations.

> A female friend of ours was startled while standing on an almost empty beach with her children, when a young man came up and asked for a cigarette. He reached gently into her breast pocket (a man's shirt over a bathing suit), took the pack and one cigarette and placed the pack gently back in her pocket, without speaking. She was left, she said, with a frightened, uneasy feeling that almost totally recurs when she thinks about it. *Rape (violence) from a stranger would almost make sense to her, but seduction (gentle touching) from a one-minute acquaintance did not.*

We have heard young teenagers who were obviously quite comfortable with themselves as sexual entities, though not terribly knowledgeable about sex, discuss the pleasures of parental touching: being bathed, cuddled, loved.

Some individuals retain the feeling of being threatened by any form of touching for a much longer time than others. It takes little insight into human behavior to consider the problems which may result for individuals who grow up in families without seeing people touch, embrace, kiss each other, or parents lying closely together, or without being touched, either casually or warmly. Reactions to this type of cool home environment may take some extreme forms when these individuals come in contact with other people. Persons with this background may literally jerk away from any contact with another, an unconscious reaction which may occur even when there is understanding of the background for the reaction. Or, such individuals may reach out for physical contact with anyone, desperate for a warmth which they know exists, and which they have never had.

They may have difficulties being aggressive in the physical sexual situation, regardless of very real desire and of previously experienced, known pleasure. Many young and older adults worry: Who touches who first? Will I be rejected? Will he think I'm a nympho (nymphomaniac)? Will she think I'm a sex-starved stud?

They may find some sexual techniques to be more acceptable than others for reasons which may not make any apparent sense; for example, total body contact may feel more spontaneous and therefore more acceptable than the seemingly calculated use of hands for stimulation. These same individuals, as new fathers or mothers, may find the cuddling and closeness difficult with the advent of a first baby (see Breast-feeding).

We have discussed touching here to illustrate, though not in detail, that the physiology and function of the body in response to stimuli in the sexual situation depends almost entirely on what experiences, not necessarily overtly sexual, one brings to it. Part of maturing, and no one is ever mature in all areas of living, is being able to sort out, subconsciously, reasons for being touched or touching. This is a phase of growing up that can create problems for some.

There are no absolutes which define total sexual response for any combination of two people, whatever the sex, though there is a point of inevitability of ejaculation for the male and, to a lesser extent, a desire for penetration and closeness by the heterosexual female, primarily, that is reached with maximal stimulation—the point of no return. It is then and only then that one can assume that all or some of the physiological reactions to be noted below are really occurring. The body takes over, if it is allowed to, and if one can handle the temporary "loss of control."

Masters and Johnson divide the total sexual response pattern in females and males into four phases: excitement, plateau, orgasm, and resolution.[2] These are almost self-explanatory. What has usually been ignored in their writing is their comment that "this *arbitrary* division provides a framework for detailed description of *physiologic variants,* some of which are so frequently *transient* as to appear in only one phase."[3] This is a slight abbreviation of their longer comment, but the reader should give some emphasis and attention to the words, "arbitrary," "physiologic variants," and "transient." Masters and Johnson further point out that "there are many identifiable variations in the male sexual reaction . . . usually related to duration rather than intensity," and that there is an "infinite variety in female sexual response. . . . Here, intensity as well as duration of response are factors which must be considered. . . ."[4] Or, to put it briefly, the male response usually varies in duration, and the female response may vary in duration and intensity.

Masters and Johnson's research is not intended to *set* standards or patterns, but to describe as accurately as possible preexisting and almost universal patterns of sexual response, which, by definition, include all of the variations, some of which are considered dysfunctions. They wish to describe these in the same way that other physiological functions of the human body have been described and for the same reasons: 1) to further understanding of sexual function, and 2) to define "normal." They do not intend that everyone should become preoccupied with the minutiae of physiology, any more than physicians (gastroenterologists) who study the gut intend to have ulcer patients preoccupied with how the circular muscle at the top of the stomach functions in response to the pleasures of food in the mouth. The imponderables of ulcer formation in the stomach are always referred back to the effects of the psyche. Masters and Johnson repeatedly refer their imponderables back to the psyche, and probably rightly so, at least until, as they say, "the mores of our society come to accept objective research . . ." in this area.

Nongenital Responses During Intercourse

The *nongenital responses in the female* during intercourse may include breast engorgement, nipple erection, muscle contractions in the pelvis (usually rhythmic), or in the arms and legs (nonrhythmic), sweating, flushing or blotchy blushing, a transient rash like that seen in measles, and changes in the heart and respiratory rates.

The one nongenital, or extragenital, response which women are most aware of is muscular contractions in the pelvis, which appear to occur without control, even though the muscles involved are controllable under all other circumstances of living. The tense female who is uncomfortable with this loss of control, even for a brief period, may consciously suppress much of it without losing the orgasmic experience, thus creating a variation in intensity for both her and her partner. If this suppression occurs early in her coital experiences and lasts for any length of time, she may have some difficulty in allowing it to return when she begins to feel more at ease about control and "letting go."

The *nongenital responses in the male* are similar to those in the female, with the possible exceptions of intensity, duration, or frequency of occurrence. The one real exception is the muscular response, part of which is voluntary and enhanced by an intense desire to stimulate the penis against the vaginal wall, to be inside, to be close. However, the intensity of the orgasmic and reflex muscular response of the entire body depends on the relative positions of the male and female during intercourse.

The need for either partner to concentrate on maintaining a particular position, whether on top, on the knees, sideways, from behind, or standing up requires a conscious effort which may block some of the involuntary, reflex muscular reactions, particularly in the arms and legs. This might be a partial explanation of the evolution among humans of the male on top of the female. This position allows the male unrestricted movement and force, and just lying out flat "on her" with male orgasm and ejaculation, permitting him to just "let go." This is the only position for intercourse which allows total body involvement of both female and male with no need to think about maintaining a position which keeps the penis in the vagina (see Chap. 3).

The horizontal position with solitary masturbation to orgasm allows the same type of total muscular response.

Genital Responses During Intercourse

The *genital response in the female* can be observed to some extent, if anyone is looking, but for all practical purposes it is one of increasingly intense sensation in response to direct or indirect stimulation. Vasocongestion is marked: the labia majora become swollen, and the labia minora darken and become slightly enlarged.* Both are more sensitive to touch.

Visual, or palpable changes in the size of the clitoris due to vasocongestion are not very remarkable, except under close scrutiny. Its basic anatomy allows for erection, but this would probably be noted only in the usual course of events if the clitoral size was at the upper limits of normal, and this limit is only about 1 cm. Its size and appearance belies its one and only function, "receptor and transformer" and central focus of sensual stimuli in the female. Stimulation of any kind which is interpreted by the receiver as sexual creates vasocongestion and awareness of the entire genital area, with an exquisite sensitivity of the glans of the clitoris which is usually the only portion visible. This sensitivity is discovered when manipulation of the genital area follows. ". . . There is a narrow margin between stimulation and irritation"[5] at this point, and irritation can quickly become pain with direct manipulation of the glans. This may also be true in the immediate postorgasmic or early resolution phase. Since the amount of pressure or manipulation which creates pain and brings the female "down to earth" again, making it necessary to start all over, varies from female to female and from experience to experience for an individual female, this clitoral sensitivity can create problems unless all of the signals are well understood by the male and are well communicated by the female (see Chap. 3).

As noted previously, the normal vagina is usually moist from cervical secretions which are cyclic in amount and consistency and usually mucoid rather than watery. Sexual stimulation very quickly causes a copious "sweating phenomenon" from the walls of the vagina. The word phenomenon is used because there are no glands in the vaginal walls, and there is still no adequate

---

* Vasocongestion may be defined here as darkening and enlargement, due to an increased volume of blood.

explanation for this sweating. Most females are aware of the wetness which occurs. The presence of yeast or Trichomonads (see p. 119) in large amounts tends to prevent this vaginal response, and some females who are on the pill for four or five months or more find that their ability to lubricate has decreased, even under optimal circumstances. Without this lubrication, there may be uncomfortable feelings with penetration and with any movement of the penis in the vagina. The lubricating effects of some of the creams and gels used for contraception are often helpful. The inner surfaces of the labia minora are frequently a source of discomfort in the presence of yeast overgrowth or Trichomonad infection.

Masters and Johnson describe a "tenting" of the inner two-thirds of the vagina which occurs as sexual tensions increase. Remembering that the vagina is only a potential space and difficult to measure, their measurements show a maximum increase in transverse diameter of only about $1\frac{1}{2}$ inches (4 cms.) and a similar increase in length.[6] This is an interesting response to stimulation but not terribly significant in the functional sense, though it is frequently used as an argument against the use of the diaphragm which has a finite measurement. However, the latter's efficacy as a contraceptive depends almost totally on the spermicidal agents used with it, and these agents do not have a finite measurement. More interesting and more important is the change in length which occurs with position (see p. 206).

Painful sensation in the vagina is said to be limited to the outer third, but in some way, the inner two-thirds certainly has a sensation of pressure transmitted to it, and it is also an area which can "itch where you cannot scratch" if there is yeast overgrowth or infection. Both pressure and itching are variations of the sensation of touch. The stretch receptors in the adjacent rectum, which normally signal a full rectum and the need for a bowel movement, are often stimulated by a penis in the vagina. Many women report a tremendous desire to *push* at the height of a "good" orgasm, similar to the pushing with delivery, or with a bowel movement. To the extent that one feels secure enough to do this at any time, it may or may not be a part of an orgasmic feeling, another variation of intensity.

To varying degrees on different occasions, rhythmic rectal sphincter contractions, which are sometimes sharply uncomfortable, are also associated with any or all phases of intercourse.

The pelvic organs of the female are normally mobile and move with deep thrusting or penetration. The after effects, or awareness of the pelvis, may continue into the next day; a female knows she has had intercourse and a male is similarly aware. This kind of feeling can be very disconcerting with early experiences, but is something which most women can choose or not choose to be aware of as their experience increases. The same is true of vaginal and introital, as well as penile, awareness the next day or two. The tenderness or sensitivity of the ovaries may vary during the ovulatory cycle; their movement during deep penetration may be more or less uncomfortable in the same cyclic fashion. Persistent discomfort should be investigated.

Although the uterus undergoes rhythmic contractions during sexual excitement, orgasm, and resolution which contribute to the aching pelvis of early sexual excitement, this rarely or never approaches the intensity of even moderate menstrual cramping; it is a "good" ache.

The *genital response in the male* is also one of total pelvic awareness and also very visible, or at least palpable. The rhythmic contractions associated with ejaculation are not only consciously experienced by the male, but they are palpable on the undersurface of the base of the penis. Once allowed to begin, they are involuntary.

Erection of the penis is the spontaneous and initial reaction to any type of stimulation interpreted as sexual at the subconscious or conscious level.

Most texts show the fully erect penis perpendicular to its usual nonerect position. If the male is recumbent (on his back), the erect penis "at rest" can lie on the abdomen, or 130 degrees in the other direction. If he is standing, the semi-erect penis may or may not be perpendicular to the body. Males can voluntarily contract muscles which insert on the connective tissue covering of the cavernous bodies and raise, or maintain, the penis at a 90-degree angle. Although uncomfortable, erections can even occur under a jock strap.

The quick response of erection is analogous to the quick response of lubrication, but in neither case need there be a completion of the act of intercourse, or an ejaculation, for these responses to disappear. With practice or training, erection can be maintained and prolonged through the plateau phase of rising sexual tension by means of intermittent stimulation, either manually or by the vaginal walls. Excessive stimulation of the male glans during this plateau phase may precipitate ejaculation (male orgasm). Manual stimulation at this time can, like direct stimulation of the clitoris, be very painful or, at least, uncomfortable.

Most males discover at some time, usually when love and affection enter into the act of intercourse, that anything which prolongs female pleasure in the sexual act also prolongs male pleasure. Therefore, intermittent stimulation during the plateau phase is extremely important for both male and female. If this technique is ignored, there is often a rather rapid progression, in the male, to ejaculation and loss of erection. If the male is able to prolong his own plateau phase (see Premature Ejaculation), this allows maximal stimulation of the female and perhaps, if not always, the repeated orgasmic phases of which the female is capable, though the latter may vary in intensity.

The longer the plateau phase prior to ejaculation, the longer the postejaculatory resolution phase, unless external factors intervene (see p. 79).

The longer the plateau phase in the male, the greater the likelihood of pre-ejaculatory secretion of seminal fluid. The amount may vary from a few drops to as much as 1 cc. This fluid frequently contains motile sperm (see Withdrawal).

Rhythmic contractions of the muscles around the urethra and the base of the penis occur during the orgasmic phase and signal the inevitability of ejaculation. This signal is very short, only about two to three seconds (see Withdrawal). An experienced female will be aware of this, but usually only if she has to be aware of it for contraceptive reasons.

The thin layer of muscles in the scrotal sac contract during intercourse raising the testes, thickening the scrotal skin, and shortening the entire sac. Stroking the inner side of the thigh or the skin of the lower abdomen will also cause the testes to rise slightly.

In the uncircumcised male, a clean foreskin, if easily retractable, will "roll back" either with erection and manipulation, or with penetration, and act exactly like the circumcised penis. The usual questions about increased or decreased sensitivity being related to circumcision are not important if retraction is easy. For the same reason, circumcision does not decrease ejaculatory control or shorten the plateau phase; it has nothing to do with premature ejaculation.

Neither males nor females can urinate during the plateau and orgasmic phases of intercourse. Of all of the reflex muscular activity which occurs during intercourse, this is undoubtedly the most reliable. The circular muscle at the base of the urinary bladder really closes. Since the excitement and resolution phases are both relatively easily reversible, or in the latter instance ended quickly, it is possible to urinate with conscious effort. But this makes it necessary to "start all over again from the beginning." Many females are aware, early in the excitement phase, of a desire to urinate and become extremely tense and fearful that they may do so. If they have urinated recently, the sensation can be ignored; if they have not, the tension and fear will prevent relaxation. Tension and fear in males does not prevent the progression of events to orgasm to the same degree that it does in females, though it may contribute to a need or desire for speed.

Dysfunction

Self-diagnosis of sexual dysfunction is frequently based on lack of real information about how the rest of the world does or does not function, or upon self-imposed, impossible, or unrealistic standards of function. Diagnosis of dysfunction in a female or a male partner may have the same origins.

Not long ago, standards of sexual behavior were not only defined by each couple, but were also limited to that definition; though changes and redefinitions could and did occur with time and experience. Honeymoons were seen as glamorous, romantic times for the establishment of these standards. In reality, they were often two weeks of frustrating attempts at penetration; such experiences seem less common today, but they still occur. The double standard of sexual behavior which allowed males to be knowledgeable and "experienced" and prohibited females from even appearing experienced did little to help newly married couples. This double standard also put a tremendous burden on the many males who really were inexperienced; it is difficult to feel and look "good" or even caring, when one is obviously clumsy and bumbling. And if a girl asked her mother, or even her physician, about sexual matters, the answer often was, "Your husband will teach you." Also in the back of her mind were those many unanswered questions about what men did only with prostitutes.

Even though a wife had to be well aware of her own desires, she could not risk looking too eager, and it might be a long time, sometimes never, before she dared to initiate sexual activity. Ten minute "quickie" acts of intercourse could easily become the pattern for many years of marriage when husbands and wives knew little else about sexual behavior. The phrase "wifely duties" is completely understandable under such circumstances. The number of women whom Kinsey found who didn't know whether or not they had ever had an orgasm, which is the same as saying they never had one, attests to the above conditions.

The overwhelming amount of information now available has value, but can be equally limiting when improperly used. Masculinity seems to be defined by how long a male can maintain an erection without ejaculation, which is not a bad goal to strive for. Femininity is defined, less by orgasmic capability than by how many orgasms per encounter, not an unpleasurable goal either. But the concerns produced by this kind of goal-setting have to be tempered with reality, which is simply saying that inadequacies, or dysfunctions, may well be an intermittent happening for the entire human population. On the other hand, males who make an attempt to discover the multiorgasmic potential of a female, friend or wife, can only improve the total sexual relationship, though even this can be rather exhausting, if pursued without some female desire and cooperation.

Some dysfunctions are found more often in the younger, inexperienced age group, and some more often in the older age group, regardless of total experience. But experience and age are not the only factors; many older males and females of parental age are aghast at the total amount of energy that they know is needed when they hear about young couples having intercourse every day, or having five or six episodes of intercourse on weekends. They forget that much of this activity in the young is not the 30 or 40 minutes they may have become used to as a once or twice a week special event, or that this daily frequency is not always accompanied by female orgasm, though it may be pleasurable in other ways, at the level of giving, sharing, and closeness. Older married women might be expected to forget their own early morning or middle of the night ten minute physical demonstrations of closeness, loving, and sharing when they think about their own frequency. Older married males might be expected to include these, when and if they count.[7]

Just as important, when talking about dysfunction, is the fact that every combination of two people is unique, and well-developed techniques which work with one individual may not work with another; nor are they necessarily the appropriate technique every time with the same individual, in or out of marriage. Males have difficulty learning this. Females who have had experiences with more than one male say that they could tell who it was "if they were blindfolded," simply by feeling fixed patterns of stimulation.

Dysfunctions should only be considered a problem when they have become an involuntary pattern of response, though defining a pattern for any one person is difficult. To call something a pattern, one must know about the frequency of exposure, the understanding that individual has of sexual response in both sexes, how many different individuals one has had experience with, and the degree of "performance anxiety" generated by the occurrence of each "failure" in what seemed to be optimal circumstances. The *snowballing* effect of increasing anxiety should never be underestimated; failures can generate failures. The power of positive thinking is not that powerful in the sexual area; it is difficult to establish control over the apparently uncontrollable. But negative thinking may have an even worse effect. We feel strongly that one of the most effective ways of thinking is "lie down and enjoy it," which is really saying, "Don't think too much at all." Whether an alliance is temporary or not, with love or at least some affection, with just being together, closely, slowly, and nonaggressively, some dysfunctions may never appear or may not reappear.

Sexual Dysfunctions in the Male

Unfortunately, if contrasted with the female, almost any type of sexual dysfunction in the male can severely limit both fertility and the pleasurable aspects of intercourse for both participants. Function means erection for a reasonable length of time under voluntary control. Dysfunction is defined as: 1) impotence, the inability to have an erection, or to maintain an erection to ejaculation, or 2) premature ejaculation, the inability to exert some voluntary control over ejaculation. Problems with failure of ejaculation are rare and usually related to an inability to ejaculate intravaginally, rather than to complete absence of ejaculation in the presence of erection and adequate stimulation.[8]

It is also unfortunate that in our present state of knowledge, putting aside for the moment, disease, trauma, and surgical problems, the origin of these problems appears to lie almost entirely in the psyche. And most young and old psyches have many unplumbed depths. This suggests that if females would be more understanding and less demanding when intermittent failures occur, there would be fewer progressions of an intermittent incompetence into a pattern of total incompetence. But, again studies indicate that self-imposed male standards contribute at least as much to this performance anxiety as a noncaring, demanding female. (Only recently have female standards become public knowledge, which, if accepted as absolutes, would tend to act in the same way, though Kinsey and Dickenson both referred to multiorgasmic women, 20 and 40 years ago.)

Premature ejaculation. This is the most common disturbance and the most readily amenable to direct methods of correction, though, as noted above, most investigators feel that it is entirely psychic in origin. But what is premature? Each male defines this for himself, and the caring male usually defines it as not being able to last long enough to please his partner. If the female routinely responds quickly, he may never feel that he ejaculates prematurely. However, if he meets someone who does not respond as quickly, or the original female has had enough experience to realize that the quick five or ten minute act of intercourse, even when orgasmic for her, lacks something in lingering closeness, he will feel premature. At the point when lingering closeness becomes part of intercourse, this same couple may find that the female is capable of being multiorgasmic, or some variation of this. Then intercourse becomes much more than penetration and male orgasm, though vaginal penetration defines intercourse in the strictest sense. Given any of these situations, which often evolve with time, experience, and love, the male may feel and be premature and be a disappointment to himself and to his partner, unless he has also evolved.

The best male reaction to the infrequent premature happening is, "Sorry, honey," while at the same time making sure that he does not then leave her at the preorgasmic end of the plateau phase without relief of her sexual tension. If this becomes a pattern, or has always been a pattern in a short history of sexual activity, a decrease in the amount of initial mutual genital contact can be effective in maintaining the excitement or early plateau phase without an involuntary escalation to ejaculation.

Masters and Johnson's "squeeze" technique requires an understanding female. One-night-stands do not always involve an understanding female, and many females with varying degrees of sexual experience, are not visually or manually at ease with the penis. Since premature ejaculation is primarily a dysfunction of the relatively inexperienced, the chances are very good that the inexperienced but understanding female may still be uncomfortable with the required manipulation. (Many males who are aware of an impending ejaculation, but before it is out of control, move away and squeeze the glans until the feeling goes away.) The slight loss of erection that occurs is usually temporary, and erection returns with either manual or mutual stimulation.

Condoms decrease sensation slightly, and their use may decrease the intensity of sensation just enough to aid in maintaining an intravaginal erection without precipitous ejaculation. Maintaining an erection intravaginally without ejaculation is the primary problem for most premature ejaculators. Even good, caring males have difficulty resisting, even temporarily, the intense desire to be "inside" (see Rhythm and Chap. 3).

Premature ejaculation is not related to a past history or continuing practice of masturbation, but there does seem to be a correlation with a long history of heavy petting which progresses into withdrawal as a method of contraception (see p. 199); neither petting nor withdrawal usually requires ejaculatory control as they are practiced early in sexual life, and both are part of almost every male's early sexual experiences. We know of several males who have practiced control techniques with solitary masturbation; they did not use masturbation as a quick release mechanism. Another possible solution, which should be combined with the above, is that of assuming some real concern for the female, whether the situation is just a friendly encounter or has the potential of becoming a long-term commitment. In the process, the male may discover that whatever prolongs her pleasure will, in turn, prolong his.

It may be difficult to understand that the same need for caring and concern is necessary within a marriage relationship in which love may clearly exist, but the "Dear Abby" letter below illustrates the situation of more women, and more nonorgasmic women, than we would like to think about:

Dear Abby:

Once again, a letter in your column from a man complaining because his wife doesn't give him enough "affection." ("I just can't get her into the bedroom.")

When a man says "affection" he means sex. Sex is great, but what most women really want is affection. The reassuring words, the warm embraces, the loving looks.

In my case, I can't show my husband the least bit of "affection" without his wanting to head for the bedroom.

He isn't the "affectionate" type. And he doesn't want to waste time with preliminaries.

Women are advised to fake orgasms in order to please their husbands. Will you please advise men to fake a little affection in order to please their wives? It could save their marriage.

Jinny

In fairness to the husband, he may be a premature ejaculator, easily aroused, who knows he doesn't have time for preliminaries. He also does not know enough about women to understand that they can enjoy and need the closeness of continuing stimulation postejaculation.

The apparent increase in premature ejaculation has been attributed to 1) an increasing number of demanding, threatening, expectant females, and 2) greater verbal and oral recognition of the problem. We would like to add a third possible cause, the relative nonuse of condoms in the past few years which puts an increasing number of uncovered penises into vaginas. Such skin to skin contact can be intensely stimulating to the relatively inexperienced male and can precipitate ejaculation. We prefer the latter two interpretations, though the disappointed female is undoubtedly a factor in some isolated one-to-one encounters. Females can be just as cruel or unthinking as males are often accused of being in a sexual situation. For example, a summary of Hubbard's description of the typical skyjacker:

In his experience, they are not strong, masculine supermen but weak, longtime losers, men who have failed at life and love. They often tend to be passive, effeminate, latently homosexual, and afraid of their eldest sisters and mothers. . . . Almost without exception the men were reviled by their wives, strove to placate them and were often cuckolded. . . . One betrayed skyjacker's wife told her husband that he had "never pleased her sexually, had a tiny penis, and not the least idea in the world about what to do with it."[9]

Impotence. This may be primary: the male has never maintained an erection intravaginally, or secondary: the male has been successful previously but isn't now. The psychic background and the resulting emotional overlay with impotence present difficult but not insoluble problems. The occasional episode of impotence in any age group does not constitute dysfunction; for example, the male setting out in an extramarital affair or a night out. A thoughtful, experienced mistress or prostitute is often much more tolerant and understanding of impotence than a chronically unhappy wife can be. Or, there may be impotence with a wife and not with another sexually available female. We have seen young women who have decided that they have to be the "contraceptors" because their males repeatedly lose their erection as soon as they put on a condom.

Performance anxiety and alcohol are the major causes of occasional impotence. The effect of drug use, whether heavy or light, is unpredictable. If an individual's usual response to a specific drug is withdrawal into "self," some dysfunction may be expected if sexual activity is demanded or exacted by a partner. A little alcohol can remove some inhibitions in both females and males. But only the fantasies work well with excessive amounts, and males are more disadvantaged at the performance level. Use of "light" drugs can also remove inhibitions, and the distortion of time which occurs with some of these drugs can make even moderately good sex feel, look, and be remembered as fantastic.

Some knowledge of the body's normal physiological response to anxiety and fear—blood vessels constrict in the peripheral organs of the body, including the skin and the penis—helps in the understanding of the relation of concerns about failure and the spiraling of occasional impotence into a pattern of failure. This information, combined with sensitive counseling (informed listening), reassurance about physical normality, and a well-informed sensitive partner, allows some urologists to treat patients with early impotence, successfully.[10] Here, too, the "slow down, don't make intercourse the end point of every sexual encounter" approach is very valuable.

Understanding this physiological response will also help those males who function well when using withdrawal, but find that they lose their erection when they put on a condom. There are many males and females who do not trust the condom, and pregnancy fears in the male can be as real as those in the female. Also, protected or unprotected intravaginal ejaculation can represent just as much of a commitment for a single male as it does for some females, regardless of how intense his temporary, conscious desire to be "inside" is.

An experienced, sensitive female can be an invaluable asset in the face of occasional or frequent impotence. She will not be threatening, or openly disappointed, and will be comfortable enough with physical sexuality to assist the male by manual or oral manipulation. She will also understand those times or that time when he is so devastated that nothing works, and he cannot even think about her intense needs at that moment.

Masters and Johnson cite a long list of physical conditions medical and surgical, which may be associated with impotence.[11] But most of these conditions do not have an absolute relationship; it should not be assumed that postoperative impotence is inevitable just because the genital, urinary, or pelvic area is involved.

After operation, the patient should be encouraged to engage in whatever sexual activity he finds himself capable of. If his potency is unchanged, he may return to activity as soon as his desires dictate. If potency is diminished, but still present, he can be reassured that full function may return, but he might be well advised against continually testing himself lest the anticipation of failure be worse than just accepting the diminished power. If impotence does occur, he should be especially encouraged to engage freely in sexual actions that please his sexual partner. Indeed, gratification by other than the usual conventional coitus can often be most gratifying to women and may even be preferred. He should therefore continue to think of himself as a sexual human being.[12]

This is excellent advice for any dysfunction regardless of origin or circumstances.

Spinal injuries. One of the tragedies of war is the return of men to civilian life with spinal cord injuries and without adequate knowledge of their sexual potential. To this group we must add males and females with diving and football injuries (broken necks), with automobile injuries, and those caught up in the increasing number of civilian gunshot wounds of the spinal cord. These injured are often paraplegic (muscle paralysis of the pelvis and lower extremities with loss of most or all sensation). The higher cord injuries, in the neck area, cause quadriplegia, or loss of voluntary muscular activity and some or all sensation from the neck down. Equally tragic is the assumption by their friends, acquaintances, and strangers that these people have no sexual function. Germaine Greer, writing about the Democratic Convention (1972) noted that "the heterosexuality of the politicians was in plentiful evidence, but their virility was almost as important. Ladies of the Wallace persuasion, worried perhaps that the Gov'nah might not appear to be holding his own, volunteered the information on three separate occasions that 'he has all of his sexual faculties unimpaired'."[13]

There is no need to look at the 50-year-old paraplegic from World War II and wonder if those four children are really his; undoubtedly they are. Or to pity the martyred wife, because ". . . a vast majority of disabled men can have erections; . . . up to 70% of those with incomplete cord damage can ejaculate; . . . most of them, given a patient and knowing partner, can have coitus."[14] There are a number of publications on the subject of sexual function in this group, and at least one training movie for sex education in rehabilitation centers. This kind of information is still not a part of most medical school curricula. Many doctors are not aware of it, but the information is available.

Sexual Dysfunctions in the Female

One group of dysfunctions in the female is entirely in the realm of lack of desire, or of total response. Both of these lacks have been defined as frigidity. Both are almost totally centered in a female's own mind or awareness; they need not even be known by a partner. The second group arises from varying degrees of discomfort with intercourse (dyspareunia). Physical discomfort can be severely limiting to the success of the sexual act for both female and male and, in many cases, is completely independent of the pysche.

In the male, lack of orgasm is seldom, if ever, a problem if there is ejaculation, though the quality of the male orgasmic experience will vary, being more or less intense with a longer or shorter resolution phase.

Females should count their blessings; in the sexual context, the advantages of being female far outweigh the disadvantages. Females can just lie there, dysfunctional, and be considered 100 percent successful at least 50 percent of the time in the judgment of many males. Females can look good 100 percent of the time if, as a well-known actress noted on TV, she adds "a grunt or a groan, rolls her eyes, gives him the 'tortured'[15] look and moves around a little." But there is no way to fake an erection. Remember, we are still discussing function, not love, affection, or caring.

Successfully faking an orgasm, even for good and true reasons, represents, at best, a kind of Pyrrhic victory: one loses while winning. This has no place in any woman's repertoire until she has become aware of her own reactions during orgasm and, more important, is with someone she knows intimately enough to know his moods and needs at a particular time, even though they do not coincide with hers. There is certainly no need to pretend for a casual acquaintance. On the other hand, if a woman knows a man very well, there should really be no need to pretend:

> ... Pretending to have sexual pleasure virtually guarantees never experiencing it. The first step toward orgasmic experience for those who have not enjoyed this birthright is to acknowledge that it is missing.[16]

However, everyone goes through a learning phase of short or long duration, during which insecurities about function arise as do insecurities about how well one really knows one's partner, even a husband. It is terribly difficult to answer the question, "Did you come?" with a "No." And to add "not yet," is almost an aggressive act and can be a very bad putdown for an insecure male who has already confessed that he doesn't recognize a female orgasm when he sees, hears, or feels one. For the same reasons, most females are not going to answer, "I don't think so."

No matter how much honesty there is in a relationship or how much freedom there is in sexual discussion between partners, this kind of question and answer game is really the moment of truth in any relationship. How one handles the situation is an individual matter, depending on all other aspects of the relationship. This is an interesting case of situational ethics.

It is usually women who feel that there are occasions when, for the male, the positive effects of admitting or pretending an orgasm that did not occur are far greater than any negative effects of the deception. Some women feel that this even has positive effects for the female who is only intermittently orgasmic under the best of circumstances. To pretend is to make a conscious effort to appear out of control. Discovering that out of control is not as embarrassing or devastating as she had imagined, may have a positive influence on a woman's future activities.

We tend to agree that there may be a time and place for this kind of deception, but we feel that perhaps a better approach is to indicate at some time to a partner that there are several different levels of very satisfactory sexual release and that while they all don't "hit the top," levels two or three are not that bad. This is true for most women; Reuben's patients called it "skimming." This approach comforts most males and may or may not comfort the female, depending on what really happened. But it does give the male partner courage for the next time, and eventually both will find out what the "top" is for her.

Sexual intercourse is very simple in concept, but it is frequently difficult to establish optimal conditions because ". . . it requires a total abandonment of civilized veneers and defences; a total exposure and sharing with another, of the deepest most primitive layers of the emotional self. It is simply not compatible with 'Sunday-best behaviour' ".[17] And this is essential for good results, even in casual encounters.

Lack of orgasm. Lack of orgasm, or infrequent orgasm, is a common feature of intercourse in the inexperienced female. We will ignore, for the moment, that she is often with an equally inexperienced male. Lack of orgasm is not necessarily a common feature of early sexual experiences which stop just short of intercourse, since the clitoral and vaginal stimulation, manual, penile, or oral, in this situation may be more intense and prolonged than when intercourse is the expected "end point."

In the past few years, even experienced females who have fairly predictable orgasmic responses have been assaulted with information which says that they are capable of being multiorgasmic. Some of these women are now wondering and insecure. "Is it the inept male or is it me?" Males may be threatened by the same information. "Am I inept or is she frigid? How come she has only one when I can stay around as long as I do? What am I doing wrong?" But there are always males who do not care about female responses and females who have either given up caring or do not wish to be involved in the sexual act to this extent.

Many females and males have difficulty believing that the female orgasm, besides being the expected result of masturbation or direct clitoral stimulation during intercourse, can also occur as the result of oral or manual breast stimulation, breast-feeding, vaginal stimulation (penile, manual, or childbirth), or visual or verbal stimulation. Even awaking in the orgasmic state from a recognized or unrecognized erotic dream is not unusual.

Regardless of its source, orgasm is an intense, brief, overwhelming awareness of all of oneself; or some describe it as a brief disembodiment, perceived as arising primarily from the genital area with a focus which may be clitoral, vaginal, or just diffusely pelvic. Words are inadequate even for the most articulate poets and literary giants. It is a feeling which, because of its intensity, is probably blessed to some degree by its relative brevity.

Recurrent imagery may be associated with orgasm, though recalling the image does not recall the feeling; during early experiences there may be tendency to measure the intensity of the orgasm with the appearance or nonappearance of a familiar image. But orgasmic experiences change over the years, and the images change, and disappear. The orgasmic experiences with childbirth are reported in auditory and visual terms: cymbals clashing, bells ringing, "the rockets red glare, the bombs bursting in air." This makes it sound like a good drug trip, though such trips frequently last too long, are unpredictable, and are followed by the most miserable of side effects. Good orgasmic experiences often seem ridiculously short, too short to be an adequate substitute for drug-oriented people, but certainly worth considering. A few years ago, we suggested somewhat facetiously but wherever it seemed appropriate, that an attempt to switch students from hard drugs to safe knowledgeable sex might be in order. There were many shocked looks. Now, 18-year-olds are promoting sex over drugs because ". . . It's a natural thing, a nice thing and a nice high. It sure can clear up the blues."[18] There are still shocked looks, but not from those who know.

Three major areas are worth examining when orgasmic experiences are either infrequent or lacking: 1) the time involved, which may be elapsed time per encounter or just accumulated experience; 2) the actual physical technique; and 3) the wide range of attitudes about sexual activity. The latter includes situational aspects such as fear of pregnancy, type of contraception, the immediate as well as the past environment,* the involvement with the male, a masturbation history and feelings about this, a woman's concept of herself as a functioning female (i.e., is she willing to be female?), and most important, some expertise in interpersonal relationships and knowledge of how other people function. But sexual activity seldom waits for all of this learning and self-examination, though physical sex will continue to improve in direct relation to the amount of information one has about oneself and others. Twenty years later, sexual activity, with the same or another partner, can be completely different and better, even though the mechanics are essentially the same, and it is the same penis and vagina.

Keeping in mind that none of the factors mentioned above may be totally to blame, probably time and experience are the predominant issue in the younger age group. There is really something to be said for the old axiom, "Girls should be taught by older men, and boys should be taught by older women." In this context, old means experienced.

In general, women are aroused more slowly than men; this is true even of females who are able to be moderately active in initiating sexual activity. Arousal includes physiology as well as the psyche. Very few women can func-

---

* One point must be made about the environment, and perhaps it deserves more than a footnote since we have not seen it mentioned elsewhere—at times darkness serves a very useful function early in sexual experience and even later. Darkness or semidarkness removes all distracting visual stimuli and allows only touch, odor, and aural stimuli to predominate. It also removes any inhibitions about seeing or being seen. This allows total involvement in the sensations arising from touching and the pleasures of what is happening—the girl who has never been orgasmic on a couch at midday, in the early morning light, or in the dimly lighted environment desired by many males who enjoy visual stimuli, may find out what her orgasmic potential is. It is not very "sophisticated" to have intercourse in total darkness, but functionally it can be very useful, at least initially.

tion well in a ten minute time span, but most males can accomplish penetration, ejaculation, and be orgasmic in this length of time or less, if that is all they are interested in. It is difficult for the premature ejaculator to maintain his interest in further sexual activity postejaculation (in the resolution phase) unless he really cares about the female he is with, and even then it requires conscious effort. Even under these caring circumstances, he may occasionally be so devastated about having been premature for the "umpteenth" time that further activity is out of the question. If a woman can help dissipate these feelings, or create an atmosphere that is not demanding, or full of disappointment or hostility, she is less likely to be ignored and left behind.

If a female feels "used," simply a receptacle for sperm, before, during, or after one of these brief encounters, she will hardly be able to abandon her "civilized veneers" and to trust. However, if both partners in a brief encounter clearly understand that they are "using" each other ("real honesty" in a relationship) and that "fun" is the end point, the chances of success are much greater. It might be better to make this assumption in all encounters, at least initially, if one can. If guilt about sex is not a major problem, and intercourse and its preliminaries can be viewed as fun, good, and an experience with someone to whom one is attracted, even temporarily, relaxation rather than performance anxiety will be the predominant mood. Even the "inexperienced fumblings and bumblings," the words of an 18-year-old (Maynard) can be enjoyed;[19] there may or may not be penetration, but the pleasures can be appreciated, if there is adequate contraception, which alleviates an additional problem.

There are a great many females of all ages, who simply want to "do something" for their men. Their expectations are low, they are not success oriented; they are giving, not taking. This group is included in any statistics about frequency of orgasm. Occasionally, we have asked girls about orgasm, when they have come in requesting contraceptive advice, and have said that the diaphragm or condom was too much trouble and interfered with their once-a-day frequency. More often than not, in the 17 to 19 age group, they had never had an orgasm, and really did not expect to have orgasmic experiences "until later" or with "one particular guy."

It takes many encounters to discover one's own needs in a sexual situation, what is good and what is effective; this frequency may take place in or out of marriage, or with a variety of partners. Having discovered some kind of pattern, each individual can guide and recreate success, vary the pattern, and allow for evolution of his or her own sexuality. The problem is, of course, communicating this to one or more partners. Not everyone speaks the same language or recognizes the signals in the same way. Seaman ended an article about orgasm in MS magazine with "men must learn to seek and receive signals from the women they love."[20] Equally important, women must understand that they have to send signals which are clear, gentle, and quiet. Initially, with any partner, there may have to be a verbal "Yes" or "No," a firm guiding hand, or an obvious readjustment of contact. Eventually, with one partner, messages will become increasingly more subtle and perhaps more infrequent, but they will always be needed because the emotions which two people bring to sexual activity, as well as the environment, are always changing.

The classic and tragic example of noncommunication and performance orientation would be the newly married couple, very well read in techniques, who spent their three month honeymoon in Europe trying every position and every technique without orgasmic success for her. They sought advice in the fall, wondering what was wrong with them; neither had had any premarital experience, either together or with others. With questioning, it became apparent that she had found many of the techniques unpleasant at this stage and had accepted them only because the instruction book had made them legitimate in her mind. The male was also unenthusiastic about some of the techniques. They really had read the books too soon and needed to start all over again (see p. 73).

Frequently women will blame some factor other than time. One college student, age 19, said, "I've been on the pill for the past five months, and I am just not interested in sex anymore except for those seven days when I am off the pill. Does the pill have anything to do with this feeling?" With questioning she told us that she was engaged, that sex was getting better, though she had never been orgasmic (she didn't think she had), that intercourse was once a day or oftener on weekends. When questioned about "elapsed" time per encounter, she mumbled something, then laughed and said "Would you believe three minutes?" We talked about time and technique; we also discussed the fairly common misunderstanding that there is a greater risk of pregnancy on the nonpill days, and that risk often increases sexual pleasure (see Contraception).*

Seldom mentioned in any books on techniques is the actual physical fit of two individuals in relation to her or his orgasmic potential. Fit, technique, and discomfort with intercourse are three physical factors which have little to do with the psyche but which require some knowledgeable adaptation or, in some cases, medical treatment.

The relative size of the penis and the vagina are seldom factors though many women think, initially, that intercourse is an impossibility for them because they "can't even get a tampon in." Many men, knowing the size of

---

*Another girl, age 21, announced to us that she didn't view the pill as the "great all American panacea," since there was still a week that one had to abstain, which was only slightly less than the abstinence required with the rhythm method. When she was enlightened on this point, she said, "My God, and I think I am reasonably intelligent; what about all of those other people?"

their erect penis and the apparent size of the vagina are also concerned. But this is not the fit we are discussing. Any woman who has been with more than one male is well aware that, when the penis is in the vagina, the prominence of the male pubic bone varies from male to male in its relation to the female clitoris. With adequate clitoral stimulation from any source, prior to penetration, the thrusting and direct contact with the clitoris is often a successful combination for female orgasm. If thrusting is combined only with soft body contact against the clitoral area, the stimulation may not be as great. This is confirmed by women who have a history, which often puzzles them, of one or more males who will "turn them on" almost immediately, even though they were not that emotionally involved and the prepenetration technique was not that different. This kind of information should not be interpreted as an absolute need to maintain clitoral contact during penetration because this can often be uncomfortable, if the penis thrusts against the middle of the posterior vaginal wall.

The comment, "I don't know if I ever had an orgasm," probably stems from that good, full feeling and vaginal stimulation that never progressed to orgasm. Firm, intermittent, or steady clitoral pressure, with direct or lateral contact, is necessary for most women, at least up to the beginning of orgasm. Direct manipulation, can be painful or become painful; there is a time to stop. But firm, total pressure in the clitoral area seldom produces this kind of discomfort. If more males who apparently "don't quite fit" took time to be quiet, to hold tightly, or firmly, or to readjust temporarily so that they do fit, moving only slightly or maintaining pressure in the clitoral area even without complete penetration, there might be more successes. If females, who are wondering why all of that vaginal stimulation isn't progressing to something more intense, would tell their partners to be quiet, hold them tightly, and maybe do some readjusting themselves, a signal in itself, they could contribute to their own success. This is a purely physical thing which, if all other factors can be eliminated as causal, can lead to a "cure" of this dysfunction.

The basic mechanism of stimulation and pleasure for the male is penetration and movement. The basic mechanism of stimulation which progresses to orgasmic release in the female is pressure and firm touch in the clitoral area, though total genital stimulation can only enhance this. In females and males, the orgasmic phase is preceded by an intense desire for closeness and penetration, which persists, in the female especially, past the orgasmic phase. Movement of the penis, in and out, with its resultant intermittent total genital pressure is not always the specific technique for every female. If the male can maintain his erection long enough, the resolution phase can be as pleasurable for the female, in a different way, as anything that has gone before. For the female who wishes, this can be expanded into some intense feelings again by her own activities. Males do not have this immediate potential of recreating after their ejaculation (see Chap. 3).

Without intending to sound militantly liberated, we can understand any male writer's view (the primary source of sexual technique books) that vaginal stimulation should somehow be the same kind of *primary* stimulation for females that it is for males. Females do not need penetration to accomplish sexual release, but most will desire it intensely as an extension of the closeness. Total stimulation, vaginal plus clitoral, is definitely more than the sum of its parts. This rather basic difference in the source of primary stimulation between the male and the female may explain some of the longstanding questions and myths about clitoral and vaginal orgasm. Tunnadine, a female physician, speaks of the very real difference between clitoral orgasm experienced with mutual or solitary masturbation and the "vaginal totality" achieved with total genital stimulation. Orgasm is a very intense sensation, but vaginal stimulation, prolongation of total genital stimulation, and the whole feeling of closeness with another individual adds a whole new dimension to physical sex. Most heterosexual and homosexual women would agree that there is a difference.

Lack of interest. This definition of frigidity includes that small group of heterosexual women who experience little or no sexual arousal or pleasure and are never orgasmic, as well as an even smaller group who have completely negative reactions to sexual approaches of any kind by any male, though they consciously desire and are happy with all other aspects of heterosexual life.

Brady, who has been quite successful in treating all types of frigidity, feels that these women are severely disabled and more difficult to treat, because they are more apt to show evidences of personality disorders in other areas of their lives which predate this type of sexual dysfunction. Treatment in this group must also be directed at the resulting problems in the marriage relationship as well, which often extend beyond the sexual area by the time treatment and help is sought.[21]

Decreased interest in sexual activity, from a previous moderate or normal level of interest, is often associated with a history of painful intercourse. The continuation of intercourse through an uncomfortable episode(s) of vulvovaginitis can lead to fears and tension after the cure (see p. 119). These fears and tensions can give rise to vaginismus (an involuntary tightening of the muscles around the introitus which prevents penetration). The need for continuing intercourse, though painful or uncomfortable, is often blamed on a demanding male. However, we have seen a number of women who do not stop having intercourse but ask only for some good lubricant so "that it doesn't hurt too much." They may be afraid of losing their man if they request or demand a period of abstinence or some variation. We question if all of these women would progress into problems with vaginismus, though continued activity does prolong their symptoms and treatment.

Every gynecologist is aware of the temporary vaginismus which occurs just prior to or at the time of a patient's first or thirtieth pelvic examination; an elbow on the patient's knee, a hand on her thigh, and the speculum or gloved examining fingers resting on, not in, the introitus for an extra 30 or 40 seconds is usually sufficient to overcome even the vaginismus with a first pelvic examination. The muscles often contract with nervous tension, even in women with previous sexual experience. Seduction reduces fearful tension, or that is its primary function; the pleasures of seduction are a secondary gain and incidental to function. Penetration, or a pelvic examination, prior to this relaxation is extremely uncomfortable, but not impossible (see Rape).

Lack of lubrication is frequently associated with vaginismus, or it may be the primary cause of vaginismus.

When vaginismus becomes the primary pattern of response to any sexual stimulation, some form of desensitization or behavioral therapy is usually required, if other factors are ruled out or at least recognized and included in the therapy (see below). Sexual counseling may take the form of asking the couple to start from the beginning again: a recapitulation of dating behavior, without intercourse as an end point. Occasionally it is necessary for the gynecologist to indicate to both partners that he or she can insert the speculum or gloved examining fingers without difficulty and that the husband can do the same. There may be results from this type of recapitulation and desensitization in from one to three months. There should be no hurry.

Other factors which may be operating and creating a need for some active psychotherapy are recognized or unrecognized sexual inhibition. The feeling that "sex is sinful"; "men are not to be trusted and are exploitative"; "all lovers are Dad"; "all partners are mother" can present major problems for males. Traumatic sexual encounters, such as rape, do not seem to contribute to later sexual difficulties, except perhaps initially.[22] As we have noted before, trauma from a stranger almost makes sense; trauma from a friend does not.

It is apparent that there are many lay and professional definitions of frigidity, and the term is often used so loosely and in such a hostile, accusatory manner by a male partner that its use only perpetuates an already difficult situation.[23] The male partner may not be as hostile as he sounds, just uninformed and trying to help in a gross kind of way. Self-diagnosis without a background of experience, time, and some knowledge of the basic physiology of males and females can also be destructive.

Dyspareunia. Dyspareunia (dys' pahr oo' ni ah), or discomfort with intercourse, stemming from a physical or mental source limits orgasmic potential. Everything else can be optimal, and the fear or threat of pain will prevent "losing oneself." This affects females more than males, though, in the latter, it depends more upon the degree of discomfort anticipated.

In the female, sensitivity of the vaginal lining to some contraceptive agents will create irritation; frequency of intercourse may create irritation because every vagina seems to have its own changing threshold for what it considers too much activity; lack of lubrication prevents easy penetration. All of these may create a temporary vaginismus. Deep discomfort with penetration may be due to a physical problem in the pelvis, such as inflamed tubes, enlarged ovaries, or a nonmobile, retroflexed uterus.

One of the most frequent types of discomfort we have seen is that occurring in females recently into sexual activity. These women are not aware that genital manipulation or intercourse has some after effects which may last 24 to 36 hours. They suddenly become aware of an area which they have never been aware of before—an awareness which their mothers and females with more experience have learned is relatively normal and of no consequence.

In the male, sensitivity to contraceptives can be a problem though it is relatively infrequent. There may be little vesicles (blisters) or a rash on the glans or shaft of the penis. A nonretracting foreskin is uncomfortable. Even in circumcised males, the variable length of foreskin may be slightly adherent and create problems. Sensitivity to the latex in condoms or to the lubricant used with lubricated condoms is infrequent, but occurs or seems to be the etiology of some sensitivity reactions (see Chap. 4).

References

1. See William H. Masters and Virginia Johnson, *Human Sexual Response* (Boston: Little, Brown and Co., 1966).

2. *Ibid.*

3. *Ibid.*

4. *Ibid.*

5. *Ibid.*

6. *Ibid.*

7. Levinger's article, "Husbands' and Wives' Estimates of Coital Frequency," *Medical Aspects of Human Sexuality* (September 1970), indicates that there are more factors than simple memory operating when each member of a couple is questioned separately about frequency, and whether or not it approaches that which he or she expects or desires.

8. William H. Masters and Virginia Johnson, *Human Sexual Inadequacy* (Boston: Little, Brown and Co., 1970).

9. See discussion of D. Hubbard's *The Skyjacker: His Flights of Fantasy* (New York: Macmillan, 1971) in *Time,* 13 November 1972, p. 51.

10. Dr. Sheldon Fellman as quoted in "Sex Counseling and the Primary Physician," *Medical World News* (March 2, 1972).

11. Masters and Johnson, *Human Sexual Inadequacy.*

12. A. S. Lyons, "Potency after Rectal Resection," *Medical Aspects of Human Sexuality* (May 1972).

13. Germaine Greer, "McGovern, the Big Tease," *Harper's,* October 1972.

14. Anonymous, "Sex and the Paraplegic," *Medical World News* (January 14, 1972).

15. Alfred C. Kinsey, et al., *Sexual Behavior in the Human Female* (Philadelphia: W. B. Saunders Company, 1953).

16. William H. Masters and Virginia Johnson, "Plain Talk for Women Who Lie About Sex," *Redbook,* September 1972, p. 76.

17. L. P. Tunnadine, *Contraception and Sexual Life: A Therapeutic Approach* (Philadelphia: J. B. Lippincott Company, 1970).

18. "Teenage Sex: Letting the Pendulum Swing," *Time,* 21 August 1972, p. 34.

19. From Joyce Maynard, *Looking Back: A Chronicle of Growing Up Old in the Sixties* (Garden City, New York: Doubleday and Company, 1973).

20. Barbara Seaman, "The Liberated Orgasm," *Ms.,* August 1972, p. 65. Adapted from *Free and Female: The Sex Life of the Contemporary Woman* (New York: Coward, McCann & Geoghegan, Inc., 1972).

21. J. P. Brady, "Frigidity," *Medical Aspects of Human Sexuality* (November 1967):42.

22. J. P. Brady, et al., "Roundtable: Frigidity," *Medical Aspects of Human Sexuality* (February 1968):26.

23. *Ibid.*

3

· · · · · · · · ·   Intercourse: · · · · · · · · ·
Reproduction and Pleasure

Reproduction

EVERY ACT OF INTERCOURSE has the potential of being an act of reproduction, if there are sperm in the ejaculate, the ovaries are ovulating, and there are no barriers between the sperm and the egg. It is as simple as that.

Fifteen percent of all married couples who find themselves temporarily or permanently infertile know that getting pregnant is not easy, but the other 85 percent know, often too well, how easy it can be.

Although there are still many unknowns, we know that:

1. Ovulation normally occurs once in every menstrual cycle. Ordinarily only one egg is released, or ovulated, per cycle. Two or more eggs may be ovulated at once, and if fertilized, may result in fraternal or nonidentical multiple births. Ovulation occurs 14 ± 1 days *prior* to the first day of the *next* menstrual flow. It is generally assumed that the egg is capable of being fertilized for a period of 24 hours postovulation, though there is some evidence that this period may be considerably shorter.

2. In the normal male, spermatozoa are produced in optimal numbers and motility when ejaculation occurs with a frequency of about two to three times a week (see Infertility). However, any two of these ejaculates may vary in number and motility of sperm. The changes in motility and number which occur with increased or markedly decreased frequency of ejaculation are unpredictable, but generally a frequency of more than seven or eight ejaculations a week is associated with a decreased number of sperm. Motile spermatozoa may be present in the preejaculatory secretion (see Withdrawal), and may be found in the semen up to three or more months postvasectomy; this depends on the frequency of ejaculation during the postvasectomy period (see Vasectomy).

3. Sperm deposited in the vagina with deep penetration may be found in the uterine cavity 30 to 40 *seconds* after deposition. Sperm from this same ejaculate may be found in the motile state in the vagina and uterus as long as five to six days after deposition. Pregnancies occurring from unprotected intercourse on Day 6 of a menstrual cycle of 24 to 28 days are not uncommon. In this cycle, ovulation would occur any time from Day 10 to Day 14. There is still doubt about the occurrence of spontaneous ovulation with intercourse in

the human, though this is common in some lower animals, such as the rabbit. Most pregnancies that "could not have happened" can be explained by either the longevity of the sperm, or the occurrence of early or delayed ovulation. The normal range of possible ovulation days is about four with regular 28 day cycles, since these cycles may vary as much as four days and still be normal. Delayed ovulation, Day 16 or beyond, with a delayed menstrual flow is not uncommon, nor is being three or four days late in the presence of a history of usually regular cycles of 26 to 30 days (see Menstruation).

Every obstetrician at some time has had a patient who is pregnant, although her hymeneal ring is still so tight that it prevents adequate vaginal examination prior to delivery. This can only mean that sperm deposited at the introitus are capable of ascending 4 inches or more to the cervical canal. Keep in mind also that the force of ejaculation is variable, even in one individual male's experience. The vagina is not a hollow tube, but forceful ejaculation against a tight hymeneal ring coupled with the normal lubrication of the vagina can certainly assist the sperm part of the way. Abortions may require dilatation of the hymeneal ring for the same reasons.

A common question from females and males concerns the "danger" of spermatic fluid on male fingers which are later inserted into the vagina. Without facts, and there do not seem to be any, we can say only that if sperm in the preejaculatory secretion should be suspect at all times, we must also keep post-ejaculatory, digital, vaginal manipulation suspect. It is difficult for some males in the middle of the sexual act to think of their ejaculate as "dangerous" or anything but pleasurable, so that a quick wiping of the hand, as if it were dirty, is not easy. However, this would seem to be a logical, if not entirely realistic approach to use.

But to be realistic, reproduction can occur with preejaculatory secretions as experienced with preejaculatory penetration, ejaculation at the introitus with withdrawal or "heavy petting," postejaculatory, digital, intravaginal placement, and, of course, the usual way. Most important, there is little one can do after the sperm are in the cervical canal to change their direction, though we must admit that douching out the remaining spermatic fluid undoubtedly decreases the continued migration of those remaining sperm into the uterus. But little is gained by leaping up and douching immediately.

There are other points which will be made in later discussions regarding sperm in the first few adolescent ejaculations, predicting the first day of the next menstrual cycle, and ovulation during breast-feeding or with grossly irregular menstrual cycles.

NO is the answer to another common question, "Do you have to have an orgasm to get pregnant?" Rape is seldom, if ever, orgasmic but does impregnate on occasion. Many of those five minute episodes of intercourse can result in pregnancy.

Yes, the penis was in the vagina. Yes, there was an ejaculation, but we thought there was more to it than that. Nothing really happened.

No, we didn't use anything. We aren't really intending to do that sort of thing (intercourse); once or twice maybe, but not regularly. We are not interested in contraception.

These comments are real, and we have heard many variations from young adults who could list every type of contraception that was discussed in their high school sex education courses, but who apparently missed some vital information in their desire to ignore the mechanics, and to learn how to "really relate to someone of the opposite sex."

There has always been a wealth of mythology about the facts of reproduction, or more accurately, about the facts of preventing reproduction. Mythology is very useful; it serves to conceal ignorance or lack of knowledge. Every culture has its own mythology about reproduction and contraception which indicates some basic desire to avoid unwanted pregnancies. This is equally true among the various cultures in the United States in which our society further imposed on many of us and our parents a morality which prohibited discussion of sexual matters. This mythology, often a street-corner or locker-room mythology, allows a female or male to say, "Look, I am a responsible person. I did not want to create a pregnancy now. I did everything I have been told would work. The people who told me are to blame if they told me wrong, not me; I tried and I really do care."

It is unnecessary to list the myths if the previous paragraphs were well understood. It is also impossible to list all of them, but none of the following works: blowing hot air into the vagina postintercourse, standing up during or after intercourse, the female urinating after intercourse, the woman on top, lack of orgasm, lack of penetration, the male ingesting codeine cough syrup a few hours prior to ejaculation, and so on. Douching is not a method of contraception. Withdrawal is poor sexually and unreliable contraceptively.

Many of the contraceptive myths, including some in recent sex manuals, are based on doing the reverse of methods advised for *infertile* couples who are trying to get pregnant. These couples are primarily concerned with methods of intercourse which insure prolonged contact between sperm and the cervical canal. For fertile couples, and all couples must assume that they are fertile until proven otherwise, prolonged close contact of sperm and cervical mucus does not seem to be essential. Nor is it often the vital factor in infertility though often a carefully taken history will reveal some sexual practices which might make fertilization unlikely.

Drugs, potions, or herbs with scientifically proven safe aphrodisiac effects are nonexistent, as are proven safe antiaphrodisiacs.* However, the use of estrogens and male hormones in early puberty may precipitate the onset of sexual awareness (see p. 246). There are drugs, including alcohol, which decrease inhibitions about any kind of social or behavioral activities, including sexual activities; if these are used in appropriate amounts they may *act* as aphrodisiacs (see Rhythm, Infertility, Endocrinology for further discussions of reproduction).

Pleasure

What I think is this; all the misconceptions about sexuality will straighten out if everyone simply grows up. For a grownup human being, what's good in bed is to be with another human being one truly cares about. And what one cares about in bed is exactly the same as what one cares about out of bed—honesty, imagination, a little mischief, and a lot of kindness.

Eleanor Perry

AND THIS IS WHAT it is all about, isn't it—love, pleasure, and affection? Making babies is easy, making love is another matter. The latter involves people caring enough, even temporarily, to demonstrate how much they care. We use the word temporarily only because we are realistic.

It is quite possible for a person to have pleasurable intercourse (our words for fun) with a casual acquaintance, with someone she or he is fond of but would never think of marrying, or with someone she or he is thinking about seriously enough to weigh other considerations besides that of sexual compatibility. With a little experience, Perry's "growing up," a person may be able to find sexual compatibility with a number of individuals, but only if they are equally knowledgeable. Or, within marriage, a marriage based on mutual interests and the ability to function together intellectually, sexual compatibility will usually emerge spontaneously.

* There is a recent discovery of LRF (Luteinizing Hormone-Releasing Factor) in female rats. It is produced in an area of the brain which has been previously identified as being associated with sexual desire. When it is given to female rats, it induces mating behavior.

This hormone has been synthesized and there are some preliminary, unpublished, and incomplete reports that when this is given to human males, it increases libido (sexual desire).

See R. L. Moss and S. M. McCann, "Induction of Mating Behavior in Rats by Luteinizing Hormone-Releasing Factor," *Science,* 81 (July 13, 1973):4095.

A tranquilizing sex pill, cyproterone acetate (an antiaphrodisiac) has been tested in England, and found to be useful in controlling oversexed men.

There is an old persuasive line which undoubtedly is still being used: "But how else can we really get to know each other?" Knowing quickly is perhaps a more accurate translation, because there really is *no* other activity between two individuals which *can* illustrate or demonstrate so vividly in 35 to 40 minutes, so many facets of either individual's honesty, imagination, sense of mischief, kindness, and we must add, sense of humor. A game of tennis, a sail, a walk in the woods, or sitting on the front porch swing can never match it. There is also no other activity in which the physical or mechanical basis stays the same and the emotional aspects can change so much with experience, with time, with changes in the environment.

But simply going through the motions does not make it all come true. Nor will the presence of fondness, infatuation, or whatever feeling one defines as love necessarily make it all come true. Caring and being able to demonstrate this caring is the most important ingredient for each partner, and this means, at its very best, caring for another at least as much as one cares for oneself.

Teenage girls from any socioeconomic group, when asked why they have intercourse when they are getting nothing out of it by sophisticated adult standards, will answer with a variation of "It's something I can do for him. It's no big deal." Their expectations are often low, but they really care about themselves and their males, though their reasoning may be obscure to outsiders.

Young teenage boys are not programmed to think that showing evidence of caring is compatible with masculinity. Many high school sex education courses inadvertently perpetuate the stud image of young males for their male and female students. Males are perfectly capable of caring, and many high school liaisons are very intense; but being able to demonstrate this to the exclusion of his own needs is almost always more than any male's well-indoctrinated stud image of masculinity will permit.

Equally important, young girls are not programmed to expect evidence of caring beyond the apparent "wanting" by the male. When this kind of thinking and expectation extends into adult life, as it seems to in many marriages, the Kinsey reports of "no orgasm ever" are understandable. This is usually considered to be a characteristic of lower socioeconomic groups. It may be more prevalent there, but upper socioeconomic groups are beginning to verbalize their problems; rightly or wrongly, they call them frigidity, impotence, and premature ejaculation. In the former group, it may be primarily the stud philosophy operating, though this can be found at any class level; single-sex prep schools have been a good, though inconstant, source of this image:

We had been in the "beast barracks" only a few weeks when we learned of the first honor violation in our class. A guy in another company had been eliminated for "quibbling" (not telling the whole truth) to his squad leader. And what had he quibbled about? The squad leader held a manhood session and asked each man in the squad if he was still a virgin. The entire squad boasted they were not. Later, the man in question confided to his roommates that he was not really a virgin, exactly, but that he was "kind of" a virgin. The roommates turned him in.[1]

Whether it is the stud approach to sex, or low expectations of one's partner or of oneself, there is little excuse today for being unaware of a partner's needs in light of the wealth of information that is freely available, though some of it can easily be misread.

Many knowledgeable couples care about each other very much, but early in their sexual experiences the act itself is paramount and their knowledgeable expectations for themselves are high. Their problems arise from: 1) trying too hard to look good, too soon, and 2) the disappointments which follow when no matter how good one looks to oneself, somehow it did not work for the other person. These are often the same people who think that if the penis is in the vagina, all else should come naturally in this most natural of activities. This feeling seems to be especially prevalent in our present era of "instant gratification."

Above all else, "good" intercourse requires a sense of humor about oneself, the most difficult kind of humor to have, and about one's temporary or transient inadequacies. When, in the face of adversity, a male can say, "Sorry, honey, I couldn't keep it up," and know that his partner will not threaten him by word or action, both are on their way to "growing up." But this will only happen if he also recognizes that he should not leave his partner in the almost orgasmic phase, and she can communicate her needs to him with some expectation that he will understand and respond to her signals.

When both partners find that they are so comfortable and trusting that they can allow themselves the luxury and freedom to laugh, cry, and become totally involved without fears of looking too aggressive (the female), or losing masculinity (the male), maturity has arrived in this area of living. "For a woman to apologize for success is as pointless as for a man to apologize for a failure. One is as one is and the love that can't encompass both is a poor sort of love."[2] This is a theme which has endless variations, all of them based on women losing their femininity with success and men losing their masculinity with failure. It takes maturity to be able to act in an "immature" fashion without fears, to lose control, to be emotional in front of another for a time, even in a clearly defined, self-limited situation. This does not come easily or quickly to most people. But when it does, what can happen in a positive way to sexual activity will astound the participants.

Attitudes *about* sex are near the top of the list of factors influencing function. How do we modify attitudes or, in some cases anxieties, to make sex more than a mechanical act? *By relieving anxieties about pregnancy.* No one should be concerned about getting pregnant during intercourse; both partners must feel secure and comfortable about this and then dismiss it from their thinking. *By relieving concerns about appropriateness of behavior in relation to the rest of the population.* Parent and peer pressures can be very real, and their influence may be felt by either partner in the middle of a sexual act. *By relieving concerns about pain, potential damage, or disease. By feeling secure about personal hygiene.* Absence of the latter security makes some contemplated sexual activity appear completely impossible.

Some of these factors have already been discussed and are mentioned only to reinforce the point that knowledge of one's own conflicts is important in more than an intellectual sense; one has to do something about them. Some factors can be eliminated completely. Some are noted in later sections which should be read in connection with this discussion of what good mutual sex is, or can be, and the wide spectrum of basically physical activity it can encompass. However, the pleasures of each combination of two people are unique and can only be defined and discovered by them; we, of necessity, have placed our emphasis on the perils and pitfalls of various techniques, where and why things can apparently go wrong, and what one can reasonably expect of one's physical self. Although this is a slightly negative or backwards approach, if well understood, it can produce positive results.

Seduction

Seduction is essential to good sex. We prefer this word, even with its connotations to heavy petting or foreplay.* Heavy petting is a little old-fashioned and foreplay implies that this activity is secondary to the "Big O," orgasm. Physical seduction of both females and males includes the excitement and plateau phases of sexual stimulation, and when well done should be of equal value emotionally, if not in elapsed time, to orgasm and resolution. The kind of physical activity involved in seduction should, or can be, a part of the resolution phase as well, even if the intensity is lacking. Maintenance of postorgasmic closeness can be one of the most satisfying aspects of intercourse. Very simply, it confirms the existence of real caring about the other person, though there are frequently acceptable variations of this for each couple. Or some women enjoy prolonging seduction, and will stop, or request stopping further stimulation for a brief period, knowing that when orgasm occurs, the pleasures of the preorgasmic phase are over. Males with good voluntary control may also enjoy this prolongation.

---

* The negative connotations of seduction stem from its primary definition which is "to lead astray" with a certain amount of guile or "artful deception."

Ignoring the effects of sound and lighting, drugs and alcohol, and verbal tenderness, the physical aspects of seduction involve touching, initially (see p. 43). The electricity of sexual stimulation can arise from almost any area of the body, providing the mind is at least partially receptive. Touching can involve hands, mouths, or total or partial body contact, and is usually gentle. We say gentle, though we are aware that wrestling and tickling serve a useful function by making total body contact quickly and almost involuntarily, emotionally comfortable. Tickling can be teasing and fun, but it usually has no place in the progression of intensity of sexual stimulation. If introduced in the middle of seduction, it often stops the progression. Some females and males are so extremely sensitive to any kind of light touch, that this cannot be used. In the seduction phase, firm touch does not mean rough for most individuals, though anything goes in the orgasmic phase which is primarily involuntary, reflex activity.

Parental and adult concern over the so-called sexual exhibitionism of dancing in the late fifties and sixties has always amused us. Ask these same adults about rhumbas or the close body contact of dancing in the forties when they were growing up. That kind of dancing was frequently against a hard penis, with the extra stimulation of a female leg between male thighs, or vice-versa, or the mons and clitoral area gently stimulated during "dipping," with the male on top. Add the whispered nothings, the cheek to cheek, breasts to chest closeness and this was real vertical seduction, with a resulting aching pelvis and testes and no consummation. No amount of visual stimulation at a three foot distance can possibly produce the effects of this kind of touching. Even "nice" girls could participate without fear of parental or peer concern, though 6 or 8 inches was a good distance for dancing just for the fun of dancing.

While public dances are obviously not as well attended or needed in the same way they once were because of the increasing acceptance of "horizontal sex," slow dancing is returning. High school junior proms, when held, are beginning to alternate slow dances with the exhibitions. "Contact Sport. Every third dance at the Cheshire junior prom is slow. 'Slow dances' are five-minute hugs, back-rubs and bottom pats."[3] *Harper's Bazaar* devoted several pages to the comeback of close dancing in its October, 1972 issue.[4] (Is it possible that it was the sexual revolution more than the financial problems caused by inflation which spelled the end of the big bands of the thirties and forties?) One other point should be made about touching. Casual, unpremeditated touch is an important source of spontaneous sex later in marriage, and also an important source of accidental pregnancies if there is no pill, or no condom is nearby. This kind of sex is also related to "diaphragm failures"; they simply are not used (see p. 204). Thus, in a subtle way, king-sized beds that look like giant-sized playgrounds to newly or recently married couples, and very desirable, are not conducive to casual sex. For most people, the frequency of intercourse declines three or four years postmarriage, and a female has to be very comfortable with being the initiator of lovemaking to be able to reach the necessary distance with a foot or a hand and touch that tired husband who fell into bed without the energy to reach over. The thoughtful husband may not waken a peaceful, sleeping wife at that distance. The king-sized bed can separate people just as effectively as twin beds. Touch is inevitable in the conventional bed, and it is difficult to continue an argument of mild proportions without the whole thing getting ridiculous, when body warmth and closeness intervene.

Seduction recapitulates the progression of dating behavior, but in a much shorter time span. Some steps are omitted, some can be. Pleasure may come from slow progression, or from aggressive speed. Optimal results, in terms of good sexual function with an end point of orgasm, come from a variety of patterns used in accord with the occasion. For example, even long-marrieds find simple handholding and thigh-to-thigh contact, while in the movies or walking on the street, to be a rare form of physical contact which may take them home to bed. The head is full of erotic areas, the ears, the mouth, the eyes, the neck. Open-mouth kissing was frowned upon for a long time because it can be a highly erotic type of stimulation, and it was thought that young people could not handle the consequences. We remember from our college freshman days being puzzled by a girl who came running into the washroom at the 12:30 A.M. curfew and desperately gargled, brushed her teeth, and drank water for at least 15 minutes. We assumed that she was anxious about "disease" or thought, as many did, that one could get pregnant from "deep kissing." This was when oral-genital sexual contact was considered a gross perversion, at least by this age group. And for the majority of students, sexual activity was essentially "vertical group sex" at the front door of the dormitory at curfew time; males were not allowed in except in the afternoon. Girls without dates made it a point to arrive back before they had to weave their way through the curfew crowd, who were apparently oblivious to everyone else around them; they had to be, for that was the only kind of sex they had. Knowledge and attitudes have improved, though other problems have emerged.

Body Contact

Patterns of physical seduction are related to clothing, and clothing covers bodies. These patterns may be constant, slowly changing, or surprisingly inconstant. Even males and females, who are comfortable nude with each other in many situations, may need or enjoy being undressed by their partner as part of lovemaking. The female who wears pajamas is not necessarily signaling unavailability, nor is the female who routinely goes to bed nude signaling total availability. There are sexually active females who "cannot" undress themselves, and prefer to be undressed by their partner. Males have the same variety of needs, desires, and pleasures, which may be evidenced only by a preference for pajama tops that button instead of slipping over the head. The male who is in such a hurry that he leaves his socks on in a casual one-night-stand can create a very disconcerting environment for some females, but there are others for whom this creates no problems at all. Sexual activity is as variable as the people involved in it, and it takes time and experience to learn about one's partner or partners. To repeat, intercourse is not just simply the penis in the vagina.

Body contact is a combination of body to body, hand to body, mouth to body. Excluding the genital area for the moment, the nipples and breasts are probably the primary erotic areas in the female, though hand to skin contact anywhere has its place in the progression of seduction. For the heterosexual male, body or hand contact any place, by a female, can be stimulating.

Breast stimulation is pleasurable for most women though there are those who say clearly " . . . not for me." It is possible that previously experienced unpleasant techniques might be a part of their problem; some women interpret finger manipulation of the breasts and nipples as too calculated and without spontaneity. They might be much more comfortable, initially, with whole hand or oral stimulation. For some, oral stimulation is enhanced with moisture, sucking, or even a transient, gentle kind of biting. Nipples, like the clitoris, may become sensitive to the point of pain with direct stimulation, often in a cyclic fashion reflecting hormonal changes during the ovulatory cycle, or during the first few months of pill taking. Painful stimuli can drop a female down from the plateau phase in seconds; then the need to start over.

Total body contact in the horizontal position is almost independent of total body length. Since height is determined primarily by leg length, shoulders, chests, bellies, and genitals always seem to coincide reasonably well, though there may be chins against foreheads and legs that don't quite match. (Look at the similarity in height of a group of people who are sitting, and then look again when they stand up.)

Weight and the size of the belly are variables which are sometimes limiting and require adaptation. We have seen articles on sexual dysfunction which assume that people who "allow" themselves to get obese are unhappy sexually and will never have good sexual lives. While true in some instances, the writers' biases may have influenced that statement. Everyone has her or his own individual and cultural physical preferences, and mild to moderate obesity may be one of them, though it can limit sexual techniques. There is little reason to believe that handholding obese-thin, or obese-obese couples are unhappy.

Genital Contact

In the female, genital stimulation and arousal occur with all of the previous activity, including firm pressure or movement of the base or shaft of the penis against the mons, the undivided labial area over the pubic bone. This may even be enough clitoral stimulation for the female, with or without clothing, to be orgasmic, and, in turn, often precipitates male orgasm and ejaculation. Manual, oral, or penile stimulation of the clitoral area has many variations.

Direct finger manipulation of the clitoris may also be interpreted as too calculated and without spontaneity, a kind of "button pushing to turn me on" approach and resented. Oral stimulation can be dry or moist, sucking or biting; again painful stimuli can break the sequence of events almost immediately. Females have an obligation to communicate their desires by moving a hand, or readjusting contact, or by a verbal "here" or "there." Males who have evolved a successful technique with one female are frequently surprised to find that it is unpleasant or unacceptable for another. The name of the game in the early stages is "getting to know you" and adapting. The female who does not succeed because she has not gently lifted a hand away, or indicated pleasure or displeasure will continue to fail. The male who is sensitive to quiet, subtle messages will succeed.

Quiet and subtle are used for a reason. As with painful stimuli, loud talking, vigorous gestures of a voluntary nature, as contrasted to the sometimes vigorous, involuntary pelvic activity prior to or during orgasm, may destroy the whole gestalt and leave both back in the early excitement phase. Female laughter arising from pleasure can be very threatening to the inexperienced or insecure male who wonders "Why is she laughing *at* me?" And loud shouts or moans can also be disturbing to him when or if they occur in the female in her immediate preorgasmic or orgasmic state, and he has not had this experience before.

From my limited experience, I believe that the degree of sexuality in women not only varies as much as with men but that the gamut is much greater. A woman thoroughly aroused is almost frightening to the average man. She can take him places he never dreamed of in his wildest flights. She can give the illusion of being insatiable, whereas most men (at least those I know) are soon satiated.[5]

James Dickey

I will reach out with my hand and find the reality of the dream woman. She exists, and lo and behold, she is alive. She is warm. She responds. She murmurs. She weeps. She is wild. She is dangerous. But sometimes, like this photograph, she will come running at me with all the beauty of the unmistakable tide coming in on the rough shore. And I lie there like a rock. . . .[6]

Richard Burton

No one need wait to be over 40, as these men are, to experience this type of relationship, but both partners do have to feel quite secure in themselves, in each other, and in sex to be able to handle this kind of intensity. More important, not every sexual encounter needs to be so intense; intensity and lack of intensity frequently occur by desire and design.

For the male, contact in any area by a female can be interpreted as erotic stimulation; the mere fact that she is there and touching of her own desire and volition is erotic in itself. The inner side of the thigh, as in the female, and the buttocks and perianal area are highly erotic areas which can survive, without pain, almost any type of sexual stimulation. The scrotum, testes, and erect penis (shaft and glans) are more sensitive to vigorous stimulation, or more likely to be uncomfortable or even painful with misguided stimulation, than the female genitals. Perhaps because of this and from real necessity, most males are able to guide females to the type of stimulation they enjoy and prefer. But many inexperienced females, who can lay their hands forcefully or gently on the erect penis and scrotum through clothing, are not yet ready for hand to skin contact with male genitals. Forced handling of male genitals will not be an erotic experience for such a female, will add nothing to the seduction, and may, in fact, detract from any intensification of desire which is supposed to occur. Some males want, prefer, or demand that females insert the penis into the vagina. This may be for the male's own increased pleasure, or it may be a less than subtle way of placing the responsibility for penetration on the female, some reassurance that he is not forcing himself on her. But her refusal to do this should not be interpreted negatively; on occasion she may have her own equally subtle reasons for refusing.

Males are much more able to stay aware of their surroundings during the excitement and plateau phases; females who are gradually or quickly becoming orgasmic reach a point where conscious activity, for example, their active stimulation of the male, is difficult to maintain. This is really the end point of seduction in the classic sense: the female receptive, desirous and not protesting. (see p. 73)

As do females, every male eventually learns how much or what kind of stimulation he can handle, and excessive stimulation may have to be stopped to avoid premature ejaculation. Males who have this problem chronically, or because of the excessive stimulation of the moment, can solve it by retreating briefly from stimulation, even moving away, but they should maintain some female contact. This retreating can be very puzzling to the female partner unless the reason is made clear. Oral stimulation of the shaft or glans may have to be stopped for the same reason. The testes swell slightly during the excitement and plateau phases and become more vulnerable to painful sensation; at this point female hands may have to be lifted away.

Insertion of the penis into the vagina is easy by this time and usually desired intensely by both partners. The feeling of having achieved the ultimate in closeness can be equally intense though "something" is still lacking—orgasm and the relief of sexual tension. Males who have some voluntary control will continue stimulation of the glans and shaft of the penis with movement and contact with the warm, moist vaginal walls. There are males who know that they ejaculate almost immediately upon penetration, and therefore postpone penetration until some optimal time for the female. The movement of the shaft of the penis against the back of the vaginal opening, the introitus, also pulls down on the labia minora and the fold of "skin" over the glans, thus stimulating the clitoral body indirectly. Pressure on the entire genital area is also effective. Signals are needed, such as holding the male tightly, a verbal "stay close." Total genital stimulation may be enough at this point to lead to orgasmic release in the female, a time of 3 to 15 seconds for peak intensity. The male who is in control can often arrange to ejaculate during this time or close to it, if such timing is desired.

Simultaneous orgasm takes a good deal of coordination, control, and communication, all of which imply intimate knowledge of and experience with one's partner and oneself. It is obviously something which is possible, and when it occurs purposefully or accidentally, it can be fun; but often it is too rapid an experience for some females who need more. And most males, postejaculation, are temporarily unable and sometimes uninterested in producing more. Simultaneous orgasm is simply another variation of intercourse as are the positional variations noted below.

Many couples prefer that the female be stimulated to orgasm first, *prior to any penetration,* or that penetration occur at the height of female orgasm. The "insatiable" postorgasmic female is still capable of giving and receiving sexual stimulation with delayed penetration. This may or may not repeat the intense orgasmic phase for her, but it will often reach some intensely pleasurable "skimming" levels. Delaying penetration also allows the male to enjoy the full force of the involuntary, rhythmic contractions around the lower third of the vagina, or the voluntary contractions which the female can initiate herself, postorgasmically. This approach prolongs pleasure for both and postpones penile-vaginal stimulation which may be of value in postponing ejaculation. It also insures female orgasm and release and allows further stimulation if she wishes. It makes the postejaculatory refractory phase in the male a relatively unimportant factor in the total act, since both male and female are satiated. This is again, simply another variation, and the environment is the primary determinant for variations, for example, time of day or week, presence or absence of children, and so on.

To a large extent, the postorgasmic or resolution phase for the couple is determined by the ability of the male to maintain at least some semblance of an erection for a period of time, either within the vagina or closely outside, thus maintaining genital contact. A semi-erect penis can be kept in the vagina, but it cannot be removed and reinserted. The full vagina is pleasurable for most females. The resolution phase can be peace and sleep, peace and talking, or just being together and more of the same later on, depending on mutual energy levels. The postorgasmic feeling is unique and, for some, the best time; it should not be lost by the compulsive female who feels she must leap up and douche for some misinformed reason, or by the male who has to "leave." There are many environmental reasons for having to leave, perhaps more so in marriage, but the act of intercourse is approached differently and with different expectations under these variable circumstances. Since the focus in this section is on sex for affection, pleasure, and love, "staying around" is one of the better indications of caring. A male rolling over and going to sleep is often perceived by *his* female, as leaving. Falling asleep together is caring.

Positions as Variations on a Theme

Any position is legitimate if it is mutually acceptable. But this philosophy has been a long time in coming into general acknowledgment, and often still requires a moderate amount of previous experience before it is acceptable to any individual.

The classic male on top and female below position has much to recommend it psychologically and physiologically, which probably accounts for its universality, both in early encounters and often later on. It allows the female to *play* the passive role or to *be* passive if she wishes, or if she needs or wishes to be seduced, or persuaded into sexual activity. (The sexually aggressive female is still in the minority, and she personifies a concept which is difficult for many males and females to handle well.) However, this position requires females to present their most psychologically vulnerable, ventral surface, and this is often difficult to do spontaneously. The seduction pattern of some females may include a desire to be physically seduced regardless of who initiated the touching, and only after this can they be supine. Physiologically, it allows total body contact from top to toe. It allows males to utilize the force of gravity for stronger thrusting, and is the best angle for vaginal penetration. The disadvantage for males is the real or imagined necessity for constant awareness of their own size or weight. They know they will lose this awareness for a brief time during ejaculation and orgasm, and sometimes care is needed not to crush the partner below. Adaptations are easily made, but initially, for the male who cares, these concerns are real and can interfere with total function.

Lying on one's side facing one's partner must of necessity be a gentler, less forceful variation. Total body contact is possible, but, anatomically, penetration and thrusting are difficult without the two partners eventually ending up in an X position and losing body contact if there is complete penetration. The penis tends to thrust into the middle and lower third of the vagina, sometimes uncomfortably so, if total body contact is maintained. Often this is also true if attempting to maintain clitoral contact in the top and bottom position.

Some females find that the female on top, male on the bottom is the only position in which they have enough control to be orgasmic. Perhaps they are not sending out the right signals in other positions. Depending on the slight anatomical variations which exist, it may or may not be possible to maintain body as well as genital contact, and it may or may not be important in any given situation. Erect penises are not always mobile enough to accommodate excessive movement, or extremes of movement, in any direction. This can be very uncomfortable, and occasionally painful.

Eventually, in any relationship, secure men enjoy aggressive females who take pleasure in male bodies. Aggressive, not necessarily vigorous, sex can demonstrate this. But females have to be relatively comfortable with sex to assume this role and males have to be equally comfortable about relinquishing their expected role and becoming "passive."

Complete posterior penetration with the female in the knees-to-chest position in bed, on the floor, on a chair, or on the edge of the bed, with the male standing or kneeling is anatomically possible. But unless a woman is comfortably and easily orgasmic without direct clitoral stimulation, manual stimulation is often necessary, and this may or may not be acceptable to one or the other of them. This need not be a problem, if the position is used during the female's postorgasmic phase (see below), or if the male has good ejaculatory control prior to female orgasm which is achieved later in some other manner.

Anatomically, complete penetration with both in the standing position, that is, in doorways, in showers, or leaning against the kitchen sink, is almost impossible. Partial penetration and clitoral stimulation may lead both through an orgasmic stage, but the necessity of thinking about the possibility of falling down, or the need to remain standing would be limiting. It is not a position for mutual total relaxation, but it is, nevertheless, an acceptable variation.

Generally speaking, variations in position other than the usual top and bottom are better functionally, at least initially, if used postorgasmically in females, immediately prior to male ejaculation, or for stimulation prior to arranging an almost, or actual, simultaneous orgasmic experience. However, many women and men routinely prefer such variations.

There have been a number of articles in magazines for young women which say that it takes two years with one man for an optimal sex life to emerge. True or not, many couples who have had what they consider a mutually good sexual life are frequently surprised at the possibilities for improvement which evolve over a time span much longer than two years, and at the almost infinite number of acceptable variations in duration and intensity which may occur from one time to the next. It is difficult and often impossible to get this point across to recently married couples who seek advice after two or three months when "nothing has worked." Many physicians, gynecologists, and urologists are given this problem, and with only a brief office time for the minute details of technique, timing, and uncovering other conflicts, marriage or sexual counseling is often indicated. The male psychology major who whiningly complained in front of his new wife, also a psychology major, that "her hands are too small, she'll never be able to stimulate me the way I need to be . . ." was obviously in need of something more than advice on time and technique. They had reached an apparent openness and honesty that good marriages should have, but there is even a time and place for openness and honesty.

There are two other variations of heterosexual intercourse, each with its own spectrum of timing and details, that do not involve the penis in the vagina: oral-genital stimulation, mutual or by only one participant, and anal intercourse. Both can be highly erotic, producing orgasm and satisfaction in the same sense as the conventional penis-vagina type, and both are obviously excellent contraceptive techniques and of value in other situations as well (see Pregnancy).

With increasing public acceptance of oral-genital stimulation, younger and older women are making more and more reference to it for any number of reasons in the patient-doctor relationship. They may question it directly as a technique or, they may be more casual and oblique: "Is oral stimulation all right while I am using these suppositories?" "My boyfriend doesn't like the taste of foam; is there anything else I can use in the same way?" Ads for flavored douches, male genital deodorants, even flavored condoms, and the emphasis on feminine hygiene are explicit acknowlegments of its increasing acceptability (see Hygiene). Actually, oral-genital stimulation is as old as intercourse, and with the increase in sexual freedom, it is no longer taboo for many people.

Twenty years ago, Kinsey reported oral-genital activity primarily as a late variation in the educated group, rather than part of the early "lets try everything and anything" approach it is for some today. However, many young people still have trouble removing parental or childhood taboos from their bedroom.

Oral stimulation of the penis (fellatio) may be a part of the early sexual play prior to intercourse, in which case many males have to stop this intense stimulation briefly, or at intervals, to avoid premature escalation to ejaculation. Oral stimulation of the clitoris, labia minora, or introitus (cunnilingus) can be immediately or quickly orgasmic for many females, depending upon experience. Mutual or simultaneous oral-genital stimulation, has been known for many years as "the 69" which is almost self-explanatory, if the reader will visualize the necessary male and female positions. But this type of stimulation can occur in any number of positions: the female on the bottom, on top, or on her side. Here, also, if the female is on top, or on her side, she often has better control over continuing stimulation, or prolonging the plateau phase just short of orgasm, than she does in the ventral position.

Portnoy and his female friends illustrate vividly some of the psychological and physiological concerns about spermatic fluid.[7] Do you swallow it and if so, is it harmful? Would I insult him if I spit out his precious "seed?" She or he must love me very much (care about me) if willing to do that. Or, is he just a stud, out for anything he can get; is she a nympho who will take her sex any way she can get it? Spermatic fluid (semen) is essentially sterile, bland, and without ill effects when swallowed. With this knowledge, the remaining concerns, if any, should be dispersed easily, but almost always in direct relation to the degree of mutuality involved.

Anal, or rectal, intercourse (sodomy)* has been called "the poor man's contraceptive" (see p. 35). The poor men are most likely to be European. It is still not a common topic of conversation in the gynecologist's office, though one woman with a chronic vaginitis finally did question whether or not her boyfriend's habit of rectal penetration prior to vaginal penetration might have something to do with her problem. The doctor who told us of this patient, modified his treatment.

Frequent references to sodomy and homosexuality in male prisons are modified by Davis' study which indicates that many participants in the prison population do not think of themselves as homosexuals, but simply as heterosexual males who have no other outlet for aggression, and no intellectual or financial power base other than physical sexuality.[8] Physical sexuality with another male is not just for relief of sexual tension. In the "old West", and even now in isolated lumbering or mining camps, absence of feminine company creates situations which might look homosexual, for example, men dancing with each other in public bars. The majority of these males do not feel homosexual, they are simply adapting to a difficult situation.

"J," who wrote *The Sensuous Woman* and apparently is enthusiastic about all types of sexual stimulation, calls anal intercourse something a woman does for her man in exchange for other favors; she includes detailed positions and procedures in her "how to" book. Masters and Johnson, discussing the physiology of rectal intercourse, note that a rectal examination, if slightly prolonged, will usually give evidence in the male or female of previous experience with penile-rectal penetration: the anal sphinctor muscle which initially tightens around the examining finger, will gradually relax.[9] The perianal area is an erotic area to touch, and the circular muscle participates in the same rhythmic contractions of orgasm in the male and female as do the muscles around the lower third of the vagina; the vasocongestion of the pelvic contents which occurs with sexual stimulation includes the perianal area. The rectum is frequently empty of fecal material, but enemas may be a prelude to intended anal intercourse, and may have, for some, an erotic potential all their own. Anal intercourse is a rare subject for patient-doctor conversation, whether it be males and urologists, or females and gynecologists, but questions do arise a little more frequently than in previous times. Perhaps this is only evidence of ease with sexuality in all forms.

Intercourse During Menstruation and Pregnancy

Intercourse during menstruation presents no physical problems and is frequently better and more free of concerns about pregnancy than any other time, except perhaps during a pregnancy (see Rhythm, Diaphragm, Menstruation). It may present some emotional problems for females or males, and neither

* Sodomy is a term which also includes female and male human copulation with animals.

should insist, if there are obvious conflicts about this. One woman, who had been married for 15 years, said that intercourse during menstruation didn't bother her, but her husband "really had some hangups about it," and that "frankly, I've never tried to dissuade him. It's a nice respite."

The only real problem which arises is that this is the time when tampons, if left in the vagina, get "lost" or disappear, and are forgotten until they are evidenced five or six days later by a watery, foul-smelling vaginal discharge.

Sexual intercourse during pregnancy frequently carries with it an intense psychological component which may have an intermittently positive or negative effect upon sexual activity during the nine-and-a-half months. The adaptations required for the increasing size of the abdomen are often the same required for large bellies in nonpregnant males or females, pillows under female buttocks, males kneeling, front-to-front positions. If pregnancy enters a couple's life before the arrival of sexual ease, the adaptation may simply be abstinence. If a couple's sexual life has been good, adaptations come easily unless distorted by misinformation or lack of information about what is possible.

Pregnancy can create a whole new awareness of what sexuality and closeness really are as opposed to the purely mechanical penis-vagina approach, and add even more experience and growth to a couple's relationship (see Pregnancy).

Personal Hygiene: Male and Female

We assume that very few will be surprised or puzzled by our placement of hygiene in a section on intercourse for affection, pleasure, and love. There is no better place. Even for long-married couples nothing is more difficult to discuss. Ease with the vocabulary of sexual behavior, and with other aspects of personal physiology, total trust and honesty, and even a satisfactory sexual life do not seem to provide any predictable carryover into the area of personal hygiene.

Habitual, or even intermittent and unknowing lack of adequate hygiene is unpleasant and can interfere with almost any kind of sexual activity. If there is difficulty in communicating, some sexual techniques which can be very pleasurable are simply eliminated from that particular encounter or perhaps never introduced at any time. If this is done by either partner without explanation, or if one simply refuses to participate, the other will be left wondering.

Many unmarried, sexually active couples would be surprised to learn of the signaling which takes place between many husbands and wives, essentially equating cleanliness with availability and desire. A wife or husband can signal displeasure, unavailability, or hostility by breaking the routine of a nighttime shower, bath, or even of brushing the teeth. It might be more than a nonverbal signal; he or she might beg off gently with "... but I didn't shower." On the surface, this is not a hostile remark; it even sounds as if it came from a considerate spouse, and it may have. A husband who usually showers in the morning may indicate his intended desires and plans with a noisy, obvious nighttime shower. These are not necessarily people or couples who are so compulsive about cleanliness that there is no sex unless they have just showered or bathed; spontaneous sex may be very easy for them, but signals are used to communicate a feeling that this particular time is special.

A 40-year-old woman, 17 years married, told us that she made herself unavailable, most of the time, after finding that her husband was seeing someone else on his trips out of town. During one of several reconciliations, her usually taciturn husband mentioned that he had noticed that she wasn't taking her usual nighttime shower and that somehow he knew then that she knew about his extramarital wanderings. She was delighted, because up to that time, she had never been aware that he was that sensitive to anything she did in the sexual area.

Among the married, "poor personal hygiene and grooming is a nonverbal expression of trying to avoid sex, and it often carries the identical message as fatigue. . . . The postscript to 'love is never having to say you're sorry' is 'That's fine, but don't forget to brush your teeth.' "[10] Or, the flippant "The reason sex and grass go together for me is I can forget what a 'dog' she (or he) is"; which may just be a put down for the listener.

Hair, mouth, underarm, and genital odors in humans and other animals are unique, but only unpleasant when the source of the odors has been around too long. There is no need to cover up good, clean body odors with perfumes or powders though some of these are erotically stimulating or, at least, pleasant. Pheromones are hormones produced by animals which cause physiological or psychological responses in animals of the same species. One of the best examples of induced behavioral changes is that seen in male dogs when any female dog within a mile-and-a-half radius is in "heat," or estrus. The effect of cats in "heat" on a neighborhood is another example. Pheromones in humans and their effects are the subject of relatively recent research (see Bibliography). Related to the latter, is the popularity of simple musk perfumes or oils which have an odor, we think, very similar to a clean, human, genital odor.

Kissing is not erotic if only one individual has been smoking, drinking, or eating exotic foods. Nor is early morning kissing with sexual activity particularly attractive, regardless of what was going on the night before. Kissing may often be omitted by unspoken, mutual consent in early morning sex, and if kissing is vital to the established pattern of female sexual arousal, morning intercouse may end up as nothing more than female participation at the skimming level of pleasure. If both participants understand that morning sex is going to be enjoyable but not orgasmic for the female, there are no problems. But there may often be a period of time when both wonder why it isn't working.

Because males do not have as many little crevices and folds as females, genital hygiene for them is somewhat simpler. They are also more familiar with handling their genitals, and soap and water, when used, almost automatically cover the area. But without some extra effort, "males can get kind of strong down there, too"* and oral-genital stimulation is simply out of the question for many experienced and inexperienced females.

On the other hand, females never really have a need to touch or look at their genital area in the same way, and have often been cautioned by word or glance to avoid the area. With all of the emphasis on the naturalness of sex, many regard the accumulated secretions and vaginal leakage as natural, too. They are, but if around too long, they become unpleasant. Soap and water and some attention to the crevices and folds are important; sitting in a bathtub is not sufficient, nor are incomplete showers.

There is a myth about the "self-cleaning" vagina which should not be perpetuated, especially in the present era of foams, gels, cremes, and pills. These, combined with frequency of intercourse, lead to almost chronic vaginal leakage. Even the leakage of spermatic fluid associated with daily intercourse, and using the pill as a contraceptive, can be unpleasantly wet and have an odor which is quite unlike any odor which might be perceived immediately postemission.

The use of feminine deodorant sprays makes sense only if the individual is trying to cover up what she considers to be unpleasant genital odors which might be perceived at a distance, for example, a male or female head in her lap. The spray cannot possibly get where it is supposed to go to do a thorough job for close contact. There have been reports of individual sensitivity reactions to some spray deodorants. Some have been removed from the market as dangerous, and some have simply had the hexachlorophene removed and are labeled as such. (Some spermicidal agents also occasionally produce sensitivity reactions in the vagina, see p. 119). Since sprays are really unnecessary, and have little effect on the source of the problem, there is no need to continue their use, if soap and water are available and used. We have noted that several of the spray manufacturers are now marketing premoistened paper towelettes. Their use makes a little more sense.

Douching (doosh′ ing), an intravaginal washing-out, was limited for many years to medicinal usage, and associated with cleanliness in high-class prostitutes. (Both male and female prostitutes of this calibre are concerned with being clean.) One of our patients said she had heard of douching, but thought that it was only an old-fashioned method of contraception, which it was, and that nice girls didn't have to do it.

There is still a rather large antidouching faction of both male and female doctors, left over from the days when condoms were the usual method of con-

---

* Comment from a 23-year-old female who requested that we put some emphasis on male hygiene.

traception, and oral-genital sex was taboo and therefore uncommon. We cannot help but think that there must be many men and women who wonder how anyone could initiate oral-genital activity when just putting one's head in someone's lap could be unpleasant. Kinsey explained this as possible because there is some loss of sensory (olfactory) perception during intercourse, but it is of note that he felt the need to explain "how." There is also some neurological evidence, as well as the personal experience of any human ever involved in sexual arousal and orgasm, that some degree of "cerebral clouding" does occur. This is evidenced by the decrease in some sensory perceptions, and the enhancement of others that one never knew existed.

But both partners must feel secure, and the increasing prevalence of sprays, douches, deodorants, portable douche machines, and the ads which only thinly disguise the need to be "feminine" or "masculine all over" will only increase a couple's awareness of what other people are apparently doing. This big business approach* to sexual hygiene can have a very negative effect on insecure people, if they allow it to; but its positive effects can only enhance sexual activity in any position. The reader may not like the following analogy, but we do think that it is important to point out that women owe their men the same degree of feminine hygiene that any high-class female prostitute would offer them. It is difficult to find a similar heterosexual analogy for males, but the same reasoning applies.

An example, will summarize this section on hygiene and indicate the need to stop, look, and listen for signals from a partner, male or female.

A young woman came in with a complaint of chronic vaginal discharge, without any itching. She had been using a diaphragm every day (or night) for the previous three months. We asked her if she ever douched out the gel on occasion and she said "Oh, my boyfriend asked me about douching, too, and I told him that I never did, I didn't feel dirty." Among other comments we made along with a vaginal examination, was a gentle suggestion that maybe he was trying to give her a message (see Diaphragm Usage).

Summary

There is no way of summarizing techniques for pleasure or to differentiate them from those of affection and love except perhaps to indicate and reemphasize the security which comes only from the slow evolution of one's own sexuality, learning about oneself, how one reacts, how others react, and some

* MS, the feminist magazine, does not accept ads for feminine deodorant sprays, not because it is against being clean, but because it is against the total sexist slant. We agree for this reason and those noted above.

awareness of the infinite variations possible in sexual intercourse. These variations depend more upon the self-awareness an individual brings to each act of intercourse, than upon variations in technique and body position.

This slowly achieved security allows freedom in sexuality: freedom from concerns about the presence or absence of orgasm on all occasions, freedom from concerns about occasional male malfunction. Both partners will be aware that there will be environmental situations, techniques, and positions which do not produce maximal results in one partner, but *give* tremendous pleasure to the other.

Everyone goes through a performance-oriented learning phase of short or long duration, sometimes with an intensity and a seriousness that is appalling to their elders who may have forgotten their own early concerns. The real essence of the learning, beyond the basic mechanics, is finding that intercourse and its variations, though a basic physiological drive, are intellectually successful only when they become relatively free of this initial intensity. Intense efforts to have fun are seldom successful. The origin of sexuality and the success of sexual performance are located in the brain, not in the pelvis.

VIEWPOINTS

In this day of group love and quartet marriages, many of us may wonder whether the personal and private side of love is lost forever. We also have heard so much about the bees and the birds that we can be pardoned for asking, "Is there any real difference at all between love and sex for human beings and for animals?"

I believe there is.

It lies in the fact that, for human beings, love is personal. At a certain point in evolution there is a shift from sex as a drive to love as desire.

If it is satisfying a drive, any partner will do; while desire centers on a chosen person. This is what makes love personal. If love were merely a drive, personal commitment would not be involved. One would just fulfill the needs. Choice and other aspects of self-awareness would not enter the picture.

The fact that love is personal is also shown in the love act itself.

Man is the only animal who makes love face-to-face. Yes, we can turn our heads or assume some other position for variety's sake, but these are variations on a theme—the theme of making love face-to-face. This opens the whole front of the person—all the parts of ourselves which are most tender and most vulnerable—to the kindness or cruelty of the partner. . . .

The two chords of lovemaking—my experience of myself and my experience of my partner—are then merged. We feel our own delight and passion, and we look into the eyes of the partner and read there the meaning of the act—and I cannot distinguish between her passion and mine. But the looking is fraught with intensity. It brings a heightened awareness of intimacy.

Indeed, to make love impersonal requires exerting effort to block off our normal intimacy. This is the case in prostitution, which is obviously impersonal, and in some impersonal kinds of homosexuality.

Casual relationships in love may have their gratification or meaning in the sharing of pleasure and tenderness. But if one's whole attitude toward it is only casual, then sooner or later the playing itself becomes boring. The same is true of sensuality, another element in any gratifying love: If it has to carry the whole weight of the relationship, one becomes satiated, and sooner or later turns against his partner.

Rollo May, "Is the Private Side
of Love a Thing of the Past."

. . . .

The adult of today has all three options—sex as parenthood, sex as total relationship, and sex as physical pleasure accompanied by no more than affection. Older people looking at the young today realize increasingly how much the confusion between these modes, which they could not foresee, or even choose voluntarily between, has often complicated their lives; when play between boy and girl resulted in pregnancy and a forced marriage between mere acquaintances, when one partner misread the other's degree of involvement, or falsified his own selfishly to overcome reluctance.

Greater choice can bring greater problems and greater opportunities. It will bring problems in any event, and these can only be reduced by recognizing how great is the range of situations in which sex relations now take place, and learning to handle them to meet our own and our partner's needs. . . .

All that can be certainly predicted for the future is that the variety of patterns will increase as individuals find the norm that suits them. For some, parenthood will still be the central satisfaction, carrying with it the obligation of giving the children the stability they require. For others, sexuality will express total involvement with one person. For others, one or more primary relationships will be central, but will not exclude others, in which the recreational role of sex acts as a source of bonding to supply the range of relationships formerly met by kin—an old human pattern in which sexual contacts were permitted between a woman and all her husband's clan brothers, or a man and all his wife's titular sisters.

Conventional morals are probably correct in asserting that all satisfactory sex is in some degree inherently relational—if it is satisfactory, and mutually so, a relation subsists. Only the wholly insensitive mate mechanically, even under the conditions of permitted nondiscrimination which characterize a ritualized orgy. A society like ours, which has traditionally feared and rejected close personal contact, has also generated a mythology of all-or-none involvement which profoundly influences us to our hurt. Unable to exclude the recreational and the partly relations modes of sex, it has set about rejecting or falsifying them. Once rid of this ideology, it might find that the relation present in purely recreational or social sex is a uniquely effective tool in breaking down personal separateness—of which the proprietary notion of love is an offshoot—so that, for us as for many primitives, social sex comes to express and cement the equivalent of kinship through a general intimacy and nondefensiveness, reinforced by the very strong reward of realizing suppressed needs for variety and for acceptance.

Alexander Comfort, "Sexuality in a Zero Growth Society,"
The Center Report (Center for the Study
of Democratic Institutions, December, 1972), pp. 12 and 13.

References

1. L. K. Truscott, 4th, "West Point: A Question of Honor," *New York Times,* 19 August 1972.

2. Marya Mannes, *Out of My Time* (Garden City, New York: Doubleday and Company, 1971).

3. Joyce Maynard, " 'Color My World,' Or, No News from Cheshire High School," *New York Times Magazine,* 18 June 1972, p. 14.

4. M. Batterberry and A. Batterberry, "Dance with Me: Ballroom Dancing," *Harper's Bazaar,* 105:72 (October 1972).

5. James Dickey, "Female Sexuality: What It Is—and Isn't," *Mademoiselle,* July 1971, p. 108-109.

6. Richard Burton, quoted in *Time,* 25 January 1971, p. 41.

7. Philip Roth, *Portnoy's Complaint* (New York: Random House, 1969).

8. A. J. Davis, "Sexual Assaults in the Philadelphia Prison System and Sheriff's Vans," *Transaction* (December 1968).

9. William H. Masters and Virginia Johnson, *Human Sexual Inadequacy* (Boston: Little, Brown and Co., 1970).

10. B. R. Berkey, "Too Tired for Sex: Fighting the Fatigue Factor in Sexual Disharmony," *Medical Aspects of Human Sexuality* (September 1972).

4

Sexual Assault and Rape

The FBI told us that violent crimes in the nation rose again last year and that forcible rape took the biggest jump of all, a whopping 11 percent. It is not exactly unrelated that at the age of 38 I have solemnly embarked on a dedicated program of self-defense instruction. . . . I have not embarked on this rigorous program of learning how to kick, elbow, twist, knee and punch where it does the most damage without a prolonged search of my feminine soul. Learning to fight is something that young boys are trained to do from childhood, and it would not be an overgeneralization to say that fighting, for men, is inextricably tied to a concept of masculinity. The converse has always held for me.

Susan Brownmiller

LEGALLY, RAPE IS DEFINED not by penetration or ejaculation, but by the act of "intruding the male genital organ in any portion of the female genitals (a female who is not his wife), without her consent and by compulsion, either through fear, force or fraud, singly or in combination."[1]

Statutory rape is defined as sexual assault on a girl under the "age of consent," an age defined by each individual state. Legally, some high school and most junior high school encounters with genital contact qualify as statutory rape, a criminal offense even with consent. Included in sexual assault are sodomy (attempted or actual anal penetration) and cunnilingus and fellatio (oral-genital contact), which are usually referred to as "forced into an unnatural act."

If we include "violation" in our thinking about sexual violence, as an only sometimes gentler form of sexual assault involving strangers, we should also include sexual contacts between adults and children and between nonconsenting adult males. This latter group made up 4 percent of victims brought to the

91

hospital by police for medical attention in a Washington, D. C. study.[2] However, only half of the total sexual assault complaints during the period studied requested or needed medical examination and treatment.

In sexual assault involving adults and children, usually defined as forced contact with an adult male genital organ, or exhibitionism (visual demonstration of the male genital organ), the adult is any male over age 13 or 14; the child may be male or female, age 13 or under. ". . . offenses of women against either male or female children are practically nonexistent," though as Gagnon and Simon point out, "the impact of some mothers on their own children may be pathological, but no one has yet suggested making them against" (part of) "the criminal law."[3] However, females may be convicted of rape as accessories.

One very important approach to conventional rape (adult male of an adult female), and necessarily a female approach, has been publicized and advocated only in the past few years. It is, very simply, a realistic approach, "don't fight it."* A late night TV show devoted an hour-and-a-half to this thesis with corroborating testimony from lawyers, police officers, psychiatrists, and two rape victims. Schiff, a medical examiner in Miami, says ". . . I do not write lightly when I urge a woman with the odds very much against her to yield to her assailant. In this instance, discretion is the better part of valor."[4] Staying alive is more important than making a token defense of one's "honor" against a male intent on rape. We have made this point many times in group discussions with young women newly arrived on a city campus, adding that one seldom reads about a 5 foot 5 inch solitary rapist, though such undoubtedly exist. In short, most females do not really have the strength for fighting off a rapist, unless they have developed a special karate skill.

Only a few years ago, it was decided in conference with the Dean of Students that we could not include this advice in the contraceptive guide we were writing, since it would certainly be misinterpreted by parents and even by some students. Obviously times have changed; many now feel that it can and should be made clear that too much struggling can enrage an already disturbed person. Inevitably, there will be some reflex attempt at defense, an attempt to escape, a scream, and if feasible, this should be done; noise is sometimes very effective. But as Dr. Mary Conroy, a physical education teacher of self-defense states:

> The all important point to remember is that if a woman is going to defend herself, she must injure—let me repeat—injure her assailant so as to incapacitate him. Just hurting him makes him more dangerous so that he can pursue her with more anger and determination.

---

* Defense attorneys like to ask: "Have you ever had intercourse before this alleged incident? Do you enjoy intercourse?" Women should be prepared for this type of questioning if they elect not to fight, but bruises on any area of the body should be noted on the emergency room record for future use in court.

Once a woman decides that she must, in fact, attack her attacker, her decision is based on the assumption that she's about to be killed. Under such circumstances, everything goes, even killing, which is morally and legally justifiable in self-defense.[5]

But if from the back of the mind comes the knowledge that no permanent physical damage usually occurs in the genital area, though there may be bruising, bleeding, and discomfort, there will be less threat to life itself. Remember also, that rapists, given the time, usually attempt more than one act of penetration if they are alone, and if in a group, this is inevitable.

With sexual activity becoming relatively commonplace among the unmarried, though the acceptance of this depends on the locale and the culture, many enlightened young women do not feel overwhelmed, embarrassed, or guilty about a rape experience. For those with a clear conscience about the amount of enticement involved in the attack, the emotional trauma does not seem to be great, though it may contribute to nightmarish fantasies for a time. There may be a tendency to equate men-sex-violence for varying lengths of time, postrape. They may think that they never want to see another man. But, if they have been previously at ease with the amount of sexuality in the environment, even though they may never have been active, overt participants, such females will probably have less difficulty recovering from the unpleasant aspects of the experience, and be more understanding of their own transient feelings of disgust or rage, guilt or fear.

Often overlooked by the woman are her obligations to society to prevent recurrence. She often bypasses this obligation in an almost conscience-free manner, knowing that police are frequently unsympathetic, or perhaps only jaded with experience, that convictions are infrequent, and that court is unpleasant and the hearing may be 6 to 18 months from the time of the attack. Some states require witnesses, which seems a little ridiculous. One of many suggestions that have been made is that proof that the rapist and victim were strangers should be enough, but this would subject many innocent males involved in *cooperative* one-night-stands to the threat of rape. There is no easy answer, but attempts are being made to change the laws to make them a little more equitable and manageable for the accused and the victim; and police are gradually being made aware, in the larger cities, that their unsympathetic approach to the victim contributes little to the apprehension of rapists in the community, and, in fact, makes it much more difficult.

The real problem is that any physician, private or hospital, is obligated to report his treatment of an apparent felony, be it gunshot wound or rape. Many private physicians do not do this, at the request of their patients. Many victims who are aware of this obligation do not seek medical treatment unless it is desperately needed. This accounts, in part, for the feeling that there may be three or four unreported rapes for every case reported to the police; in larger cities, police feel that this ratio is much higher, even ten to one. It also means that women are not treated for venereal disease or pregnancy which might have resulted from the attack until it is too late to prevent the consequences of delayed treatment. VD and pregnancy are unpleasant realities which do not constitute a large percentage of most studies, but which do occur, singly or together, in 10 to 30 percent of reported rapes. Young women have asked us if it is really necessary to be seen by a doctor if "there is no real harm." Rape victims, who feel they have not been harmed, frequently ask university officials to "please not send them to the hospital."

Contact with venereal disease is often assumed to have occurred, and the victim is treated for this even prior to a positive diagnosis of gonorrhea or syphilis. Cultures and blood tests should be done at the time of the initial examination (see VD). Pregnancies resulting from rape can usually be prevented from implanting, if the victim is seen within 24 to 48 hours (see below). Most hospital emergency rooms offer both services. In addition, physicians must note the presence or absence of sperm, though sperm are not essential for conviction if there is sufficient evidence of physical assault; there usually is, but it must be documented. If necessary, the victim should be sure that all bruises are indicated to the examining physician; some emergency room physicians fail to examine areas other than the genital area.

Most hospitals offer the morning-after pill to prevent implantation of any acquired pregnancy (see p. 225). No patient need accept this treatment, but she should be aware that it is available from private physicians, if not from the hospital. If menstrual extraction is available, this might be a pleasanter and more reliable method, two or three weeks later, though we are not promoting this method except in emergencies (see p. 208). One gynecologist we know, routinely inserts an IUD (see p. 208) in addition to giving the morning-after-pill, orally. *If rape occurs in a woman who is unknowingly pregnant,* that is, prior to a missed menstrual period, or two or three weeks past a missed period, and she is given the morning-after pill, there are two points to consider which might alleviate concern about a desired pregnancy. 1) The dosage of DES (the morning-after pill) which is used is very small when compared with the large amounts used several years ago to "maintain" pregnancies, and which apparently are related to vaginal lesions in the female offspring of these pregnancies. 2) If DES is given prior to a missed menstrual period, it is doubtful that the beginnings of the genital system in the embryo are developed enough to be influenced by this medication in the dosage given.[6]

Treatment for psychic trauma is important and may be simply mild sedation, tranquilizers for a period of time, or a stay in the hospital. A four to six week follow-up visit is essential for a number of reasons: blood tests for syphilis, if acquired, become positive in six to eight weeks; a repeat gonorrhea culture is needed; and a pelvic examination and pregnancy test are needed, if there has been no menstrual period. Frequently emotional trauma is evidenced only by absent menstrual periods for one or several months, which of course will look like pregnancy until proven otherwise. The morning-after-pill is no guarantee against pregnancy.

Follow-up should be available and used, because frequently the mental state of the patient may have changed from apparent bravado at the time of the incident, a not uncommon reaction to gentle rapes, to something more profound and disturbing. To a large extent this is determined by how the people around her react to the attack, family especially, but also friends.

Medical treatment of children, postmenopausal females, and males involved in sexual assault is directed primarily toward venereal disease, trauma, and the psyche. But any girl with early signs of puberty, even if she has not had a menstrual period, should be considered potentially pregnant if there is any evidence of ejaculation in the genital area or even attempted penile penetration in the absence of demonstrable sperm. This group of assault cases usually requires more attention to the effects of physical trauma resulting from attempted penetration (digital, penile, vaginal, or anal) than does the conventional rape victim. Some rather damaging items have been reported found in what would appear to most as an impenetrable rectum.

With regard to child assaults, Gagnon and Simon state that " . . . for most children, in most situations, the victim situation is transient, minimal, and of short duration."[7] This does not negate emotional trauma, in particular the emotional trauma induced in the child by the attitudes of the adults immediately concerned, normally the parents and the police. These attitudes may serve to exacerbate what might have been only a slightly fearful and curious reaction. Children's reactions to sexual content or mild experiences should never be equated with adult reactions to the same stimuli, but they often are.

The same writers report that the largest category of sexual acts involving children, other than exhibitionism, involve genital touching. This touching can range from a minor contact to an attempt to stimulate orgasm in the child. In some cases, commonly those that occur repetitively over a period of time, usually with a person known to the child, there is an attempt to get the child to reciprocate the contact "though this would seem to be more common in homosexual contacts than heterosexual."[8] A summary of research studies indicates that 85 to 90 percent of all female child victim experiences are either visual (about one-half) or single occasion touching (about one-third), primarily hand-genital. For male children, the bulk of the approaches are verbal with about another one-third involving only brief genital contact.

Group, or gang rape, represented 43 percent of all rapes reported in Philadelphia from 1958 to 1960, and over half of these involved more than two male offenders.[9] Or, to look at it differently, 71 percent of all reported rapists during this period were involved in gang rape. These figures must be interpreted in light of the word reported. The physical and emotional trauma resulting from group rape more often requires medical attention which, in turn, requires reporting. Also, a girl can report this type of assault with some assurance that something will be done about it, and with fewer implications of enticement from investigating authorities. Frequently the older girl involved in this kind of assault is one who is known to one or more members of the group as available or sexually experienced on at least a one-to-one basis. In talking with a group of ten high school girls from a rough but wide-ranging neighborhood, eight of them knew girls who at age 13 or 14 had been walking along the street and had been dragged into a deserted house, or a house where the occupants were gone, and raped by a group of three or four boys. "But," they said, "they didn't all 'get in'."

Who Rapes?

". . . because of the clandestine nature of the act he is not often apprehended and hence little is known concerning his intelligence, occupation, nationality, religion, and psychiatric mood."[10] Again, it is important here to remember that gentle rapes with no medical attention are seldom followed up and probably represent three out of four incidents. However, the feeling of those in close contact with this problem is that the majority of rapes are committed by opportunists, males who take advantage of women whom they find alone and defenseless or who are apparently "asking for it." In contrast, the true rapist must repeat until he is caught and even afterwards while out on bail, or during probation after serving a sentence, or out of the psychiatric wards on a weekend pass. The true rapist carefully puts himself into situations, sometimes with great difficulty, where rape is the prime motive, rather than incidental to robbery, burglary, or a chance encounter. The two examples below are from one edition of the *Philadelphia Evening Bulletin:*

> . . . A 57-year-old woman was raped and robbed . . . by a man who entered through a partially opened window from a fire escape at 1:45 A.M. The woman was asleep in her living room . . . After the man raped her he took $100 from her pocketbook.

> . . . testimony that X (age 23) climbed a ladder to the second floor of the victim's home, threatened her and her two children with a knife, and forced her to accompany him through the backyard to a spot in front of a home on Y Lane, where he assaulted her.[11]

Rape probably has little to do with sexual desire; the rapist seems motivated by aggressiveness and hostility toward women; thus no matter how available sexual relations are to him, or to any males in our society, rape will undoubtedly continue to be a problem.

"What is most apparent," say Gagnon and Simon in discussing who "offends" children, "is the low order of sexual experience had by men who offend against children and their not only sexual but general ineptitude in life management."[12] There is a wide age range in this category of males. As with rapists, the compulsive offender is a minority of all of those who offend, and the opportunist offends in direct relation to stressful situations inside or outside of marriage. Homosexuality is not a major factor in offenders of male children.[13]

"Group rape is not rape by a number of rapists convened for the occasion. It is the group which rapes."[14] This is generally a lower-class, adolescent phenomenon, with intensified desires and experimentation with sex. Some elements of the game of "chicken" seem to enter in, with the usual paradox of feeling safer in a group, but also of fearing the threat of humiliation in front of that same group. It may even be the leader who is least secure.[15] A previous pattern of aggression as well as violence in the environment is also associated with this type of rape. Some psychiatrists see symbolic homosexuality in the mutual involvement with the same object.[16] Or, it could simply be a part of that adolescent male-to-male stage of maturing, prior to being able to relate to females in any rational way, but with much sexual tension and curiosity that has no other outlet. And in many of the lower socioeconomic living situations (schools, homes, streets), there is no other outlet, and little guidance or opportunity for active sublimation in sports, academics, or even a job.

The female, of *any* socioeconomic class, who makes herself available to males in sequence, whether at parties, in cars, or wherever, may find that she has asked for more than she can handle and cry rape, that is group rape, though no group was really involved. Even the prostitute can cry rape if she has not been paid, though she has more difficulty than most in proving her case.

There have been many privately and federally funded studies on the role of explicit sexual material and frank pornography in its many forms as a causal factor in the increasing frequency of rape and sexual assault. We must include here, also, studies on the influence of real and fictional violence in the communications media.[17] Very probably the answer will never be available in a form that can be tabulated neatly; too many variables exist which do not fit into the statistical world of Chi Square. We do know that sexual material can act as a stimulant to almost anyone who allows himself or herself to give it more than a passing glance. It may stimulate sexual hostility or sexual desire, each with its own spectrum of reactions. Or, it may simply satisfy a curiosity about the apparent needs of other people. The effects of repetitive violence in the environment and in the media depend entirely upon the fertility of the ground it reaches. It is each individual's previous pattern of aggression and hostility which determines the conversion of these stimuli into fantasy or potential reality for that person, or into a socially acceptable modification, or whether they are simply added to a store of vicarious experiences.

The X and R ratings limit movies to adults who are theoretically mature enough to direct the sex and violence stimuli into legitimate channels. The dark of the theatre, like bedrooms, is very protective. But, if X- and R-rated films were shown in lighted theatres or outdoors on a sunny, summer afternoon, what kind of people would one see there? And how would they react? Or, to take this one step further, the same questions could be asked about "softcore" and "hardcore" movies and "live shows" as described in "The Selling of Sex: A Look through Solemn Sodom":

> *They had arrived . . . one at a time . . . sitting one seat apart until that was no longer possible, and then taking seats on the aisle . . . No one willingly sits next to anyone else and indeed, except for a quick sometimes furtive glance, they do not even look at anyone else.*
>
> *Thirty men watch her. They are distinguished by absolutely nothing, and they could be the first 30 men off a BMT local in Brooklyn. They are, however, enormously polite.*[18]

Who Gets Raped?

By legal definition, females of all ages but primarily older teenagers, young adults, and the unmarried.* In Philadelphia, about half of the rapes reported at any length in the newspapers are of women, age 40 to 80, and occur in their homes. The remainder are simply listed in the daily crime statistics; these females are usually in the wrong place at the wrong time. Those closely associated with the problem feel that some of these women thought they were in the right place at the right time for whatever "trouble" they were looking for. This is undoubtedly true, and while they may not consciously be equating trouble with rape, in the present state of city and country life, rape is what they usually get. Or with a gentler male friend, they get pregnant.

These women may be looking for and enjoy good aggressive sex and fantasize that the stranger whom they entice with their apparent availability will be so overcome with their charm that the raping tiger will be turned into a playful, but aggressive, "fun" kitten, someone who really cares about them. What better way to demonstrate one's power over the male, possibly a form of hostility, or to prove one's femininity to an insecure self? This may sound naive, but naiveté is not uncommon when there is no acceptance or recognition of reality. An old story will illustrate this point: the self-fulfilling nightmare of the lady who dreams of being raped. When she asks her dream attacker to be gentle with her, he responds, "It's your dream, lady."

---

* For a very explicit discussion of male rape in prisons, the reader is referred to Alan J. Davis' study, "Sexual Assault in the Philadelphia Prisons and Sheriff's Vans," *Transaction* (December, 1968).

But what does one tell women who work late and have to walk to or from a bus or home besides "carry Mace, hairspray, hatpins, learn Karate, find another job, or 'don't fight it'"? Many are finding other jobs. Inner city hospitals have difficulty staffing their night and evening shifts unless they provide escort services, but even that service is only part of the answer.

There is a rather prevalent feeling among the young, who are idealists about people if not about the environment, that all humans are their brothers and sisters and inherently good if treated well and with respect. "If I radiate love and goodwill nothing can happen to me that will be anything but a reflection of this love and goodwill." A 30-year-old psychiatrist acquaintance was curious about the extent of this kind of thinking in hitchhiking college women. He and a friend devoted a few weeks to the project, picking up these women, taking them in the direction they wanted to go, and asking questions. The almost invariable answer was that the inherent danger was not a major concern and, besides, "We do not get in just any car." The obvious fallacies here are that there may be occasions when a female standing in or beside the road cannot avoid getting in a car, and, also, this particular psychiatrist, with his beard and long hair could have been a murderer, a rapist, or a saint. Hair is not the criterion, but in this situation, there really are no adequate criteria. The most deceptive offender can look like the clean-shaven, square-faced, blond, All-American boy, for example, the male rapist and murderer in a mid-Western university community a few years ago.

Hitchhiking males may be physically assaulted (robbery), but the homosexual proposals usually come in the form of gestures, verbal offers, or requests.

Daytime rape is increasing. We will never understand how door-to-door salesmen or women make a living now, or how they did so in previous years. Nor do we understand how even well-identified interviewers for a national study on violence are going to get a foot in the door to ask their questions, without ending up with a skewed sample of females and males who are apparently willing to open their doors to strangers for any reason, even allowing them to use telephones. Even telephone interviews about the previous year's experience with any type of violence would be met with a slammed-down receiver and no answer from sensibly cautious people.

Deserted subway stations as well as the hidden recesses of parking garages also require more than casual alertness. A recent group rape occurred one Saturday at high noon in a deserted subway station. A new student nurse walking from the hospital asked a group of four boys the way to the entrance, and they offered to accompany her. This is the point at which she should or could have done some thinking. When they arrived in the deserted station, they each raped her, in turn.

But is it really rape when a young woman is raped after meeting a stranger a 9 P.M. on a campus walk and agreeing to help him carry his paintings into a nearby, unlighted building? With this amount of information, the experts would classify *him* as an opportunist. How would you classify *her*? An opportunist? A romantic? An ingenue?

There is no need to live in fear, but common sense can become so reflex that fear need not be omnipresent: common sense about locks, being alone on the streets, late night sorties for cigarettes or groceries, about who is behind or in front of you. What is really needed is a realistic appraisal of the "it can't happen to me" philosophy, because if this is a female's point of view, it can happen. One *should* be able to walk the streets at any time of day or night, but it has become perfectly apparent that one *cannot,* without, at least, the minimal precaution of awareness of the possibility of assault.

More pragmatically, what is also needed, especially on city college campuses, is an adequate communications system for students so they can be aware of the rapes which occur or of unapprehended rapists in the vicinity. After a series of four or five group rapes on and near a city campus, a newspaper reporter went out to ask students how they had modified their activities and discovered that few knew anything about the rapes, though they had been widely reported on television and in the city and campus newspapers. These students had obviously not changed their activities in any way.

But if rape does happen, and many times rape is inevitable and unavoidable, the present tenor of the times in the United States and the culture have practically eliminated any need for guilt, a feeling of loss of honor, or of being spoiled for any other males or a prospective husband.

If there is unmanageable guilt, it would be well for the victim to seek help in examining the how's and why's of the incident: was it avoidable, was there an element of enticement, an element of defiance, or just naiveté? Is the guilt being imposed on her by others in her acquaintance? The victim must also be assured that if she has had good relationships with males in the past, overtly sexual or not, she has known some good males, and she will have good relationships in the future, regardless of any immediate or lingering negative feelings about males and physical sexuality. If she has never had such relationships, or after having been involved in physical sex, has always felt "used," or if this was the first sexual encounter of any kind, the victim will probably need much more than self-help and understanding friends to get over the initial shock and disappointment of discovering that sexual activity can have very ugly and unpleasant parameters. ". . . Equating sex with violence does change the nature of each. . . ."[19]

Prostitution

The existence of prostitutes in the community may be denied, although it may be common knowledge that there are some females and males who are hustling.

Alfred C. Kinsey

PROSTITUTION, THE OLDEST PROFESSION, is a business or occupation which has always been identified as sexual activity associated with selling, emotional indifference, and promiscuity. The line has always been clearly drawn for the majority of the population; any stepping over this line was clearly recognizable: the female was seeing or being seen with too many males, and she was doing very well with no visible means of support.

Sexual freedom has created problems and questions not only in the minds of the onlookers, but in some of the active participants as well. As a result the line between sexual freedom and promiscuity is now less clearly drawn. Accepting prostitution as a fact of life requires little exercise of the intellect, but questioning one's own activities in light of a definition is quite another matter. The concerns created by indiscriminate self-labeling can be destructive.

When intercourse becomes a part of dating behavior, it automatically becomes associated with all of the variables of conventional dating practices, which include: several male contacts, occasional emotional indifference, and even selling and buying in one form or another. Kinsey discussed this problem, but with less reason than we now have, if we think of absolute percentages of people actively participting in sexual activity outside of marriage.[20] The existence of any two of these three factors in a relationship or a particular life style may give rise to the questions: "What am I doing?" "What is it that I really want?" These are not bad questions to ask oneself in any relationship, male or female, but the self-questioning and self-doubts are often resolved with a quick, easy rationalization which seldom gives workable, lasting answers.

These questions and doubts arise primarily in the minds of females, but males are not immune. Kinsey mentioned heterosexual male prostitutes in only one or two lines, acknowledging that they exist, but with no evidence that any of his interviewed females used male prostitutes. Winick and Kinsie note "there have been recurring rumors of brothels with male inmates which had female clients . . . which have never been substantiated."[21] Later, they also mention Joe Buck, *The Midnight Cowboy,* as one of the best examples of "the near impossibility of a stud earning a livelihood from prostitution."[22]

An important consideration which we have not seen mentioned elsewhere is that the physiology of the male does not usually allow him to function well under pressure, or frequently enough to be able to make prostitution a profession. In heterosexual male prostitution, an impotent stud would be a financial failure. The fee before service, a characteristic of female prostitution, would have to be changed to service before fee.

Male houses of prostitution catering to homosexual males do exist, primarily in metropolitan areas. A composite description of several indicates that their operation is similar in financial and sexual arrangements to female heterosexual houses.[23] These prostitutes can see several customers over a relatively short period of time who may request any one of a variety of sexual acts, some of which do not require an erect penis or ejaculation on the part of the prostitute.

The problems associated with frequency of performance and performance under pressure do not exist to the extent they would in a heterosexual situation.

The nature of female to female relationships in general, and among female homosexuals in particular, appears to make the existence of female homosexual houses unnecessary.

The Nonprofessional Female

Our concern for the moment is not with the professional prostitute; she is identified by others and by herself. Rather, it is with the female who may wonder, even briefly, if she qualifies as a nonprofessional. Fear of being labeled by others is also limiting, and will often keep a woman in a relationship that has gone from bad to worse, and has nothing going for it except the fact that there was or is sexual intercourse; and she may even have become emotionally indifferent to and bored with this. Males have always had fewer personally or publicly imposed conflicts about leaving this kind of relationship. But even in this enlightened age, the female who leaves is often still suspect.

Realistically, and with no intent to promote premature sexual activity, decisions about intercourse in relationships in the seventies often represent little more in the emotional sense than the decisions the previous generations had to make about heavy petting in relationships. "Older generations . . . were themselves once faced with the question of crossing the fine line between necking and heavy petting. Today, for many, it has become a matter of intercourse or no intercourse and, if so, when in relation to the initial encounter."[24]

Once the emotional decision is made about the "first time," accidentally or with forethought, the sexual act itself becomes progressively easier, and it may or may not have any *mature* emotional meaning. It certainly becomes easier for the younger group of females and males who are in the "giving" and "taking" stage and not expecting too much; this is especially true if their first encounter was a ten minute "in and out" which did not give the female that much physiological or emotional satisfaction. Their response is likely to be "It's really no big deal, what's all the fuss about? I'm saving this for marriage? Marriage should be more than sex." The real emotional pleasure for this female is in allowing a male whom she likes to get a few moments of uniquely male pleasure from her.

At the other end of the spectrum, after the first time and whatever reasons prompted the "loss of virginity," it also becomes easier *not* to have intercourse with just anyone who comes along. This "I can take it or leave it" philosophy is just beginning to evidence itself. Intercourse has become an available option, and options and opportunities are part of what most minority groups are fighting for. And, rightly or wrongly, male and female virgins almost always consider themselves members of a minority group among their peers.

Thus it can happen that within a relatively short time, it becomes easy to have intercourse with friends or lovers without commitment; that is, there is sex, relative emotional indifference, and a variety of partners. Even sex with only two people in one's lifetime, without benefit of a marriage license, can represent promiscuity in the strictest interpretation of the word, a defiant gesture against an old almost universal taboo, though for many this taboo may exist only subliminally. The word promiscuity must be redefined or declared obsolete before many of the present generation or their elders can become comfortable enough to enjoy some of the pleasures of the new sexual freedom which can and should include the equally pleasurable option of saying, "No, thank you," without appearing completely out of phase with the rest of the world. This same word, promiscuity, has kept and is still keeping venereal disease underground, because its connotations are simply not yet acceptable.

Sexual freedom is not an end in itself. If one does not see today's sexuality in its proper perspective, it is difficult to view the activities of others and the results of these activities—venereal disease, pregnancy, abortion, the need for contraceptive information and facilities—realistically. And without this perspective, it is often difficult for "beginners" to recognize that sexual freedom creates many more problems than it seems to solve, namely, the basic one of availability of options. And the point that is often completely missed is that many of the problems which are created are not related to the sexual act itself, but to the fact of sexual activity *outside of marriage*.

So, the stage is quickly set for transient feelings of being a nonprofessional because there are so many possible variations of "selling" and "emotional indifference." These pose questions which can only be answered by the participants in the context of each individual relationship.

Some of the more militant feminists use only the *sex plus payment* part of the definition of prostitution, and take the extreme view that *hausfrau* wives are literal prostitutes, and high-priced ones at that. "When Gloria Steinem dismisses marriage as 'prostitution' in a speech to the League of Women Voters, the assumption is that no woman would ever want to go to bed with a man if she didn't need to sell her body for bread or a mink coat."[25] Feminists in 1886 felt the same way:

The man who has been accustomed to gratify his passions promiscuously seeks and marries a lovely virtuous girl. She is not supposed to have needs in this direction. Neither has she learned that her body is her own and her soul is her Maker's. She gives up all ownership of herself to her husband, and what is the difference between her life and the life of a public woman? She is sold to one man, and is not half so well paid. Is it too strong language to say she is the one prostitute taking the place, for the man, of many, and not like her, having a choice of time or conditions?[26]

Or regarding marriage, "It's not such a great job, but it pays well and offers a lot of security."

Mistresses receive gifts in all forms, but are seldom condemned as promiscuous. Nor are they accused of prostituting themselves. Males with mistresses, or females with studs, do not seem to fall into either category, though the stud label is not appreciated by males, possibly because it can give rise to some of the same concerns as the word prostitute.

Inevitably, even in a college population, there will be a few females who are selling drugs to their sexual contacts. Are they *selling* sex and drugs for money, or *buying* sex with drug availability, the money being incidental?

Or, assuming sexual activity is part of the following examples of current dating behavior, who is buying, and who is selling? The male pays for a conventional date. They go Dutch. She pays for both, and provides bed and, occasionally, board. They are living together because two or three together can live more cheaply than separately, and *she* is a good cook; in addition, they enjoy each other's company and the privileges of "home" and a "nest." Good friends are sleeping together on occasion because they both need and enjoy sex and have an understanding and trust they feel is unique. The latter situation is almost payment "in kind," sex for sex. There may be two or three good friends who fit into this category. Is this promiscuity? None of these examples may represent a long-term commitment, nor are they devoid of emotional involvement. But the intermittently insecure female or male caught up too soon in this life style may have some doubts about the degree of commitment; it does not seem to approach anything that she or he expected, or was led to expect, should be associated with intercourse. Again, the degree to which buying and selling enters into these arrangements can only be determined by the individuals directly concerned.

There are many accidental one-night-stands which have progressed into good relationships, even marriage. But what about the girl who misjudges and finds $10 under her pillow? Does she keep the money, call it a learning experience, and do a little thinking about her image? Or, does she return it gently, tearfully, or angrily, knowing as *The Respectful Prostitute* did, that if she were "that kind" she would have charged more?[27] Or, what is the difference between money and other tangible gifts?

Many young people with experience and insight, who know their own personal needs and priorities, have learned to recognize the bases for their brief moments of discomfort and doubt, are able to be comfortable with their own activity, and do not make judgments about others; they have learned the real lesson: sexual activity cannot be categorized in or out of marriage. It is really a continuum ranging from prostitution to good sex for pleasure which may not always include a penis in a vagina. Within this continuum, one can place marriage and heterosexual and homosexual activity, as well as solitary masturbation. Inevitably, all of these variations will have some things in common, above and beyond the genital area, and any one of the variations will share some of the characteristics of another.

There are many young people and their elders who are in continuing conflict with some of the taboos and mores of previous generations, some of which do not apply to the present scene, or are misapplied. When misapplied, they may create many more emotional problems than does the simple physical act of intercourse.

The Professional

Among the initial questions which come to mind when one first discovers the word prostitute and has it explained and justified are, "How do they keep from getting pregnant?" and "Why don't they get VD?" The answers are simple. Prostitutes *do* get pregnant, and they *do* get VD; furthermore, a gonorrheal episode early in their careers frequently leaves them with closed tubes which prevent pregnancy. Pregnancies are undesirable because they remove these women from the marketplace. (Menstrual periods have the same effect briefly, unless a diaphragm is used to contain the menstrual flow, see p. 206). The pill has been a boon for those prostitutes who think they are still fertile. Police raids on "houses" frequently yield the vital equipment for the practice of prostitution: a large supply of contraceptives (to prevent pregnancy), a number of wigs (to provide variety), and cameras (for later visual entertainment, or blackmail).

It has been noted that prostitutes have a poor reproductive history and a high incidence of spontaneous abortion.[28] A study of 37 jailed prostitutes revealed that prior to their careers they had 40 pregnancies resulting in 27 live births (68.5 percent); afterward, they had 35 pregnancies with only 12 live births (34.5 percent) and 23 spontaneous abortions.[29] In the general prostitute population one must also consider an unrevealed incidence of illegal abortions (nonprofessional abortions) and resulting infections which may also create sterility or a poor reproductive history (see Abortion).

"In 1871 Darwin suggested that a direct relationship between sexual promiscuity in women and infertility may exist on the basis of exposure to semen."[30] This relationship is still under investigation in infertile couples and in prostitutes; antibodies which "clump" and immobilize the sperm have been found in the blood of both groups of women. A wife may create antibodies to her husband's semen, and a prostitute to several different samples of semen. The significance of this in the treatment of infertility is still not clearly established.

Prostitutes have always been considered the reservoir of venereal disease, thus some of the poor connotations associated with contracting VD in the past. Expensive, high-class houses pride themselves on not being reservoirs. They insist on weekly medical checks and constant attention to douching between customers for whatever value this might have. In areas where prostitution is legal, some parts of Nevada, weekly medical checks are mandatory. Good houses cannot afford bad reputations.

The independent streetwalker, as opposed to the call girl or house prostitute, who depends more on volume than on reputation, undoubtedly represents a reservoir of VD, but such a woman is often clever enough to take care of herself in public clinics or with local doctors (see VD). The more organized and cared for prostitute, one of a stable maintained by the organizer, a pimp, or a madam whom they support, frequently has some initial attention and instruction about the disease and pregnancy aspects of her profession.

Condoms *can* be used prophylactically (preventively) and acquired one of their other names (pros or prophylactics) for a good reason (see p. 200). Massive distribution of condoms in the armed forces along with lectures and vivid, visual aids have been effective in reducing VD and, more important and more realistically, encouraging early treatment in this very susceptible group of isolated males.

Questions also arise concerning "wear and tear" caused by the necessary frequency in the practice of prostitution. Many women and couples find that every time *they* increase the frequency of intercourse over their usual norm there is either a bladder infection (see Traumatic Urethritis, p. 118) or so much discomfort that they have to cease activities for a while. According to *The Happy Hooker*, "One of the working girl's best friends is a little product called Koromex jelly. . . . Too much friction can injure a girl's vagina."[31] No one is immune, apparently.

Hirschi writes of prostitution as a profession, arguing against the claim that only girls too lazy to work become involved:

In order to survive, she must be able to 1) find customers, 2) "sell" them, 3) provide a suitable place in which to transact business, 4) please the customer, 5) collect the money, 6) protect herself from disease, pregnancy and physical injury, 7) avoid the police.[32]

He feels this is at least a partial answer to the question of why so few females become prostitutes or stay in the business very long.

The skills needed to survive are common to the whole profession, but the relative importance of each skill varies with the clientele and the mode of operation. Bryan notes that "it may well be that the verbal exchange required of the call girl requires greater knowledge than that required of the streetwalker, but the nonverbal skills required of the streetwalker may be considerably greater. . . ."[33] He quotes a pimp who manages call girls and "high-class streetwalkers":

The girl that goes out into the street is the sharper of the two, because she is capable of handling herself in the street, getting around the law, picking out the trick that is not absolutely psycho . . . and capable of getting along in the street. . . . The streetwalker, as you call her, is really a prima donna of the prostitutes . . . her field is unlimited, she goes to all of the top places so she meets the top people. . . .[34]

Who and Why

This is the land of opportunity; money and what it can buy are the primary reasons for anyone needing an occupation or profession. Talent, interest, and acquired skills determine which profession. With luck and careful planning, a vocation may even coincide with an avocation. The home environment and the external environment are certainly determining factors for all of us, but neither need be the definitive factor in sending a young female into prostitution.

The more one reads about prostitution and prostitutes, the more varied and less stereotyped the group becomes. Undoubtedly masochism, poor or confused self-image, infantile mentality, and so on are present in some of these females. But not all of them are defiant or hate their parents or even hate men. Not all of them are lesbians who like the female environment of their leisure hours, and not all of them fail to have orgasms, deny themselves orgasm, or make bad marriages. Some drop in and out of the profession for quick money, and some drop out because they couldn't make it, the money just was not there for them. Many drop in because they have a child or children to support, and the pimp provides day or night care facilities for his stable of working mothers.

One attitude prostitutes must have in common is a relative lack of concern about the illegality of their activity; if ambivalent feelings about the *immorality* of their occupation exist, these women can usually handle them without losing their effectiveness as prostitutes. If they are clever enough or have good supervision, they can stay out of trouble with the law. But if they are picked up, they are not overwhelmed by police, magistrates, courts, a night or two in jail, or the threat of longer jail sentences. Police vice squads in the larger cities say that it requires a major effort just to keep prostitution from becoming a public nuisance in any neighborhood, not to mention trying to control the drug traffic, blackmail, and other criminal activities often associated with this occupation.

Another characteristic which seems to be common to prostitutes as well as to those females who are rented out by escort services for the day or evening, is the great pleasure they take in their ability to be in control of the situation at all times. The female escorts from New York and Miami who were interviewed by the *New York Times* and on TV talk shows vigorously denied any sexual activity, but were clearly very pleased with their ability to handle sexual overtures with a firm hand. This seems to be an underlying theme in many of the interviews and quotes of prostitutes working at almost any level of their profession with the exception of teenagers. The seller is obviously in control. For money, she will appear to *lose* control as judged by ordinary standards. *When wives or girlfriends are that controlling they are called "castrating females."**

The need for money to support a drug habit may start or prolong a hustling career. "I was hustling before I got on narcotics, I liked the fast money. Now it's a must."[35]

Creating a need for narcotics will create a stable of girls for an ambitious pimp. In an article about "teeny hookers," *Time* reported a "desperate culture of emotionally troubled rejects largely from working class and even ghetto families . . . easy pickings for professional pimps who use a combination of terrorism, drugs, and ersatz affection to lure confused girls into prostitution." "The street life" (for runaways) "is hard, the kids get down fast to the basic fact of finding money for food. The boys deal drugs or panhandle, even becoming male prostitutes. The girls become whores." These were teenagers who, as one older hooker said "ain't even got their period yet!"[36]

Barclay, discussing "white slave traffic" at the international level, describes girls only slightly older, but no less caught up in the traps set for them. He emphasizes the futility of trying to implement any of the UN's Human Rights Commission's concerns for these girls.[37]

Who Buys?

Why aren't prostitutes out of business? Why should a male with anything on the ball pay for sex when he can get it free? But not all males are lucky enough to get it free, nor do all of them want it free. Not all of them get either the frequency or the kind of sex they want from their wives or girl friends (perhaps their women do not get it either) but many would hesitate to request this of their women, for a variety of reasons. Their reasons for not asking might include any of those briefly discussed under sexual dysfunction as well as a fear of impregnating a wife who would not or could not take the responsibility for contracepting.

In discussing the increased frequency of premarital intercourse up to 1953,

---

* Women have no comparable, neat, common phrase to use for men. How do men castrate women? Or, how does a man castrate a woman on the one-to-one level? By ignoring them, not listening to them, not showing any evidence of caring while using them.

In the much larger social arena, the feminist movement is basically a response to many years of "castration" of females, of not being listened to, or cared for except in the physical sense, and of lack of concern for their plight from a male-oriented and dominated society. Naturally, the response of the more militant feminists is "We don't need men."

Kinsey noted studies which indicated that after World War I, the number of males who had had some experience with prostitutes did not change, but the frequency with which American males went to prostitutes decreased to about half of what it had been in the prewar generation. This could be directly correlated with the increase in premarital coitus with "nice girls." The change in attitudes and sexual behavior of American youth began in the twenties. What we have in the seventies is only the result of a geometric progression of attitudes over two or three generations; that is, sexually permissive parents begat sexually permissive children, and the definitions of sexually permissive changed to include more activities and a greater age range. This, in turn, created peer pressure on those whose grandparents did not give them such a legacy. Those grandparents who were sexually defiant in the twenties may each have influenced twenty or more of their descendants in the seventies.

If we extrapolate the information about the decreasing frequency of visits to prostitutes to today, forty to fifty years later, we could postulate that there is now a core group of males who visit or use prostitutes—a group, which if studied in depth, might be more uniform in its psychosexual makeup than the prostitutes they are visiting and which also might possibly be more uniform in its psychosexual makeup than its predecessors in the twenties, thirties and forties, regardless of socioeconomic level. These would be interesting males to study in quantity and in depth, but they are difficult to find.

VIEWPOINT

The laws against prostitution are a good example, for surely they cause far more harm than they have ever done good. Prostitution has been going on since the dawn of history; and no civilization has ever been able to dispense with it. And for good reason. It's a necessary profession, every bit as essential as the corner grocery store. As long as men have a sex drive, there must be women to satisfy them. Naturally, our romantic natures would prefer that the act of love be accompanied as well by feelings of love, but obviously this is not always possible, or even desirable. There are innumerable situations in which individuals and society as a whole benefit from the existence of prostitution. Thousands of men, the world over, engaged in lonely jobs away from home must have some way to fill their bodily needs. Other thousands are mentally, physically, or emotionally handicapped in their ability to find willing partners. Surely being able to visit a prostitute is a far healthier solution than unwilling homosexuality or rape.

Girls who sell their bodies for a living are performing an important service for these men, and frequently for their families, as well. Personally, I'd much prefer to have my man engage in a meaningless encounter with a prostitute when he's away from home or needs a change, than to have him become emotionally involved with a nonprofessional. I seriously doubt that many wives would demand a divorce because of a husband's occasional, perhaps necessary, visit to a prostitute. I'm certain that any sensible woman would choose that alternative over an extramarital love affair as a solution to every man's natural desire for variety.

Yet despite the obvious benefits they provide, the girls who engage in this occupation are persecuted, hounded, and treated as the worst kind of criminals. Of course, it's unfortunate that many of them are forced into the profession by circumstance, and I'm sure it can't be the happiest existence. But there are innumerable unpleasant jobs which must be performed for the good of society. How many men, for instance, really want to collect garbage for a living? We're grateful that there are some who are willing to serve the rest of us in this way. By the same token, we should be thankful that there are girls who are willing to provide their bodies to men who need them. And we should be delighted that there are some who enjoy their work, doing it through choice, rather than necessity. How nice for them!

From Ruth Dickson, "Essay,"
(Sexual Latitude: For and Against),
pp. 44-46.

Venereal Disease

Venereal disease and the family have a common origin; and while, if authorities like R. D. Laing are to be believed, the latter is a far more potent source of misery, madness, and human waste than the former, VD may still constitute the more serious problem. The family, though still highly pathogenic, is said to be losing power and may be dying out. Venereal disease is more prevalent than ever.

E. Z. Friedenberg

IN ANY SEXUALLY MOBILE POPULATION, venereal disease is inevitable. Sexual mobility need only involve three individuals of any sex. Now that it has become not only a part of the middle-class life style, but is involving relatively more women than previously, we are seeing an active anti-VD campaign in many not only a part of the middle-class life style, but is involving relatively more "Even nice people get VD." "We don't care where you got it, let us help you get rid of it." "Penicillin is the gift for the guy who's had everyone."

* Venereal disease is not a new problem in the United States, but when drugs, pregnancies, unavailability of contraceptives, abortions, venereal disease, or the Vietnam War intrude into the daily lives of the middle class, they suddenly become social and moral problems worthy of national concern.

Venereal simply means associated with sexual intercourse or the genital area. Used in its broadest sense, venereal disease includes venereal warts, vaginal infectious with Trichomonads, yeast overgrowth in the vagina, herpes lesions which are similar to cold sores, infestation with crab lice, as well as the potentially disastrous syphilis and gonorrhea.

There are three other venereal diseases which may extend slightly beyond the genital area into the groin in their primary disease state and frequently also have lesions similar to those of syphilis. They may be chronic, that is, last for a long time, but if untreated they do not appear to have delayed or permanent effects on other areas in the body. These are: lymphopathia venereum, granuloma inguinale, and chancroid. Although these are still rare in the United States, the incidence is increasing, but their actual incidence has never been known since they are not reportable diseases. To the extent that they exist, they have probably long since moved out of the lower socioeconomic groups which older texts and some new, popular sex books claim is their almost exclusive range.* The signs and symptoms of these diseases, such as painful ulcerations, enlarged lymph nodes or glands in the groin, are sufficiently obvious to send anyone, female or male, for medical attention.

Four or five years ago college health services believed that they were not seeing the increase in VD noted in the noncollege population because their students, especially females, were reluctant to admit sexual activity. Though there has been an increase in the incidence in the college population, health services are still not seeing that much VD.[38] One possible reason for the relatively low incidence is that the anti-VD advertising is working. Most people are now more aware of and less self-conscious about VD and, if sexually active, at even a minimal level, they have become very suspicious of every discharge or bump on the genitals, which causes them to go for diagnosis and treatment rather promptly. If, in fact, the discharge or bump is VD and it is treated, this makes the spread of the disease through multiple contacts unlikely.

However, the sexual mobility necessary for the spread of VD clearly exists, even if it is merely a brief overlapping of one-to-one relationships, each of which may be three or more months long. There is also a certain amount of honesty and caring, even about the fellow or girl who was just left behind, so that informing sexual contacts is considered the right thing to do. Another possible reason, though we do not see it as contributing that much to the lower incidence in this group, is more attention to genital hygiene and wider use of occlusive contraceptive methods such as diaphragms and condoms rather than universal reliance on the pill or nothing for casual encounters.

A sizable percentage of the accidental, "it just happened" type of contacts in the adolescent and late adolescent groups uses no contraception. This is the

* This is similar to the spread of gonorrhea and syphilis out of lower socioeconomic groups.

group in which the incidence of reported VD and pregnancy has risen so sharply (see p. 194). This is also the group that is so bombarded with information about VD, pregnancy, sex, and relationships that much of it is only half-heard, and very little of it has any real meaning until these individuals become sexually active. They hear that condoms prevent VD, but they do not hear how to use them properly: no genital contact without a condom; they are seldom used this way. A letter to the editor of a teen-age magazine criticized their article on VD prevention for its emphasis on douching after sexual contact and its failure to mention the danger of douching out contraceptive foams or gels before the end of the six or eight hour postintercourse period. The writer's "friend" was so concerned about VD that she "douched out the foam immediately and became pregnant."

Prevention of gonorrhea and syphilis is extremely difficult and requires that two virgins with no previous genital contacts with anyone begin their sexual life together and stay together forever. Many couples operate this way and have no concerns about VD. The remaining individuals must accept the risks realistically, with full knowledge of the possible consequences of casual attitudes about these diseases.

There is no other way to prevent *getting* VD, but one can prevent spreading it to others and suffering the personal consequences of lack of treatment. There are exceptions to this general statement: silent infections with no *known* contacts do exist in males and females, but there is little one can do about these at the present time, unless there is a known contact (see Blood Tests).

Patients and physicians must have what the latter call a "high index of suspicion" about physical signs and symptoms as well as about their friends. No female likes to admit to herself that her man could possibly have had the time or the desire to be with anyone else. No male wants to think that the great female whom he has finally found, and who really understands him, has been getting or giving instructions elsewhere—which may just be the reason she is so understanding. It is this kind of ostrichlike "head in the sand" thinking which gives rise to the bedclothes, toilet seat, doorknob theories of transmission of VD.

You might contract VD from the proverbial toilet seat, if you happen to have a toilet that was kept at the invariant temperature of 98.6 F. and flushed with lukewarm blood plasma; but this is a luxury beyond the resources of all but the most decadent.[39]

We do not know the origin of the "split" toilet seat used in public facilities, but it was obviously designed to avoid contact with male urine or the genital area while sitting, a prophylactic measure very effective against the more active, sturdy crab lice, but of little preventive value in the transmission of VD.

The hundreds of different pamphlets on VD which are directed at all ages and educational levels, are written to be effective using the "fear" approach. Blindness, insanity, sterility, and death are frightening terms. The reader remembers to associate this kind of fear with any vaginal or penile discharge, any burning with urination, and any lesion on the genitals, with or without sexual activity. If these have been diagnosed two or three times as benign (no VD), and treated, there is a tendency with further recurrence to say, "Well, I've got it again," and use the leftover antibiotics, creams, or suppositories. The signs and symptoms of gonorrhea and syphilis do go away spontaneously without treatment, but the disease lingers on silently. These should be seen by a physician whenever they occur, even if neither partner is aware that a third person exists, and even when it is embarrassing to appear overly concerned.

Marriage relationships are more secure than dating relationships, but there is the old story about the husband who always comes back from his out of town trips with the "flu," desperately needing some penicillin. In this age of sexual freedom, often the only persons who are surprised or dismayed by the physical effects of sexual conduct are the persons who are sexually active; they are frequently very self-conscious and apologetic when requesting diagnosis and treatment.

But some doctors are self-conscious and ill at ease, too, which presents another problem which will continue to be with us for some time. Some young and old physicians have difficulty telling their patients that they have either syphilis or gonorrhea. They mumble and think that the patients understand. Or, they say "you have a venereal disease and we will treat it," and fail to tell them which one they have, or to explain the need for follow-up studies, or to request names of contacts. Requesting abstinence from genital contact for 10 to 14 days is also a sensible request, though not absolutely necessary posttreatment; but not all gonococcal organisms are sensitive to penicillin or to the other antibiotics which might have been used; resistant strains are becoming more and more common. It is also easy for physicians to assume that with all of the available literature about VD, patients automatically know that the diseases have serious consequences if not treated thoroughly and followed for a time. We have found that this is simply not so, even among graduate students.

Many state legislatures who tend to be very self-righteous about other side effects of sexual behavior, such as contraception, abortion, or deviance from the norm, approve treatment of VD in minors without parental consent or knowledge. At the present time, even in less lenient states, most physicians and clinics treat and look the other way; but they cannot advertise this fact. The patient of any age does have the responsibility of either informing his contacts or allowing the physician to do this, and he also has a responsibility to be reexamined in at least six to eight weeks; to be free of symptoms is not necessarily to be free of disease, even with treatment.

Common Characteristics of Syphilis (Sif, Lues, Bad Blood) and Gonorrhea (Clap, Dose, G.C., A Strain, The Drip)

Although these diseases are quite different from one another and gonorrhea is more prevalent than syphilis, they have many things in common.

1. With rare exceptions, both are transmitted through sexual contact—penile-vaginal, oral-genital, anal-genital, manual-genital (syphilis usually and this is rare), oral contact alone (rare)—and both involve the mucous membranes or nonskin areas of the body, again with rare exceptions to be noted.

2. Both may be transmitted from an infected pregnant woman to her fetus in utero (syphilis), or at the time of delivery (gonorrhea), with devastating results (see below).

3. The nature of the symptoms and signs of both diseases and the structure of the male and female genitals are such that most males are always aware that they have "something," and females are almost always unaware. This is frequently noted as one more advantage the male has over the female, but there are no advantages for either sex. What is forgotten is that, with rare exceptions, no one sets out to give or get either disease; what women do not know about themselves their men will not know either.

4. They may be contracted and exist simultaneously. The sexual activities of the rapist, other than rape itself, do not seem to be frequent or widespread enough within the female population to cause a constant VD threat, but in all emergency rooms it is usually assumed that both diseases have been acquired at the time of the rape. Therefore the physician cultures the cervix and perianal area and treats immediately, sometimes for both diseases, if he or she does not expect to see the patient again. A blood test for syphilis is usually done to determine whether or not there has been previous syphilitic infection (see p. 116). A change in the blood test from negative to positive six to eight weeks later would indicate that syphilis was acquired at the time of the rape and treatment would be necessary, if not done previously; the possibility always exists that it was acquired a few days later in a new encounter. Statistics are difficult because the follow-up on rape victims can be erratic, but of about 800 alleged rape victims in Washington, D. C. in 1970 there were 36 cases of gonorrhea which were probably the result of the attack. Five cases of syphilis were seen but could not be directly related.[40]

5. Promiscuity, with all of its connotations, is frequently associated with the occurrence of venereal disease. As noted previously, it takes only one sexual contact with two different people during a period which may be as long as two-and-a-half to three weeks or even much longer if we include the infectious secondary lesions of syphilis, to acquire and transmit the disease. This is hardly promiscuity by any current definition, and the second contact may even be a virgin female or male.

6. The responsibility for informing contacts takes many strange forms. We

have been questioned about the safety of having had intercourse three days after treatment of either disease when both partners were fully aware of treatment at the time. Again, one cannot assume that treatment automatically causes the disease to disappear. No one should feel completely free of disease until cultures become negative or the more sophisticated blood tests for syphilis have changed from positive to negative (see footnote, p. 116). Couples who do not practice abstinence for 10 to 14 days posttreatment are very likely to create a "pingpong" infection from one partner to another and back, which can go on for weeks. This is especially true of gonorrhea. Some gonococcal organisms are resistant to penicillin, and some individuals are sensitive (allergic) to penicillin and have to be treated with other less specific antibiotics.

Occasionally, patients refuse to inform their contacts or to name them. "I got it from X and it serves X right." Or, "I couldn't tell him, he'll know I got it from someone else and we're engaged." Some males are apparently unwilling to submit to the minimal physical examination of their genitals necessary for diagnosis and, instead, send their girlfriends for examination. If they are infected, the males will be treated as contacts, often without examination. Females are often treated as contacts of known gonorrhea without examination or culture, since "cultures cost too much," and are not always reliable.

Occasionally there is calculated and malicious false reporting of VD, or it might be simply a misunderstanding of the nature of the penile or vaginal discharge, pimple, rash, or ulcer due to a failure in patient-doctor communication. Or it may be the male with a positive diagnosis of gonorrhea who calls his female contact and says she is a "carrier," because he is loathe to admit that he has had other contacts. Females may make the same kind of calls.

Syphilis: The Disease, Diagnosis, and Treatment

The hallmark of syphilitic lesions at any stage and wherever found, is their painless nature. This keeps hidden lesions in the female hidden, and the obviout lesions very suspect because primary and secondary lesions invariably look as if they should be very painful or, at least, uncomfortably itchy.

The primary lesion is often a small, raised papule or pimple with a white head but no pus, occurring from 9 to 90 days postcontact, averaging about three weeks. It may enlarge gradually and ulcerate, has a firm feeling to touch, but is painless. In contrast, cold sores which it resembles, are painful. There is usually one lesion or three or four, occurring in a break in the mucus membrane of the glans, lips, mouth, tonsils, vagina, cervix, or the introital area. The lesion may occur anywhere on the body; the organisms enter any break in the skin which has been in contact with the infecting lesion. The open lesion is highly infectious, but the organism (a spirochaete, Treponema pallidum) is also in the bloodstream at this time. These lesions heal spontaneously, without treatment, leaving no evidence of entry, but leaving the blood still infectious.

Secondary lesions, which appear eight to ten weeks after the primary or sometimes simultaneously with the subsiding primary, are usually multiple and bilateral, on the hands, feet, elbows, face, or genitals. These are also infectious to touch. The blood test is positive by this time, if there has been no treatment or inadequate treatment. The lesions mimic many common skin disorders and are often associated with lymph node enlargement or generalized "flu" symptoms. Both doctor and patient must have a high index of suspicion to consider some of these signs and symptoms as syphilitic in origin. These, too, will disappear without treatment.

The tertiary signs and symptoms may occur a few years to many years later and are the progressive kind which cause the "blindness, insanity, heart and large blood vessel complications, and death" described in the pamphlets, as well as other late, progressive symptoms; meanwhile, if untreated, the blood continues to be infectious for only four or five years, but those blood tests which indicate only the previous existence of the disease will continue to be positive (see below).

Diagnosis of the primary lesion may be presumptive—"it looks like syphilis and we will treat is as syphilis"—or it may be made by examining a smear of the contents of the lesion under a "dark field" microscope. For this, doctors and laboratory people usually wear gloves. Diagnosis of the secondary stage is made from blood tests, biopsies (tissue under the microscope), sometimes spinal fluid examinations, and general appearance of the lesions. Diagnosis of the tertiary stage is made from spinal fluid examination, tissue examination, blood tests, physical examination, and history.

Until four or five years ago hospitals could not be accredited unless they did screening tests for syphilis on all entering patients. These tests became increasingly expensive, and the yield was so low that they were removed from the list of necessary procedures, though many hospitals have continued to do them routinely.

Blood tests prior to marriage are mandatory in most states. Their primary function is to prevent infection of any fetus in utero in subsequent pregnancies. A positive blood test must be treated before a license is issued.* Blood tests early in pregnancy are routine. Blood tests late in pregnancy are done routinely in some clinics. Syphilis may contribute to early abortion, premature delivery of dead babies, or to severely damaged babies from full-term deliveries. Depending upon the amount of damage, these babies may continue to live, but with marked and characteristic external and internal physical deformities.

---

* Blood tests (serology) for syphilis are confusing because there are several kinds. The significance when any one test turns from negative to positive should be clear, but some of the screening tests remain positive after adequate treatment is given. Laboratories use combinations of two or three of increasing sensitivity for diagnosing and following infections and reinfections.

Treatment of any one of these stages or phases is easy and simple for the patient: penicillin in adequate amounts is specific for the organism. Follow-up examinations and blood tests are essential. The damage of the tertiary stage cannot be reversed, but it can be prevented from progressing if treatment is obtained. THERE IS NO KNOWN IMMUNITY CONFERRED BY ONE INFECTION. REINFECTION IS ALWAYS POSSIBLE.

Gonorrhea: The Disease, Diagnosis, and Treatment

In the male, gonorrhea is characterized by a burning, penile discharge. This is usually of sudden onset, perhaps only four hours from the beginning of symptoms to severe discomfort which may occur several days after contact. (see Nonspecific Urethritis). The discharge may disappear without treatment, but there will be a few days of acute discomfort. The gonococcus will still exist in the prostate or in any of the connecting "tubes" and can create intermittent prostatic discomfort and the possibility of permanent tubal blockage, that is, sterility or a narrowed urethra with urine blockage. However, there are other causes of prostatic discomfort (prostatitis) and urethritis. "Silent" infections, those without signs or symptoms, are possible in the male; this is a rather discouraging fact, but does serve to emphasize the need for informing contacts.

In the female, the classic description is vaginal discharge and urethral burning with or without discharge. The problem here is that these symptoms are common to all females, intermittently, in their sexual and nonsexual lives. Cultures of the cervix, urethra, and anal area* are done empirically if there is known contact, possible contact, or a threat to a fetus from previously undiagnosed disease. The primary threat to the fetus is contact with the gonococcal organism in the birth canal (vagina) at the time of delivery. Fetal eye infections with this organism may lead to blindness. All 50 states have legislation requiring routine treatment of *all* newborns' eyes immediately upon delivery. Penicillin drops were used for several years, but most delivery rooms have returned to the use of silver nitrate drops.

The major threat of untreated gonorrhea in the female is the infection ascending into the Fallopian tubes, with subsequent tubal deformity or closure, sterility, and intermittent symptoms of pelvic inflammatory disease (PID). Gonorrhea which has ascended prior to treatment may create enough damage in the tubes to give rise to other problems (see Ectopic Pregnancy).

PID may become a chronic disease, flaring at odd intervals, often related to the immediate postmenstrual phase of the menstrual cycle. There may be moderate to severe chronic pelvic pain and temperature elevations, with discomfort during intercourse and deep penetration at any time. PID may also

---

* The rectum is a common source of gonococcal organisms in both males and females whether or not they are present in the genital area.

be related to postabortion infections and other less common causes; tuberculosis was a major cause of tubal sterility at one time. Adequate initial treatment does not always insure open tubes or prevention of PID; it only makes the patient noninfectious. THERE IS NO KNOWN IMMUNITY CONFERRED BY ONE EPISODE OF GONORRHEA. REINFECTION IS ALWAYS POSSIBLE.

As with syphilis, treatment is adequate amounts of antibiotics. Penicillin is specific for most strains of the organism, but other antibiotics may be used if there is an allergy or a resistant strain. Treatment of severe and incapacitating PID is drastic: removal of the involved pelvic organs, namely the uterus, tubes, and ovaries, and maintenance therapy with estrogen.

The long-term effects of this disease are confined primarily to the pelvis in males and females, but joint disease and heart complications are not unknown. With the increasing incidence of gonorrhea in the general population, arthritis* and tonsillar† gonorrhea are being seen more frequently, even though the actual incidence of these as complications of gonorrhea may be no higher than previously. There are as yet no blood tests for this disease, but much research is being directed toward such tests and toward vaccination, as possible methods of control.

Other Venereal Diseases Which May Mimic Syphilis and Gonorrhea

Nonspecific urethritis (NSU). Symptoms and signs are burning with urination and a penile discharge which are usually much slower in onset, two or three days, than the same symptoms seen with gonorrhea. NSU is being seen more and more frequently, partly because males are concerned about gonorrhea and perhaps partly because of decreased use of condoms which leaves the male urethra directly exposed to the flora and fauna of the vagina. It is also seen in males who have been treated adequately for gonorrhea, two or three weeks before.[41] Or the individual male may be sensitive to contraceptive creams and gels. Diagnosis requires culture of the discharge and demonstrated absence of gonococcal organisms. NSU can arise spontaneously in the absence of sexual activity, and may be related to generalized "flu" symptoms; it may occur in almost epidemic fashion in isolated groups of males in military camps.[42]

Honeymoon cystitis. This is almost the female variation of NSU except that it is usually related to sexual activity, genital manipulation, or increased frequency of intercourse (trauma); hence the name honeymoon. Diagnosis re-

---

* Arthritis may accompany the early symptoms of gonorrhea or, especially in the female, it may be the primary symptom; that is, a single, swollen, tender joint or diffuse joint involvement of sudden onset, a polyarthritis.

† Tonsils may become infected with gonorrhea or syphilis. Gonococcal tonsils are difficult to get positive cultures from, but they do serve as a focus for disseminating the disease in the body. The increasing prevalence of oral-genital sexual activity may increase the incidence of this complication.

quires culture of the urine, the urethra, the cervix, and the demonstrated absence of gonococcal organisms. Females who get this frequently are advised by some physicians to urinate at some time, reasonably soon, after intercourse. This is apparently effective for some. Neither NSU or honeymoon cystitis (traumatic urethritis) are related to specific bacterial infection which can be demonstrated by culture of the urine.

Vaginitis. Yeast organisms are the most common cause of vaginitis. Many physicians are gradually coming to believe that these are part of the normal flora of the vagina and become symptomatic only when the physiology of the vagina changes and allows them to overgrow. Symptoms and signs of overgrowth are an unpleasant, white, cheesy discharge and burning and itching deep in the vagina and around the introitus.

Fourteen-year-old virgins can get yeast symptoms for no apparent reason, though they may be related to a high carbohydrate diet. The mechanics (irritation) of sexual activity, sensitivity to some contraceptives, antibiotics taken for complexion problems or for acute infections, the change in carbohydrate metabolism created by the pill, all increase the possibility of yeast overgrowth in susceptible females. And all females seem susceptible for some period or periods in their lives. Yeast overgrowth is also common in pregnancy and diabetes.

The vagina is normally slightly acid; douching with a weak acid solution once or twice a week, depending upon the amount of sexual activity and gels and foams, will wash out alkaline materials and keep the vaginal physiology and the yeast organisms under reasonable control. Medical treatment is available when the organisms become symptomatic.

Yeast organisms can be transmitted to the male, but usually without symptoms, though repeated contact with the vaginal discharge without adequate postcoital hygiene may result in a rash or minor skin irritation on the shaft of the penis, or small white placques on the glans. To the anxious viewer these look like primary or secondary lesions of syphilis. The organisms have been found in specimens of spermatic and prostatic fluid resulting from prostatic massage, but they are seldom symptomatic; nor are they necessarily related to recurrence in females since there are so many other reasons for recurrences.

Trichomonads, the less common cause of vaginitis, has the same symptoms, and is a venereal disease in the classic sense; that is, it is transmitted by intercourse.* The "steady" male may harbor the Trichomonads and reinfect a treated female. Some vaginal medications act upon both yeast and Trichomonads since they often occur together in sexually active people. If there is repeated recurrence of the Trichomonads, and only one male is involved, he

---

* The vaginal discharge associated with Trichomonads is usually yellow and foamy, looking more like the classic description of the yellow discharge of gonorrhea. Other causes of vaginitis may be bacterial, but are associated with painful burning during intercourse and some itching, but very little discharge.

should be treated also with an oral medication. Use of a condom might improve the aesthetics and decrease transfer of Trichomonads.

The most frequent question about vaginitis and treatment concerns intercourse during treatment. Many couples have to stop because it is too uncomfortable; many stop for aesthetic reasons; others will not or cannot stop, or perhaps need someone to tell them they must stop. Continued intercourse during treatment only prolongs the symptoms. There are those who feel that the longer the discomfort is associated with sexual activity, the greater the frequency of posttreatment vaginismus (see p. 64). Vaginismus has such a large psychic component that its occurrence, postvaginitis, in those females still not quite at ease or comfortable with intercourse would seem quite possible. We would suspect also that the female who is not secure enough to request or demand abstinence in the face of temporary discomfort would also be a good candidate for posttreatment vaginismus (see Frigidity). Very judgmentally, we must add that the male who demands sexual access despite female discomfort is much more likely to be faced with the problem of a fearful female, posttreatment.

Venereal warts. These are one of the more unpleasant venereal diseases. They look and feel unattractive. There is no immediate cure and no known way of avoiding them. They are relatively rare, but not rare enough to omit from this discussion. In addition, some of the warts look a little like granuloma inguinale (p. 111) when they are relatively large and flat. Some girls appear to be wart-prone for a period of time in their lives. Some gynecologists associate these warts with lack of genital hygiene, but if this were true, they would be more common. Increased hygiene may prevent their spread, but this is not well documented. They are even more rare in males, usually occurring around the base of the glans. However, there is little evidence of direct transfer, that is, they do not seem to be very contagious, and if left alone usually disappear spontaneously. We have seen one patient who had warts frequently, but not constantly, on her hands and who also had venereal warts, another patient with venereal warts whose "steady" had venereal warts, and another patient with venereal warts whose "steady" had warts on his hands. Our lack of knowledge about warts is due, we believe, to the fact that it is not a terribly interesting field of research, except to dermatologists (skin specialists) who see very few venereal warts and do not experience the emotional discomfort of these patients. At present, they are best treated chemically with repeated local applications; or, when extensive, they can be removed with electrocautery or cryosurgery (freezing).

Herpetic lesions. These lesions, looking like early cold sores, are painful and appear and disappear spontaneously. They are usually located around the introitus, looking like some primary and secondary lesions of syphilis, and should be suspect if they are not painful. They do not usually ulcerate to the same depth as the latter. As yet, the only effective treatment is ointments to relieve discomfort, although some physicians are trying cleaning, drying, and fluorescent light with local medication.

Sebacious cysts. These worrisome, single lumps, or pimples, look like the early stage of a primary lesion of syphilis. They are found in the nonhairy areas of the genitals, though similar white-headed bumps may be found associated with hair follicles in the hairy areas of the genitals. They are frequently reddened with infection and slightly sore to touch. Hot compresses (not too hot) will aid in opening them, draining the white material, and allowing healing. Maintaining genital cleanliness will prevent them from becoming reinfected while healing. The "white" look should be suspect if not painful, and if there is no discharge from the center.

Bartholin's glands. These are bilateral glands, one each in the base of the labia minora, whose ducts open near the introitus. Under ordinary circumstances they are not visible or palpable. One or both may become infected and painfully enlarged, partially blocking the introitus. Infection is always assumed to be gonococcal until proven otherwise, though this can seldom be demonstrated from the gland itself. Antibiotics and minimal local treatment (hot soaks, packs) are usually sufficient, but if they are intermittently or chronically infected, surgical treatment is sometimes necessary.

Crab lice. This is another unpleasantness which is becoming increasingly frequent in a sexually mobile society that is also casual about sleeping accommodations, for example community sleeping bags, cheap hotels, and sitting on any and all toilet seats. Crab lice are supposed to stay fairly close to the pubic hair, the eyebrows, and hairs on the back of the head, but we have seen them on examining table sheets after the infected patient has left, and they have been seen on toilet seats. The symptoms are itching, and the signs frequently are minute, red specks of blood on underclothing. If one looks, there may be red, dark brown, or grayish dots, 1 to 2 mm., at the base of the pubic hairs, and attached to the skin. If one feels one or several pubic hairs, they may feel bumpy or irregular because of attached eggs or nits. The lice will be killed with medicated ointments and shampoos,* but the eggs are often more resistant, hatching out more lice later. A second, and sometimes third, application of ointment and shampoo are indicated in about four to five days. Shaving gets rid of the eggs with the hair. Normal, hot laundering is sufficient for linens and clothing, or dry cleaning for woolens. Transfer is primarily by direct contact, for example, people-to-people, bed linen-to-people, or toilet-seat-to-people, and may occur during intercourse. Lice still cause consternation, but less so than a few years ago. The infected individual is often ostracized if living communally, but two hours devoted to shampooing, washing, maybe shaving or clipping, removing and laundering bedlinen and underclothes should take care of any infestation.

---

* Kwell and A-200 Pyrinate are the most common anti-crab lice medications.

In summary, some brief generalizations can be made about these mimicking diseases and patient's reactions to them. The itching diseases like vaginitis, herpetic lesions, vaginal discharges, and crab lice are usually scratched, and scratching creates additional skin irritation. Unless it is a recurrence, patients usually call every lump, bump, or pimple, regardless of size, "a lump in my vagina." Pain with intercourse can be pain with entry, during intercourse, or a few hours afterwards, deep or on the outside. Pain with urination can be pain just prior to urination, after urination, or when the urine goes over the irritated area, or when using toilet paper near the introitus. For females especially, many of the concerns about these various symptoms which arise prior to obtaining medical attention, could be alleviated if they would use a mirror occasionally and became acquainted with what "normal" looks and feels like, so that the abnormal would be recognized more readily; for example, hymeneal tags felt for the first time are often interpreted as abnormal. Males do not have this kind of problem; they do not need a mirror, and they can even treat their own warts, at home.

Summary

Unfortunately venereal disease, along with pregnancy and abortion has now become epidemic. It is reported that only the common cold is more common than VD now in the United States.[43] Prostitutes are no longer the major carriers and spreaders of VD. And since it is no longer a class-limited disease, it is found as readily in the suburbs as in the cities, and among bankers and professionals as among truckdrivers and housewives. The epidemic has strong roots among the young, but cuts across age lines, as only one in five of those who were *reported* to have gonorrhea last year were under 20. If preventive measures are not successful, it is estimated that among the preteenagers, the probability of contracting VD before age 25 will be 50 percent.

Open, frank, and helpful discussions about venereal disease, its causes and cures, has lagged far behind other aspects of the sexual revolution. If history is any lesson, not even an epidemic of VD such as we are now witnessing is likely to have much of an impact on the new sexual ethics. What is called for is a program to bring preventive medicine practices in line with the new sexual ethics. Not to provide funds for education about VD and for basic research which might lead to a vaccine is to continue to say, subtly but really, that the new sexual ethics are wrong and that those who would live by them must be willing to pay the consequences.

References

1. A. F. Schiff, "Rape," *Medical Aspects of Human Sexuality* 6 (May 1972):5.

2. See C. R. Hayman, et al., "Rape and Its Consequences," *Medical Aspects of Human Sexuality* 6 (1972):2. See also C. R. Hayman and C. Lanza, "Sexual

Assault on Women and Girls," *American Journal of Obstetrics and Gynecology* 109 (February 1, 1971):480.

3. John H. Gagnon and William Simon, "Sexual Encounters Between Adults and Children," *Siecus* Study Guide No. 11, 1970.

4. Schiff, "Rape."

5. Lloyd Shearer, "What Every Woman Should Know—About Self-Defense," *Parade,* 26 August 1973.

6. Personal communication from Dr. Luigi Mastroianni, Jr.

7. Gagnon and Simon, "Sexual Encounters Between Adults and Children."

8. *Ibid.*

9. Menachem Amir, *Patterns in Forceable Rape* (Chicago: University of Chicago Press, 1971).

10. *Ibid.*

11. *Philadelphia Evening Bulletin,* 10 August 1972.

12. Gagnon and Simon, "Sexual Encounters Between Adults and Children."

13. *Ibid.*

14. Gilbert Geis, "Group Sexual Assaults," *Medical Aspects of Human Sexuality,* 5 (May 1971):5.

15. Amir, *Patterns in Forceable Rape.*

16. Geis, "Group Sexual Assaults."

17. U. S. Surgeon General's Scientific Advisory Committee on Television and Social Behavior, *Television and Growing Up: The Impact of Televised Violence,* U.S.P.H.S. (Washington, D. C.: U. S. Government Printing Office, 1972).

18. J. Corry, "The Selling of Sex: A Look Through a Solemn Sodom," The *New York Times,* 10 October 1972, p. 41.

19. G. Vidal, "The Fallacy of the Male Imperative," *Intellectual Digest,* October 1971 (from the *New York Review of Books*).

20. Alfred C. Kinsey, et al., *Sexual Behavior in the Human Female* (Philadelphia: W. B. Saunders Company, 1953), p. 62.

21. Charles Winick and Paul M. Kinsie, *The Lively Commerce: Prostitution in the United States* (Chicago: Quadrangle Books, 1971).

22. *Ibid.*

23. David J. Pittman and Lee Rainwater, "The Male House of Prostitution," *Transaction* (March-April, 1971):21. Excerpted from: *Deviant Behavior: Social Process and Identity* (New York: Holt, Rinehart, and Winston, 1972).

24. Elaine C. Pierson, "New Sexual Pressures on Youth," *The Pennsylvania Gazette,* May 1971.

25. Betty Friedan, "Beyond Women's Liberation," *McCall's,* August 1972, p. 82.

26. Alice B. Stockham, *Tokology, A Book for Every Woman* (Chicago: Alice B. Stockham and Co., 1886).

27. Jean-Paul Sartre, "The Respectful Prostitute," *No Exit and Three Other Plays* (New York: Vintage Books Edition, 1955).

28. W. Schwimmer, K. Ustay and S. Behrman, "Sperm-agglutinating Antibodies and Decreased Fertility in Prostitutes," *American Journal of Obstetrics and Gynecology* 30, 2 (1967):192.

29. *Ibid.*

30. *Ibid.*

31. Xaviera Hollander, *The Happy Hooker* (New York: Dell Publishing Co., 1972).

32. Travis Hirschi, "The Professional Prostitute," *Berkeley Journal of Sociology* VII, 1:33-39.

33. James H. Bryan, "Apprenticeships in Prostitution," *Social Problems* 12, 3 (Winter 1965):287-297.

34. *Ibid.*

35. H. G. Toland and L. Antosh, "Streetwalker Needs Fast Money—for Drugs," *Philadelphia Evening Bulletin,* 30 July 1972, p. 3.

36. Anonymous, "White Slavery," *Time,* 5 June 1972.

37. S. Barclay, *Bondage: The Slave Traffic in Women Today* (New York: Funk and Wagnalls, 1968).

38. See *American Medical News,* 17 April 1972, p. 14.

39. E. Z. Friedenberg, a review of Theodore Rosebury, *Microbes and Morals: The Strange Story of Venereal Disease* (Viking Press, 1971), in The *New York Review of Books,* 30 December 1971.

40. Hayman and Lanza, "Sexual Assault on Women and Girls," pp. 480-486.

41. Steven T. Knee, "Complexities of Gonococcal Infection," *Medical Aspects of Human Sexuality* (April 1972).

42. Personal communications from Peter F. Kohler, urologist.

43. See also *Newsweek,* 24 January 1972, pp. 46-50.

5

· · · · · · · · · Reproduction: · · · · · · · · ·
Endocrinology, Menstruation, Infertility

Endocrinology

WE HAVE ALWAYS FELT that the study of endocrines, the secretions of ductless glands in the body, was best left to the endocrinologists. But since estrogen and progesterone have almost become household words, or at least relatively common because of the pill, readers and users of the pill should be aware of some of the fundamentals in this area of endocrinology.

The pill is made up of *synthetic* steroids* which have estrogenic and progesteronelike activity. At present, about four or five synthetic "estrogens" and "progesterones" are being used, each with slightly different properties and effects. Each brand of pill has one estrogenic, and one progesteronelike steroid.† The slightly dissimilar properties of each and the differences in dosages required to prevent ovulation account for the varying effects of each brand. Several females may also react differently to the same pill.

The activity of *naturally occurring* hormones during pregnancy is simply a variation of their cyclic activity during the ovulatory cycle; only the cycle in pregnancy is nine-and-a-half months long. Simply is a poor word to use because it is not simple; there are many missing arrows in the classic diagrams which are used to illustrate some of the relationships between the pineal gland, the hypothalamus (base of the brain), the pituitary gland, the ovaries, the uterine lining, and the embryonic tissue.

In many respects, obstetrics and gynecology are empirical medical specialties. There are many unanswered questions, and also many treatments which work for reasons that are not completely understood. For example:

1) The Fallopian tubes play an important role in the establishment of a pregnancy, in particular, fertilization and transport of the eggs and maybe even the sperm. These relationships are not yet clear, and the tubes have never been included in any diagrams of hormonal activity in pregnancy.

---

* Steroids make up a group of organic compounds with a basic chemical formula in common, and are associated with many of the sex hormones.

† Exceptions are the minipill which contains only progesterone and the sequential birth control regimen: estrogen only followed by progesterone only.

2) The pill. Appropriate combinations of estrogens and progesterones prevent ovulation; estrogen alone will prevent ovulation; progesterone alone in small doses (the minipill) will prevent implantation but not ovulation. The pill and the various other types of hormonal contraception also produce intermittent and *unpredictable* bleeding in some women.

3) Menopause. Why do the ovaries cease functioning? Do they cease completely? Symptoms which may arise with cessation of ovarian function are often attributed to erratic hormone levels which may occur prior to cessation. Some of these symptoms are rightly or wrongly attributed to the mental state of the patient; or, perhaps, it is vice-versa.

4) The influence of stress and emotions on hormonal balance is very clear in a clinical or patient setting, but it is not clear in the laboratory; for example, women who menstruate completely out of phase with their regular cycle on carefully planned wedding days; girls fearing possibility of pregnancy, who may miss a menstrual period, or delay a menstrual period, but who are not pregnant by any test available at the present time.

5) Regular, cyclic menstruation does not necessarily mean that ovulation occurs with each cycle. Grossly irregular menstruation does not mean that ovulation has *not* occurred.

However, there are some things we think we know that will help your understanding. But do not look at the diagram below with any hope of discovering how the pill works.

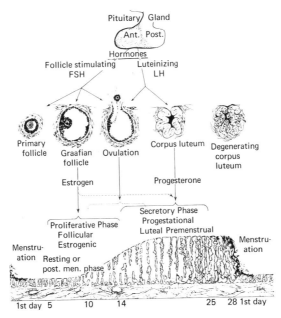

Figure 5-1. Hormonal control of the normal menstrual cycle.

Omitted from the above diagram is the anatomical connection of the posterior lobe of the pituitary gland with the hypothalamus which lies just above it. Also omitted are the usual arrows which indicate a feedback mechanism of hormonal action, the body's internal computer; for example, increasing amounts of hormone #1 trigger the release of another hormone which then causes a decrease in hormone #1. The absolutism of this feedback mechanism is beginning to be questioned in other areas of human physiology, and it may, in time, be questioned in the reproductive cycle, as well.

The structures labeled follicle and corpus luteum (or yellow body) show the sequential changes in a single follicle during a menstrual cycle, from menses to menses. A single follicle ovulates or releases an egg in each cycle. Two or more follicles may ovulate and, if the eggs are fertilized, will produce multiple births (see Superovulation, p. 140). Ovulation does not alternate regularly from side to side, though this may happen spontaneously; only the egg which is exactly at the right stage of development is ovulated. Only one ovary or even part of one ovary is necessary for fertility, if the tube or tubes are open and functioning.

The diagram of the uterine lining illustrates the sequential changes occurring during a normal menstrual cycle. The muscular uterine wall is several times thicker than the lining and is not illustrated. If the egg is fertilized and implants in the uterine lining, about Day 5 after ovulation and about Day 3 after fertilization, the corpus luteum does not degenerate as seen in the diagram, but continues to produce progesterone and maintain the lining of the uterus in its lush state. There is no breakdown of the lining, and therefore no menstruation. Spotting (bleeding from the uterine cavity) may occur at the time of implantation, Day 16 to Day 19 of this average 28-day cycle.

Most women are more aware of the progesterone phase of their menstrual cycle than the estrogen phase. Progesterone production may be associated with symptoms and signs of breast tenderness, salt and water retention, and with the slight rise in basal body temperature (BBT) in the postovulation phase of the cycle. Girls who are taking their BBT every day will be the first to know if they are pregnant because the continuing progesterone secretion associated with pregnancy maintains the elevated BBT beyond the expected day of the menstrual flow, which is 14 days after ovulation in a menstrual cycle of any length. If a temperature chart shows ovulation, a pregnancy can be diagnosed from the chart as soon as 17 days past ovulation. No chemical test is yet available for three days past a missed period.

During pregnancy, the estrogen and progesterone continue to circulate in gradually increasing amounts. The body adapts to these increases over a two or three month period. This is comparable to the adaptation with the pill which may also take two or three months. The symptoms of early pill-taking and early pregnancy may be very similar.

The source of estrogen and progesterone after the first four or five weeks of pregnancy is *not* the ovary but the placenta, which is tissue from the developing fertilized ovum, but not part of the embryo itself. Ovaries can even be removed after these first few weeks without affecting the pregnancy, though surgical trauma should be avoided unless absolutely indicated.

At about 26 days, from the date of conception, the early placental tissue is producing a hormone called chorionic gonadotropin (derived from the chorionic portion of the placenta and affecting the gonads or ovaries). This hormone is found in the urine and is the basis for pregnancy tests done for many years on frogs, toads, and rabbits and now in the more sensitive "slide" tests.

The relatively high levels of these hormones drop rather abruptly just prior to and at the time of delivery. This is similar to the drop seen prior to menstrual bleeding. The normal ovulatory cycle resumes about four to five weeks post delivery and is evidenced by menstruation; ovulation may precede the first menstruation (see Breast-feeding and Prevention of Pregnancy). The uterine bleeding which continues after delivery usually ceases in about ten days.

In summary, perhaps the important information about reproduction is not endocrinological, but simply a matter of numbers and averages:

1) The average woman ovulates about 500 eggs during her reproductive lifetime, and

2) She may average 2500 episodes of intercourse during her entire reproductive lifetime of about 30 years.

This means that on the average, one out of every five sexual encounters has reproductive potential.

Menstruation

No swimming today, I just fell off the roof.

My redheaded cousin *came to visit today.*

WE THOUGHT WE WERE at some distance from these 1930 euphemisms for menstrual periods, but some physical education teachers are still asking their students to hand in slips of paper noting their names and the dates of their menstrual periods so they may be excused from sports. This practice makes it unnecessary to say anything out loud about menstruation; it also encourages the whole "sick" approach to menstruation.

The word menses and all of the related words come from the Latin *mens* meaning month. Many of the real and imagined problems with periods stem from the idea of monthly or periodicity. Menstrual periods in the adolescent and young adult may be regular, but frequently are not. Girls who are irregular are really in limbo because they "never know when." In addition, they, or their mothers, often think that something is wrong. When mothers and daughters cannot talk easily about menstruation, and this also includes those mothers who hand their daughter a book and a box of menstrual pads or tampons, the daughters never get to a physician who can reassure them, and there are enough problems in adolescence without this additional concern.

If part of the evolving definition of healthy sexuality includes a girl's self-image as a normal, functioning female in the physiological sense, it is clear that anything as intimately and frequently related to sexuality in all of its aspects as menstruation must also be understood at the emotional and factual level by males of any age. But boys almost never see the *Girl to Woman* movie, and girls seldom see the *Boy to Man* movie or hear discussions about the other sex in the fifth and sixth grades, and both have many questions at this age which they never ask.

Menstruation is only the visible evidence of the complicated and important cyclic hormonal process described previously (p. 125). However, since most females are not aware of the hormonal process itself, with exceptions to be noted later, many of their feelings about "growing up" or "being a woman" are frequently focused on this visible evidence of proper female functioning (see Pill).

When periods occur in a reasonably regular fashion, they can be a "drag," a "bore," the "curse," or "sick." When they do *not* occur (e.g., delayed menarche or the beginning of menstruation, skipped periods, delayed periods), there are concerns about "really being a woman," "something being wrong and they are not telling me," or "being able to have children with these crazy periods." And, of course, there may be concern about pregnancy, if there has been unprotected intercourse.

In the face of sexual activity, the presence or absence of a menstrual period can represent failure: failure to get pregnant, failure of a contraceptive, or a personal weakness which allowed the couple to ignore contraception "just that once." This monthly questioning, if only for a few days, can be a fairly intense emotion to carry around, even if only in the subconscious.

Most adolescents are aware of some facts about menstruation before they are ten or eleven, but ease with vocabulary and a facility with the facts and mechanics still leaves many prepubertal and pubertal youngsters and teenagers with a kind of floating unease with the subject, especially when it becomes a reality for them. (Many sophisticated and intelligent adults, female and male, have a similar unease.) This is even more true when the realities of dating, petting, dancing, and intercourse intrude into their menstrual lives: "...the pad is bulging, they can see it," or "...he can feel it," "...can I really use tampons?" "What about the odor," "...the hymen?" "...do people really have intercourse during menstrual periods?" "...swimming?" "...bathing?" Pads and strings cause problems in some casual or steady dating situations which can be solved easily with a word or two, if the word or two can be spoken with ease to a knowledgeable partner.

And what about hygiene? The area is very sensitive to touch and temperature, which would make anyone think that it is also a very delicate and easily injured area. Carrying this thought further, as many do, one thinks of permanent injury with too much manipulation. But intercourse and delivery of babies probably subjects this area to more physical trauma than any other area of the body, the skin surface excepted, with less harm, which illustrates very well its unique adaptability to function.

There are some other rather basic reasons for the floating unease about menstruation, which though they may not apply to everyone are worth being aware of, because if the physical aspects of dating, marriage, and sexuality are based on, or limited by, some of these subconscious or conscious attitudes in either partner, an individual's sexual behavior and performance may be incomprehensible to a partner and be misunderstood completely, if the right words cannot be spoken.

One of the most common feelings is that something is *unclean*. Even the Bible says "unclean," though there are those who feel that this is not an accurate translation of the original. The word *sanitary* to describe menstrual pads has been with us for a long time and has had its effects, thought it is gradually being replaced by *feminine*. The word napkin has never seemed quite appropriate either. The uterus is not getting rid of the body's "poisons" on a monthly basis, nor does intercourse during menstruation push all of those poisons back into the uterus.* Menstrual blood is essentially sterile until it reaches the vagina, and at that point it remains as clean as the vagina is at that moment.

Another common feeling: Blood or bleeding from any area is not a comfortable concept for many, and it makes little difference whether the blood is one's own or someone else's. Nor does it matter that the total amount of blood in the average menstrual period is only about 35 to 45 cc.'s, or seven to nine teaspoons total, though it often looks like more. Add to this, bleeding from an area which has never been considered quite clean, emotionally or physically, and the feelings about menstruation are understandable, though hardly valid. Even an understanding that urine and spermatic fluid (semen) are basically sterile fluids does not help most people. The close association of menstruation with the rectum and feces can give rise to somewhat more universal feelings about odor and being unclean.

To a certain degree, the very real, daily taking care of a period becomes mechanical and reflex, but it can involve up to seven or eight days of every month in the adolescent and older female. Menopausal females have some very

---

* We still hear this in high school and college age groups, even with all of the "education" that is available today.

real, confining problems with unpredictable, profuse bleeding. Girls always have to be prepared: "Where can I keep (hide) the tampons or pads?" "How many today?" "Am I leaking or showing?" "Damn, I can't wear those white shorts today."

Some girls enjoy the privilege extended to them to "play female" with a Mona Lisa smile that says "No, not today . . . ," whether it be sex or sports. Some girls resent the real or imagined limitations of activity. There need be no physical or hygienic limitations, even when mild cramping exists.

Many girls resent or simply do not fight their parent's attitudes about not using tampons and wait until they are away from home. Frequently this is a father's attitude transmitted directly or indirectly through the mother. Fathers' negative attitudes about tampons usually center on manipulation of the genital area (an accidental discovery of the "pleasures" of masturbation), or dilating the hymen prematurely. For most fathers, using a menstrual pad would appear to be a relatively asexual procedure, but it isn't always. A fresh pad, tightly in place between the thighs can feel rather good, but it does not stay fresh or in place that long. This leaves girls constantly aware of the genital area and readjusting pads.

Some tampons come in three sizes and absorbency for reasons which are unclear to us, since the difference in size is minimal, and the largest size is only about one-third the size of an erect penis. Initially, there should be no difficulty, except emotional, in inserting the "super" tampon. (We always use the latter with lubrication, when patients come asking for help with learning to insert them. They are pleased and surprised, and only rarely is instruction about manual or mechanical dilatation needed, see p. 323). Palpable evidence of virginity will still exist, if this is important to the girl or to her parents. More important, there is very little genital manipulation required after the first few insertions, and there is no constant awareness of the genital area when the tampon is in place. Some visually handicapped girls who have difficulty finding restrooms in unfamiliar places often use two tampons at all times without discomfort and without excessive dilatation of the hymeneal ring, since they are inserted one at a time.

Rarely, a vagina is constructed so that a tampon must be directed slightly differently than the instructions on the package indicate; or the anterior wall of the vagina may be shorter than average. The usual complaint is that "something seems to be in the way" just beyond the opening, or simply that "the tampon just won't stay in," or "I can feel it when it's in." These problems, or simply the inability to insert a tampon, are worth a gynecological examination in any age group, and can usually be taken care of with explanations of how to dilate the hymen, or to adapt to the slight anatomical variation.

Encouraging the use of tampons "from the beginning," to quote the ads in the Girl Scout magazine, will go a long way toward keeping young adolescents and others at ease with menstruation.* The ability to live a normal, unhampered life every day of the month will eliminate many if not all of the unpleasant feelings which may have been communicated by mothers or friends for real or imagined reasons (see Menstrual Cramps). Use of tampons from the beginning will also serve another very useful function: acquainting a girl early with her anatomy and the fact that one can touch and exert pressure on one's own genital area without automatically arousing sexual feelings, and that sexual arousal depends almost totally on the intent and desires of the mind.

Physiology

Menarche (men-ar-key), the beginning of menstrual periods, may occur as early as age eight or as late as age 17 or 18; these appear to be the absolute limits of normal physiology. Any girl who menstruates before age 11 or does not menstruate by age 14½ should be examined by a gynecologist. Gross examination of stature, breast development, pubic hair, and external genitalia in the "under 11" girls, along with a rectal examination† to rule out ovarian disease can quickly reassure the parents and the girl that all is well. The same type of examination can be done for the 14-year-old girl who has never menstruated to reassure her that all is within normal limits. This examination should be repeated at least at yearly intervals, if menstruation does not occur.

We do not know any woman who is really mentally comfortable about going for her "checkup" (see Pelvic Examination, p. 320); this even includes women doctors who are often the prime offenders in postponing the recommended annual or semi-annual visit to two or three year intervals. However, this postponement and hesitancy is even more true the first time, whatever the age. The ideal gynecologist will adapt to the specific needs of the patient, or her mother if necessary. Occasionally her father insists on being there, too, but most gynecologists take time to evaluate the needs of the patient before they permit parents in the examining room or in consultation. The increasing number of adolescent clinics is making this easier in some areas of the country, but there are simply not enough women doctors or women doctors interested in adolescent gynecology to insure that the first or subsequent adolescent examinations will have the female surroundings desired by many 11- and 14-year-olds.

---

* Small, soft, plastic, tulip-shaped cups with a very short stem may also be used during menstrual periods for "catching" the menstrual flow. They are folded slightly and inserted into the vagina where they effectively seal off any area of possible leakage by conforming to the contours of the vaginal wall. These are not in common usage, but those who use them are enthusiastic. Removal almost requires that one be able to get two fingers into the vagina; this would limit their use in many girls who can use tampons easily.

† Enlarged ovaries and tubes and the uterus may be felt through the anterior rectal wall when the hymen will not admit an examining instrument.

Many girls have their first pelvic examination during the first few months they are away from home, either in college or working. There are often many questions to be answered which may have been submerged during high school years, the kinds of questions that were not asked in sex education classes or of one's parents. They may not have trusted their mother's gynecologist to keep their secrets, or perhaps they were just unable to insert a tampon after several trials.

About a year or so postmenarche, a pattern of menstruation is usually established which is not always constant, but which is reasonably reliable. The variables include the amount of bleeding, the degree of cramping, the length of the intermenstrual cycle, and the duration of the menstrual period.

Backaches and lower abdominal cramping with menstruation (dysmenorrhea) are very real for some girls, but only rarely incapacitating. For a period of four to five hours or longer, this cramping may even involve the whole genital area and also be felt in the thighs, or it may only be increased awareness of the whole pelvic area. A few girls have no cramping at all, especially during the first few years of a menstrual history. There is no need to cease activity because of cramping; in fact, activity often decreases the intensity of the cramping. But it may be severe enough to require curling up with a heating pad and some form of pain relief, or it may even be associated with nausea and vomiting.* Often girls will live with this kind of monthly "day off" through high school and early college or work experiences until the stresses and demands of graduate school or a good, responsible job become so great that they cannot "afford" to take a day off every month. But patterns of cramping do change over time, often for no apparent reason.

Anxieties can emerge about having babies "if this is what it's like." Reassurance that the discomfort of contractions of labor is quite different, more diffuse, and most important, self-limited and productive is occasionally effective. The severe sharpness of some menstrual cramps is more like that associated with spontaneous or induced abortions (p. 222).

Girls who are incapacitated for a day or more are often treated with cyclic hormones (the birth control pill) to eliminate ovulation; nonovulatory periods will occur without cramping, *but* not all painless periods are nonovulatory. Most physicians are reluctant to use this treatment for the adolescent because the use of the pill invites a safe feeling in the girl and, often, extreme parental unease. Everyone, parent, child, physician has to handle this in his or her own way. Treatment is usually limited to five or six months and then normal periods are allowed to resume. The periods which follow are usually more comfortable, but they may gradually return to their old crampy pattern, or the cramping may

---

*Nausea and vomiting are frequently labeled as psychosomatic in origin, but for the girl who is nauseated and vomiting, they are real, no matter the origin. This problem has to be approached both directly and indirectly.

never recur. (Meanwhile the girl may have become addicted to safe sex.) A few years ago, a complaint of severe but undemonstrated dysmenorrhea was one of the circuitous routes by which girls obtained birth control pills. This is not necessary anymore, but many girls still justify a request for pills, in their own minds, with a complaint of dysmenorrhea.

Menstrual cycles in the adolescent can be very irregular ranging from every three weeks to every six or eight weeks or even once a year (see Rhythm). A normal cycle can vary as much as four days in either direction and still be called normal. A year or two of irregularity can revert to regularity for no good reason. If, by the age of 17, cycles have always been grossly irregular, a gynecological investigation should be done. Here again, if there is a history of previously regular cycles, birth control pills used for five or six months will often regulate the cycles which occur after the pills are stopped. If there has been no previous regularity, the use of birth control pills will regulate periods or cycles artificially (withdrawal bleeding), but when the medication is stopped, the periods will usually revert back to their old irregular pattern. This all sounds very empirical, and it still is.

Skipped periods create a feeling of irregularity when no accurate record is kept. Skipped periods during summer months are common, or during periods of emotional stress or illness, or during the first few months of a new job or a new college year. Any new emotional situation may evidence itself only as skipped periods. Guilt or concern about unprotected sexual activity will delay a period, or appear to cause it to be skipped entirely. If the pelvic examination is negative, most doctors will use progesterone by mouth for five days, or an intramuscular injection to bring on uterine bleeding. This is primarily a test of ovarian function and will produce bleeding in five to ten days *if no pregnancy is present*. If it does not produce bleeding and there is no pregnancy, further investigation may be necessary if the amenorrhea (no menstruation) persists more than six or seven months.

"Am I ovulating?" is the primary question when periods are so irregular. There is evidence to suggest that ovulation does not always start with menarche, but no assumptions can be made in any individual girl without daily temperature charts or vaginal cytology. There is also evidence that pregnancy can occur *before* menarche. If one considers the amount of unprotected intercourse in the adolescent group alone, one almost has to assume that ovulation does not necessarily occur regularly even with regular menstrual cycles. If it did, there should be many more pregnancies in this group than are actually seen. However, ovulation can occur even with twice or once a year periods, or with any of the variations of regular "irregularity," though establishing a pregnancy when one is wanted is more difficult for these girls.

Spotting or bleeding may occur between menstrual periods. This may be associated with ovulation, or with a cervical polyp (a small, usually benign growth), or postintercourse in the presence of cervicitis (an inflammation of the cervix). Carcinoma (cancer) of the cervix is very rare in this age group, but not unheard of. Any spotting or bleeding should be investigated. Bleeding may also occur with rape or the initial dilatation of the hymeneal ring, if this was done too forcefully.* Intermenstrual bleeding lasting more than two or three days and requiring pads or tampons may be the onset of a series of every two week periods. In addition to being a nuisance, this kind of cycle may give rise to an anemia (how iron in the blood), if it continues for more than two or three months. This type of bleeding is usually self-limited, but can be treated also, with the birth control pills for a few months, to break this frequent cycle. (See also, Intermenstrual Bleeding with the Pill).

There are two other periodic, cyclic occurrences which are troublesome to some girls early in their menstrual history, or to others later on. These are the *premenstrual syndrome,* the group of signs and symptoms associated with fluid retention, and *mittelschmerz,* abdominal pain at the time of ovulation. These two do not necessarily occur together, nor are they predictably present in each cycle in an individual girl or woman.

Mittelschmerz, the German word for middle pain, is associated with ovulation. This pain may be mild or acute lower abdominal discomfort of one or more hour's duration. There may even be a slight temperature elevation which can lead to some confusion when trying to differentiate between this and an acute attack of appendicitis. The occasional uterine bleeding at this time was mentioned above. The reason for the pain is not well defined, but it is believed to arise from irritation of the lining of the pelvic cavity by bleeding which occasionally occurs from the ovary at the time of ovulation. Intercourse at this time can be painful, especially with deep penetration. Using mittelschmerz as a guide for the practice of rhythm is not reliable because a few gas pains in the bowel can be misinterpreted, and also it is not a constant sign or symptom.

The symptoms and signs of the premenstrual syndrome are related to fluid retention in the latter 14 days of the menstrual cycle when progesterone exerts its effects (see Fig. 5-1). Symptoms may be all or some of the following in varying degrees of severity: feeling of pelvic fullness, irritability, emotional lability, four or five hours of moderate to severe headaches usually just prior to the onset of bleeding, lightheaded or dizzy spells, migraine headaches in girls with this tendency, breast tenderness with such acute sensitivity to touch that even bras can be too much. The signs may be: a weight gain of 4 to even 8 or 10 pounds, increased breast size, increased urinary frequency, disturbances in bowel function which may be diarrhea or constipation. Hemorrhoids can often be a cyclic nuisance as well, and skirts and jeans often get too tight with a distended abdomen.

---

*If there has been no intercourse for several years and the female is menopausal, there may be bleeding with penetration the "first time." Estrogenic compounds may be used locally or by mouth so that this does not remain a problem.

Not all of these signs and symptoms occur together, though they may, and they are variable in degree. The week immediately after ovulation (two weeks before menstruation) may be the time of acute distress, or it may be the week prior to menstruation. In either case, the signs and symptoms subside rather abruptly with the onset of menses. Girls who are plagued by this syndrome are often those who have more problems with menstrual cramping, especially in the teenage group. Married women with this syndrome need very understanding husbands and children. But sometimes the very understanding husband labels *all* of his wife's irritability as premenstrual, even when she is really preovulatory. This effectively frustrates any attempt she might make to sound angry or unhappy for legitimate reasons. There is nothing more irritating to the premenstrual female than to be told she is acting in a premenstrual fashion; she may be aware she is overreacting, but the source of the irritation still exists in her mind and should not be ignored.

The use of birth control pills in this group of females may accentuate what were only minor symptoms before, or create some premenstrual problems where they did not exist previously. Medical treatment is quite effective if used in cyclic fashion. This treatment is directed at removing the excess fluid by decreasing the sodium (salt) intake, and the cyclic use of diuretics to remove salt from the body and with this, the extra fluid; decreasing one's fluid intake is *not* indicated.

One other interesting phenomenon which mothers and daughters very soon become aware of, and this awareness gradually includes sisters and female friends who are living in reasonable proximity, is that they find that their menstrual cycles are overlapping or are occurring in some cases on the same day quite regularly. One of the recent studies explored most of the possible parameters in a large group of girls in a single dormitory and found no correlation with any factor except "proximity."[1] The investigator could only conclude "that in humans there is some interpersonal physiological process which affects the menstrual cycle."

Also noted in this article, and clinically by other physicians, as well as personally by many girls, is the fact that increasing exposure to males, even just dating without sexual activity, tends to regulate cycles, decrease cramping, and even improve complexions in some instances. All of these things may happen *without* the use of the birth control pill which, as we have seen, is also used to treat these problems.

Another exotic direction of research in menstrual irregularity is the use of increasing amounts of light, for example, leaving lights on all night for two or three months to regulate cycles. Lower animals are affected by varying the dark-light proportions of a 24-hour period and perhaps humans are also. More interesting, we think, is the very real fact that females do not like to be irregular; it is difficult to cope with emotionally as well as physically.

Infertility

23-year-old graduate student has plan which will interest barren woman with fertile husband. If sincere, write P. O. Box yyy, Wall Street Station, NYC.

Classified Ad, New York Review of Books

BABY MACHINES? PERHAPS. A baby from a baby machine represents a conscious deliberate act, a wanted child. Is a baby adopted for money from an accidentally pregnant female who either did not believe in abortion or could not afford an abortion that much different in origin? It is, if one considers it to be a life already in existence which must be cared for. But infertile women also have lives that are already in existence, and they also have a right, with their husbands, to have children that have some familial resemblance and genetic ties. Donor insemination has been available to fertile women with barren husbands for at least 25 years and is more or less acceptable to society if not the law in many states. Why should this be more socially acceptable than baby machines?

The next step, the subject of a recent science fiction TV doctor show, is transplanting the early embryo from a mother unable to carry a pregnancy to a healthy female who can.* Another variation is transplanting an ovary or ovaries to a woman without ovaries. The eggs would carry the characteristics of the donor, but the conception and pregnancy and father would be "in the family." This has been done in Argentina, and an early pregnancy was established.

The above is not all in the realm of science fiction. Physicians working in infertility are just beginning to be approached by wealthy couples or their lawyers who feel that since sex and pregnancy are being treated so casually, there surely must be some young women on a large university campus who could use $10,000 for a year out of their lives. However, no one should plan on $10,000, as the price would inevitably go down with increasing acceptance. We are obviously not advocating this, but a casual and irresponsible attitude toward sex and pregnancy might easily be extrapolated into this approach by an uninformed individual who does not know that a baby carried in one's uterus for nine-and-a-half months becomes a very personal possession.

It is even difficult to find males for donor insemination since many males do not like the thought of creating a child which they will never see. Many unwed fathers are distraught at the idea of their pregnancy being aborted; not all of them are callous about the product of conception, though they may have acted in a callous, unthinking manner toward the mother. Frequently the

---

* This has been done with frozen embryos in cattle.

unwed mother does not tell the father that she either had an abortion or is carrying the child to term, because she does not want him around anymore.

These same physicians are seeing more and more infertility related to post-abortion infections, abortion instrumentation, and venereal disease. A review of the literature up to 1968 indicates that the female was the source of infertility problems 60 to 65 percent of the time, with tubal factors representing about half of the female problems.[2] It has become evident in the past few years that with the prevalence of treated and untreated gonorrhea and legal and illegal abortions, the tubal factor is on the increase and there may even be an increase in the total percentage of infertile couples. Gonorrhea may also affect male fertility, but the signs and symptoms are generally so recognizable and often treated early enough to prevent any significant contribution to a change in the number of infertile couples. But the male-female ratio of responsibility may change in the next few years; that is, females, because of the tubal factor, may represent a higher percentage of the total than previously.

"For every 85 married couples producing offspring there are still 15 couples in this country who are unable to conceive" or who cannot maintain a pregnancy.[3] The latter are known as habitual aborters (see p. 223). Of this infertile group, about 10 percent, and some feel as high as 25 percent, can be helped with the methods and procedures known at the present time, but about half are apparently normal in all areas which can be investigated and still do not conceive. The remaining 25 percent have some disorder of the reproductive system in the male, female, or both, which cannot be treated, or some disorder which affects the reproductive system secondarily.

One of the major treatable causes of infertility is ignorance. This may seem unbelievable in an age when sexual information is all around us, but available information is not necessarily read, listened to, remembered, or used. Timing intercourse with ovulation is important, and for a long time infertility specialists were loathe to ask their patients to time intercourse with mittelschmerz or temperature charts. They didn't feel that couples could or should have intercourse on demand. Ambivalent feelings about a pregnancy, even in the face of apparent infertility, are common, and impotence should not surprise any male who is having intercourse because he is supposed to "make a baby this time." However, such timing is an excellent way to get pregnant, and is certainly worth trying before getting involved in long-term studies. Any couple who has used a temperature chart for five months and has not conceived when ovulation is clearly shown on the chart, should begin investigating other areas which may be at fault.

Frequency of intercourse is important, if temperature charts look too mechanical. The usual definition of infertility is failure to conceive in one year after adequate exposure. There is no real definition of adequate, but intercourse two or three times a week for a year approaches it. Many newly married couples find it easy to postpone having children, especially with the pill, and may postpone them for four, five, or six years. By that time the frequency of intercourse may be down to once a week, or simply very irregular, or just on weekends. If the female is not ovulating on weekends, she may not get pregnant.

Another examination which is easily, quickly, and inexpensively done is an evaluation of the spermatic fluid: the number of sperm, their motility, and their reaction to the vaginal and cervical environment. This is called a postcoital test. No specialist in infertility begins studies of the infertile couple without this knowledge and a discussion of sexual frequency and techniques unless there are extenuating circumstances, for example, a husband who absolutely refuses to accept the possibility of his responsibility or partial responsibility. This is not uncommon even in the present age of sexual enlightenment. Sterility is a devastating concept for both males and females. Even voluntarily discarding previous fertility presents problems (see Sterilization).

There are always women with grossly irregular menstrual periods who are concerned about their fertility, even prior to marriage. Irregularity does not mean lack of ovulation in all cases; it just makes timing ovulation more difficult.

Very few young males are secure enough to have their spermatic fluid checked prior to marriage or early in marriage, but if we are talking about increasing male responsibility for contraception, this simple little examination might fit into some relationships easily, though it would ultimately affect only a very small percentage of males. We are thinking about those couples in which the female may have been on the pill for four or five years prior to marriage, and though neither she nor her husband are terribly comfortable with it, they know that it is the only answer to their particular contraceptive needs. She stays on the pill for another four or five years until they are ready to have children, and then finds they are infertile because he is sterile. We have presented a problem which is soluble only in the context of each individual relationship; semen evaluation early in marriage might or might not be a demonstration of caring.

Diagnosis and Treatment

The diagnosis and treatment of infertility are too extensive to summarize, but in view of the increasing tubal problems and the prevalence of newspaper accounts of multiple births, these two areas of treatment should be noted.

The mechanical aspects of the tubal factor are relatively easy to diagnose but always require surgical repair. This is specialized surgery and the results, even in expert hands, vary depending on the extent of tubal involvement. Husbands should not automatically assume that their wives' need for tubal surgery means previous VD or postabortion infections. Appendicitis, with or without a scar, is a major cause of adhesions in the pelvic cavity. Adhesions are connective tissue strands of scar tissue which distort the relationships of ovaries and tubes and may even cause closure of the ends of the tube. Lysis of these adhesions and reapproximating the ovaries and tubes are quite successful, and pregnancies can even occur in the following ovulatory cycle, if all other factors are normal.

Some women whose endocrine system seems to be normal, fail to ovulate. Clomiphene, a relatively new drug, is being used to induce ovulation in these women. It apparently acts through the pituitary gland, and the amount needed to stimulate ovulation varies from one patient to the next. This accounts for the number of "supermultiple" premature births (up to nine have been recorded) reported in the newspapers. The ovary is superovulated, putting out several eggs, all of which are fertilized. The human uterus does not seem to be able to carry more than five viable babies to term delivery, and that only rarely. Most multiple births, even twins, deliver slightly earlier than the estimated due date. However, the newspapers do not report on the many infertile couples who have had successful single pregnancies with this treatment of their ovulatory failure. They accept this treatment of their reproductive problem, knowing the risk and possibility of disappointment and pregnancy wastage which often follows superovulation.

I feel great. I'm anxious to get out of here and go home, to be able to feel the babies, to touch them and get the mother instincts.

We knew the risks and the possibilities of multiple births, but if I had to do it again, I would do the same thing.

Mrs. Lynn Baer, mother of quintuplets

The role of the psyche in infertility should not be underestimated. Long before infertility specialists had as many procedures and tests as they now have, it was well known that a certain percentage of couples would get pregnant after one office visit which might consist entirely of conversation and a reassuring pelvic examination. Some of these so-called normal couples who have been told after exhaustive studies that adoption is the only answer, find themselves pregnant, before or after adoption.

Fifteen years ago, a 35-year-old couple in this normal group arranged through a lawyer to adopt the baby of an unmarried pregnant girl. After delivery, they found themselves with twins. They also found themselves compelled to use contraception for the first time in their married life. They were afraid the psyche would work its wondrous ways, and they felt that they were too old to have more than two children, even if the third was one "of their own."

Artificial insemination from a donor or the husband also plays a role in the treatment of infertility. Both procedures require a very special and unique husband-wife relationship. Artificial insemination with the husband's semen is usually done if he is unable to ejaculate intravaginally, a devastating dysfunction in itself. There are other less common reasons for needing or trying artificial insemination with husband's semen, none of which are too successful in establishing pregnancies (see Frozen Sperm).

Donor insemination, especially, requires another type of husband-wife relationship which requires careful investigation before any reputable physician will participate. And recently, there are single females who are requesting donor insemination because they would love to have a child but are not interested in getting married or living with a male. And there are couples who discover with one or more pregnancies that they have either a lethal gene combination, or a combination of genes which produces deformed babies, or chronically ill babies. Some of these couples are asking for donor insemination.

Facilities for freezing sperm or semen for later use are available in several large cities. Many medical authorities in the field of reproduction feel that these facilities for humans are a little premature, though prize bulls have been inseminating prize cows at great distances for many years with semen which has been frozen.

The commercial semen banks have suggested that men about to undergo vasectomy may store their semen as fertility insurance. In the opinion of the Committee, the storage . . . is not wise . . ., promise of fertility insurance is misleading . . .; it may lead to the persuasion of the immature or poorly motivated individuals to undergo vasectomy . . .; collecting successive specimens from men with low sperm counts is not feasible since the semen quality is not likely to survive the freezing process.[4]

The factors involved in habitual abortion are incompletely known and treatment is, to some degree, empirical. Mechanical factors do not seem to play a major role, but one is emerging as therapeutic abortions become more frequent: the incompetent cervix.

Prior to the increase in the number of induced abortions, the incompetent cervix was characterized by an apparent weakness in the cervical tissue which though it might be able to stay closed through one term delivery, could not maintain any subsequent pregnancies much beyond the fifth, sixth, or seventh months. Or, the weakness might be so marked that no pregnancy could be carried to term. Some figures from Sweden and the eastern European countries indicate that the increasing incidence of incompetent cervices in first postabortion pregnancies is directly related to the number of induced abortions, though not an inevitable result of these. In Japan, almost all *first* induced abortions are done with *laminaria* (a number of thin sticks of special wood inserted into the uterine cavity and left there to swell and slowly dilate the cervix "naturally" over a period of 20 to 24 hours) to avoid the rapid mechanical dilatation of the cervix used with suction or D and C's (see Induced Abortion). Their experience with induced abortion since the late forties has indicated that there are fewer complications in later desired pregnancies, using this method.

The treatment for the incompetent cervix is mechanical: a plastic band is placed around the cervix so that the latter is prevented from opening prematurely. The band can be placed before or after a pregnancy has been established, and removed or not removed at the time of delivery. If not removed, the delivery must be done by Caesarian section (see p. 181). Occasionally there are some complications, but the band works very well and should be considered effective treatment.

References

1. Martha K. McClintock, "Menstrual Synchrony and Suppression," *Nature* 229 (January 22, 1971).

2. S. J. Behrman and R. W. Kistner, eds., *Progress in Infertility* (Boston: Little, Brown and Co., 1968).

3. *Ibid.*

4. Planned Parenthood-World Population, "Memorandum: Human Semen Cryobanking," May 1972.

6

· · · · · · · · · Reproduction: · · · · · · · · ·
Pregnancy, Labor, and Delivery

God, I had a crazy pregnancy; I tried to learn all of those things like you are supposed to. . . . I bet I'm the only one who's ever been kicked out of a childbirth class and for nothing . . . all I did was ask if they'd run that film backwards . . . now I ask you. . . .

Joan Rivers

FOR THE PURPOSES of what will be a sexually-oriented but factual discussion of pregnancy and delivery, we are going to assume that the pregnancy is planned, or at least desired.* This will allow discussion of all of the pleasures and joys of expectancy as well as the ambivalence and questions, without a constant need for qualifying comments. It also means that a husband and wife have decided that they are ready to share with a child the feelings which they have for each other, and that they have not simply succumbed to societal pressures, or to boredom with each other or with the marriage; nor do they find pregnancy a legitimate excuse for the wife to quit working and stay home "where she belongs." This may sound overly calculated, cynical, idealistic, or improbable, but the fact is that there are many children created within marriage in this manner, and for these reasons.

A female and male have to know each other quite well to be able to understand and handle the intermittent, though frequently brief and disturbing feelings of mistrust, being overwhelmed, paranoia, and the whole gamut of emotions which a pregnancy can create in both individuals, even in the best circumstances. These feelings, and all of the variations, are especially prevalent in some ethnic and intellectual groups of our society in which individuals tend

---

* "Love child" is a phrase born of the necessity for explaining discrepancies in time between marriage and childbirth to a child old enough to count. It has a romantic, spontaneous sound, and the current prevalence of pregnant weddings has already caused it to lose some of the unpleasant connotations of the past. However, this kind of pregnancy can, and often does, create a different set of feelings, dependent on the relationship of the couple.

to analyze each of their own emotional ups-and-downs, as well as those of others. Prospective parents who are less introspective are more apt to handle these ups-and-downs by viewing the pregnancy as "her," or "my," project, a result of female desires, or the woman's role, and on some occasions, her fault or her baby. In this situation, the pregnant female has the options of a feeling of martyrdom on the bad days, or the delights of expectancy, something to look forward to, on the good days. The expectant father has the options of tuning out, in essence, leaving, on the bad days, or enjoying the good days "as a husband," but not necessarily as a prospective father directly involved in the pregnancy.

The Pregnancy

Diagnosis

Pregnancy may be diagnosed as early as ten days after the first missed period, or, if using a BBT chart, three days after a missed period. At ten days past the missed period, the embryo is 24-days old. A few drops of urine, obtained at any time of day, are all that are needed for the five minute slide tests (p. 127). At ten days, there is a small percentage of false negative tests, but virtually no false positive tests. If the test is negative, the doctor may suggest returning the following week for a repeat test, or if there is anxiety or concern, he may prescribe progesterone by mouth or by injection to induce menstruation. This is effective only if there is no pregnancy. In the dosage given, it does not harm the embryo, if it exists. Many contraceptive clinics are now doing free or low-cost pregnancy testing.

The symptoms of pregnancy prior to and after the first missed period may simply be an exaggeration of breast fullness or tenderness, and the pelvic awareness that are common premenstrual symptoms in many women. Or, there may be no increase in these symptoms. There may or may not be a mild, prebreakfast nausea. This is not usually a dizzy nausea; it is more like the nausea associated with hunger, and can often be relieved by nonfat foods, such as crackers or fruit drops. Feelings of nausea may also occur at other classic hunger periods, such as prelunch, late afternoon, or evening. They are much like the feelings of nausea some women experience with the pill.*

At the time of the expected period, there may be no menstrual period, only mild cramping, perhaps only spotting (bleeding), or, rarely, a woman may con-

---

*Hyperemesis gravidarum is a relatively rare condition of early pregnancy which is, as its name implies, associated with severe nausea and vomiting of several weeks duration which may require hospitalization and intravenous fluids to treat the severe dehydration which can occur.

tinue to have cyclic, menstrual bleeding, though usually scanty, for the first four or five months (see Spontaneous Abortion).

For the first three or four months there may be an increased frequency of urination and some urgency about the need to urinate immediately (see discussion of last trimester).

A pelvic examination at this early stage will not usually establish a diagnosis of pregnancy, but it will reveal whether or not the pregnancy is later than the assumed 24 days. Also important, it may give an early indication of whether or not the pregnancy is in the Fallopian tube instead of in the uterus, or it may reveal some other reason for menstrual delay.

The frequency of ectopic pregnancies, pregnancies in some area other than the uterus, has increased, and varies from 1 in 80 to 1 in 200 pregnancies, depending on the population studied. The greatest number of these are in the tube, and the incidence *has been* much higher in the disadvantaged than in the affluent population, correlated with the incidence of previous tubal infections (salpingitis) in these populations (see VD). Increase in the incidence of tubal pregnancies has closely paralleled the expanding use of antibiotics in the treatment of tubal infections, and many physicians feel that the increasing number of *treated* gonorrheal and postabortion infections in the female population of *all* socioeconomic groups will tend to close this essentially racial gap. If the above seems paradoxical, we should add that treatment only cures the infection, it does not reverse any prior damage which might have occurred. *Untreated* gonorrhea or tubal infections usually result in completely closed tubes, or sterility. *Treated* tubal infections appear to leave fertility intact; that is, the sperm and the egg can reach each other, but the movement of the fertilized egg through the tube is often impaired.

Concern about tubal pregnancies is well founded, since by the twelfth week the embryo, if in the tube, has either outgrown its blood supply and dies, or just as frequently has outgrown its space and ruptures the tube. This is a surgical emergency accompanied by severe pain and rapid blood loss. Early attention to the signs and symptoms of pregnancy can sometimes avoid such emergency aspects, though surgical treatment is always necessary. The earlier the diagnosis and treatment, the greater the chance of salvaging the tube for future use.

The estimated date of confinement-delivery (EDC) should always be regarded as a date to which two weeks must be added or subtracted. If menstrual cycles are 28 to 32 days, it is calculated by counting back three months from the first day of the *last* normal menstrual period and adding seven days: if Day 1 was May 16, the EDC would be February 16 plus seven days, or February 23. If menstrual cycles are longer or shorter, or slightly irregular, adding 273 days ± seven days to the approximate date of conception will give an equally approximate date of delivery.

Prenatal Care

It has been amply demonstrated that prenatal care from the second or third month, as compared with no care, or care from the seventh or eighth month, reduces the incidence of maternal and fetal complications of pregnancy and delivery. Teenage and "elderly" pregnancies (ages 32 to 45 and beyond) have always been considered high risk pregnancies. Osofsky and others have shown that the risk of complications in a group of pregnant teenagers can be reduced to the expected average of any age group with good, interested, early, and very supportive prenatal care.[1] However, this requires a more substantial medical effort than is currently available to match the number of pregnancies, so this young age group must still be considered high risk. Advances in obstetrics in the past few years, combined with careful watching and good obstetrical judgment, have reduced maternal and fetal risks to almost average in elderly pregnancies in which there are no preexisting complications.

After the diagnosis of pregnancy, prenatal care is a series of about ten office visits during the eight-and-a-half to nine-and-a-half months, on a monthly, biweekly, and then weekly schedule. They often seem like a great deal of effort for so little office and doctor time. But the routine checking of blood pressure, urine, and weight, checking the size of the uterus, and just looking at the pregnant patient can be very revealing. Five minutes of time is often enough to determine normal progress, or potential or real problems. If the doctor has been chosen carefully, there is also time to ask questions about any of the new feelings and sensations which may require some reassurance.

Because they feel very experienced, women with second and third pregnancies tend to wait for this careful watching until the fourth or fifth month unless they have had some previous problems. Teenagers and women in lower socioeconomic groups who may have neither time nor baby-sitters for their other children, tend to wait until the seventh or eighth month, with their concerns centered primarily on delivery care (see p. 159).

Every pregnancy and delivery differs slightly, and prenatal visits sometimes pay off in spite of the boredom and the effort they require. For the doctor, much of the pleasure of obstetrics, beyond establishing some kind of relationship with the patient is in the early diagnosis of problems, and the assurance that he can handle these problems and deliver a good baby. It is a devastating challenge to see a patient at seven or eight months with a problem which might have been prevented or have been easier to treat if it had been recognized earlier.

Choosing an Obstetrician and a Hospital

Many husbands still become very possessive of their wives' bodies and minds, temporarily, and insist that they see only female doctors, on the mistaken assumption that no male doctor can look at female genitals without arousal of some feelings, however minor (see Gynecological Examination, p. 320). Stories of women becoming infatuated with their doctors are relatively commonplace and contribute to this wariness in husbands. The reverse is extremely rare (see p. 322). And many women feel that only female doctors, childless or otherwise, will really understand them. This is also a fallacy. Caring and understanding, whether derived from intuition or experience, are not confined to either sex in the medical profession. There are some women doctors who stride around and demand or imply that the patient must keep a stiff upper lip and not embarrass "our sex," or who put off all questions from the patient as "foolishness." There are male doctors who treat all women like ignorant little girls who are incapable of thinking, and who are certainly dreaming impossible dreams if they believe that they can go through labor and delivery by themselves. (Someone pointed out that the writing style of most prenatal booklets sounds like "Run, Spot, Run.") Some women obviously enjoy being treated harshly or gruffly by a father or mother figure in the guise of an obstetrician, and even come back for the next delivery. Often they married the same kind of man.

Shopping around for doctors is legitimate activity, as is changing doctors in midpregnancy, if a woman is not getting what she is looking for. But she may never find what she is looking for because it may not exist, or it may not be that well defined in her own mind, or even possible in her community. There is no need for allegiance to a particular obstetrician just because of a few visits. Friends can be helpful informants, but pregnancy needs are so personal that a woman may not be aware of even a good friend's most personal needs, which often may not coincide with hers.

There are several important factors to consider when looking for hospitals, in addition to the factor of the doctor's affiliation: Are fathers allowed in the labor rooms? Are they allowed in the delivery rooms? Are they allowed to look through the delivery-room window? Is there rooming-in with the baby? Is this compulsory or optional? Whether or not a woman wants her husband in any of these places, or wants to be with her baby full time is incidental. The fact that these options are available indicates a hospital policy which is flexible and aware of the niceties of delivery and postpartem care. Also, individual labor rooms indicate some dedication to the principles of privacy and a good experience, though this is not always available in every community. Two laboring mothers in one room is tolerable, but the curtains separating patients are never soundproof; nor are most walls, but they do help.

Midwives

The gradually increasing use of midwives in the United States, women who assist other women in the "maternity cycle" from conception through the post-delivery period, is not due to a lack of doctors, but to the increasing desire of all women and their doctors to make normal pregnancy and childbirth a good experience. It is also partly due to the decreasing number of registered nurses who are available for direct patient care. Today, more and more, patient contact with hospital personnel other than physicians is almost entirely with nurses' aides and licensed practical nurses (LPN's). Registered nurses in many hospitals are supervisory and in charge of medications. The trained nurses who love obstetrics take further training and become nurse-midwives. A good obstetrical nurse with long experience always served, and still does in some areas, almost the same function as the nurse-midwife, but she never had the legal right to "manage" any labor or delivery without doctor's orders. Nor was she closely acquainted with the patient prior to her arrival on the delivery floor. But emergencies often required that she assist many normal, spontaneous deliveries.

Untrained, but very experienced granny midwives* almost disappeared in the late 1800s, when it became apparent that physicians were having fewer complications among their patients, and a lower maternal and fetal morbidity and mortality rate. This became more important than whether or not the attending personnel were male or female. Granny midwives are still doing some home deliveries in the Southern states, but without legal sanction.

Today, trained nurse-midwives are recognized by law in almost all of the 50 states—the law allows them to deliver babies for a fee, and usually establishes some criteria for training. "Nurse-midwifery is an extension of care of nursing practice into the area of management of care of mothers and babies throughout the maternity cycle so long as progress meets criteria accepted as normal."[2]

However, "The American nurse-midwife always functions within the framework of a medically directed health service; she is never an independent practitioner."[3] She is trained in all aspects of pregnancy and delivery, and, most important, trained to recognize potential problems and emergencies when they arise. As noted elsewhere, 90 percent of all deliveries are without maternal or fetal complications, but 100 percent of all pregnancies can use that extra supportive and personal touch. It is often impossible for an obstetrician, who has one or two patients in labor and an office full of pregnant patients, to be with his laboring patients constantly. The patient and the doctor may be more comfortable when someone is there who is trained to recognize emergencies and who is capable of managing a normal labor, and, if necessary, delivery in his or her own way, without a constant need for telephoned orders.

A final note: A patient never chooses between a doctor *or* a midwife to deliver her baby; she chooses a doctor who does or does not use midwives, or a clinic which does or does not employ them.† The ultimate responsibility is always with the doctor.

---

*Granny midwives are older experienced women who deliver babies for a fee. Sometimes this profession is passed down from mother to daughter.

† A very competent and caring nurse-midwife who is knowledgeable about the growing field of midwifery requested that we make this point very clear.

Living With a Pregnancy

Pregnancy is a normal, physiological function and even desirable and fun for a great many women who "just love being pregnant," completely aside from having the child. The expectant feeling can create interest in a life grown dull for whatever reasons, or add a whole new dimension to a good life. However, pregnancy and illness have doctors and hospitals (and their procedures) in common, and this can cause a number of problems which, if their origins are recognized, might be minimized.

A tendency to deny that pregnancy has the potential of being a medical problem because it is so "natural" indicates lack of awareness of the fact that the marked decrease in maternal and fetal mortality is due to increasingly good and available medical watching, which is really *care*. The other extreme is the tendency in more educated societies to consider pregnancy, at some point, as illness and to treat it accordingly.[4] Treating pregnant women as if they are ill, and women treating themselves as if they are ill, may encourage the adoption of certain roles which are characteristic of illness. On the other hand, in some situations when women cannot maintain themselves under the physiological strain of pregnancy, a "sick role" behavior pattern has some reality.[5]

Parsons defines the sick role as: 1) The sick person is allowed some exemptions from the performance of normal social obligations, and 2) the sick person is allowed exemption from responsibility for his own state. But, in addition, the sick person has certain obligations 1) to be motivated to get well as soon as possible, and 2) to seek competent help and to cooperate with medical experts.[6]

Some recognition of how these allowances and obligations may be used and responded to during pregnancy and delivery, either consciously or subconsciously by both females and males, is vitally important to the maintenance of good relationships during a pregnancy. The allowances may be used to excess by the expectant mother for brief or long periods of time; depending on the response she gets, and her absolute need. The expectant father may even encourage prolonging the sick role, sometimes damagingly so, if he has not recognized what is really happening and why.

One example, and there are countless others: There is, or should be a necessary, temporary change in roles demanded by a few weeks of morning nausea which may extend into a temporary change in dietary habits for the entire day. Who makes breakfast? Who makes dinner? Is the morning nausea, or the abhorrence of afternoon cooking odors prolonged over several weeks because the change in roles is so pleasant and unexpected, because the expectant mother has failed to get some advice from her doctor, or because it is still really a major problem? She cannot stand the smell of perking coffee in the morning; would he please switch to instant coffee, even though he doesn't like it as well? These are basic day-to-day, hour-to-hour little problems of living together which can balloon out of all proportion, and assume a significance that a cup of coffee does not really deserve.

Although he cannot put himself in his wife's place, a male can demonstrate love and caring in this situation by indulging her without question; or, he can encourage her, without pushing, to get some medical advice. Some caring males may be overwhelmed by their wives' needs, if they become numerous, and pretend they do not exist, or tease about some requests which may have real meaning for their wives. Life goes on badly, though usually only temporarily so. It is also easy to use these or similar situations to give vent to previously hidden resentment or hostility which predate the pregnancy.

Most of the unpleasant symptoms associated with some pregnancies are unfortunately of such brief duration—minutes, hours, a few days, or a few weeks—that adaptation is difficult for either partner. Therefore, these often must be treated as brief indispositions which carry with them all of the elements of illness and role-playing noted above.

Vaginal bleeding during early or late pregnancy, or just the fact of pregnancy itself, can threaten a sexual life if there were sexual problems previously, or if there is misunderstanding about what is possible. Breast tenderness, genital sensitivity, and the growing uterus require modifications of sexual techniques. The man who "leaves" during his wife's pregnancy, is either forced out of the home (bed) or, because they have had problems in the past which are now magnified, he feels justified in finding temporary solace elsewhere.

Those men and women who have had experience with the emotional upheavals of premenstrual tension should not be surprised by an extension of these symptoms when there is no menstruation, because the same hormone is operating, only at increasing, noncyclic levels. The body does finally adapt, though emotional lability may continue for other nonphysiological reasons.

It is much easier for the pregnant woman to be pleasant to strangers than to her family. The woman who works outside of the home or has some absolute need for structuring her daily life within the home, even if she has to make a conscious effort to do this on some days ("bootstrapping"), will be in a much better position to avoid the temptation to sit all day and "contemplate" her growing belly. Working is easier with a first pregnancy, of course, but a good experience with the first will often speed the adaptation to a second, even with another child in the house; children can structure the daily lives of their mothers extremely well. Whether or not there are children, a flexible work schedule or a flexible boss helps, and this is the most realistic approach to either part-time or full-time working during any pregnancy. The physical aspects of pregnancy are so unpredictable that to plan on working until the day one goes into labor is unrealistic, though frequently possible.

The kind of work is important to consider, both its emotional and physical aspects. Despite 15-minute breaks, standing, sitting, or walking all day can become uncomfortable, even early in pregnancy, and can result in exhaustion at home every night. An intellectually fulfilled but exhausted wife can put unreasonable demands on a husband who is also working. The pleasures of

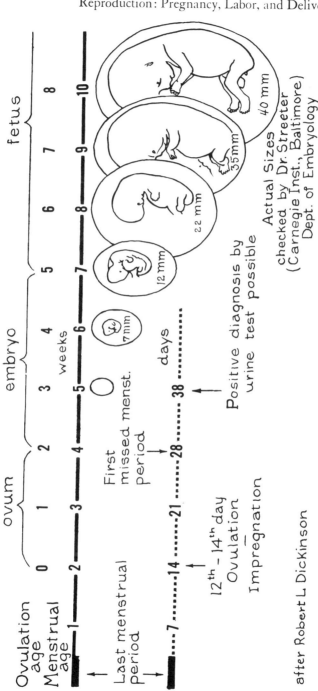

Figure 6-1. Growth of ovum, embryo, and fetus in early pregnancy.

working with 30 small children all day, as in elementary or nursery school teaching, can become a nightmare on some days for the pregnant teacher *and* the children. The need for personal interaction with adults or adolescents with social problems, or simply the need to be pleasant to a large number of people every day, can limit one's emotional resources at home.

These are some of the reasons why we dare to say that "there is more to pregnancy than the fetus." Expectant parents react to each other and to those outside of the home in somewhat different ways resulting from the *fact* of pregnancy, but there is *no direct interaction* with the fetus until it is born. It is important to consider any pregnancy as a new experience and an opportunity to learn about one's own interpersonal relationships. If the expectant mother stays emotionally and physically healthy, she will have the best opportunity to create a healthy child who will not be a destructive or disturbing factor in a previously good marriage, and both individuals will be better parents. The fetus will inevitably turn into a baby, the uterus will contract, and the baby will emerge; there is little one can do about this sequence of events except to let the doctor worry about it *and* the mother, if she will give a doctor the opportunity to do this.

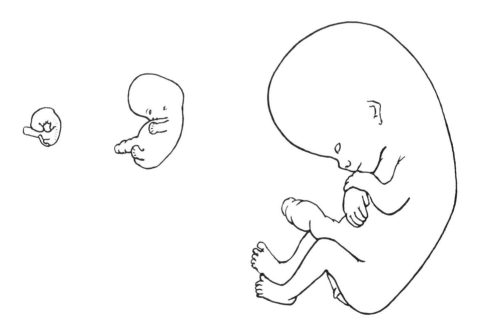

Figure 6-2. Actual size of fetus at approximately one month, two months, and three months, respectively.

The Physical and Sexual Sides of Pregnancy

There is some physiological basis for dividing the nine-and-a-half months of pregnancy into trimesters; questions from expectant parents and the potential problems seem to fit into this pattern as well. Our emphasis here will be primarily on the physical and sexual aspects of the adult side of pregnancy rather than on the fetus, though it is important for everyone to have some knowledge of the appearance of the embryo and the fetus in the first 16 to 20 weeks of pregnancy, especially in today's abortion-oriented society. *Pregnancy must be regarded as something more than a missed menstrual period and an abortion.*

The First Trimester: First through Twelfth Week or First through Third Month

The baby. Figures 6-1 and 6-2 illustrate the rapid growth in the first 12 weeks. By this time, the embryo has become a miniature infant; the external genitals have become differentiated to the expert eye, and the living fetus may show some movement in response to stimuli. The measurements noted are "crown-rump" up to the time of delivery. The length at delivery is a "crown-heel" measurement.

The pregnancy. Primary consideration is, of course, diagnosis of pregnancy, but the first visit often includes blood tests (hemoglobin and syphilis), a medical history, a chest X-ray (though this may be deferred), a blood pressure, urine examination, a Pap test for cervical cancer, a pelvic examination, and, in this day and age, a cervical culture for gonorrhea (see also Spontaneous Abortion and Tubal Pregnancy).

The parents. The nine-and-a-half months of pregnancy can be one of the most anxiety-free, spontaneous sexual interludes of a couple's life, but only if there is understanding that intercourse poses no threat to the pregnancy, with rare exceptions which are noted elsewhere, and if both partners have been reasonably comfortable with their sexuality prior to pregnancy. This is only one of many good arguments for a period of living together and getting to know one another, and oneself, prior to a pregnancy. The excitement of creating a wanted child adds a whole new dimension of closeness to a relationship and, therefore, can only improve the physical aspects of that relationship, since these are almost totally centered in the psyche. A couple may even discover that this closeness does not depend on intercourse for expression, though this should not be interpreted as meaning an "active" act of abstaining by either partner.

In the first trimester, pregnant women are very aware of their pelvises—the fullness, the increased sensations, the sharp, round ligament twinges which may occur in the groin with sudden movement; with the first, second, or even third pregnancy, they tend to contemplate these physical signs and symptoms as a threat to the pregnancy. Although occasional spotting is common, it puts legitimate thoughts of a threatened abortion in their minds (p. 222). Deep penile penetration with an enlarging, soft uterus which is still entirely in the pelvis creates feelings entirely different from those usually experienced. This does not mean that the penis cannot be inserted, or that thrusting and movement are against the rules, but it does mean that if a pregnant female is busy thinking about this during intercourse, she is not losing herself in the pleasures of sexual stimulation, and may not be orgasmic on all occasions or as often as is usual for her.

If there are times when intercourse should wait for a few days, this should not limit any of the other variations of sexual stimulation and orgasmic release for the female, male, or both. Sexual techniques may need modification because of increased sensitivity of breasts and genitals. Secretions increase and change in character, and the genital odor is unique to pregnancy, but not unpleasant, if previous standards of hygiene are maintained at a daily level. This even includes an intermittent douche if desired, but the douche tip should not be inserted as deeply as in the nonpregnant vagina. Yeast overgrowth in the vagina is common during pregnancy, as it is with the pseudopregnancy of the pill, and often requires medication and douching to keep it under control.

This is also the time to start learning a little of the anatomy and physiology of pregnancy and delivery, or to think about looking for courses given in many hospitals at intervals during the year. The more it knows about normal, the more secure a couple is going to be in all other areas of its life.

> . . . have in your mind very clearly an intellectual picture of the sequence of labor (and pregnancy) for an intellectual picture is the only one possible until you experience labor (and pregnancy).[7]

The prospective father should go to the doctor with his wife at least once during the pregnancy, either on the first visit or in the seventh or eighth month when the baby is a reality. She will feel less as if it is her project by default, and he will feel less left out, an inevitable feeling when he finds her confiding in her male obstetrician, or joining forces with a female obstetrician. The doctor also likes to know that there is support and understanding at home, beyond the usual patient comment, "He's being just great." There are many husbands who do not like anything about doctors, hospitals, or medical offices; they should keep in mind that perhaps their wives have the same feelings, but are in no position to have options. It is not unmasculine to care, to be curious, not to know all of the answers, or to ask questions.

There is a tiredness and a hunger during the first trimester which are easily taken care of with brief daytime rests, and frequent, well-balanced small feedings. These feelings are characteristic of the first three months and seldom continue into the second and third trimesters, though it can be very depressing to think that the nine months are going to be "like this." Usually the yawning wife is not bored, just tired. About half of the total weight gain (20 to 30 pounds) occurs during this first trimester, though it may be safely less with care, or be much more without care. Generally speaking, thin obstetricians like to keep the patient's weight gain around 20 pounds; obese obstetricians are more lenient; medium-sized obstetricians favor 20 to 30 pounds. There are exceptions to this. Keep in mind how hard it is to take off an extra 10 to 15 pounds at any time, and then add the weight of the average baby (about 7 pounds), the weight of the placenta and the amnionic fluid (about 6 to 7 pounds), and 4 to 5 pounds of retained water in the body tissues. This means that only 14 to 16 pounds will disappear at the time of delivery, and 4 to 5 pounds of fluid in the first few days, postdelivery. The rest is excess. We have seen moderately obese women, who were well motivated, lose weight during a pregnancy because they finally decided to eat properly "for the sake of the baby."

The Second Trimester: Thirteenth through Twenty-Fourth Week or Fourth through Sixth Month

The baby. By the end of this period, the baby is about 14 inches long and weighs about 2 to 3 pounds. He is floating and kicking (quickening) during the fourth month. If born late in this trimester, the fetus may live for a few days or, in rare instances, survive. The fetal heartbeat and brain activity can be detected electronically early in this trimester. This is relevant to some definitions of the "Beginning of Life," but, perhaps depends more on the sensitivity of present-day electronic techniques.

The pregnancy. Spontaneous abortion of a living fetus during the fourth month is not uncommon, but it is usually associated with some abnormality of the reproductive tract, for example, a cervix that dilates too soon (see Infertility and Techniques of Abortion).

Recent advances in genetics and cytogenetics and the availability of abortion have created a use for a procedure known as amniocentesis (the removal of a sample of amnionic fluid). This cannot be done before the fourth month, or until there is enough fluid and space around the baby to decrease the risk to the fetus. The risk must be balanced against the value of the information desired; this method is not to be used casually for sex determination, though this is possible.* It does help anxious expectant parents who may have had

* However, determination of sex is important when there is a question of sex-linked hereditary diseases: see "The Antiseptic Baby," *Newsweek*, 20 December 1971.

previous children with congenital defects, or who have reason to think that there might be a problem, make a decision about terminating the pregnancy. There are, surprisingly, a number of parents who refuse the option of knowing, because to know is to be almost committed to abortion.

If the mother is over the age of 35, and has been told that the incidence of Down's syndrome (mongolism) is increased in pregnancies in this age group and increases rather sharply to 1 in 44 live births from mothers age 44 or over, this may be a welcome procedure. This method may be used to diagnose some of the hereditary, metabolic diseases of children which are associated with inevitable and marked mental retardation, or early childhood death. Some of hereditary bleeding diseases can be diagnosed while the baby is in the uterus. The procedure is not difficult, and analysis of the cells obtained is, as yet, done in only a few medical centers in the country, but these are within the reach of anyone who is concerned.

Vaginal bleeding during the second trimester is very unusual. Even fourth month abortions or premature deliveries in the fifth and sixth months are not usually preceded by bleeding, but by cramping and a gush of amnionic fluid. Stress incontinence of urine (losing urine with coughing or sneezing) and urinary frequency may continue into this trimester; the uterus is out of the pelvis, but leaning on the bladder. This incontinence can sometimes be confused with the gush of amnionic fluid noted above, and can also be very embarrassing in a public place. With conscious effort, urine can be stopped; amnionic fluid cannot.

The parents. Early in the fourth month the uterus becomes an abdominal organ instead of a pelvic organ and may enlarge rather rapidly, causing the parents and the doctor to think about the possibility of twins, or multiple births. Adaptation to the pelvic awareness has usually occurred so that intercourse is not approached as gingerly as previously, but concerns about crushing the fetus may become real, though not valid concerns. The fetus is well protected, but the uterus can get in the way of the usual top and bottom intercourse by the fifth month, and modifications are often needed. However, the uterus is not pressing down in the vagina, and the feeling of hitting an immovable object with penetration is less apparent for both female and male.

Intercourse with both partners on their sides can be successful and, from a purely mechanical point of view is, of necessity, gentle. As the uterus enlarges, women are much more comfortable sleeping on their sides, often with a pillow under the uterus for support. If the expectant mother is on her back, the uterus presses against the large blood vessels causing some problems with blood pressure and lightheadedness, if this position is prolonged, or if there are quick or sudden changes of position. Using a pillow under the hips for a brief period only during intercourse often avoids blood pressure problems and the protruding uterus.

It is difficult for caring, thoughtful husbands to initiate a sexual approach to a wife who is lying on her side, a pillow under her uterus, and two pillows under her head to help with breathing, but they should be aware that warmth and closeness are always desired, even though not always defined as intercourse. Wives may push away any attempts at warmth and closeness, if their experience has shown that these attempts always lead to intercourse. They may not want to be seduced. Just as important, wives should know and remember that it is difficult for males *only* to be close every time, without eventually needing and desperately wanting some kind of orgasmic release. A husband should not have to roll over and masturbate, or get up and disappear elsewhere to get some solitary relief from *his* aching pelvic congestion. This is especially true if there has been any kind of frequent regularity in a couple's sexual life prior to pregnancy.

Females are in a much better physiological and psychological position to adapt to any abstinence desired for physical reasons than the males who, no matter how involved they are with the pregnancy or the mother, can never be more than onlookers. Females with small babies, inside or outside of their uteri, frequently have long moments of dreaming contemplation and fantasy which exclude everyone around them, husbands, children, and friends. Fleeting moments of jealousy in the excluded group are natural. Most males, even those who would have been mildly disturbed by aggressive female sexuality previously, will welcome any indication of caring and awareness of their needs at this time. This is another dimension of sexuality which often begins during a pregnancy, and once established, easily becomes a nonthreatening part of future sexual activity. The caring male does not like to be the aggressor only to be rebuffed or set aside, even for legitimate reasons. He may find it much easier to tune out completely. However, though possible, the female on top position which connotes female aggressiveness for many males, is often uncomfortable during pregnancy, but it does keep the uterus out of the way. Simply initiating sexual activity, or hand-genital or oral-genital activity, if acceptable, is an easily recognized act of caring by the female.

There are occasional references to "pseudopregnant males" who have all of the signs and symptoms of pregnancy, and abdominal discomfort with delivery. More often, the male reacts by becoming preoccupied with something of *his own,* a car, an avocation, even a vocation, just as his wife is preoccupied with her own being. Before any female allows herself to become resentful about a husband's activities, which could also be directed in an almost total fashion toward the other child or children, she should examine the real extent of her concerns about herself, and to what degree they may be a causative factor.

A medical student wrote a very sensitive article for the *Philadelphia Bulletin* about being with his wife during the delivery of their first child. He did not mention their predelivery relationship but noted, almost in passing and without apology or explanation, that she was alone when she went into labor about 4:00 A.M. He did say that he had been playing soccer the previous day, about 50 miles away, had partied briefly, had decided to sleep off the effects along the road, and had come home in the morning. We were briefly outraged when reading this, but knew that no outsider could hope to understand the rationale for this casual approach without extensive, privileged information about the couple's interpersonal relationships.[8]

The need for change of dress in the fourth month is frequently full of ambivalence. There is delight with maternity clothes, "I'm really pregnant now," and dismay with the fat belly, and a feeling of distortion, if not downright ugliness. Stretch marks, if they are going to appear at all, may have begun on the breasts and abdomen; pregnancy becomes a very personal thing that is doing something "to her," in contrast to the abstraction of the first trimester.

Constant reassurance from a husband that "you look lovely to me" can sometimes be destructive by its very constancy. It may be heard through the intermittent paranoia of the pregnant female as "methinks thou dost protest too much," or "lovely to me" means lovely to you but not to anyone else, because we both know I really am ugly. There may be weeping and the feeling that "You're just saying those things without really meaning them." That lovely old phrase, "keep 'em barefoot and pregnant" cannot help but come to mind occasionally, regardless of any real strength which she knows exists in the relationship. Also, any previous, unclothed freedom may disappear for varying periods, a day, a night, a week, or more.

All of these attitudes would be easier for both to handle, if they were consistently present, or present and then absent forever. But they are inconsistent, and require constant adaptation. This is a very fine line for the expectant father to tread, and his inability to handle these attitudes well every time should be no more suspect than the female's ups and downs. The pregnancy is perhaps more of a reality for the expectant father at this time than it is for the mother; he can see it and is less caught up in personal physical feelings. He can also see financial and emotional responsibility for another human being for another 20 years.

The "glow of pregnancy," the Mona Lisa smile when the baby kicks her, if it doesn't kick too hard, is very real. But the female ego is best served by a conscious effort, sometimes difficult, to look great in spite of the pregnancy, if that is the way she is feeling on some days. The glow of pregnancy will not cover all of the sins of omission, of just giving in and giving up on one's physical self. Maintaining previous standards is really all that is required, though it frequently takes a little more effort.

The Third Trimester: Twenty-Fifth to Thirty-Eighth Week or Seventh through Ninth Month

The baby. "It" will grow about 4 inches and gain about 3 pounds during this period, to a delivery weight and size which averages about 7 pounds and 20 inches in crown-heel length. The seven-month infant has a fifty-fifty chance of survival, if the premature delivery is otherwise uncomplicated. "It" is very active at times, occasionally turning completely around, and at other times being so quiet that the mother becomes worried.

The pregnancy. The uterus becomes very irritable; it contracts at odd intervals and for varying periods of time; these are called Braxton-Hicks contractions. The first few times can be very disconcerting. Some of the contractions, though not uncomfortable, are strong enough to give pressure sensations in the bladder and rectum, and the mother just knows that everything is coming out, including the baby.

In the first pregnancy, the head descends into the pelvis early in the ninth month or before, which relieves some of the pressure on the diaphragm, making breathing much easier and lying down more comfortable. Dropping is the word that is used when this happens.

The ligaments which hold the two pelvic bones together, back and front, become soft and elastic enough to create the unstable "waddle" of late pregnancy. The pressure of the head against the nerves in the pelvis occasionally causes sharp shooting pains down into the labia or into the legs. There is nothing one can do about this except stand on the good leg or side, lean against the sink, the desk, or the counter in the store until it goes away. Coughing or sneezing, without doubling up first, can cause very uncomfortable cramping, or pulling, on the ligaments which run from the groin to the top of the uretus (the round ligaments). In subsequent pregnancies, the head does not usually descend, or drop, until the last week or, often, until labor begins.

Visits to the doctor are now every two weeks and finally every week in the last month, if the pregnancy is normal. A second test for syphilis and a culture for gonorrhea are done routinely in most clinics and by some private doctors no matter who the patient is. This is also the time when one finds how labile the weight is, regardless of careful eating habits. This is due almost entirely to salt and water retention, some of which is unavoidable. This water retention and the pressure on the venous return through the pelvis often creates edema, or swelling, in the legs, and varying degrees of varicosities of the veins in the legs and the labia. There are as yet no elastic stockings made which look reasonable. Hemorrhoids are varicosities of the veins around the rectum and anus, and these can be a real problem when combined with a preexisting, or resulting, constipation. Breasts need support for comfort now, if not before, and there may be leaking of early milk (colostrum).

During the thirty-second to thirty-eighth weeks, the doctor is listening to all of the above problems, and evaluating and making decisions about the fetus:

Rh problems if they exist, scheduling Caesarian sections if needed, discussing anesthesia or analgesia in real terms (though they were undoubtedly discussed previously in a more abstract form), arranging visits to labor and delivery floors if desired, answering questions about the signs of labor, or perhaps discussing the induction of labor (p. 176).

The doctor's primary concerns are still blood pressure, weight gain, and the urine. Six or seven percent of all pregnancies are complicated by the toxemias of pregnancy. This is a disease of pregnancy which can be mild, moderate, or severe, and if severe can threaten both mother and baby. It is characterized by elevation of blood pressure, the appearance of protein in the urine, swelling of the face and hands, and, in its later stages, if it progresses, maternal convulsions and even fetal death.

The patient is unaware of the sudden elevation of blood pressure or the appearance of moderate amounts of protein in the urine, though she will be aware of the onset of swelling in the face and hands, which is a slightly later phase of early toxemia. She will frequently feel quite well until she starts seeing the puffiness of the face and hands; thus early diagnosis from the routine urines and blood pressures are important aspects of prenatal care, and this disease in particular. Bedrest and sedation are essential to the treatment of early or late toxemias, to avoid the progression of the disease into convulsions and fetal complications. The incidence of toxemia is high in females who do not seek or get good prenatal care; for example, the pregnant teenagers, the poor (in nutrition and services), the elderly pregnant patients who may have had mild blood pressure or kidney problems prior to the pregnancy, and the diabetic pregnant patients of any age. Difficult toxemias can also occur with good care, watching, and good nutrition with no apparent predisposing causes, though this is rare. A previous history of even mild toxemia predicts, for all practical purposes, the possibility or the potential in the next pregnancy.

Two other major complications of the last trimester are intrauterine: placental bleeding and intrauterine infection. These are also emergencies which require bedrest and sedation and often early delivery of the baby.

The placenta is usually located in the upper portion of the uterus behind the baby, covering a rather large oval to circular area of the uterine wall. If the edge of this very vascular circle is near the cervix instead of higher up, there may be vaginal bleeding as the cervix becomes softer and begins to dilate slightly. If the placenta lies completely over the cervix, Caesarian section delivery is necessary because the baby cannot deliver through the placenta. Partial separation of the edge may cause intermittent bleeding which may cease when the head is firmly down in the pelvis. The bleeding cannot be trusted to stop, or even continue slowly. It has to be watched carefully, and is a threat to mother and baby. If the patient is in good hands and is being watched near the labor and delivery floor, an emergency Caesarian section can be done in about six or seven minutes, with anesthesia.

Intrauterine infection is primarily a threat to the baby; the baby develops pneumonia, the mother a fever. The primary cause appears to be allowing prematurely ruptured membranes (leakage of amnionic fluid) to go beyond 18 hours without delivery of the baby or treatment of the mother with antibiotics; often treatment involves both, if the baby is large enough.

In the face of any of these complications, delivery is the best solution, but waiting even a few extra days to deliver the baby is often indicated. This gives greater assurance of getting a slightly stronger, healthier baby. Inducing delivery in the face of complications is always a compromise, and requires experienced judgment.

The parents. Psychiatrists who have pregnant patients in *nonemergency* therapy often note a "marshalling of forces" in the seventh or eighth month which makes patient-psychiatrist communication difficult. This seems to be true in later as well as first pregnancies. Mental (emotional) vision narrows down to the task at hand, even though there is really very little for the pregnant woman to do except to wait it out. The baby is becoming a reality, and there are finally things to do for it. Some women are so enthralled with the fact of pregnancy, or perhaps they refuse to acknowledge the reality, that they forget or ignore the physical needs of this real baby until "nesting" time comes. Why else would so many couples wait to think about a name for the baby until the day "it" is born? They have had nine-and-a-half months to decide on one girl's name and one boy's name. There is no real evidence of a nesting hormone in humans, but there are a number of women who find themselves, very late in pregnancy, cleaning shelves and places that have never been cleaned before, making curtains for the baby's room, and painting the walls. This even happens to some premenstrual women.

The working mother often stops about this time, even if the work is not physically demanding. Sometimes creative people become less creative, though they may have more time, and be spending more time on their writing, knitting, or macrame. The surprises of physiology, even of a nonemergency nature, demand some preplanned flexibility. Continuing normal activity at a lesser pace is the best approach.

Traveling is no problem for an uncomplicated pregnancy, if the travel is in civilized areas, near some medical expertise, and does not involve prolonged sitting or standing.

Most women have adapted to the changes in themselves by this time, and the ego-threatening distortion of body contours does not seem to loom as large in their thinking. Even the awkwardness of gait is viewed as only a temporary thing, three to six weeks at most. They handle this well, as they do their other physical problems because the baby is almost out; an end is in sight.

In contrast to previous thinking about sexual activity in late pregnancy, many doctors are now encouraging maintenance of sexual relations during this period, or if not actively encouraging, certainly not discouraging it as they used to do.

The threat of possible infection from penile penetration, or of stimulating vaginal bleeding does not seem to warrant abstinence, nor do any contractions associated with orgasm warrant adherence to types of sexual stimulation just short of orgasm for the female.

Caution about deep penetration is often in order for reasons of comfort, but with a first pregnancy, when the head is down in the pelvis, this is difficult anyway. In subsequent pregnancies when the head stays relatively high, and the cervix does not usually dilate until labor begins, there is even less reason for abstinence.

However, maintenance of sexual activity does not have to include intercourse per se, and often the female genital area is so sensitive that she is not really interested in anything but good warm arms and a loving body close by. Though brief, the uterine contractions which may occur with orgasm can be marked, and are often disturbing. The concerned husband who brings the equally concerned wife to the emergency room because of postcoital spotting, or apparent labor is not uncommon.

> A patient of a friend of ours had heard from someone that the fetal heart stopped with contractions, and she became hysterical each time the Braxton-Hicks contractions seemed to last longer than 30 seconds. She was helped, and, indirectly, her husband was too, when she was allowed to observe the continuing fetal heart tracings (a fetal electrocardiogram) during some of her contractions. She simply could not hear the fetal heart when listening with a stethoscope.

Many of the vague, transient symptoms and signs, all within the range of normal and previously regarded as only a personal discomfort, are now interpreted and analyzed in relation to their possible effects on the child. The welfare of the child becomes a reality now, and the mother feels almost incidental; in her worst moments she may even feel like a baby machine. This is in contrast to the previous six or seven months when concerns about the fetus were all rather abstract.

Pregnant mothers of any socioeconomic class, who have had no prenatal care up to the seventh or eighth month may come to the clinics or the doctor at this time. They also want a good baby.

Fathers share some of this same concern and do not want to do anything to endanger the child; thus abstinence is often a mutual, unspoken decision. This commonly occurring mutual concern is the rationale for allowing sexual activity during this period, or saying nothing to discourage it unless medically indicated. The really demanding husband will continue to require sexual access, and telling the expectant mother to abstain will just put her in an even more difficult position in relation to him, and cause worry over what it might do to the child. But frequently she can control the vigor of the act. Others modify their sexual activity almost by instinct.

Labor and Delivery

Now all my world is divided into two parts—pain and absence of it. The interval between contractions becomes a positive thing . . . an air of waiting in the delivery room. . . . The doctor asks me to "push, push hard!!" Nurses gently reassure me. I push with such force my ears ring and the grip bars on the sides of the delivery table rattle in my hands. A kaleidoscope of sound and color surround me. Lights, clanking, suction, wetness, moaning, emptiness, warmth! . . . Peace. Out of nowhere rises a lone sound. . . . It travels around the room and finally enters the corners of my brain. My baby is crying! . . . Tears fill my eyes. They brim over and fall down my hair. I feel laughter rising in me. It bursts out. I am full of rainbows and symphonies. . . .

Jan Seale

A POSITIVE APPROACH to what is a rare experience in anyone's life (an average of 2.3 deliveries per family and decreasing) can make labor and delivery the truly exciting, unique experience that it is becoming for increasing numbers of women and those husbands who are not hesitant about getting involved. And more and more female and male obstetricians are beginning to believe this; they also have husbands or wives and children.

But, there is no way to alleviate the fear-tension-pain syndrome which haunts almost every pregnant female approaching delivery, except with knowledge of what is being accomplished in each stage of labor and some understanding of what the "doctors and nurses are whispering about." When a laboring mother understands the language, she will discover that doctors and nurses are not really whispering. If they have something of consequence to say which might disturb a patient, they do their talking elsewhere.* She may even discover that she can speak the language and have intelligent conversations about her progress instead of existing in an uncomfortable, even painful isolation.

But do not mistakenly assume that the information which may have been acquired prior to the fact of pregnancy is sufficient. The necessary details of information in this area, as in any other sexual area, do not become relevant until they are actually needed. Much is forgotten, much is never really heard. Even prepared childbirth classes, or reading in the first or early second trimester will not carry one through. At this time the reality of the pregnancy is not yet felt, even though the baby may be kicking. There is a difference

---

* We are using the word patient in spite of the illness connotations, because in the hospital setting, a doctor-nurse-patient relationship is established.

between knowing "our baby is here in my belly," and knowing, often with a little panic, that "I'm going to have this baby in three or four weeks, or maybe even tomorrow. I'm going to do this labor thing and deliver." Prior information, if accurate, is of value, but the emphasis should be on rereading, classes if desired, and visiting labor and delivery rooms late in pregnancy, during the last trimester.

Fear of pain and discomfort in childbirth is a legitimate fear that no amount of observation of others or reassurance about its self-limiting nature can dispel. But with knowledge and understanding, the fear of the unknown can be turned into an excitement about the unknown. Fears about pain, and pain itself, are so very personal that even females trained in obstetrics (nurses, doctors, midwives) wonder how they will handle it, or, perhaps more accurately, how they will behave. They may have seen every possible variation of responses during labor and delivery from Christian Scientists sitting Yoga-fashion from early labor through complete dilatation of the cervix, communal home deliveries with the mother delivering on her hands and knees, and the midwife or doctor also on her or his knees on the floor, or the terrified teen-ager, without previous prenatal care, who walks in in labor, and understands nothing about what is happening "to her," to the other extreme: the bare light bulbs, side rails, Charles Addams kind of labor floor and delivery room with every patient "knocked out" with medication (see scopalomine, below).

"A pain willingly born" is the common phrase—as if one ever had a choice. Mothers have talked this way to their children and husbands since time began, as have doctors to questioning patients. It may be nice for a husband's ego to think that his wife willingly martyred herself for him, even though this is not the case; and some wives push the martyrdom potential of childbirth in an attempt to gain some reward: "Look how I have suffered to give you a child. Where is that new car (or fur) that you promised?"

No one can completely prepare a woman for *childbirth*, just as no one can be prepared for *sexual activity* or for *parenthood*. Each couple is a unit unique unto itself, and each delivery and pregnancy has different emotional components. But there is a greater fund of predictable knowledge about childbirth than there is about sexual activity or parenthood. If this knowledge is actively pursued at the right time, by one or both expectant parents, labor and delivery have a better opportunity of being described by all of those superlative adjectives which always seem so suspect and unbelievable until one has really been there and had the experience.

It may be difficult to tell one's children at some point, as a friend of ours did, that "with no disrespect to your father, you were the biggest and best orgasmic experience I have ever had." But this type of approach is certainly much better than "You were a pain, willingly born." Since childbirth will probably be a once or twice in a lifetime experience, one should make the most of it, if not the first time, then the second.

Obviously females have more to gain from being prepared than males, but living with an anxious pregnant female, or a female who is fearful of getting pregnant because of the discomfort of a previous delivery experience, leaves much to be desired. It is in the male's own best interests to encourage and to support any preparation, even to the point of participation, if necessary.

There are three almost classic paperback publications which we can recommend as bedside references worthy of reading and rereading: Guttmacher's *Pregnancy and Birth*, G. Dick-Read's *Childbirth Without Fear* (occasionally referred to as *Childbirth Without Terror*), and Bing's *Six Practical Lessons for an Easier Childbirth*.

The first answers all of the large and small, general and specific questions, about pregnancy and birth.* The second discusses the fear-pain-tension syndrome at length, and suggests effective ways to deal with this fear. The third is a do-it-yourself Lamaze (La mahz') approach to childbirth. This is simply an extension of *Childbirth Without Fear*, with the addition of gimmicks, for example, stroking the belly, using talcum powder, doing exercises, panting. There are details in each book which are unique to specific hospitals and not necessarily transferable to another, but these are minor.

A woman should not be disappointed in her husband if he is not interested in childbirth books, babies, or pregnancies the first or even the second time around; the whole medical aura is difficult. He may be very interested in the mother, but not in the delivery; he has heard the same things that the expectant mother has heard, and may be just as fearful at times. There may even be some occasional brief guilt about what he has "done to her." However, none of this means that books cannot be placed at his disposal. A male and female may choose to live together and have a child because, in addition to some sexual attraction, their general philosophies of living coincide, or because they have interests in common. But they should not expect that all of the nitty gritty details of living should also coincide in all respects. Pregnancy, labor, and delivery fall into this latter category for many.

A male's interest in his "own" pregnancy may be one of curiosity, or it may be a primary concern for the mother, or the baby. He might be thinking about having a boy, or wondering how he could possibly tell anyone that he would really prefer to have a girl. There are an infinite number of other interests in many combinations. He may not want to be prepared.

Some females and males are unenthusiastic about the sensitivity session, encounter group, or group therapy look of some childbirth classes. The common bond of pregnancy concerns and questions does not make friends or aquaintances of unlike personalities. Classes in techniques (as opposed to information classes) are not effective unless there is some degree of participa-

---

* In this respect it is similar to Benjamin Spock's *Baby and Child Care* to which we must also add Lee Salk's *What Every Child Would Like His Parents to Know*.

tion. Verbal and physical participation in this personal area demands an exposure of mind and body that is often unacceptable to some females and males.

If the doctor and hospital have been chosen well, motivated and solitary reading can produce excellent results. The doctor does not have to be an active practitioner of any particular cult, but he or she must show some understanding of how the prospective parents feel and what they are trying to accomplish. If this is not the case, they should change doctors; both the couple and doctor will be more comfortable.

We see no need to parrot an abbreviated version of any of the recommended texts noted above, since more than an abbreviated version is needed. We would like to clear up some persistent misconceptions about certain obstetrical procedures and perhaps give a little more insight into the obstetrician's end of the labor bed and the delivery table.

First, a word about husbands in the delivery room, or labor room, or both. We use the word husband because this is the role that the male should assume, to be with his wife, married or not, at a time when the potential for closeness and the need for evidence of caring is perhaps maximal. Here again, for the male, the baby should be secondary; the father role is a few hours away in relation to this pregnancy.

But not all women want their husbands around. Some know their husbands well enough not to insist. Husbands should know their wives well enough not to insist on being there, if they are not wanted. Some women want their husbands during labor but not during delivery; this may only be for aesthetic reasons which they may not be able to state openly. If a woman can make this clear, no remonstrations from her husband that he "doesn't care about aesthetics" are likely to convince her otherwise. It might be the second or third delivery before a wife is willing and comfortable enough with herself to want her husband to be present, especially if she is one of those who likes to be well put together at all times.

Many husbands will sit through labor,* read, hold a hand, and, on request, put pressure on an aching back with ease and equanimity, but will find "delivery watching" to be quite another matter. A father of our acquaintance who disliked everything about hospitals, did get as far as the window outside the delivery room for his wife's third and final delivery. He was not going to look until he heard the baby cry. He glanced, accidentally, just as the perineum was stretched over the baby's head (crowning) and, in his words which were not those of the academic philosopher that he was, "Nothing, but nothing, could have torn me away from that point on."

---

* In a discussion about furnishing a new labor floor, the question of cots for husbands came up. It was quickly dismissed for reclining chairs; no expectant father should be encouraged to sleep, no matter how tired or how long the labor.

If a husband is in the labor room, the wife has a certain responsibility to acknowledge that he is there, and that his mere presence is useful. She should not consider him simply as an observer, though many do, and, in essence, that might be his total visible contribution. Inevitably there are moments when he will feel completely helpless and sometimes overwhelmed, just listening.

The aesthetics of the shaved or clipped, darkened, engorged perineum are seldom attractive, except in cultures which are accustomed to the shaved perineum, and it does not need exposure to husbands, especially during vaginal or rectal examinations. Husbands are usually asked to leave briefly, or drapes are used. Husbands are also not admitted during admission procedures which usually include enemas and vaginal examinations. No husband or wife should assume that previous carefree, unconcerned attitudes about bodies and natural functions carry over into the necessary exposure of childbirth, for either partner. Privacy often becomes redefined for a period of time. For females, this kind of exposure is frequently easier with relative strangers. For males, it is sometimes better and easier not to know some of the realities. Relatively few women or men want their friends and neighbors present, even in a home delivery room—in another room, perhaps, but not right there.

Stages of Labor

Classically, and in most lay texts, labor is divided into three stages: 1) the beginning of labor (contractions) to full dilatation of the cervix, 2) delivery of the baby, and 3) delivery of the placenta or afterbirth. These stages all involve contractions of the uterus, or labor. The immediate postdelivery period of about one hour is equally important to a mother's health, in contrast to the first and second stages when the fetus is the primary concern. This period is called the fourth stage of labor. We will put some emphasis on this and the third stage, not to frighten readers or potential parents, but to point out as graphically as possible, that *no pregnancy or delivery can be considered normal before, or until, the fourth stage is over.*

If one visualizes the baby, head down, chin on chest, inside a large (15 inch) ovoid balloon (the uterus), with the neck of the balloon representing the thick cervix, the work of the uterine contractions and the dilating force of the back of the fetal head may make some sense. Contractions of the uterus create pressure on the fetus and on the cervix. The cervix flattens out and opens (effaces and dilates) in response to the pressure of the head against this area. It flattens to paper thinness, and dilates to a maximum of 4 inches (10 centimeters). The initial work of the uterine contractions only flattens the cervix, and contributes little to dilatation. This is, or seems like, the longest phase of the first stage of labor, to complete effacement and 2 centimeters dilatation. By this time, most women think that labor should be all over. With first babies, effacement and dilatation begin three or four weeks before labor starts. In later pregnancies, early labor often begins with a soft but essentially closed, thick cervix, and effacement and dilatation proceed together during labor.

There is no way to predict the length of any labor but, in general, first labors are four to five hours longer than subsequent labors, and a history of rapid labors usually predicts another of similar duration. Two hours of good labor is probably the minimum, and twelve hours of progressively good labor, effective contractions, is about maximum in this day and age. The stories of eighteen to twenty-four hours, or two days, in labor are just about past; good obstetrical care demands that the obstetrician either enhance labor with medications, or get the baby out from above (a Caesarian section). However, what the laboring mother and husband think is good labor may not be the doctor's definition of good labor, so it is best not to count the hours but to keep the above flexible limits in mind. Breech babies (bottom or legs first) do not dilate or efface the cervix as efficiently as babies who are "head first." Also, positions of the head, other than the usual chin on the chest, may also prolong labor, for example, the top of the head, or the face, or simply failure of the baby's head to rotate in the pelvis so that it is facing toward the back of the pelvis.

Analgesia and Anesthesia in Labor and Childbirth

We have read that childbirth in China has never been considered a fit subject for acupuncture, though it is used for tubal ligations and other pelvic procedures. If it eliminates all sensation, it would not be acceptable to many of today's women; hypnosis* could present the same lack of sensation. Many of the European countries see no need for analgesia† or anesthesia** in childbirth, except with complications. The right amount of analgesia is the minimum which allows labor to progress normally, which keeps the mother comfortable, cooperative, in contact with the world, and most important, which has no negative effects on the baby. Within the range of normal obstetrics this can mean anything from literally nothing to being "knocked out," which is unnecessary, but is still a common request, almost a demand, from fearful women.

Complications during labor and delivery require an immediate shift to an appropriate anesthetic for a particular procedure. The mother has no control over these complications or their solution and, at that point, generally does not

---

* Hypnosis for childbirth is designed to eliminate the need for medication by creating amnesia for the discomfort. Good hypnotic subjects can separate the painful discomfort from the pleasurable discomfort (see p. 173) with selective amnesia. The increasing popularity of the Lamaze method in the past few years has almost eliminated requests for hypnotic childbirth, according to an obstetrician who used hypnosis very successfully for a number of years, and was sought out for his expertise in hypnosis.

† analgesia: medication to take the intense edge off discomfort.

** anesthesia: medication to eliminate discomfort.

care. Everyone has heard about that very rare patient who has absolutely no discomfort during labor; the uterus contracts efficiently, but she feels nothing except perhaps fullness and rectal pressure. However, labor is usually uncomfortable and many women have difficulty dealing with their discomfort, being able to cooperate with requests, and keeping their composure without some form of analgesia. But even these women, who represent the majority of laboring women in most hospitals, do well with what is really minimal relief of discomfort—minimal, if compared with the needs, desires, and routine practices of previous generations. But there must be emotional support from the people attending them, including husbands if present.

One of the best ways of enjoying oneself and keeping comfortable and aware for a normal delivery includes the use of infrequent, medium doses of intramuscular Demerol (an analgesic) during the first stage, perhaps even only one injection; whiffs of nitrous oxide (laughing gas) for the height of contractions in the second stage; and a pudendal block (local anesthetic) for the perineal discomfort associated with the stretching and the stitching up of an episiotomy (see below).

Demerol and nitrous oxide. Using this approach, a woman still needs and can use all of the knowledge, training, and techniques that she may have learned, but the acute edge of the discomfort is gone. A moderate amount of Demerol is a superb analgesic, and most people do not get to use it under such potentially pleasant circumstances. Carefully administered in relation to the actual time of delivery, it does not appear to affect the baby adversely, and can give a very good "high" to the mother. It still leaves one able to count, breathe, pant, or rub the belly, all techniques for distracting oneself during a contraction. Deep draughts of nitrous oxide, used only with the longer contractions in the delivery room, allow one to push effectively and remain alert except for five or ten seconds at the height of a sixty second contraction.

Pudendal block. The pudendal block is anesthesia injected deep in the perineum, anesthetizing only the perineum and the lowest part of the vagina. It leaves most, if not all of the vaginal feeling intact, the fullness, the desire to push, the total genital stimulation which is the basis for the superlative adjectives attached to childbirth *and* intercourse. Once the fetal head is delivered, the mother needs nothing else. Though the uterus continues to contract, the cervix has dilated to its utmost. This regimen leaves the baby, mother, father, and doctor comfortable, and no one has to play heroine or martyr, or try to do a controlled, slow delivery with the mother's hips intermittently eight to ten inches off the delivery table, in uncontrolled discomfort.

Spinal anesthetics. Other methods of analgesia and anesthesia are frequently used in normal obstetrics at the request of the patient, or if the doctor feels that the patient and the baby will benefit from them because of the patient's generally negative attitudes towards the whole procedure. The doctor has to have a cooperative patient to get a good baby, and fear and tension can prolong labor, sometimes to the detriment of both child and mother. Depressants (analgesics) are not advisable with premature babies (under 5½ pounds), but the importance of controlled delivery with prematures cannot be overemphasized. Rapid delivery of a small baby through an incompletely dilated cervix may be associated with minor and major fetal complications.

Several variations of spinal anesthetics are often used in the labor and delivery room. They have in common the elimination of all sensation from the lower abdomen down, including the legs. Caudal anesthesia and epidural anesthesia are *continuous* spinal anesthetics started in the labor room at about 4 to 5 centimeters dilatation. Spinal anesthesia may be used in the delivery room just prior to delivery, and is given in one single injection which lasts for at least an hour, often longer.

Spinal anesthetics came into popularity in the early and mid-1940s at about the same time that natural childbirth was beginning to attract attention and become cultish. Common to both was being awake and seeing one's baby born; mirrors to view the perineum went up in all of the delivery rooms. Doctors were happy because there was now no need for excessive use of drugs or general anesthesia which almost always resulted in "sleepy" babies. "Sleepy" babies do not give that initial cry when they emerge, and they are often a little limp for a while.

There is pleasure in seeing one's baby born (in the mirror), if the appearance of the bloody perineum or the newly born baby covered with blood-streaked, waxy material (the vernix caseosa) is not too disturbing. These are some of the reasons why seeing the movie in the prepared childbirth class or looking at pictures of a newly delivered child are important. They are good preparation and eliminate the surprises. There is pleasure in hearing the first cry and seeing and holding the baby immediately after birth. The pleasures of being awake during delivery do not rest entirely upon vision, however. Anesthetizing the entire pelvis and lower abdominal area with spinal anesthetics does not allow the total genital sensation which is essential for the ecstatic comments from the true devotees of natural childbirth (see p. 171).

Some complicated deliveries require the total relaxation of the pelvic organs and tissues which occurs with general or spinal anesthetics. General anesthesia is seldom, if ever, needed for normal obstetrics, though ether and sodium pentothal are undoubtedly still being used in some parts of the United States for normal, uncomplicated deliveries.

Scopalomine. Some mothers and grandmothers may say that they cannot remember a thing about their deliveries, but they will imply that it was all pretty horrendous. This amnesic nightmare is usually associated with the use of large doses of scopalomine, a drug used for its amnesic qualities as well as for its additional property of decreasing secretions in the mouth. The latter is necessary when general anesthesia is being used; most commonly this was ether. Those women who walked, or were wheeled, onto labor floors where scopalomine was being used often needed some quick "amnesia" themselves to forget what they were hearing, seeing, and feeling. Patients on "scope" look and sound as if they are in terrible pain. They do not respond to requests or questions, and often lack verbal or physical control; but they will smile at you four or five hours later, postdelivery, and tell you that it was great, that they didn't feel or remember a thing. Their next question is usually, "Is it a boy or a girl?" because they have not yet seen the baby.

If hospitals allow prenatal visits to their labor and delivery floors, one can rest assured that they do not use this drug routinely anymore. Otherwise, no expectant mother would ever come back after such a visit. If there are side-rails up on any bed (which used to be 100 percent of the time with "scope" patients), they are probably up for an early toxemic patient who must always be considered as potentially convulsive and about to fall out of bed.

It was obviously very difficult in the 1940s and 1950s, and in some hospitals even now, for those women who were really intent on natural childbirth not to lose their composure when they arrived on some labor floors. There are still moans and groans to be heard, but there are sometimes moans and groans with intercourse, too.

Natural Childbirth

The advances which have been made in medical science have added much that is good to everyone's life, including a marked decrease in maternal, fetal, and perinatal (postdelivery) deaths. These advances have also caused pregnancies to become special events, rare, and therefore "unnatural." No longer does one need to have eighteen pregnancies and three wives to obtain three viable children who will grow to adulthood and take over the farm, or the business, or support one in old age. Though we often seem to be surrounded by pregnancies, we never have the opportunity, as previous generations did, of annual or biannual childbirth in the other room or upstairs. For many emotional and physical reasons this is probably just as well. But remember, these women had no choice. What was happening in the upstairs room was defined as natural because it was inevitable. It was also natural to lose mothers, babies, and often subsequent fertility, due to complications of infections associated with long labors, or from hemorrhage. In the United States today, it is difficult to find either doctors or midwives who will do home deliveries *by choice*. Home deliveries are almost always a necessity when they occur, and the mothers and midwives or doctors* know that they are working with very poor odds, if an obstetrical emergency occurs.

Today, the extreme definitions of natural childbirth ignore all of the advantages of good obstetrical care and equate natural delivery with the home

* For example, the Frontier Nursing Service, Kentucky.

deliveries of the 1860s, or even of the 1920s and 1930s.* Home deliveries today have one statistic in their favor, but it is the same statistic that has been associated with all deliveries for a long time: namely, that 95 percent of all deliveries are uncomplicated, if we ignore prolonged labor. That percentage drops down to 90 percent if we include fetal complications; these latter complications may only be prematurity, but premature babies require special care and their needs are not always predictable. Even out of a carefully chosen group of expectant mothers who were selected for home deliveries (at their request), 10 percent eventually went to the hospital for delivery because of threatened complications.[9]

There are other factors which operate in favor of home deliveries now, which were not available in the past: antibiotics, fast transportation (highways and cars) for emergencies, and a world so full of people that it is difficult to be very far away from emergency care and expertise, at least in the urban and suburban areas of the United States.

But what is an emergency, and who recognizes it at home? We are concerned especially about the fourth stage of labor, but the first, second, and third stages have their problems, too. Such emergencies are notoriously unpredictable; there is no other medical specialty where seconds and minutes are so *routinely* important to fetal life (the first and second stages) and maternal life (the third and fourth stages). The absent or grossly irregular fetal heartbeat, or the bright red vaginal bleeding which appears suddenly are two signs of emergencies during labor which immediately gather all available expertise for instant diagnosis and treatment, if in a hospital. Neither of these signs are necessarily known to the mother who is either at home and wide awake, or in the hospital and wide awake. The primary emergency during the third and fourth stages is continued vaginal bleeding, either from failure of the uterus to contract, or expel the placenta, and rarely, failure of the blood to clot, before or after the third stage. These two emergencies are absolutely unpredictable.

If the mother is Rh negative and has had a previous abortion, with or without treatment (see p. 228), she should consider even a first pregnancy as potentially hazardous to the fetus, requiring close prenatal care as well as immediate postdelivery care. Some wives do not admit previous abortions to their husbands, and generally there is no need to do this. But often they will only admit them to their doctors when they feel they can trust them not to tell the husbands.

Also, the Maternal and Infant Care (MIC) program in Philadelphia has become increasingly concerned about the number of three- and four-day-old babies of home deliveries (exact percentages are difficult to obtain) who are

---

*Both authors were delivered at home in the 1920s. The physician parents-in-law of one continued to do home deliveries in decreasing numbers through the early 1960s.

being brought into the hospitals with pneumonias or other infections. Though very loving and concerned, casual "natural" households tend to be casual about babies, too.

We are being realistic, not judgmental, when we emphasize that couples who find themselves weighing fetal and maternal mortality statistics, which vary with the population studied, against their home definition of natural, should do some more reading. We are not forgetting the financial aspects. "No insurance" and "No money for doctors and hospitals" are some of the common reasons which determine a desire for home deliveries. Mothers and fathers can live on very little money, food, or clothing with relative ease and fun, especially if they know that it does not need to last forever. But babies cost a minimum of 60 cents a day (200 dollars a year) once they are out of the uterus. Contraception costs between 25 and 50 dollars a year (not calculated on daily frequency). If there is no money, perhaps weighing these figures is more to the point. Most states have some type of medical assistance for indigent care. It is available to those who choose to live indigently, and to those who have to live indigently.

If we define natural childbirth as it should be defined in the 1970s, as the wife and husband participating in a rare, mutual, sexual experience that is relatively risk-free and comfortable, but that needs some help and expertise, this kind of childbirth is possible in most hospitals and with many doctors. There are even doctors who allow the husband to deliver the baby after the head is out.

"Natural childbirth is NOT necessarily painless, an endurance test, a failure when anesthesia is used, a denial of achievements of modern obstetrics, a denial of the importance of the doctor . . . an hypnotic episode, or a cult."[10] "Natural childbirth is fearless, trained, relaxed, easier and satisfying."[11] Realistically, the latter definition is slightly exaggerated in its use of the word "fearless," but when done even reasonably well, training in natural childbirth decreases anxiety and allows mothers and fathers to stay in control.

The potential of pleasure. Perhaps the reader has noted a paradox here in our approach to two sexual areas which we say can have the same or a similar end point. In intercourse we have put some emphasis on being knowledgeable enough and secure enough to be able to *lose* control; in childbirth, our emphasis has been on being knowledgeable and secure enough to be able to *stay* in control. The genital orientation of childbirth and intercourse, which also defines them as sexual areas, has obscured information on both activities for generations. As a result, many conflicts involving guilt, shame, and the inability to verbalize feelings and questions still remain.

Invariably, mention of the sexual aspects of any genital stimulation which occurs without the benefit of the penis, whether it be abortion, childbirth, intercourse, or homosexual stimulation, is cause for denials and qualifications, not all of which come from males. Some women have had bad experiences in childbirth, or are so terrified, before the fact, that they are unwilling to inform themselves enough to make it a good experience. Denial of the potential for a good experience in childbirth takes much less effort, and fits neatly with what is still the opinion of a majority of women and men about childbirth. The emotional overlay in any one of the above sexual situations is extremely important, and just feeling "loose" and knowledgeable will not always make genital stimulation orgasmic, though the experiences need not be that intense to give pleasure. It is enough to know that the potential of pleasure exists, and may be comparable for some to the "skimming" mentioned previously (p. 57). The adjectives "fantastic," "exhilarating," "unbelievable," were used many, many times in the 1940s and 1950s in women's magazines to describe, inadequately, a childbirth experience which was for the writers, clearly an intense orgasmic experience.

Even men should be able to understand this, if they can acknowledge the pleasurable feelings associated with bowel movements; the pushing feels good, even though occasionally uncomfortable, and often it is a reflex pushing which is not under conscious control. There is even the sense of relief and peace afterwards. For women, the pleasurable feelings are far more intense, at least once or twice in their lifetimes, but only if they are secure enough to allow them to be, and if there are no complications which tend to distort the experience.

The urge to push is an amazing thing. It takes everything out of you and in some ways reminded me of a terrifically strong orgasm.[12]

Some observers feel that "prepared" women who seem unable to push when requested to do so late in labor, lose some of the intensity of the experience. Their difficulty in pushing may be related to fear of fecal discharge, which is not valid if there has been an admission enema, or it may be related to a reluctance to permit themselves the necessary grunts, groans, or moans in public. This kind of "holding back" can also limit orgasmic experience in intercourse. The rectal stretch receptors are receiving stimuli in intercourse, childbirth, and anal intercourse. The same pleasurable feelings, though intensified, are clearly present in childbirth. They are also associated with the tortured look of orgasm, and followed by a tremendous sense of relief, exhaustion, and contentment, postdelivery.

There is often some real resentment from the delivered mother when her contented stage (which might be compared with the resolution phase of intercourse) is interrupted with another request to push, or help with the third stage of labor; there is often a very real "don't bother me" look and sound. There is no need or even desire for multiple orgasms in this situation. Many women report well-remembered imagery, music, or simply the kaleidoscope of visual and aural sensations noted in the beginning of this section. Mothers who deliver with this kind of experience will almost immediately reach, indiscriminately, for the nearest living thing for warmth, closeness, and sharing. This may be the baby if it is in her arms soon enough, or her husband if he is lucky enough to be standing in the right spot, though he may be passed over for the nearby nurse or anesthetist.

These observations are not based solely on limited personal experience but also upon observations in several hospitals with a "natural" orientation, questioning of friends, and discussions with obstetricians who prefer to practice their obstetrics this way *when they are allowed to* by their patients.

> *However, I can't be sure I won't be scared again in future labor. At this transition point, a woman is very close if not actually in another plane of existence. Our society doesn't recognize these other planes of existence, and therefore most of us have no training or familiarity with it. Without fear this might possibly be the highest moment in a woman's life.*[13]

The Lamaze method.   The Lamaze method of natural childbirth is extremely popular and effective and does not have to be as cultish as some of its practitioners would lead one to believe (see p. 173). We would like to point out some areas where trouble can arise, if some of the procedures are taken too literally. We feel that it puts too much emphasis on the father's participation. There is even the implication that it will not work if the father is not there and trained to be strong when the laboring mother has lapses. The father's function is carefully spelled out: He is supposed to stand or sit by the labor bed and make sure that his wife does everything she is supposed to do at the right time. If she gets momentarily overwhelmed, he is to speak in a firm voice and get her to compose herself again. This is supposed to work because he, too, has been practicing with her. But we have seen fathers get carried away with their duties, and those firm voices become "Teutonic commands." Laboring mothers do not need Teutonic commands from anyone, especially husbands, or a figurative slap in the face to cure momentary hysteria. On the other hand, the trained, prepared father rarely gets overwhelmed with the realities; he is usually informed and anxious to help. But even some trained fathers are there under duress, "See how I'm suffering, but don't touch me." This is disturbing for hospital personnel to observe unless they are comfortable with the knowledge that the male-female relationship in marriage has many different and apparently workable bases.

The home and class exercises associated with Lamaze require male participation, and can put a shy, pregnant woman in many ungainly and, perhaps to her or her husband, unattractive positions. Not everyone feels this secure about herself or even wants to. The value of many of these exercises would seem to be primarily that of desensitizing oneself in private, or in small groups, to the awkward and ungainly positions which must be assumed later in public.

Actually, most pregnant women could "do" the Lamaze method quite effectively by leading instead of following instructions, by telling their husbands how they can help, and by being sure that the doctor and the hospital have been chosen for their understanding of what these women would like to accomplish. We wish more of the Lamaze teachers would recognize this potential for resentment of male authority figures, and modify their techniques, for those who need techniques, so that all women might have some reassurance that they really can handle the details of this childbirth by themselves, if necessary, or if desired. The unmarried woman, and the married woman with an absent husband, need and should have the same assurance. We have recently discovered that we are not alone in this feeling about this very popular method of preparing for childbirth.

Comments, Questions, and Answers about Labor and Its Procedures

Contractions. For generations, uterine contractions during labor have been referred to as pains and often still are. "Have your pains started yet?" It is not a word that induces a positive approach to childbirth, and it is only slowly disappearing from literature and usage.

Contractions are best described as an increasingly intense, but dull, ache in the low back area. They can be very intense, but seldom if ever are they perceived as sharp, stabbing, or knifelike. In the front pelvic area, they are more like diffuse, very intense menstrual cramping, but again, seldom if ever sharp. Also, quite unlike most severe menstrual cramping, the discomfort disappears between contractions.

The uterine cramping and discomfort with early spontaneous abortions and premature deliveries (seven months or later) appear to have a much sharper quality than the contractions experienced with labor at term. Contractions, even at their strongest and longest in the late second stage, just prior to delivery, seldom last more than 55 or 60 seconds. The height of the discomfort is perhaps only the middle 10 or 15 seconds of that period.

The gradual onset of *spontaneous* labor, which allows one to adapt slowly to the increasing intensity, is in contrast to the rapid onset of good contractions when labor is artificially *induced* with medicine (pitocin) by vein or injection. One has to be very practiced and knowledgeable to adapt quickly to this rapid onset of intense contractions. They are no more intense than those experienced in late spontaneous labor, but there is little time for adaptation. If the intention of the expectant mother is to do her labor and delivery as naturally as possible, induction of labor for the first experience tends to make this difficult. Induction of labor should not be selected without good reason; there are a number of medically good reasons, but some inductions are often scheduled only for convenience.

However, adaptation in both situations is possible, even when contractions are occurring every two minutes and each lasting for a minute, as they do in the late second stage. It is difficult at times not to get preoccupied with the pelvic pressure which continues to exist between contractions, and makes one forget about the need to relax during that free minute that is available.

Practicing counting to eight slowly over a forty second interval is extremely helpful and a variation of Lamaze; when five is reached, the height of the contraction is over, and it can only get better from that point on. Husbands can count, put firm pressure on the sacral (lower back) area when it feels as if it is about to burst. The firmer and larger the hand, the better it feels; this almost makes it a masculine job. The skin of the back and the lower abdomen can become extremely sensitive during labor, and the rubbing and light stroking recommended by Lamaze can be very irritating, even with talcum powder on the skin.

A few grunts, groans, or moans are the consequence of the reflex desire to push, and the evidence, also, of some breathholding with tension. These sounds should not be interpreted as failures or lapses. Women with high expectations for themselves, frequently spend time apologizing to personnel for these noises, "I'm sorry I'm not a good patient." Good patients are not defined by absence of lapses or noises, but by their ability to bounce back into a cooperative, cognitive state with a little assistance.

We have heard teenagers and adults say that their first experience with intercourse was so painful, or their menstrual cramps so overwhelming that they just know they were not meant to have children. These activities and feelings may involve the same area, but labor and delivery have a wholly different gestalt and feeling; different emotions are brought to it.

At the other extreme, are the women who wish to appear casual about impending delivery or, when describing how casual they were with their last delivery, will go into detail about how they were in early labor at a dinner party and didn't want to disturb the hostess, so they continued with their dinner and then went off to the hospital to deliver two or three hours later. This kind of bravado can be dangerous. The need for general anesthesia is never predictable and the anesthetic risk in obstetrical patients is notoriously higher than with other surgical patients. This risk is related to vomiting (a characteristic sign at 8 centimeters dilatation) and aspiration of solid food particles into the lungs. This regurgitation may occur reflexly in the early stages of general anesthesia. The stomach stops working during early labor; ingested food stays there. The doctor may have carefully said "Nothing by mouth except fluids" with the onset of early labor, but the dieting, pregnant female with the end clearly in sight, often forgets and eats joyously, or simply for the bravado effect.

Why do you have to be on your back when you deliver when the side is supposed to be more natural and more comfortable? The position is a compromise to allow the advantages of good obstetrics: a controlled delivery, an episiotomy, the use of forceps if necessary, and a good visual field. The real comfort during labor and delivery comes from the knee-chest position, whether on the side or on the back. This is approximated during delivery by having the legs up and supported under the knees, and a pillow or pillows under the head and upper back. During labor, the knee-chest position is easy to assume in the side position and requires very little energy to maintain. It is also a reflex reaction to the discomfort in the pelvis, much like "curling up" with menstrual cramps.

The birthchairs of antiquity allowed the knee-chest position, but remember that gravity has very little to do with enhancing the effectiveness of contractions. Also, there were no analgesics used at that time; their use tends to make the laboring mother a little unsteady in the walking or squatting position, or on her hands and knees. Experience leads us to believe that even those mothers who used birthchairs were probably strapped in for a portion of the time. There is no need to be lying down during labor unless or until it becomes uncomfortable to be walking, standing, or squatting, or until some form of analgesia is used to take the edge off the discomfort.

Why the straps on the wrists and the leg supports?   Initially the trapped feeling is real, but 1) the straps are not tight, 2) the wrist straps keep hands aimed at the handles on the side of the delivery table; these handles are very useful to pull back on, which enhances pushing down when the pushing feeling comes, and 3) the straps keep uncontrolled activities of the hands and legs under some control. This is not a very convincing argument for some women who know they have control during delivery and want to hold their own knees up to accomplish the pushing, but realistically, until *all* women feel that childbirth is a good, nonfrightening experience, and until they and their doctor are very sure of their control and reactions during late labor, straps will continue to be used. If a patient has a good relationship with her obstetrician and feels strongly about some procedures which will not interfere with the doctor's ideas of what delivery should be, there are always modifications that can be made. But from the physician's point of view, it is almost impossible to do a good, controlled delivery and be prepared for all emergencies, with the bed or delivery table out flat. This means that legs have to be supported either by a laboring mother who is in complete control at all times, or by leg supports, which allow relaxation between contractions.

> Now, if you ever wondered about the word labor I can tell you that it means what it sounds like—hard work. Sara would grab her knees until her breath gave out, take another breath and push again. Push until her face was beet red. Push until the blood vessels in her squeezed eyelids stood out purple and large. Push until the contraction was over and exhaustion overcame her and I would let her slump back against her pillow to sleep until the next contraction.[14]

Why the episiotomy?   Good uterine contractions will push the baby out eventually, regardless of what kind of anesthesia is used. But spinal anesthetics eliminate much of the pushing reflex. The mother can push on request, but she cannot determine how hard, or how successful she is. Forceps are usually used with spinal anesthesia to shorten the second stage. An episiotomy is almost essential when forceps are used. During natural or pudendal block deliveries, the perineum quickly stretches to a paper-thin consistency over the baby's head, before complete dilatation of the introitus occurs. The lower vaginal wall is also stretched. If a mother is pushing indiscriminately, without control, or too hard, tears of the perineum may occur and occasionally these extend into the rectum. Repair of a straight incision gives a much better postdelivery result than repair of a spontaneous, often jagged, and elongated tear. An incision also gives immediate room for the head without prolonged or excessive stretching of the vaginal wall. The primary reason for using an episiotomy, is to maintain a firm introitus and lower vaginal muscular control, postdelivery, as well as to prevent prolonged stretching of the anterior and posterior vaginal walls which may cause uncomfortable bowel and bladder symptoms in later life (see Cystocoele and Rectocoele, p. 325). Episiotomy techniques have changed, even in the past five or six years, and seldom give more than minimal discomfort, if they are done in the midline rather than extended laterally. If done through the paper-thin perineum, the incision causes no discomfort; there seems to be a natural anesthesia at the time. If the incision is done prior to this time, it would be uncomfortable unless spinal anesthesia or a pudendal block was used.

Why the intravenous bottle and the needle in the arm when the mother is in the delivery room? This is usually preventive medicine. If an emergency occurs and there is a need for blood or rapid anesthesia, the vein is open and ready. Veins disappear very fast with shock from loss of blood, are often difficult to find, and valuable time is lost. Also, long labors with nothing by mouth, or minimal fluids and ice chips, cause patients to lose body fluids and become dehydrated. Replacement of these fluids is often necessary for the well-being of the patient.

Is shaving necessary? More and more doctors are writing "no shave" or "clip only" orders for their obstetrical patients, and even more frequently for other pelvic procedures, such as dilatation and currettage. Most women do not feel quite whole, or feel very naked with a shaved perineum; also, the time when the pubic hair is growing back again is certainly the most uncomfortable and itchy part of the postdelivery period.

Is the enema necessary? Why can't it be done at home? Admission enemas are also beginning to disappear, as vaginal examinations during labor are replacing rectal examinations. However, see delivery and pushing and make a decision (p. 174). Enemas do not stimulate the onset of labor, but they often stimulate the onset of good labor when given in early labor. Therefore, enemas at home could result in good labor at home, which is often quite uncomfortable and frightening when one is alone or en route to the hospital.

Why a catheter to remove urine from the bladder? A full bladder gets in the way and is more likely to be damaged during delivery; it is often difficult to urinate after delivery even if the bladder has been emptied and there has been no apparent cause for damage. Contamination of the perineal area, or the baby, is not a problem; urine is not unclean, but repeated catheterization post-delivery because of damage, can create further urinary problems.

Why must forceps be used? See Episiotomy. Forceps are not inherently bad instruments when used properly. They are used only with contractions, to assist and guide the head in its downward path, creating a controlled delivery, and shortening the second stage when the head has not rotated properly or is in somewhat less than optimal position.

There is a higher incidence of "posterior labors" (labor which is prolonged because of failure of the head to rotate even though well down in the pelvis) in the black population. Posterior labors are not only prolonged, but create much more intense back discomfort. The back discomfort of any labor is usually related to this position of the head prior to its normal rotation; the discomfort is relieved somewhat when spontaneous rotation of the head occurs (from facing forward or to the side to facing the back).

Breech labors and deliveries (bottoms, one leg, or two legs first) are also often prolonged because the breech is not a good dilator of the cervix. They can and do deliver spontaneously, but are frequently assisted by hand to shorten the second stage for the sake of the baby and the mother. There are forceps designed to assist the delivery of the "aftercoming" head in breech deliveries.

Only rarely is the face or the forehead the presenting part of the baby, but in such cases, labor will be prolonged and require obstetrical assistance.

*Why do doctors "rupture the membranes?"** Rupturing the membranes through the dilated cervical opening releases amnionic fluid to the outside by

---

* One way to visualize the relation of the fetus to its membranes, which enclose the amnionic fluid around the fetus, is to imagine pushing your fist and arm into the side of a large, soft, ovoid, fluid-filled balloon. The fist represents the fetus, the arm the umbilical cord, and the larger shoulder area, the placenta; all of these structures, including the balloon, are derived from the fertilized ovum and are enclosed in the intrauterine cavity, with no attachment to the wall of the cavity except a tenuous, vascular one at the placental site.

The layer of the balloon over the fist represents the skin of the fetus; this is continuous with that over the arm, and represents the covering of the umbilical cord. At the point where the umbilical cord arises from the placenta, its covering reflects back on the wall of the intrauterine cavity. Thus the fist (fetus) is floating in a fluid-filled, completely enclosed cavity. The membranes which reflect back closely over the wall of the uterine cavity are therefore covering the opening of the cervix as well. As the cervix dilates, the membranes are visible with fluid behind them, or in late labor, the baby's head behind the membrane.

way of the vagina. This may happen spontaneously either with the onset of uterine contractions and the resulting increase in fluid pressure, or usually by the time the cervix has dilated to 4 or 5 cms. The intensity of the uterine contractions and their effectiveness usually increases after some or all of the fluid is released. Doctors may choose to enhance spontaneous labor by artificially rupturing membranes early in labor or, if labor is induced with medication, they will rupture membranes with the onset of good contractions. Experienced obstetricians, who have judged that the cervix and the uterus are at the right stage to respond with the onset of labor, may rupture the membranes to induce labor without medication.

To be *born with a caul* is to be born with the membranes over the face, which usually means that there was a prolonged labor without spontaneous rupture of the membranes until the moment of birth. A *dry birth,* no amnionic fluid released, also implies a long labor for the same reasons. Both phrases have been in pregnancy mythology for a long time and have the connotation of difficult labor and delivery.

Does having one Caesarian section mean that the next delivery must also be by Caesarian?   This depends on why the section was done and, to some extent, on the doctor's experiences with previous postsection deliveries. If it was done because the pelvis was too small, repeat sections are usually indicated. If it was done because of placental bleeding, fetal distress, or a poor labor, repeat sections are not always indicated. Labor may be induced or sections scheduled for early delivery of babies with Rh problems, or in the diabetic or toxemic mother. The bad reputation of Caesarian sections stems from the days prior to antibiotics and more refined surgical and anesthetic techniques. It is still best for the baby to be delivered "naturally," from below, though women with six or seven repeat sections are not unknown, and in fact, repeat sections may be maternal option and decision, if the risks of vaginal delivery and labor with a scarred uterus are explained and well understood.

Is the postpartem (postdelivery) depression, or "third day blues" common to everyone?   It may seem strange, but the baby's arrival is often an anticlimax to nine-and-a-half months of expectancy. The "third day blues" are usually brief, if they occur at all, but they can be very weepy, even with a second or third child. "I can't cope" is also a part of this feeling; the physical taking care of this baby is exhausting and demanding at a time when the exhilaration of delivery is leaving. There is no time to enjoy the baby; his or her physical needs dominate. The techniques of breast-feeding do not come that naturally to many mothers and may initially create additional problems of inadequacy. Even sterilizing bottles or figuring out how to use the throwaway kind looks overwhelming for a brief time. If it isn't the third day blues, it can easily be the first or second day home with the baby, or a week later when the baby's schedule has not yet meshed with the other demands of homekeeping. Severe prolonged depressions are rare and are often related to evidence of marked, emotional instability prior to the pregnancy, or the responsibility for the baby may be the last straw which triggers depression. It is not predictable.

Breast-feeding

Breast-feeding is another natural experience. Sex is natural. Childbirth is natural. But "natural doesn't always mean easy or trivial. . . . Sexual intercourse is not like shaking hands and having babies is not like blowing bubbles. Being fully human isn't always easy—ecstasy has its price."[15]

Perhaps this is why Dr. Spock's *Baby and Child Care* devotes its second longest chapter (28 pages) to breast-feeding versus twelve pages for bottle-feeding. Also, women have been liberated for so long from some of the drudgeries of homekeeping that there are few experienced mothers around to instruct their daughters. Instruction must come from peer groups, such as the La Leche League, or a superb, candid, gutsy book on breast-feeding by Elger and Olds which we will refer to again.[16]

Besides washers and dryers, the liberating advances of technology and attitudes have also included a variety of nursing bottles and sterile substitutes for mother's milk.* These were such a welcome addition to living that it is now extremely difficult for any individual to fight the tide and go back and restore any of those "drudgeries" of the past which they think still have some value. To restore breast-feeding, which was once called confining, and to give it legitimacy by calling it pleasurable, requires a special kind of thinking. It can create ambivalence, and demands great strength of convictions. Nursing mothers are still a minority group, as are natural childbirthers and sexually liberated women.

Girls and women who have grown up in a noisy "breasts equal sex" culture may find breasts and babies an unattractive combination. They may be appalled by the idea of self-stimulated pleasure (perhaps a difficulty with the concept of masturbation). They may fight the whole "keep 'em barefoot, pregnant, and at home" feeling, a feeling which may be unwittingly prompted by a husband's active encouragement of nursing. "Goddamn it, I'm neither a cow or a baby machine."

A woman who finds herself pregnant and then with a child in her arms before she has really become used to being close to anyone (and this can happen in the best of marriages) may have difficulty doing anything more than the essentials of diapering, feeding, and bathing that baby. She is not prepared for

---

*A World Health Organization (WHO) official noted that new mothers in emerging countries considered bottle-feeding to be one of their newly gained luxuries; breast-feeding is considered primitive, and is declining in popularity.

the closeness demanded and resulting from nursing this child. By the time the second or third child comes along, nursing may look attractive and even desirable, if she has become able to enjoy this closeness and not be threatened by it.

A woman who has been living with the right man long enough to be comfortable with her own sexuality and, more important, has the time (a flexible working schedule in or outside of the home) is usually a very successful nursing mother, if she wishes to nurse. The anxious, harried mother, who needs her sleep or her work, may not fare so well, at least initially; it is the first three-to-five-weeks experience which really determines how long nursing will continue.

Bottle-feeding should not be considered a "bad" thing. If strong, warm arms and a broad chest, with the sound of a heart beating underneath, are essential to those first few months of security for the child, fathers as well as mothers, sisters, and brothers should be able to participate and share the pleasurable feelings. Given all of this loving and closeness, it hardly matters what the nipple is made of as long as the nutrient is there and the child is sucking.

Some new fathers are content to be onlookers and truly enjoy this. Some feel left out of the close relationship between mother and nursing child, a feeling possibly accentuated by having been excluded for a time prior to delivery, too. But some mothers have no other real closeness in their sexual and nonsexual lives except this relationship with their nursing child.

Nursing or not nursing has become such a personal thing, a real option, that it is only the mother who can make the decision. It should not be a decision based on coercive propaganda from either side about the benefits to the baby or to the family, but rather a decision made on the basis of her desires, her needs, and her life style. Having made this decision, she will need emotional support and cooperation, and must always be aware of the need for adapting, if nursing or not nursing becomes a negative rather than a positive experience for her or her family.

Proselytizing literature about breast-feeding often utilizes guilt or selfishness as motivating factors: guilt about what one is not doing medically and emotionally for one's baby, and selfishness about not wanting to devote the time or energy to breast-feeding, whether or not one really has the time. The vast majority of babies are bottle fed and thrive and survive and have for several generations. It can be equally selfish, depending on family circumstances, to have the entire household revolving around the nursing mother and her schedule and her unique pleasures. Both kinds of selfishness can create guilt. Even the awareness that comes to some nursing mothers that the pleasure of nursing sometimes can approach or attain an orgasmic level (with uterine and clitoral sensations as well as brief feelings of pelvic congestion) can be guilt producing. The Elger and Olds book is excellent on the need for maintaining sexual relationships with the father while nursing.[17]

Again, nursing a child is a *maternal* option because it truly is natural even for flat-chested women and for women who have never been pregnant and who adopt small babies.[18] It is the rare woman who cannot nurse her child if she feels positive about it, and is surrounded by people who feel the same way; it is the equally rare child who absolutely needs mother's milk and will not thrive, physically or emotionally, without it.

To some women who believe in nursing, it is still an act that should be confined to the home.

"What are you talking about, nursing or showing the world what you can do?" Mrs. I. W. asked. "Too often, girls want everyone within two miles to know it."

She conceded however, that done correctly, it was possible to nurse almost anywhere without attracting attention.

"But they are such shimmering moments, and there are so few of them in a lifetime, that I didn't care to share them," she added.[19]

References

1. Howard J. Osofsky, *The Pregnant Teenager: A Medical, Educational, and Social Analysis* (Springfield, Ill.: Charles C Thomas, 1972).

2. Elise Fitzpatrick, Sharon Reeder, and Luigi Mastroianni, Jr., *Maternity Nursing*, 12th ed. (Philadelphia: J. B. Lippincott Company, 1971).

3. *Ibid*, pp. 572-574.

4. *Ibid*, pp. 174-190.

5. *Ibid*.

6. Talcott Parsons, "Definitions of Health and Illness in the Light of American Values and Social Structures," *Social Structure and Personality* (Glencoe, Ill.: The Free Press, 1964); see Fitzpatrick, Reeder, Mastroianni, *Maternity Nursing*.

7. *Birth Book* (Dallas, Texas: Genesis Press, Inc., 1972).

8. C. DeLeon, "The Day We Had a Son," *Philadelphia Bulletin*, 14 November 1971.

9. "Birth on the Kitchen Table," *Life*, 18 August 1972.

10. Grantley Dick-Read, *Childbirth Without Fear*, 4th rev. ed. (New York: Har/ Row Books, Harper & Row, 1972).

11. *Ibid*.

12. "The Birth of Erie, by Judy, November 1971," *Birth Book*.

13. "The Birth of Ariel, by Estelle, April 30, 1970," *Birth Book*.

14. DeLeon, "The Day We Had a Son."

15. Sidney Callahan, "Childbirth Backlash," *National Catholic Reporter,* 5 November 1971.

16. Marvin S. Elger and Sally W. Olds, *The Complete Book of Breast-Feeding* (New York: Workman Publishing Co., Inc., 1972).

17. *Ibid.*

18. "Adopt and Breast-Feed," *Newsweek,* 13 August 1973.

19. Enid Nemy, "Breast-Feeding in Public a Growing Trend," The *New York Times,* 29 January 1973.

7

. . . . .Reproduction:. . . . .
Contraception and Abortion

Q: What were you using for contraception that time?

A: We didn't use anything. It has only been two or three times, and we aren't really ready to make that kind of commitment yet.

Nineteen-year-old female

IF THERE IS real concern about preventing pregnancy, every act of intercourse and some of its variations must be regarded as having reproductive potential at any time in the menstrual cycle. We will discuss some high-risk methods of contraception which many couples use successfully; but when a pregnancy occurs, the degree of risk with any contraceptive method is irrelevant. The fetus will either deliver spontaneously nine-and-a-half months later, or it must be removed from the uterus (an induced abortion). Those opposed to abortion should remember that 10 percent or more of all diagnosed first pregnancies abort spontaneously in the first three months. Awareness of this fact may prevent an unwanted marriage or at least postpone one. But many individuals are surprised at the quick turnabout their thinking takes when they are suddenly faced with the reality of an embryo in their uterus; abortion often becomes the only answer.

It was one of those crazy, wild nights. All of my friends were virgins when they married. It never occurred to me that I would be any different. But there was this guy and he was fun, and it happened. There was no alcohol or drugs or anything like that. It just happened. I haven't seen him since. I didn't tell him. I've always been against abortion. I couldn't understand how people could do that. Now I know. Sometimes they have to. I had to. I certainly understand my patients better, and probably myself, too.

Twenty-four-year-old graduate student, six months postabortion,
still a little emotional about the abortion, but sexually active with a
"nice, good guy," and now using adequate contraception

Our discussion will be directed primarily at methods of contraception, their pros and cons, their perils and pitfalls, and some points of good and bad usage; attitudes about methods and the need for mutual agreement on methods will be discussed later with respect to specific age groups. However, there are some attitudes toward contraception which are common to almost all age groups which we will note here so they may be considered in relation to specific methods.

The *desire to have children,* to reproduce, to perpetuate oneself in some form is a very real part of human nature which is quite aside from pure physical sex. This desire can even take the form of adoption of a child by a single male or female, or the wish of a single female to have a child of her own. What appears to be more universal is the *desire to retain the ability to reproduce;* this delays many decisions about sterilization, often at the subconscious level. Even those who do not want any children and resent societal pressures to have them, are less intense about eliminating the ability to reproduce.

I strongly resent your use of the terms "extended honeymoon" and "empty nest" to describe childless couples under and over 30. My husband and I are 29 and we neither view ourselves as on an extended honeymoon nor heading toward an empty nest. We enjoy our childless life-style and have made a choice to continue it for a number of years, if not permanently. . . . The life-style we have chosen is a viable alternative—and the choice of many couples.[1]

The need for sexual activity, homosexual or heterosexual, is also a real part of male and female human nature, and we have a responsibility to ourselves and to other human beings to use these natural drives wisely; we need not eliminate them, but we can modify them. What is frequently forgotten, if only temporarily and at the wrong time, is a responsibility toward the potential embryo, the "other human being." Those who oppose abortion are concerned about the embryo's right to live, and also have legitimate concerns about destroying life. Those favoring abortion are equally concerned about the embryo's right to live a good life in a healthy environment. Any act of intercourse that is unprotected by contraception involves a responsibility to this potential third person. Obviously there is legitimate concern for human life on both sides of the controversy, and it must, therefore, be regarded as a significant aspect of our discussion and of the reader's thinking.

To contracept adequately, we have to give up temporarily the ability to reproduce. This can affect individual behavior in the sexual area in many subtle ways which, in turn, can affect performance and pleasure.

. . . nothing can come

Of us: of me with my grim techniques
Or you who have sealed your womb
With a ring of convulsive rubber:[2]

It is not often that diaphragms get into poetry, but in one sentence, James Dickey has illustrated his sorrowful acknowledgment of the reality of contraception, adultery, and risk, and their influence on pleasure.

For many, much of the pleasure and excitement of sex stems from the risk involved; the risk of pregnancy, the risk of being discovered, the defiance of parents and of generally accepted mores. When the risk is absent, interest may decline. Much of this may be subconscious, and these individuals may wonder why sex is not as good as it once was. But, consider heightened interest in sex during ovulation (which may have some basis in physiology), or when someone mistakenly thinks she is ovulating, or during those seven days when she is not taking the pill (see p. 61). Sometimes there is decreased interest in sex when young women start using the pill—the 100 percent, "no risk" contraceptive, if used properly. Occasionally, there is a decline in interest after vasectomy, tubal ligation, or hysterectomy, none of which affects hormones in any way (see p. 215). A marriage license obtained after a few years of living together legalizes sexual activity and decreases that risk, and occasionally will also decrease interest.

Another important factor, which is perhaps a corollary of the influence of risk upon pleasure, is that when the risk of pregnancy is *voluntarily* decreased to zero, the individual has clearly committed himself or herself to the philosophy of "sex for fun." There was even a brief period when some Catholic theologians felt that use of a condom was within their definition of sex as procreative activity, but only if there was a pinhole in the end of the condom. This would maintain the semblance of risk of pregnancy with intercourse, but, in their minds, would allow the pleasures as well. Actually a pinhole in a condom, or in a diaphragm, presents only one problem: It is a defect which may give rise to a much larger hole which *will* allow sperm to pass through.

Many individuals can talk about "sex for fun" at the intellectual level, but indulging in it, and "indulge" is the word that describes their feelings most accurately, is an active statement which goes against many of their own subconscious taboos, taboos which even the present generation of teenagers has grown up with. Guilt about sex for fun can be real, though often hidden, and this kind of guilt and good sex are not usually compatible.

Giving up the ability to reproduce via voluntary sterilization or involuntary hysterectomy should be regarded as a permanent method of contraception (p. 323). For some, the thought of being sterile primarily, or secondarily as a result of a voluntary act, is a little like "dying," and it is also often equated with loss of one's femininity or masculinity. It is an equally strange and paradoxical feeling for a couple to know that there really should be no more children in their family and to know, also, that neither of them wishes to be sterile. This is a problem which now faces "finished" families constantly, with the increasing availability and ease of sterilization procedures.

It is not uncommon to find adolescent girls or early menopausal women being casual though knowledgeable about contraception. These two groups often have in common an insecurity about their femaleness. Their conscious rationalization may come from their feeling that they cannot become pregnant because they are not yet women, or they are past being womanly. Their unconscious feelings must stem from a very real desire to have proof, in the form of a pregnancy, that they are both women and womanly. The child is incidental to their feelings about themselves at the time when they are being careless about contraception. Where abortion fits into the picture in these two groups, after they have proven their fertility, will vary with the individual.

Adolescent, and some adult, males may have some of the same feelings about manliness and virility; they may be desperate to impregnate a girl, any girl. One of the classic bits of male humor is boasting about how many babies have been left behind. Whether or not the babies or pregnancies in fact exist, the apparent demonstration of fertility, the ability to impregnate, and the just plain sexual prowess, somehow compensate for any negative stigmata.

A male's failure to use contraception may also indicate that he is very much in love: "If she gets pregnant, maybe then she will marry me; I have to have her." Any male who thinks along these lines should be forewarned that abortion often becomes the only reasonable solution for women faced with an unwanted pregnancy and an unwanted man.

If we disregard the spontaneous one-night-stands or unpremeditated sexual activity, another frequent reason for avoiding contraception is that it is not natural. For those naturalists, all of the publicity about population control or responsibility to a third person has no meaning; these arguments seem to have little bearing on "you and me, now." "We don't have any children, we are just making love naturally, the best of all possible ways."

But who has defined what is natural, civilized sexual activity? To contracept adequately, something foreign has to be introduced, directly or indirectly, between the ovum and the sperm. For the naturalists, this something cannot be any form of abstinence, because abstinence is not biologically natural.

Until recent years, romantic literature had little or nothing to say about contraception, partly because it would intrude on the romanticism, but also because the authors would be unable to sell their books.* There were a few

---

* We must acknowledge the assistance of Dr. Robert F. Lucid, Professor of Contemporary American Literature at the University of Pennsylvania in confirming our suspicions about contraception in American literature prior to *The Group* by Mary McCarthy, and *Goodbye, Columbus* by Philip Roth.

accidental pregnancies, but no contraception in the novels of Fitzgerald. There were no contraceptives in Robert and Maria's sleeping bag.[3] Hemingway mentioned condoms only in the abstract:

> . . . the worn light bulbs of our discoveries and the empty condoms of our great loves float with no significance against one single, lasting thing—the stream.[4]

The mechanical and peripheral aspects of lovemaking were described by him only when love had clearly become a disaster:

> . . . you loved me so much that love was all that mattered. Love was the greatest thing, wasn't it? Love was what we had that no one else had or could ever have: And you were a genius and I was your whole life. I was your partner and your little black flower. Slop. Love is just another dirty lie. Love is ergoipiol pills to make me come around because you were afraid to have a baby. Love is quinine, and quinine and quinine until I'm deaf with it. Love is that dirty aborting horror that you took me to. Love is my insides all messed up. It's half catheters and half whirling douches. I know about love. Love always hangs up behind the bathroom door. It smells like Lysol. To hell with love. Love is you making me happy and then going off to sleep with your mouth open while I lie awake all night afraid to say my prayers even because I know I have no right to any more. Love is all the dirty little tricks you taught me that you probably got out of some book. All right. I'm through with you and I'm through with love. Your kind of picknose love. . . . I've tried to take care of you and humor you and look after you and cook for you and keep quiet when you wanted and cheerful when you wanted and give you your little explosions and pretend it made me happy, and put up with your rages and jealousies and your meannesses and now I'm through.[5]

Lady Chatterly had many sexual encounters before she became pregnant. Even Casanova used condoms; this is a rather vital and perhaps disillusioning piece of information recently made public by the British Family Planning Service in a small pamphlet urging the use of condoms as an historically masculine and virile method:

There is no campaign to ban romantic fiction because it may lead to disillusionment, but if pornography is condemned because of its supposedly harmful consequences we must call attention to the social harm of a class of fantasy which is mistakenly regarded as innocent.[6]

Many of the young women we have seen professionally have wondered aloud how their parents managed to have only two children in so many years. TV cigarette ads were selling sex and cigarettes in the rain, on boats, and in grassy glades. Ads for feminine deodorant sprays have the same settings with no contraception in sight. Romantic images become distorted when the reality of contraception intrudes.

Regardless of how well informed some young people and their elders are prior to any need for contraception, at the vital moment when sexual intercourse becomes inevitable, romance and this very inevitability frequently take over. This is the moment when the intellectual and emotional aspects of contraception collide:

Their first mistake is thinking they can appropriate that romantic fantasy as their own. Their second mistake is forgetting the reality. Their third mistake is getting pregnant.[7]

The factor of commitment is related to this romanticism and also to the nonuse of contraception. Many couples prefer to live in an unreal world which allows them to think that contraceptive usage represents a commitment to each other which they are not yet willing to make. The logic of this is difficult to comprehend, but the emotional aspects are not. These couples are saying simply that they want to keep their sexual activity spontaneous and unpremeditated. Contraceptive availability or usage implies premeditation. If contraception could only be regarded as a pregnancy preventive and *without philosophical overtones*, there would be fewer unwanted pregnancies. But this is just as difficult for the young, inexperienced couple to accept as it is for either of their parents to inform them about contraception. Information from parents about contraception also has philosophical overtones connoting parental approval and expectations.

Our only answer to all of this is to point out that contraception has been common practice for hundreds of years and is therefore a natural, rational action. And if people were not actively contracepting, they at least recognized a desire to limit families in some way, even if it was only evidenced by labeling some pregnancies as "accidental" or "gifts of God," or by the husband going to a prostitute or having an expendable mistress to avoid pregnancy risks for his wife.

. . . he said that ever since he had seen his wife give birth in agony, he could not bear the risk of impregnating any woman, of bearing responsibility for their pain and deformation. I knew he worshiped strong and tensile bodies from his talk of the ballerinas who were his intermittent mistresses. Pregnancy would, of course, destroy their careers; he could love them and leave them free.[8]

More important to recognize when discussing methods is that there is no single contraceptive that will be mutually acceptable in all circumstances for the 30 or more years of contraception needed by most females, and the 40 or more needed by some males. Just as the parameters of sexual intimacy change and expand over time, so do attitudes about methods. Most couples end up having used all of the available methods during their contraceptive life. The 30-year-old male, faced with a disinterested wife who is tired of pills and who is fearful of another pregnancy, even the remote possibility with the IUD which she also tried for a while, is more likely to reconsider his previous feelings about condoms and vasectomy. He has been the route of masculinity, he has proved himself fertile and virile, and his feelings of security in this area of his life now allow him to reorder his priorities. What is important for him now? For *them* now? Resuming a previously good sexual life with a contraceptive method that never appealed to him, or an enforced abstinence leading to a downhill marriage?

Not only is there no single method which is appropriate for one's entire contracepting life, but every method used requires a backup method for emergency use (see Condoms, Foam), and some people are much more comfortable and secure if they are using two methods at once, for example, foam plus condoms, foam plus IUD's, even condoms plus diaphragms. The backup method when condoms are absent is some variation of abstinence (see p. 193). Even the pill is sometimes forgotten.

For the concerned female and male, there are only three periods in their lives when worry about pregnancy does not lurk in the background of every sexual act, even if it is just a pill a day at some time remote to the act: 1) when they are trying to get pregnant, unless they have been trying too long and too intensely, at which point their concerns can loom even larger; 2) when they are between their first and second child and perhaps do not care when the second one comes along; and 3) when the female is two years past her last period and clearly past menopause. We should also include the seven or eight months of each pregnancy, though frequently there are other unfounded concerns which can create as many problems in a sexual relationship as contraception (see Pregnancy).

Clearly, contraception must be included in any definition of natural sex which includes the use of reason. Though it is always a compromise, a method should be found which is mutually agreeable, and, therefore, natural for a particular couple and their circumstances of time and place. The circumstances of time and place will change, often resulting in a change in contraceptive methods.

No contraceptive is totally satisfactory, emotionally, 100 percent of the time, but neither is the act of intercourse. If 75 or 80 percent is the best *average* one can achieve in either area, a couple may find that the emotional aspects will reach the upper limits more frequently when fear of pregnancy and resentment of a contraceptive are gone.

METHODS CURRENTLY AVAILABLE

MALE AND FEMALE	MALE	FEMALE
Abstinence	Withdrawal	Spermicides†
total	Condoms	foam, cream, gels
periodic	Vasectomy	diaphragm with . . .
rhythm	*	Ovulation prevention**
basal body temperature (BBT)		oral
nonvaginal variations		injectable
masturbation		implanted
solitary		Unknown action
mutual		minipill
oral-genital		morning-after pill (MAP)
anal intercourse		intrauterine devices (IUD)
		mechanical
		chemical (R)
		hormonal
		heavy metals (copper)
		Tubal sterilization‡

R Research method.
* See "Contraceptive Research: A Male Chauvinist Plot?" (p. 218).
† Douching is not a contraceptive method.
** Breast-feeding is not a contraceptive method.
‡ Abortion is not a contraceptive method.

Of these, only abstinence (total, BBT, or nonvaginal variations), condoms, diaphragms, some IUD's, ovulation prevention, and male and female sterilization have good track records. But these records are good only with knowledgeable and motivated usage (see Table 7-1). Injectables and implanted hormones are included here because they are currently being used in some individuals who are considered to be in the "high-risk of pregnancy" group, and who are without motivation to use any other type of contraceptive; breakthrough bleeding and irregular periods make them unacceptable in their present form to most females.

The perfect contraceptive should be reversible, should not interfere with the act of intercourse, and should have no immediate or long-term side effects. Obviously none of the above methods fills these requirements, but neither does unprotected intercourse. Again, the need for compromise is obvious.

No discussion of methods can supply motivation, but it can improve effectiveness, and help in the understanding of the emotional aspects of any method being used. This kind of information can also improve any sexual relationship pre- or postmarriage.

Almost every handbook of contraceptive methods includes "percentage effectiveness" tables. Realistically, any method that works for a motivated, sexually active couple for a year is virtually 100 percent effective; though for good, significant conclusions, the couple should have first proven its fertility. Even research statistics from a carefully supervised study population can *only* indicate high-risk and low-risk methods; the absolute numbers mean very little. The best and most convincing proof of this can be seen in the startling numbers in Table 7-1.

Table 7-1

Pregnancy Testing Clinic   17 months (August 1970 to December 1971)

Age Group	−14	14 to 16	17 to 20	21 to 25	26 to 31	32+	**Total***
Number of Patients	17	281	1,419	1,324	496	290	**3,827**

Pregnancies in Relation to Methods "Used"

Methods "Used"	Pregnant	Not Pregnant	
Pill	143	162	
Diaphragm	65	45	
Rhythm	134	30	
Condom	134	70	
Foam	196	58	
IUD	49	22	
Withdrawal	73†	28†	
	794	415	
Nothing	1,700	376	**Total 3,285***

Statistics furnished and used with permission of the Planned Parenthood Association of Southeastern Pennsylvania.
* The 542 discrepancy in total figures represents early patients not questioned.
† Twelve months only.

The only conclusion which can be drawn from these figures which represent a reality situation is that simple methods are often misused and a rigid approach to statistics concerning contraceptive methods is unrealistic. Even carefully controlled studies cannot totally avoid the human element; here we are referring not just to the contraceptive user, but also to the physicians and clinics and their medical and interpersonal techniques, for example, the physicians' experiences with the insertion of some types of IUD, or their ability to instruct the patients thoroughly on the usage of any given method.

Half of the girls who skipped a period and *thought* they were using the pill were pregnant. About two-thirds of the girls who thought they were using the IUD were pregnant. We find it difficult to believe that two-thirds of the condoms broke or slid off at the wrong time of the month. And just over half of these girls, and their partners, were using no contraception.

Most important, these patients represent a self-selected group of females who were motivated and aware enough to 1) be concerned early about a pregnancy, since most had skipped only one or two periods, 2) go to a facility, which in Philadelphia is considered somewhat middle class even though the socioeconomic background of the entire group was mixed, and 3) recognize the importance of early pregnancy diagnosis in relation to safety of abortion. Almost 80 percent of those with positive pregnancy tests requested abortion counseling.

About one-third of the total number were motivated enough to "use" a contraceptive method, or guilty enough about their failure to use a contraceptive that they felt the need to falsify information. Or, possibly, they were affluent enough to be able to afford to take chances. Abortions cost money even when they are easily available. Affluence allows girls or couples to take chances that the less affluent might not take.

Come on honey, just this once. I'll get you an abortion if you need one. I know somebody.

This is a reality expressed by some males at that inevitable stage of sexual stimulation, and by some females we have seen who have either surfaced with a pregnancy, or are "checking out" a delayed period.

It has become perfectly apparent to us in the past five years of seeing girls (about 450 a year) that chances are being taken constantly. We have also come to the conclusion that many of these girls are not ovulating in any regular fashion, regardless of the regularity of their periods because, on the basis of the reported frequency of unprotected intercourse, there should be many more pregnancies than there seem to be.

Admittedly the figures in this table are derived from a skewed population (they all thought they might be pregnant), but our point about the reliability of statistics and numbers in the area of contraception is not affected by this, though these figures should not be used to draw any other conclusions.*

One other point can be made which is supported by these figures and has been made by others: the increasing availability of contraceptives *does* increase the amount of sexual intercourse and, therefore, the number of pregnancies. This seeming paradox can be explained by the numbers in the table. Girls who

* See Norman B. Ryder, "Contraceptive Failure in the United States," *Family Planning Perspectives,* 5, 3 (Summer 1973) for some similar conclusions in a nonskewed population.

might not have been having intercourse when contraceptives were unavailable, get pregnant when they use contraceptives incorrectly. It is also fair to say that contraceptive availability creates an aura of sexuality which tempts females and males into sexual activity, even if only briefly and infrequently, often without contraception.

Methods: Male and Female

Abstinence

This method applies to both male and female because it requires cooperation and mutual consent. It can mean anything from complete absence of physical sexual stimulation, to masturbation, to mutual masturbation, to periodic abstinence, to avoidance of penile-vaginal penetration (oral-genital stimulation, anal intercourse).

Masturbation. In the pubertal and postpubertal female or male, complete absence of deliberate, physical sexual stimulation is practically unknown, though it may not be interpreted as sexual by the individual, nor is it always done with orgasmic intent. Even castration (the surgical or traumatic removal of both ovaries or testes), if it occurs after a good sexual life has been established and before any decline in interest has occurred, does not make abstinence or disinterest a foregone conclusion.

As is also true in prepubertal children, the pleasurable sensations resulting from self-stimulation may not be interpreted as having sexual content. Deliberate self-stimulation or masturbation can be pleasurable without proceeding to orgasm in the female or to ejaculation in the male. But, since most of the erotic areas that one can reach, other than the head and neck, are those which society and most families would prefer to be covered, this self-stimulation requires privacy. And, even thumbsucking and pacifiers are frowned on in some families, even among those who recognize the pleasurable sensations of this kind of activity. So, nailbiting and thumbsucking in the slightly older child are carefully relegated to the privacy of the bedroom. This kind of activity in any individual, like other kinds of self-stimulation, only becomes a problem when it is compulsive, guilt-ridden, and a substitute for something missing in other areas of one's life.

Masturbation lost its aura of sinfulness because of new understanding, and this sudden metamorphosis in an almost universal attitude is more significant of the changed temper, philosophy and morality of the 20th century than any other phenomenon I can think of.[9]

Karl Menninger

Masturbation is relatively common and few can say that they have not, at one time or another, discovered some pleasurable type of self-stimulation, again, not necessarily orgasmic. Kinsey's report that about 90 percent of all males and a similar percentage of all females have masturbated to orgasm is disturbing to some who think themselves completely out of step because they have never masturbated. But these figures include those individuals who can recall only one or two experiences; even prepubertal playing "doctor" would qualify for some. Sarrel mentioned that some preliminary data, from a study he was doing seemed to indicate that in his group of college males, the incidence of masturbation on a more or less regular basis, was much lower than Kinsey's figures, even in the absence of available females.[10]

How does one define masturbation? Most females can remember nights when "the sheets were too smooth," they couldn't sleep, and they tossed and turned and finally fell asleep with a pillow, a towel, or their hand between their thighs. A pleasurable, satisfying sensation, a passive variation of masturbation, sometimes even guilt-producing, but generally nothing most of them would label as masturbation. For females an active act of masturbation, with direct or indirect clitoral stimulation, requires acknowledgment of sexual needs and ease with touching the genital area; masturbation is emotionally and physically easier for the majority of males. They are more at ease with touching their genitals, since this is required four or five times a day with urination, and they are also accustomed to spontaneous erections. But, when asked to produce a semen specimen for analysis (e.g., infertility studies), many prefer to bring the specimen from "home" rather than produce it at the moment.

Many males and females who are experienced in masturbation to orgasm prior to any heterosexual or homosexual contact are often disappointed when they find that the speed and physical intensity is not there when they become involved in mutual masturbation as a form of sexual release, or with intercourse. The vaginal wall, or the hesitant female hand, does not supply the same firm stimulation of their own hands. And females are often with males who, initially, are not well acquainted with the specific techniques they need, or who are so intent on vaginal penetration that they omit any concerns about direct or indirect clitoral stimulation. Solitary masturbation and mutual masturbation should not be equated, even though they have many things in common.

The "heavy petting," seduction phase of early sexual encounters can also be a real part of the practice of rhythm or satisfactory mutual sex in the absence of contraceptives. This assumes orgasmic release for both partners.* If mutually acceptable, oral-genital stimulation or anal intercourse can be satisfactory stimulation without fear of pregnancy.

---

* There are no sexual emergencies so urgent that they cannot be resolved in this manner for those times when contraceptives are not available.

A twenty-two-year-old tore up her six-month birth control pill prescription in a dramatic gesture to "punish" her steady who had become addicted to heroin. Three months and a new "steady" later, she came in for another prescription. As she told us, when we asked what she had been using for contraception in the interim, "My mouth was and is the best emergency contraceptive I could possibly have."

Rhythm. This is a poor contraceptive method, especially in the teenage and early twenties group when the "next" menstrual period is so unpredictable, even though usually perfectly regular. Rhythm can work most of the time if the principles are well understood. Very simply, intercourse is avoided during ovulation, and six or seven days before ovulation. What isn't simple, as we have noted before (p. 67) is knowing when ovulation occurs, that is, $14\pm$ days before the *next* menstrual period. Even regular cycles have a normal variation of two to four days. Grossly irregular periods which may occur after a few years of regularity are frequently anovulatory (without ovulation), but there is no convenient method of determining this. Periods that have *always* been irregular (with variations of up to three or more weeks, or even longer) are apt to be ovulatory periods, but this is still difficult to determine. If we add to this the longevity of the sperm in the cervical mucus or uterine cavity (five to seven days in some instances), it is obvious that abstinence, or some of its variations, are necessary to the practice of rhythm. Abstinence from Day 5 to Day 19 of a 28-day cycle is almost essential for safety. A 21-day cycle is not uncommon and places ovulation on Day 7! This has posed problems of *apparent* infertility among Orthodox Jewish couples, since intercourse is proscribed for almost the first two weeks of the cycle. Most if not all of the Day 6 or Day 22 pregnancies which "could not have happened" can be explained on the basis of delayed ovulation or longevity of the sperm.

The practice of rhythm presents other problems. It is always the female who has to say "No, it's Day 10, or 11, or 8." If she has been provocative enough to encourage the male, there is a moment when even the most understanding husband in an advanced stage of sexual arousal will take this "No, not today," or "No, it's the wrong day," as a personal insult, a rejection, or an affront. He may apologize later, but at that moment the male-female relationship seems impossibly bad. Women can intentionally or unwittingly be very cruel by encouraging that warm body next to them, and the security of those warm arms around them, and ignoring the potential for male arousal that this can create. For the caring woman, this is the time and place for the variations of abstinence, or, if she is not interested, for helping him with some form of release of his sexual tension, but it is not the time for pushing him aside, physically or verbally.

Basal body temperature (BBT). As a contraceptive method, taking the temperature every morning is very cumbersome, though reliable if correctly interpreted. Abstinence must be practiced for two or three weeks prior to and during the temperature elevation associated with ovulation. Misinterpretation of occasional temperature rises due to stress, illness, late nights, intercourse, or sexual stimulation is a hazard. This method is more useful to the infertile couple, or any couple who is looking for the "right day" to "make a baby." It is frequently suggested that if a temperature chart is kept for two or three months and the pattern noted, intercourse can be scheduled without the need for additional charts. However, this approach to the BBT method completely ignores the normal and unpredictable variation in periods, or delayed ovulation.

Methods for the Male

Withdrawal

When we hear "but withdrawal is the most common method of contraception used around the world," our only comment has to be that "this is the best indication we know that sexual techniques in most parts of the world are male-oriented, and contraceptive techniques are primitive." Even the male is deprived of a fair idea of what good sex is or can be. It is no wonder that Kinsey found women who had never had an orgasm, or were not sure if they had had one, which is the same thing. Coitus interruptus is just that, interrupted intercourse. It is a contraceptive method which distorts everything that sexual intimacy can be, should be, and is supposed to be for the female and the male. It should be eliminated from any list of contraceptive techniques, especially high school lists, but its universality demands that it be included.

Imagine the young, inexperienced male with poor ejaculatory control saying to his girl, "Don't move around too much, I might come inside," and then wondering why she is not orgasmic, or how she got pregnant. To relax at all, the female has to be able to trust the male completely, and he is often not in an emotional position to trust himself. There is a period of only three to five seconds from the time the male is aware of the inevitability of ejaculation to actual ejaculation. This requires control and awareness at a time when emotions often eliminate rational thought, and this "cerebral clouding" (p. 87), or "trip," is one of the nice things about orgasmic release.

There is also a preejaculatory secretion ranging from a few drops to as much as 1 cc. This fluid frequently has motile sperm in it.

Even this piece of information occasionally gets intellectualized; for example, a couple went "off the pill" for two months because of chronic yeast vaginitis in the female. They investigated all kinds of contraception and found them wanting in one respect or another, and decided to use withdrawal because "he does not have a preejaculatory secretion."

We have noted elsewhere that ejaculation in the introital area puts sperm in a position to migrate to the uterus (p. 68). It is not the optimal situation for establishing pregnancies, but pregnancy does happen occasionally. Why is withdrawal used at all? It is an emergency technique when the female does not really care about herself or her own satisfaction, and wants only to "give." It allows natural, skin-to-skin contact with nothing interposed. But that is the only natural part of the technique. The rest is grossly unnatural and a compromise, an impulsive kind of sexual touching, a learning and growth experience at best.

Condoms

Condoms work if used properly. In fact, they work very well. Proper use means 1) using prior to any penetration, thus containing the preejaculatory secretion, 2) leaving some space at the end of the condom for the ejaculate, and 3) holding the condom when withdrawing, which should occur before complete loss of erection. Stimulation of the vagina by the penis* is not limited by the use of the condom, nor does it need to be held when there is complete erection.

Condoms are available in colors, with monograms, or just plain. They are still all one size. Some have modifications at the end which provide room for the ejaculate. Some are designed for increased sensitivity (e.g., lambskin). Lubricated condoms have a useful function, but are aesthetically unpleasant for some males and females. They are cold, initially, and slippery to roll on; they also may create a stinging sensation in some sensitive vaginas. One expensive, lubricated condom comes folded in a plastic case, and is pulled on like a stocking. If lubrication is needed, a waterbase, surgical lubricant, used by the female, is certainly much pleasanter than some condom lubricants or vaseline. The need for lubricated condoms may indicate that there is already a problem with vaginitis, or prepenetration sexual techniques (see below).

Condoms do break, but relatively rarely.† They are manufactured according to federal standards, and undergo inspection and random sampling for strength. Couples will often report a broken condom to their physician when they are looking for the morning-after pill, or their usual question is, "Is there something you can do?" Careful questioning often reveals that either no condom was used, or that the couple was trying to reuse a condom. They are difficult to roll up again for reuse, if there is any hurry. Sometimes condoms get left behind in the vagina, leaving them free to empty their contents. Occasionally, penetration is difficult because of lack of lubrication, and the condom really

---

* Thrusting movements.

† A personal observation: In five years we have heard only four verified stories of broken condoms, all lambskins.

does break. Lack of lubrication exists if the seduction phase is neglected or shortened, if there is a vaginitis, or if the vagina has reacted to the use of the pill with decreased lubrication.

One college contraceptive guide suggested putting used condoms in a glass of water for reuse later. As there was no discernible humor in this advice, we are assuming that the writers were serious. Reliable condoms cost about 30 to 35 cents and should be considered expendable. All other types of contraception are relatively inexpensive, at least relative to abortions and deliveries which are quite costly. The dollar variety of condom does not represent much improvement, and the price often only reflects the supply and demand in a particular setting.

Do condoms reduce the risk of or prevent VD? If used prior to any genital or oral contact, they undoubtedly reduce the risk of the male acquiring or transmitting VD. But many males use them only at the last possible moment and are lucky if they get them on in time. Recent increases in VD have been attributed in part to the decreasing use of condoms. This may be partly true, but the most pronounced *reported* increase in VD has been in the high-school-age group (the primary condom-using group, if they use anything). VD increase is probably more closely related to the increase in casual, unprotected sex, as well as more sexual activity generally (see VD).

If used properly, condoms also protect against infection and reinfection of the female and male with Trichomonads and occasionally yeast organisms (see Vaginitis and Nonspecific Urethritis).

There are two classic comments about condoms which are usually attributed to males, but are also frequently voiced by females: 1) condoms decrease sensation, and 2) they do not allow total freedom. Both comments are true to some degree, but all things are relative and, again, a compromise. The slight decrease in sensation can occasionally be useful to males troubled with premature ejaculation, and thus may also be indirectly useful to females.

We have heard single and married women complaining about the contraceptive method they were using, and blaming their husbands or boyfriends for not wanting, or refusing, to use condoms. Further questioning often reveals that these women are not enthusiastic about condoms, either. The aesthetics and the need to stop at some point in the progression of sexual stimulation and wait while he puts it on, are not pleasant. (Experts can roll them on with one hand and maintain female contact with the other.) Women afraid of losing their men will often allow them to proceed rather than make a request to use a condom; "Oh, I couldn't ask him to do that."

Some males do not trust their female partners, often with good reason, and prefer being in control of the contraceptive method: There is always the woman in a bad-to-worse marriage who hopes that an accidental pregnancy will *keep* the marriage together, or the single girl who thinks that a pregnancy will *get* them together.

For several reasons, every heterosexual male of any age or marital status should keep at least two condoms on hand at all times. Pills may be forgotten. Foam and diaphragm gels may be used up. There may be accidental one-night-stands with "strangers" whose contraceptive motivation may be low or non-existent. The woman with chronic vaginitis may not wish to risk reinfection, though unable to abstain for a brief time during treatment. There may be spontaneous morning or afternoon sex with a seduced female who is in no frame of mind to get up and contracept for herself. The IUD string may have disappeared. And there is even the rare homosexual or heterosexual male, who is very tense about VD, who says, "Hell, I even use them for blowjobs (fellatio)."

There are an equal number of good reasons for every heterosexual female to carry condoms with her. But it is impossible to look like a virgin or, at the very least, untutored, inexperienced, and nonaggressive if she is carrying condoms for "his" use, whoever "he" may be. But pregnancy is not a minor event. Some of the teenage programs working with "high risk of pregnancy" girls advocate and distribute condoms to them for this type of use.

There are some free condom distribution programs around the United States which have shown some degree of success with distribution in candy and grocery stores; Thursday seems to be the primary pickup day. Entrepreneurs, who sell the free condoms they pick up, do not seem to be a major problem, and the program directors feel that, in any case, this represents usage.

Vas Ligation

With rare exceptions, the male who has had his vas deferens "tied," "cut," or "ligated," is either married, separated, or divorced, and has had at least one child. There are no laws governing *voluntary* vasectomies, but there has always been a feeling among the lay public that there are or have been laws. This stems from the longtime hesitance of physicians (notably urologists) to do them. Vas ligation is so permanently sterilizing that the threat of postoperative law-suits is very real, and physicians feel that the potential harassment is hardly worth the time, effort, and money. Since vasectomies are usually office pro-cedures, these physicians do not have the protection of any hospital policy simi-lar to that which has governed female tubal ligations in the past, and which still exists in many hospitals (i.e., approval by a special review committee). Also, many physicians know that they do not have the time, emotional energy, or expertise to investigate a marriage relationship and the reasons why vasec-tomy is the method of choice for a particular couple. This requires doctor, husband, and wife consultation.

With the increasing availability, ease, and acceptance of tubal ligation and vasectomy, married couples in their thirties are whispering to close friends that they have had one procedure or the other. Married couples in their twenties, with or without children, are being quite open about their vasectomies or tubal ligations, and their desires to have no children of their own, to adopt, or to have no more children. Some single males and females in their late teens are requesting these procedures because they are tired of contracepting. Few physicians will assume this responsibility in this late teenage group of singles, unless there are clear hereditary or medical reasons for sterilization, and these are few and far between.

As we have seen, male function is so intimately tied up with the psyche that it is probably best not to question the need to advertise, or to hide, the fact of vasectomy, but, if there is a question about contraception in a one-night-stand, one should never regard the presence of a vasectomy pin in the lapel as absolute proof.[11] There are males in public professions usually associated with masculinity (e.g., football and baseball players) who advertise the fact of their vasectomies for purposes of encouraging others to do likewise. This kind of advertising seems to have been very effective in increasing the acceptance of the procedure.

Ligation (cutting, removing a section of the vas, and tying the ends) should still be considered a permanent procedure. Reanastomosis (reuniting) of the ends of the vas can be done, usually requiring three days in the hospital, but there is evidence that the chronic obstruction in the portion of the conducting system at the level of the testis sometimes affects the kind and number of sperm one gets after reanastomosis. Fertility cannot be guaranteed even with a reopened vas.*

The liquid portion of the ejaculate is not affected by vasectomy; only the sperm are missing. An important point here, one that is seldom mentioned in magazine articles on vasectomy and occasionally overlooked by physicians or not heard by the patient, is that the first ten or twelve ejaculates after vasectomy may still have active sperm in them. Patients are usually advised to have intra- or extravaginal ejaculations *with contraception* as soon as they desire. Only when the specimen is free of sperm by microscopic examination should the male consider himself sperm-free or sterile. Postvasectomy pregnancies have occurred because males had either not been informed, so they said, or because they made their own judgment without microscopic examination, about how many ejaculates were necessary to become sperm-free.

If the decision to have a vasectomy originates with the male and is not forced upon him, the potential psychological problems of vasectomy will be reduced or simply nonexistent. "Men with healthy egos and self-confidence apparently can accept the condition . . . without dysfunction."[12] But on the interpersonal level, this decision making does "represent a new jousting field upon which

---

* There have been preliminary reports in the lay press about possible generalized effects on the body resulting from the permanent blockage of sperm release; to date, they represent only 9 out of 12 vasectomized males. See bibliography in Segal article for earlier reports on the effects of vasectomy.

the sexes can carry their traditional skirmishes to new lengths."[13] Consider the possibility that a vasectomy can represent freedom for the male, and essentially a chastity belt for the female he is married to.

Recent efforts to design an on-off valve to be inserted in the vas are interesting, but will probably give rise to a whole new set of physical and mental problems, as well as the old ones of just how long the valves can be turned off before there may be irreversible changes in sperm morphology and numbers (see Infertility and frozen sperm).

Methods for the Female

Spermicides

The major problem with this type of contraception, used without a diaphragm, is that one can never be sure that the spermicides are going to stay in place over the cervical opening. However, they do have a very useful role in conception control, though not usually if used alone. They may be used with condoms for "150 percent" contraception: The female can use the foam and the male can use a condom; or, as one prominent New York clinic was advising, the male can also use the foam at the end of the penis before rolling on the condom. This represents real motivation. The woman who is motivated enough to worry about the small risk of pregnancy with the IUD, can use foam or gel in addition.

Couples who have been on the pill and wish to get pregnant during a particular month, can go off the pill a few months earlier than the desired conception date and use foam as a contraceptive for those few months. Sometimes ovulation does not return promptly after cessation of the pill (see p. 213), and a "foam failure" near the time when they want to have children, would not be a major catastrophe.

Besides being an unreliable high-risk method, having to be used almost immediately prior to intercourse, and leaking out, the chief complaint about unrestricted spermicides heard from women is, "I can't really use it. We tried it, but he doesn't like the taste."

The Diaphragm

Used with spermicidal gels or cremes, the diaphragm solves the problem of placement, but requires some extra motivation and manipulation that many females do not like. However, when it is used well by the motivated female, it ranks along with the pill, the condom, and the IUD as a low-risk method.

The diaphragm is a circular, flexible, rubber dome which, when inserted rests above and behind the pubic bone in front, and extends *over* the anterior vaginal wall and the cervix to the upper end of the vagina (see Fig. 2-2). The spermicide lies between the cervix and the diaphragm. It is effective even if inserted two hours prior to use, and also has the added advantage of increased lubrication.

Diaphragm failures are almost always related to: 1) Nonuse. Even good friends will not confide carelessness in the sexual sphere. 2) Use related to the rhythm method, which is a variation of nonuse. 3) Insufficient spermicide. 4) Overuse. Extra spermicide has to be added prior to a second ejaculation, without removal of the diaphragm, if the second ejaculation occurs within a six-hour period after the first. 5) Improper placement.

Diaphragms have to be fitted to each individual. Sizes range from 2 to 4 or more inches in diameter; the size bears little relation to the length of the vagina which is fairly uniform, but only to the length of the anterior vaginal wall, including the cervix. The size may change with a year of sexual activity, or postchildbirth, but never markedly. If fitted correctly, diaphragms cannot be felt during intercourse by either partner.

At present, there are two types of diaphragms: the flatspring which is flat in sideview when compressed for insertion, and the alflex, or arcflex, which forms an arc when compressed. The latter was designed for ease of manual insertion, and it also fits some "relaxed" anterior vaginal walls better than the flatspring (see Cystocoele).

When filled with spermicide, both types of diaphragms are slippery and difficult to insert, and aesthetically unpleasant for some. It takes a well-motivated woman to continue using a diaphragm after having had to retrieve it from the floor, or, occasionally, from the toilet during attempted insertion. This is why some physicians have always suggested using an introducer. The diaphragm fits on this, and is automatically shaped to insert in the vagina. At most, only one finger is required to apply the spermicide. This makes it all very neat, and as easy and nonmessy as inserting a tampon, though many women prefer the security of knowing exactly where it is, and are quite at ease with manual insertion. There is no introducer yet designed for the arcflex diaphragm; a sensitive, mechanical engineer, female or male, is needed.

There are a number of contraceptive clinics and individual physicians who refuse to acknowledge the existence of the introducer, thinking that the female should get used to her own vagina and to touching her own genital area. They fail to recognize that often sexual activity comes *before* emotional constraints about the vagina and self-manipulation have disappeared. Many women are hesitant to put their fingers in their vaginas at any time, and for some it can be particularly unpleasant if there has been sexual stimulation prior to the need for insertion. Removing a diaphragm six or eight hours later does not present the same emotional problems. Some couples manage to include diaphragm insertion as part of their lovemaking. One 24-year-old female who had difficulty touching her genitals, but whose sex life was otherwise good, orgasmic, and loving, routinely had her very cooperative and caring fiance insert the diaphragm. Another very sexually active and successful young woman could not bear to insert a tampon, much less a diaphragm; she and her partner relied on condoms. Constraints about genital touching do not necessarily preclude a good heterosexual or homosexual experience, though if they are unduly prolonged into adulthood or if they cause concern, they can hamper the evolution of a fuller sexual life.

Emotional constraints are not the primary reason for the use of the introducer, since it also eliminates much of the messiness so frequently associated with the diaphragm. Diaphragms need not be messy. A washcloth will wipe off the excess cream or gel and avoids the taste problem associated with non-confined foams.

Many women, early in marriage, insert diaphragms every night as part of their usual nighttime rituals. Intercourse, without removal of the diaphragm, is really confined to twice in any six- or eight-hour period, with additional gel being used. Any frequency greater than this gives rise to unpleasant leakage. Douching before and after removal of the diaphragm minimizes leakage, even with single usage, and males should always have condoms around for any emergencies.

Other subtle advantages in having a diaphragm available include using it to contain the menstrual flow temporarily. Days 1 through 5 can be a very relaxed time to have intercourse without fear of pregnancy. For the woman who is only intermittently sexually active, and sometimes surprisingly so, it is portable and available at all times, and makes her independent of condoms and pills.

The fact that the diaphragm cannot be felt by a male partner allows for another bit of deception which can be very instructive to the female, and to the male, involved in accidental encounters. This is not dishonesty; it is just that we must acknowledge reality situations. The female is protected against pregnancy with a diaphragm in place. She can relax and be seduced, if an early relationship goes in this direction, but she can also listen for the timing of the vital question, "Is it all right, or should I use something?" Often, this question is disappointingly late in coming, if it comes at all. Knowing she has found a male who cares and is just not making assumptions that she has taken care of herself can help the development of a relationship tremendously. The real problem with this bit of deception is almost the same as the problem which arises if a female carries condoms with her: Does she really want to look that experienced? Does she really have the ego to explain that her primary interest is in not getting pregnant, and she doesn't care if she looks experienced?

Slight dislodgement of the diaphragm during intercourse is referred to by Masters and Johnson and others. We have mentioned previously that when the hips are elevated, or the female is in the knees-to-chest position, the likelihood of dislodgement is greater. Checking postintercourse, or prior to subsequent intercourse while inserting more spermicide, is probably worthwhile in these situations (see p. 41). Some women after one or two deliveries cannot be fitted adequately because of this problem of dislodgement. Some girls or women who are chronically constipated cannot be fitted with a diaphragm.

We have devoted extra space to this method, more than in most texts, because it is often neglected. It is a good method, nonhormonal, female-oriented, and works extremely well if there is some mutual understanding and knowledge. No one has to be a college graduate to use the diaphragm, just motivated not to get pregnant. Most physicians under age 35 have very little personal or professional experience with it. Most physicians over this age have had much personal and professional experience with it and know that it requires motivation. When they fail to discern motivation in many of the present-day life styles, they discourage its use. The diaphragm also takes more physician or nurse time for fitting and instructions than the pill, which is 100 percent effective if used properly, and is much easier to dispense (see p. 211).

Unknown Action

If abortion is defined as interfering with an *implanted* pregnancy, many antiabortion groups would have no difficulty in accepting the minipill, the morning-after pill, and the IUD as methods of contraception. However, we feel that it would be less than honest to discuss these methods without indicating that their probable mode of action is *preventing implantation of the fertilized ovum,* a 32 to 64 cell embryo. Some gynecologists refer to them as *interceptives;* that is, they interfere with implantation. We must also include here, menstrual extraction of an undiagnosed pregnancy as an interceptive (see p. 208). The Supreme Court decision, based to some degree on the absence of legal rights for a conceptus at this stage, has directed the efforts of antiabortion groups toward establishing legal rights for the conceptus of any age. If successful, this could create moral and legal questions about these methods.

Morning-after pill. The basic physiological effect of the morning-after pill and the minipill is a change in the lining of the uterus which interferes with implantation. They may also modify sperm and ovum transport. The basic mechanism of all types of IUD's has only been under intensive investigation for the past few years, though this type of contraception has been known for many years. Changes in the lining of the uterus occur and seem to be the reason for its effectiveness as a contraceptive, though it, too, may affect ovum transport; fertilization can and does occur in some individuals with the IUD in place (p. 208).*

The morning-after pill (MA pill) is not really a single pill, but a number of pills taken over three, four, or five days after unprotected intercourse. These pills, an estrogenic substance (diethylstilbesterol, DES) should be started no

---

* For an excellent review of "Intrauterine Contraception" see Dr. H. J. Tatum's article in the *American Journal of Obstetrics and Gynecology* (April 1, 1972).

later than 48 hours after exposure to spermatozoa. There is no positive evidence that this regimen works; no one has seen the fertilized ovum emerge from the uterus in such cases. Studies have been published and noted in the lay press which indicate that on the basis of expectation of the "probability of pregnancy" occurring in an exposed, treated group of females, no pregnancies occurred. These studies had no controls; this would require that some girls be given placebos,* and this kind of therapy and human experimentation would constitute gross malpractice, since there is sufficient evidence to justify MA pills routinely, if acceptable to the patient, in the face of rape, the broken condom, or lapses in judgment (see Rape). The MA pills are all that is available in these situations, except waiting for a missed period or perhaps using menstrual extraction (see below). No one should be under any illusion that the dosages of DES needed are benign. They do not appear to harm the body (see p. 225) but this much DES can be extremely unpleasant, usually nauseating, and hardly fits into the category of routine contraception. It is emergency treatment only.

Menstrual extraction. Menstrual extraction (suctioning out the lining of the uterus at the time of the expected menstrual period) is a new and possibly useful method of accomplishing the same kind of emergency "contraception" in a nonhormonal and more definitive way. This method is not in common usage and it is certainly not a do-it-yourself procedure for two good reasons: 1) routine insertion of objects into the uterine cavity always carries with it the potential of introducing infection which can lead to sterility, and 2) it is difficult to insert even small objects into some cervices, and every cervix and uterus presents a different degree of flexion and closure of the cervical canal. Experience is essential to prevent perforation, or undue discomfort.

The IUD. The IUD returned to favor a few years ago with the development of a plastic which is better tolerated than the heavy metals used previously. Pregnancies do occur with the IUD in place. The failure rate depends to some extent on the type of IUD, but in careful studies, it is in the range of 2 to 3 percent with the plastic only, and down to 1½ percent with the addition of metallic copper.† The overall failure rate, which means pregnancies which occur with the IUD in place or having silently fallen out without the patient's knowledge, again depends on the parity of the patients (the number of previous pregnancies) in the population being studied, and the type of IUD. Delivery at term is normal in those pregnancies which occur. There is no indication that the presence of the IUD causes abortion in the early months of pregnancy. This should not be confused with preventing implantation. There is some evidence which indicates that among those few pregnancies

* Placebo: a pseudomedication without pharmacological effect, e.g., a "sugar pill."
† The copper modification is still under investigation and only approved for research studies (August 1973).

which occur with the IUD in place, there is a higher incidence of tubal and ovarian pregnancies (ectopic pregnancies) than are seen in the non-IUD population.

The insertion of most IUD's is a two to five minute office procedure which may or may not be uncomfortable, and may or may not produce some light-headedness, or even fainting. There may or may not be mild to moderate cramping or spotting during the first 24 hours, or the first two to three months. Perforation of the uterus is the only real risk at the time of insertion, and usually only represents a risk if it goes unidentified. This is most likely if insertion is done during the six-week postdelivery or postabortion period, when the uterine wall is still soft. There have been reports of routine insertion of IUD's (if the patient wishes to have one) at the time of currettage for abortion, with no increase in postabortion complications. This offers almost immediate protection for women whom the clinic knows they will never see again for contraceptive counseling, and whom they feel are in the high risk of pregnancy group. It also offers the added advantage of controlled insertion under what-ever type of anesthesia is used for the abortion.

The IUD works, theoretically, from the moment of insertion; however most physicians advise waiting two weeks, or past the first ovulation, before using it as a method of contraception. The IUD is usually inserted during a men-strual period because: 1) insertion is somewhat easier at this time, 2) this avoids the possibility of traumatizing an unknown early pregnancy which is already present. (This was a major concern before abortion was legalized, and it still is because there are women who can use contraception with ease, but cannot condone abortion in any form.) 3) Any bleeding or cramping which might occur is better tolerated by the patient at this time; it is less traumatic, emotionally. Obviously, none of these reasons are really absolutes, and the IUD can be inserted at any time in the cycle.

Statistics with this type of contraception are just as difficult to evaluate as are those with other types (see Table 7-1). The never-pregnant uterus has a greater tendency to expel most IUD's that work well in a previously-pregnant uterus. This might be correlated with the tendency of the uterus to expel even first pregnancies at an early stage (see p. 222).

The copper-T and the copper-7 are being investigated and are the smallest of the IUD's; they are therefore easier to insert into any uterus, and they appear to stay in the never-pregnant uterus better than most and with fewer immediate side effects. To date the failure rate has been low in most studies, but the long-term effects of exposed copper in the uterus and in the abdominal cavity, if there is perforation, are still under investigation. The copper is present in the form of an external coil on the stem of the T and the 7; and appears to exert its own special magic; though still experimental, other metal coils have been used successfully.

The Dalkon shield which is crab-shaped with many legs, stays in the never-pregnant uterus very well. In fact, it is somewhat difficult to insert properly and equally difficult to remove, without some form of analgesia. The failure rate in the initial studies was comparable to other IUD's, but with increasing usage, and, therefore, an increasing number of physicians inserting it, the failure rate in any one small series from individual gynecologists, and some clinics, has been high. Failure rate means pregnancies with the Dalkon shield in the uterus. The instructions for insertion now include the suggestion that local anesthesia is needed for proper insertion into never-pregnant uteri.

The IUD is equipped with strings which extend into the vagina. There are two reasons for this: 1) to aid in removal when necessary, and 2) to enable the patient to check for its presence. Checking means reaching into the vagina which, again, requires motivation, and those girls and women who insist on using the IUD "because it seems like the neatest and easiest kind of contraception" are not necessarily noted for their motivation on a daily basis; often they will even admit that this is why they chose this method, they couldn't trust themselves with any other method. The IUD should be checked every day or so for the first seven or eight months or always before intercourse (see p. 204 for IUD plus foam).

A large group of patients who likes the IUD and is well motivated, is composed of young marrieds with one or two children who have used the pill off and on for as long as they really want to, and have not yet come to grips with the idea of sterilization. This group either feels relatively secure about obtaining abortion if necessary, or keeping any accidental pregnancy. It is also not too concerned about the IUD stirring up any latent infection in the internal pelvic organs which might lead to sterility, or about any remote possibility of perforation which might affect future ability to conceive.

The IUD is very useful in the teenage (age 13 and up) *postabortion* population where motivation is low for any other method, even the pill, and the risk of pregnancy is high. The postabortion uterus acts much like the previously-pregnant uterus, which it is, and the retention rate for these two groups is the same for all common types of IUD's; age is not a factor.

Multiparous patients (two or more pregnancies) who use the IUD are less likely to request removal because of any mild cramping or spotting. They are used to being semi-aware of their pelvises, and are willing to compromise. After about two years, IUD's often become coated with calcium, and there are heavier menstrual periods, or spotting. The device can be removed, and another reinserted immediately, if desired. Often this is the time when these women decide to have their tubal ligation.

Also being investigated are IUD's that slowly release hormones which act locally to prevent implantation.

Emotional reactions to this method are just as strong as they are to other methods. We have heard males (ages 19 and 20) say that "the whole idea of something like that inside you is just, just . . . ."; they usually cannot find the word they want, but it ends up as "unpleasant." Many females feel the same way for purely emotional reasons, or because they heard of one case where the IUD ended up in the abdominal cavity and had to be removed. Generally, there is no urgency about removing IUD's, but this should be done some time soon after it is discovered by X-ray that they are no longer in the uterus, but in the abdominal cavity. Some gynecologists can remove them through the small tube that is used to do tubal cauterizations (see p. 215); this leaves no scar.

Ovulation Prevention

If ovulation is prevented, the conception rate should be zero. The pill, in use since the midfifties, is the classic example of hormonal prevention of ovulation in humans; it was discovered to be effective in lower animals (rabbits) in the midthirties, before synthetic hormones were available.

Questions about the effects of long-term usage of these hormones are still being investigated 17 years later. However, it appears that it is not in the nature of the human female to take any pills in a regular fashion for this or any other reason for longer than 10 or 12 years unless there is a specific chronic disease.* Though still incomplete, the pill experience has been quite well studied to the present time, and should be reassuring to most women and their men with regard to the immediate side effects of this dosage (see p. 214).

However, studying long-term side effects (20 to 25 years) of previous pill-taking will not be easy, because even now, many of the 23- and 24-year-olds who have been on and off the pill over a period of five or six years, not only cannot remember the name of the pill or pills they took, but they often do not know the name of the one they are presently taking.

The entire thrust of research in this area of hormonal contraception is directed at finding the lowest dosage of a hormone or hormones which will prevent ovulation, prevent implantation or fertilization, and have the fewest unacceptable side effects.† Also being studied are hormones or other drugs which might prevent spermatogenesis in a reversible fashion (see p. 218).

The pill used at the present time contains combinations of synthetic estrogens and progesterones (really steroid chemicals which have estrogenic and progesteronelike qualities). The majority of the present pill-taking generation still likes to have a monthly or cyclic menstrual flow, because this makes the physiology look normal. The 20 or 21 day regimen was chosen for that reason, to allow withdrawal bleeding, which is not menstruation in the strictest sense,

---

* A recent study of the effects of vasectomy on males, noted that the average length of marriage prior to vasectomy was 12+ years.

† Some current research is directed at finding a chemical which will block LRF and interfere with ovulation.

once a month for the psyche, not for the uterus.* The packages which contain 28 pills, in contrast to the usual 20 or 21, are designed to maintain a pattern of daily usage. The extra seven pills are usually a different color and sometimes contain iron (for the blood), or are simply placebos.

Pill-taking can be juggled or extended, under supervision, so that special events like wedding days, ski trips, boyfriends home for the weekend can be free of uterine bleeding. Some women try this on their own, but often become very upset when the bleeding does not occur on time, or if spotting occurs in the next cycle. Frequently, they neglect to start taking the pills a week after stopping because they have not yet had a withdrawal flow. When they use the pills this way, waiting more than seven days for some uterine bleeding, they are occasionally surprised by a pregnancy (see Table 7-1 and also p. 213).

Unpredictable bleeding, regardless of amount, is unacceptable to most females on the pill, and is still a problem with some of the "minipills," injectables, hormonal tampons, or implanted hormones. Perhaps attitudes will change about spotting or the need for withdrawal flow, but it is much more likely that new methods will be found which again approximate the overt signs of normal function.

The secondary effects of the pill are decreased cramping and decreased menstrual flow; these hormones are also used to prevent ovulation and thereby decrease the severe cramping which some young women experience with ovulatory periods. They are also used in menopausal women who often have profuse and irregular uterine bleeding.

We are including some routine advice about pill-taking which every female and male should hear from a physician, or be aware of; many do not hear it, sometimes because it isn't said, and sometimes because they are not listening.

1. The pills should be taken at some regular time each day. Even casual life-styles have one element of regularity in them.
2. They should be carried with you at all times. Some of the packs fit nicely into a glasses case at the bottom of a purse.
3. A missed pill should be taken as soon as it is remembered, even if this means taking two in one day, or two at once. If you miss three or more pills in one cycle, either in sequence or on separate occasions, use some other form of contraception for the remainder of the cycle, even if the missed pills were taken later.
4. Breakthrough bleeding (spotting) in midcycle should be noted and an extra pill may be taken that day and for as many days (up to four or five) as spotting occurs, though this is not absolutely necessary. One pack of pills should always be set aside during the first three or four

---

* This would look to some as if men are deciding what women need for their psyche. But experience indicates that the majority of women still equate normal functioning with cyclic uterine bleeding regardless of the etiology.

months of any new pill and labeled "extra;" do not take extra pills from the regular pack.

5. Always start the next pack seven days after stopping, regardless of the amount of withdrawal flow, for example, if still bleeding, or if no bleeding or only minimal bleeding occurs. Seek advice if this happens for two cycles. If you have missed some pills, or taken them erratically, you might be pregnant.

6. Watch weight gain. Carbohydrate metabolism changes during this pseudo-pregnancy, just like the first three months of real pregnancy; you are hungry all of the time, "faint with hunger" and nibbling. Some of the weight gain, about five pounds, in the first few months is water and salt retention, and this can be kept under control with diuretics if the signs and symptoms of water retention become a problem (see p. 135).

7. Initially, breast tenderness or enlargement is not uncommon. This can be uncomfortable and, if a major problem beyond three months, may require a change in pills. Different combinations of synthetic hormones have slightly different side effects.

8. Going on and off the pill every other month is not recommended even if the "steadies" are intermittent, but there is no clear evidence to date of harmful effects due to this type of usage.

9. Since the mechanism of action of the pill is still not completely understood (see p. 125), many gynecologists suggest going off the pill every two years or so and allowing the ovaries to resume their normal functioning. Some ovaries ovulate the very next month; some wait three or four months or longer. This does not appear to be related to the length of time ovulation has been suppressed. Going off the pill would seem to be a good idea for the unmarried woman who has never been pregnant and might be on the pill for as long as eight or ten years prior to marriage. At the time of marriage, or when children are desired, it can be very devastating to find that she is having difficulty getting pregnant; while this problem may have nothing to do with previous pill-taking *(it has never been demonstrated to be a factor)*, a tremendous amount of guilt can be generated over what is, in reality, still an unknown. If the woman has reassured herself, at intervals, that she is still ovulating, as demonstrated by the return of normal menses, there will be much less guilt about the infertility, though there is always some whether the source is male or female. This is one more reason to be well acquainted and at ease with another method of contraception besides the pill.

10. A Pap test (p. 320), a pelvic, and a breast examination should be done initially and at least annually thereafter, preferably semi-annually. There is no evidence that cancer of the breast or the cervix is related to pill-taking, but the long-term effects are not yet known, and any sexually

active woman should have a Pap test every year, pill or no pill. A blood pressure should be taken during each checkup.

11. Thrombophlebitis* has been the subject of much discussion and has created an enormous amount of anxiety. The original study done in England has been suspect because it was a retrospective study, but it did succeed in lowering the estrogen dosage in most of the pills and in discontinuing the routine use of sequential pills for contraception. These still have a use in special circumstances. A recent study with a control group indicates that the incidence of phlebitis is no greater in the pill population. The reader with a statistical bent is referred to these two studies.[14,15] Clinically, some women with varicose veins and poor circulation in the legs, get swelling and mild edema when on the pill; this increases aching and awareness of the legs, but does not necessarily lead to phlebitis, though it has given patients and their physicians some anxious moments. Using a contraceptive which creates this kind of anxiety for real or imagined reasons contributes little to a sexual relationship, even though it is 100 percent effective as a contraceptive.

12. There are many preexisting medical conditions which some feel are contraindications to pill usage, for example, migraine headaches, previous liver disease, cystic disease of the breast, a family history of diabetes or hypertension (high blood pressure) on either or both sides of the family. Use of the pill should be individualized in these cases: get two opinions from people with experience with these diseases or who are knowledgeable about the pill, but the final decision, as with almost all contraceptive methods, is your own.

Among the uncomfortable, unpleasant, and unattractive side effects of the pill may be decreased vaginal lubrication in some females, hair loss, the mottled pigmentation of the face which is also seen in pregnancy, and overgrowth of yeast organisms in the vagina causing vaginal discharge and, sometimes, severe vaginitis. These are not universal, but if a woman is chronically disturbed by any one of them, she has two options: 1) she can go off the pill for two or three months, substituting some other form of contraception, or 2) she can try a change of pills, with supervision.

The yeast overgrowth which causes itching, burning, and discharge is quite common (see p. 117), but can be kept under reasonable control with some attention to weekly douching, though it usually needs medication for acute symptoms. In the presence of the pill, women with diabetic family histories seem particularly susceptible to yeast overgrowth, as are women who are on antibiotics for complexion problems, or for acute infections (see Dyspareunia, Vaginitis).

* thrombo- =clot, -phleb=vein, -itis=inflammation.

In the past few years we have seen a change in contraceptive usage among college females. Though the pill is still very popular, more and more young women are changing to the diaphragm, or condoms plus foam, after one or two years of the pill, or are going off the pill between boyfriends, or while their man is away at another school, or out of the city for a semester. There seems to be a little more flexibility about methods after using the pill initially. It is quite possible that the availability of abortion allows these women to be a little more comfortable with a contraceptive which they might misuse, or would not have trusted completely previously. Feminist groups and their "consciousness raising" discussions have been effective in making some young women stop and take stock of "what are they doing to themselves with this kind of contraception, and for whom?" At least, this is the general content of the comments we hear.

Tubal Sterilization

Ligation means cutting, separating, and tying each Fallopian tube, thus permanently separating the sperm from the egg. But it may also be accomplished by cauterizing (electrocoagulating) the tubes, which permanently closes the lumen of the tube. These procedures can be done through the abdominal wall (from above), or vaginally (from below).

Cauterization is a recent technique and a number of clinics are doing cauterizations on an outpatient basis.* This is done through a small incision in the umbilicus which leaves no visible scar. Experience with the technique is relatively short, about four years to date, but successful and without major or even minor side effects in most instances. Long-term results are not yet available. Recanalization of the lumen of the tube is always a concern when the ends are not physically separated.

Vaginal or abdominal ligation takes a little more time, though vaginal and some abdominal procedures are done on an outpatient basis in some clinics. The abdominal incision required for ligation needs to be slightly longer than that for cauterization. Ligations are often done at the time of Caesarian section (see p. 181), or on the first or second day postdelivery when the uterus and the tubes are still high in the abdomen.

Silver clips have been used to crush the tubes; they remain on the tubes. This clipping is a quick technique, but initial results seem to indicate that either the crushing is not always complete and pregnancies occur, or that the desired effect of crushing the tubes is not always complete for three or four months; pregnancies occurred more frequently in the first three months, postclipping. This technique was devised in an effort to find some way of closing the tube which might be more reversible than cutting or cauterization.

---

* Outpatients are hospital patients who do not stay overnight; inpatients are hospital patients who stay overnight.

There are no laws about voluntary sterilization in females except those established by any hospital, or in the absence of hospital policy, the physician's own criteria. Some of these rules are rather archaic by present standards of medical practice, but they did and do serve to protect physicians from irate patients or their husbands who may not understand that this should be considered a permanent procedure. Women who have had their tubes tied have had at least one child, usually more, and are either married, separated, or divorced. As yet, the never-married mother of two or three children has difficulty in obtaining a tubal ligation in most hospitals; if she is over 30 and has five or six children, she may find it a little easier. Some physicians will tie the tubes of a woman who has had one or two children, without the permission of her husband, if she has been separated from him for six months or more.

Reuniting the tubes is a major surgical procedure and only successful in expert and experienced hands. Success is defined as the presence of open tubes, and even experts are not always successful (see Infertility). Open tubes do not guarantee fertility; a woman's fertility potential changes from year to year, or may change, whether tubes are open or closed. Tubes are usually "untied" because of another marriage. The fertility of the new husband should be demonstrated either by examination of his spermatic fluid, or by the existence of previous children, before surgery on the female is contemplated.

A 32-year-old divorced woman with three children by a previous husband requested that her tubes be "untied." Her new husband, a divorcee with children, had had his vasectomy "untied." When examined prior to his second wife's contemplated surgery, his sperm count was extremely low on two occasions, but there had been no sperm counts done prior to his vas ligation, and he had fathered three children. He may have fathered these children with a low sperm count, or the count may have dropped postligation. The surgeon could only outline the risks of surgery, and the low-pregnancy potential for both partners, for the couple's own personal decision.

There are no hormones involved in tubal ligation, and unlike the potential of vasectomy, the reproductive cells (ova) are never affected. The feeling of being sterile, once the sterilization procedure has been decided upon and done, seems to affect women less than it does men who have had vasectomies. Here again, the need for performance is not essential, and the negative feelings of these women, if they exist at all, can dissipate slowly with no one being the wiser. The loss of the ability to reproduce is primarily a factor in *considering* ligation by the male or female, rather than being a major conscious factor after the fact. If complications arise from either procedure, or there has been some coercion, the chance of marital problems, sexual or not, surfacing is much greater.

Many wives prefer to have a tubal ligation rather than to ask their somewhat reluctant husbands to "do something." There may be an element of martyrdom, but actually women have more to gain, emotionally and physically, since more children are their work, primarily. Caring, knowledgeable females also know that their husbands must be uncoerced volunteers. Even teasing about vasectomy can be a threatening type of coercion. There are more and more males who feel secure, and know that the anesthesia risk, which is the primary risk in female sterilization, is reduced to zero with a vasectomy.

There are other subtle factors which present themselves in this sterilization quandary besides "Which one of us does it?" Not all marriages are made in heaven, and the poststerilization problems often seem to be directly related to presterilization problems in the marriage. A male might think that his vasectomy will insure that his wife will not be seeing some other man; any pregnancy would not be his. On the other hand, sterilization of either partner allows each to wander in an extramarital affair quite safely. Or, as we have noted, if the pill is used for medical conditions other than birth control, how does a wife explain her use of the pill to a vasectomized husband? Does her doctor know something that he does not know?

This brings us to another important bit of realistic advice for the single or married female or male. If you find yourself with someone, temporarily or on a long-term basis, who says that he or she had had a ligation or has a very low sperm count, it would be well to use a contraceptive until the relationship matures to a point of real trust. The surgical procedures can be done so neatly that after a few months there is no point in looking for a scar; it isn't there.

Breast-feeding

Breast-feeding does delay ovulation, but for an unpredictable period of time. The onset of ovulation and subsequent menstruation may be delayed as long as nine months, if breast-feeding is continued for this long in a regular fashion. This seldom happens in the United States, where solid foods are introduced early in the infant's life. Supplementary bottles are often used, and the babies are seldom weaned directly from breast to cup. This irregularity in breast-feeding and the gradually decreasing breast stimulation are apparently factors in the resumption of ovulation prior to the end of lactation.

Therefore, ovulation, which will occur *prior* to any return of menstruation, is unpredictable. Some form of good contraception is necessary at *all* times. Some obstetricians and pediatricians are comfortable advising the use of the pill in breast-feeding mothers; most are not. The IUD is usually not inserted until the sixth week examination, postdelivery. Spermicides should not be used until the uterus and cervical opening are back to normal. A previously-used diaphragm should be refitted. Condoms, or some variations of abstinence, are the only methods available during the first six weeks. Most doctors suggest abstaining from penile-vaginal penetration for the entire six weeks, though adherence to this is seldom, if ever, 100 percent.

"Contraceptive Research: A Male Chauvinist Plot?"[16]

One of the major issues among the feminist groups is the limited number of male contraceptive methods. "Feminists switched off from the decades-long battle to take contraceptive decision away from men . . . now demand more sharing by males of the responsibility and the risks of contraception."[17] This is a perfectly rational request. The basic problem is that "the number of targets—spermatogenesis, sperm maturation, sperm transport, and possibly the chemical constitution of the seminal fluid is far more limited in males than in females"[18] (see Fig. 7-1).

In females, the target areas, each with several approaches, are ovulation, ovum transport, sperm transport, fertilization, fertilized egg transport, prevention of placental development, and maintenance of pregnancy.

The "handy placement of the male genitals outside of the body"[19] is of little advantage in male contraception of a chemical nature, though very convenient for occlusive methods (the condom) or preventing transport (vasectomy).

Also, in females there is usually only one egg at a time, about five hundred in a lifetime. In males, there are millions of sperm involved, between 150 to 300 million per ejaculate. Care must be taken so that no changes occur in even a small number of these, which would create abnormal offspring.

The great success of the pill is not entirely due to male doctors forcing it on their patients. It also happens to be easy, convenient, and theoretically foolproof for females. It is very difficult to discourage anyone from taking it once they are used to its convenience and, like the majority of women taking it, are suffering only minimal or no side effects. The physician-patient dialogue about any type of contraception is difficult. The patient may ask questions about various types but has almost invariably made up her mind ahead of time about what she doesn't want, and only seeks confirmation of her own decisions. The physician is often put in the position of prescribing a method against his own better judgment of what is appropriate for this female and her sexual activity at a particular time, unless there are real medical reasons for or against a particular method.*

Barbara Seaman and others note that certain doctors still like to point out that the risks with the pill are less than the risks of carrying a pregnancy to term. She resents the logic of this argument. We find it wanting, too; there *are* other good methods. But it took us several years to recognize and become accustomed to the reality that not all females are as equally motivated and anxious about unwanted pregnancies as we are, nor are they equally concerned

---

*Contraception is perhaps the one area of medicine where a physician is almost forced to do what the patient requests. This is her decision (or theirs, if it is a compatible couple) and hers alone. She should expect to hear the pro's and con's about *all* methods available, but this is not always the case, and the physicians' individual prejudices inevitably creep into the conversation, if there is a conversation.

MALE

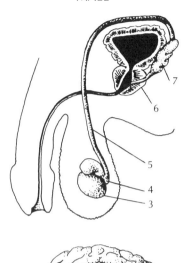

PITUITARY CONTROL (1)

STEROID NEGATIVE FEEDBACK (1 & 2)

SPERM FORMATION IN TESTIS (3)

SPERM MATURATION IN EPIDYDIMIS (4)

SPERM TRANSPORT IN VAS (5)

SEMINAL FLUID BIOCHEMISTRY
(6 & 7)

OVUM TRANSPORT
Ovum pickup by fimbria (5)
Cilia activity (6)
Tubal fluid secretion (6)
Tubal musculature (7)

OVULATION
Steroid negative feedback (1 & 2)
Central nervous system drugs (2)
Gonadotropin antagonists (3)
Local action on follicle (4)

ZYGOTE TRANSPORT
Tubal fluid secretion (6)
Tubal musculature (7)

FERTILIZATION
Shedding of zona pellucida of ovum (6)
Sperm capacitation (11)
Sperm penetration of egg membrane (6)
Pronuclei fusion (6)

FEMALE

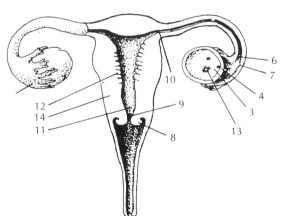

SPERM TRANSPORT
External os of cervix (8)
Cervical mucus (9)
Utero-tubal junction (10)

PREVENTION OF IMPLANTATION
Estrogen binding (12)
Corpus luteum function (13)
Progesterone binding (12)

PLACENTATION
Trophoblast formation (12)
Chorionic gonadotropin
production (12)

MAINTENANCE OF PREGNANCY
Embryogenesis (12)
Placental function (12)
Myometrial activity (14)

Figure 7-1. Vulnerable steps in the reproductive process, male and female.

about risks of any method as long as it works well and doesn't interfere too much in their daily lives. There was even a time when we sincerely believed that all that was needed was information, and then the logic of using contraception and the need for several methods would be apparent to all. Not so.

Militant feminists who have little contact with the wide variety of female attitudes beyond their own, make the same error. They assume that their goals and concerns are those of the entire female population. This is not so either, especially in the areas of contraception, abortion, and sexual behavior.

As a corollary of the above, we would like to suggest and have the reader consider that female and male gynecologists and general practitioners, if at all sensitive, probably have a more realistic view of the wider range of female attitudes toward these matters than psychiatrists, marriage counselors, or any individual female or small group of females with a common cause. The latter groups of specialists see a number of females, but often only the extremes of attitudes. The gynecologist described by Blair Sabol (see below) is a very sensitive, tender-hearted male, who adapts to individual patient's needs, but we doubt if her description and concept of what *she* likes in a doctor would be as universally appealing to others as it is to her. The thinking, knowledgeable patient seeks out the doctor who fits her or his needs.

The fact that Dr. F., or Harry the F., as he is affectionately called, delivered me, my 30-year-old brother (plus over 65 percent of all 30-and-under Philadelphia), dated my mother when they were C.I.T.s at Blue Mountain Camp, was my father's best man and is my father's best friend (he manages to give my father free rectal examinations in the middle of their golf game . . . in the men's room of the club house), and gives my brother his monthly VD shots at a moment's notice, couldn't make him anything less than God in my eyes. Maybe it's because Dr. F. was the first human being I ever laid eyes on, but religiously thereafter (for 23 years) he has been instilling the fear and fun of sex into me and all of my Philadelphia family and friends. He gave year's-supply packets of Ortho-Novum as Christmas presents long before anybody knew what the Pill was. He sex-lectured us biannually while we were still in Carter's undershirts, and up until two years ago I was still afraid to sit on a toilet seat for fear of pregnancy. And since Dr. F. was considered "family," I had the status of being the first on my block to get "an internal," and that's why I was the last on my block to ever get pregnant or need an abortion. But then I always knew that big Harry the F. would, after all, take care of "anything like that." He has the quality. Why else would I shlep down to Rizzo's wretched West Philadelphia (switch-blade-by-day country) twice a year and sit in a waiting room *that reeked of vinyl floor wax, torn leather sofas, and three-year-old* Vogues *and baby-care magazines thrown about? Not to mention the wall-to-wall menopausals fanning their hot flashes mixed in with a few frightened fifth-month "difficult" pregnancy cases. But Harry the F. always takes me immediately. I never have time to think if he'll find cancer of the cervix because I'm too preoccupied with his nurse hustling me to empty my bladder and get my heels in the stirrups. At this point, six-foot-four-inch, 200-pound Harry the F. makes his Lee J. Cobb entrance and delivers his shtik, which is mindless conversation, and it's therapeutically terrific. Constant patter as he pushes, clamps, thrusts and, wide-eyed, examines my interior. "How are ya," he'll ask even though he just saw me at lunch five minutes earlier. "How's school?" I've been out of school for five years. This is the man who's supposed to know me best? Well, what do I care if he can't tell one spread eagle from another as long as he tells me (and everyone) "You're looking gorgeous down here, dear." That's all I care about.*

And that's the secret to the Harry-the-F. addiction. (Even my 78-year-old grandmother comes all the way from Miami just to see him, and for what we don't know.) No matter how bad things are, Harry the F. will always calmly talk you out of it. There's something soothing and marvelous in how predictable he is. "Harry, I haven't gotten my period in three years." His answer: "So, what do you need it for?" An alarmist he's not. And his set cure for everything, from sterility to constipation to weight control, is to "lay off of salt" and "douche with vinegar twice a week." Nothing ever rattles him . . . so why should it rattle you? I'll stick to Harry the F.[20]

Similarly, females with a wide range of interpersonal contacts with males as role-playing mothers, sisters, wives, lovers might be expected to have a more realistic view of the diversity of male sexual attitudes than any individual male. Relatively few females have had this "privilege" and most of those who have, are still naturally reticent about discussing their experiences.* Also, males have no routine, predictable medical needs directly or indirectly involved with sexuality, or which allow, permit, or encourage sexual discussions. Therefore generalizations about male attitudes, even from a medical standpoint, are even more difficult.

* Among the not-so-reticent are Germaine Greer in *The Female Eunuch*, though she devotes only one page to contraception, and Marya Mannes in *Out of My Time*. N. Mailer's *The Prisoner of Sex* also reveals many vulnerable areas of the male, which are seldom exposed.

Women should use caution in assuming that all males, whether they be gynecologists, contraceptive researchers, or their next love, are all like the last one or two males they have had contact with. Many males, whose ideas, words, and phrases appear to have some of the unpleasant and unacceptable characteristics of male chauvinism, often recognize very quickly how unacceptable these are when this is gently but firmly indicated to them. Many are educable, but they have to be carefully taught.*

Abortion

Mother: Did I ever tell you that we had seven abortions including two that were twins?

Daughter (age 13): You did!! Why? Didn't you want them?

Mother: Of course we did. It just took that many to get the three we wanted. Abortion doesn't just mean you don't want it; they can happen accidentally for no good reason that we know. Maybe "miscarriage" is the better word now.

Spontaneous (the miscarriage)†

Spontaneous abortion occurs in 10 percent or more of all *diagnosed* first pregnancies by the end of the tenth week after conception or by the time of the third missed menstrual period. It is believed that the *real* incidence of spontaneous abortion may be closer to 25 percent, if *undiagnosed* first pregnancies in the first four weeks (a delayed, heavy menstrual period) and those occurring in the twelfth to sixteenth weeks are included.

Vaginal bleeding from a pregnant uterus, with or without cramping, signals the possibility of an abortion occurring. This bleeding may be scanty or heavy. In a *threatened abortion*, bleeding without dilatation of the cervical opening occurs. Treatment is watching and waiting. In an *inevitable abortion*, bleeding and dilatation of the cervix occur. The latter is almost always accompanied by moderate to severe cramping. Currettage (removing the lining of the uterus and the products of conception) is frequently necessary to stop the bleeding and complete the abortion. In an *incomplete abortion*, some of the products of con-

---

*Michael Korda's *Male Chauvinism! How It Works* is a good source book for this kind of teaching.

†Miscarriage is a lay term. Patients resent hearing the word "abortion" with its criminal or voluntary connotations, but it is often used in hospitals.

ception, usually the embryo, have been aborted, but the placental tissue has been left behind. This almost always requires currettage. In a *complete abortion,* all of the products of conception, the embryo and the placenta, have been aborted, and the uterine bleeding and the cramping stop. Currettage is rarely needed. In a *missed abortion,* the fetal tissue and the placental tissue are dead, but there has been no aborted material. The signs and symptoms of pregnancy disappear, the uterus is slightly enlarged but does not continue to grow, and there has been no menstrual period or perhaps only irregular spotting with little or no cramping. The missed abortion may be retained as long as three or four months and almost always requires currettage. *Habitual abortion* is defined as three or more consecutive spontaneous abortions, whether or not there have been previous pregnancies which have gone to term delivery. *Tubal abortion* indicates a tubal pregnancy which has died without rupturing the tube; the embryonic tissue is often resorbed (see p. 145).

We are devoting space to spontaneous abortion because it is so common and raises so many questions. Not all uterine bleeding during the first trimester of pregnancy is associated with abortion, and not all threatened abortions become inevitable abortions. It is important to save any aborted material for inspection by a physician, even if the abortion is so early and so spontaneous that it occurs at home and is complete. Abortions in the first three months are almost always of dead embryos, and usually occur about six weeks after the death of the embryo. This can be determined from the size of the embryo in relation to the date of conception and the date of abortion. As high as 70 to 80 percent of abortuses in this period are abnormal embryos, or are abnormalities of the fertilized ovum with no recognizable embryo. The latter are called "blighted ova." (We sometimes call them "blighted sperm.")

There is evidence that an emotional shock of moderate to severe proportions may play a role in spontaneous abortion, if the six-week interval between shock and the abortion is kept in mind; this embryo would probably show no gross abnormalities. Severe trauma (automobile accidents, pelvic surgery early in pregnancy) can also be a factor in immediate or later abortion, but this need not be a foregone conclusion.

Abortion may also be related to abnormalities of the reproductive tract or maternal disease of an acute rather than a chronic nature. There is beginning to be some evidence that excessive manipulation of the cervix during induced abortion is related to later spontaneous abortions (see p. 225). Also, previous tubal disease with extension into the pelvis, immobilizing the uterus so that it cannot rise out of the pelvis as it enlarges, seems to be a factor in some spontaneous abortions. Habitual abortion may be related to abnormalities of the reproductive tract, for example, a double uterus. This diagnosis may be made on pelvic examination, or it may require X-ray diagnosis with dye injected into the uterine cavity; surgical repair is often possible.

Given the high incidence of abnormalities in the early abortions, there is no need for concern, or a feeling of failure, with the first or even the second consecutive abortion. The uterus is simply getting rid of poor protoplasm. Tiptoeing around, lying in bed, or demanding something to "stop" the abortion is not indicated. Disappointment, the need to start all over again, is probably the paramount feeling. Months suddenly look like years. When or if a couple reaches the category of habitual aborters, some medical expertise is needed, and it is of value to know the kind of aborted material that existed previously.

Of the maternal viral and bacterial infections which appear to cause abortion, and do cause abnormalities in a percentage of exposed embryos, syphilis was one of the first recognized; rubella (German measles) and its effects were noted in the midfifties and, other than syphilis, is the best documented infection to date. Twenty percent of all embryos exposed in the first four months of pregnancy are affected to some degree by the rubella virus. This percentage was the basis for therapeutic abortion in many hospitals several years before early changes in abortion legislation were prevalent. The younger the embryo, the greater the danger of malformation of the eyes, ears, and heart. In the pregnant mother, the disease itself may be so mild and transient that it may not be noted; a skin test has been developed which indicates whether or not the mother who has been exposed acquired the virus at that time. Any girl who has not had German measles should have the vaccination now available *before* she does any baby-sitting in young families with potentially pregnant mothers. Any mother who has not had German measles or the vaccine is advised to have the vaccine immediately *after* the birth of the first child, and use adequate contraception for at least three months, so that any future embryo will have the benefit of the maternal antibodies to the disease. Any acute infection during pregnancy should be reported because there is continuing information on fetal abnormalities and probable causes.*

Drugs and hormones of any kind should be avoided during this early developmental period through the twentieth week, unless essential to treatment of real disease. Little is known, even about common drugs, and animal studies are not necessarily transferable to humans.

There is no indication that the pill, if accidentally misused in one cycle with a resultant pregnancy, has any harmful effects on the four-to-six-week-old embryo, if it is taken, or continued unknowingly, for another cycle. The dos-

---

* There is recent evidence that congenital toxoplasmosis in the newborn is related to a pregnant mother's close association with cats and cat feces, if she has never been in contact with cats prior to her pregnancy, and therefore has no antibodies to the disease. In the newborn, the disease affects the retina of the eye with symptoms of patchy blindness.

ages of synthetic estrogens and progesterones in the pill do not approach the high levels of similar hormones *once* used for habitual aborters to "maintain" a pregnancy.*

Sexual activity, in the face of threatened abortion, is not advisable and most couples, even with an accidental pregnancy, do not even consider it. Introducing infections through a cervix which may be silently dilating is the best reason for some form of abstinence. There are some physicians who feel that the temporary pelvic congestion of sexual stimulation or the uterine contractions associated with orgasm arising from any source are particularly dangerous, if they occur at the time of any of the first three missed periods. There are also many gynecologists who feel that there would be more spontaneous abortions if this represented any real threat to a pregnancy, and that any fetus that loosely attached would abort sooner or later anyway. But, there can be much intramarital guilt, blame, and hostility when sexual activity appears to bear some relation to the occurrence of spontaneous abortion of a wanted, or even an unwanted, pregnancy.

Induced Abortion

In Athens (Greece), during 1966-68, 29 percent of 8,312 previously pregnant women admitted for delivery acknowledged one or more previous abortions, induced or spontaneous. Of this group, the percentage of stillbirths (born dead) and premature births was double that of the control group (the remaining 71 percent). They note studies from other countries which agree with their findings, and also note a study from Greece which indicates that about one-third of all women subjected to induced abortion were permanently infertile.[21]

There are those who consider induced abortion benign, if done early, and an entity separate from sexual behavior; we find these opinions difficult to comprehend. It is obviously futile to try to legislate sexual behavior. Some legislators keep trying, and they are keeping local abortion legislation (regarding age

---

* There are some recent disturbing reports indicating that the high doses of DES (diethylstilbesterol, see p. 207) used 20 years ago to "aid" habitual aborters may be the causative agent of benign and malignant lesions in the vaginas of some of the female offspring of these pregnancies. Any girl born of a mother who had "difficulty" holding a pregnancy, 15 to 25 years ago, should check with her, and with a gynecologist if DES was used. High dosages of progesterone were also used for a time for the same reason, but tended to create a large clitoris in female offspring. The hormone was said to "masculinize" the clitoris!

of the embryo, financing, and setting up criteria for safe abortion clinics) in such a continuing state of flux that we must still consider the methods and dangers inherent in criminal abortions.*

Even when abortions are legal, criminal abortionists will still exist and thrive on misguided girls and women, and their men, who find the price is lower because of the legitimate competition. In those states with few legal abortion facilities, women who cannot afford to get out of the state may have to use these individuals, whatever their price.

The dangers inherent in any induced abortion, legal or illegal, depend to a large degree on the age of the embryo (the size of the uterus). This is determined either from the date of conception, or from the date of the last menstrual period, which is usually a difference of two weeks with monthly cycles. This two week differential does not seem to be defined in any abortion legislation and therefore offers physicians the same leeway in determining whether or not the age of the embryo is within the legal definition; and there are many, many females who cannot remember the date of their last menstrual period or a possible date of conception. Experienced gynecologists can usually tell the age of the embryo, within a week or two, after a pelvic examination in the first trimester.

The incompetent abortions of the self-induced, friend-induced, or motel-hotel variety, or even the inexperienced lunch hour quickie kinds, are frequently incomplete abortions which eventually require completion in a hospital. Not much money is saved. However, in areas where abortions are difficult to obtain, this intrauterine interference does create the situation known as an inevitable abortion (p. 222), and no hospital will refuse admission to an inevitable abortion. This is usually a medical emergency.

Self-induced abortions with catheters, broomstraws, or instrumentation of any sort require some knowledge of the vagina, the cervix, and the direction of the uterine cavity, plus the dexterity needed to find the opening in the cervix; no other method works (oral drugs, local drugs, or chemicals) without severely compromising the life or health of the mother.† The dexterity needed is next to impossible even for someone who is well acquainted with the female pelvis. The do-it-yourself menstrual extraction kit advertised in the underground newspapers generally requires more knowledgeable assistance than just someone to hold the mirror, or the speculum. Without anesthesia or analgesia, dilatation of the cervical canal or inserting anything into the uterine cavity, is extremely uncomfortable, crampy, and painful. But desperate girls and women have always ignored the risks to themselves and endured almost any discomfort.

---

* A retired Scotland Yard detective thinks he has evidence that the infamous Jack the Ripper of the late 1800s was really a female criminal abortionist getting rid of her abortion complications.

† See Quinine and Ergoipiol, p. 190.

The motel-hotel abortionists use very little analgesia for their brief encounters with the "patient"; they cannot have sleepy people around too long. The "best" of this group of abortionists, and the word "best" is used advisedly, send their women to the hospital immediately after the procedure. Here they can be watched and a completion currettage done if and when necessary.

As an intern in a city hospital, our weekends "on" coincided with the local abortionist's schedule; he (or she) sent the girls to different hospitals on alternate weekends. Friday and Saturday nights on the gynecology service were spent running to and from the blood bank through a long, deserted tunnel. Girls came in bleeding and cramping from the abortionist's intrauterine interference, or hemorrhaging from trying to insert potassium permanganate pills into their own uteri. The pills usually ended up in the upper end of the vagina, eroding the tissue and causing massive bleeding. Only rarely did the pill get in the cervical opening, where it also caused massive bleeding. The pregnancy remained in the uterus, untouched.

Precautions after abortions of this type should be directed at watching for signs of infection and for excessive bleeding. These may occur within one or two hours, twelve to twenty-four hours, or even two or three weeks later. Infection is indicated by a low to high grade fever and maybe a foul-smelling vaginal discharge. There may or may not be cramping. Excessive bleeding is one pad or more per hour after the procedure, or the onset of bleeding requiring five or six pads a day, even two or three weeks later. Tampons should not be used during the first two or three weeks, and intercourse is contraindicated.

The long-term effects of infection in the reproductive tract may be sterility (closed tubes) and chronic PID (see VD). The immediate complications of infection may be severe kidney or liver dysfunction requiring long, intensive hospital care.

The other complication, which can be lethal and may arise if the patient is not watched carefully, is shock from loss of blood: hidden bleeding into the abdominal cavity because of perforation of the uterus, or excessive vaginal bleeding because of incomplete uterine currettage. The uterus does not stop bleeding until all of the products of conception are out. *This can be a complication of any induced abortion that is not watched for the next 24 to 36 hours; even those done in legal, in-and-out-the-same-day clinics carry this risk.*

Case History: Twenty-year-old single female, legal early abortion with local anesthesia in a "three-hour" clinic. Vaginal bleeding increased two days later; she was seen in the emergency room of a nearby hospital and treated with drugs to contract the uterus and told to return the next day if bleeding continued, or before if necessary. The bleeding increased the next day while she was traveling three states away against the doctor's advice. She was admitted to a hospital in that area for currettage; the bleeding could not be stopped; the uterus was removed.

This is the lawyer's story; she wanted to sue somebody, but even the lawyer was not sure whom to sue. She may or may not have had a case, but she was the one traveling against advice, and the uterus may have been perforated while the second currettage was being done.

The incidence of perforation of the uterus in a study of complications of 6,000 abortions done in four hospitals over three years was one in 200. One-third of the perforated uteri had to be removed in order to stop the bleeding.[22]

Also, if a woman is Rh negative, it is important that she be treated for the possibility of having been sensitized to the probable Rh positive blood of the embryo during the procedure. Failure to treat could affect the children of subsequent pregnancies.

Women who have what seems to be a quiet postabortion course should expect a menstrual period in about six weeks. We have seen two young women (ages 18 and 19), four months postabortion of the motel variety (250 dollars); neither had had a menstrual period. They were both five-and-a-half months pregnant at the time of examination, too late to do anything legally. The four- or six-week postabortion pelvic has some very real value.

Methods of therapeutic (legal) abortion. Abortions are comparable to tonsillectomies, but not for the reasons usually given. Neither are simple or without risk, though D and C's and tonsillectomies are the two most frequently performed surgical procedures. If general anesthesia is used, an anesthesia risk is common to both. The potential of emergency blood loss, postoperatively, in tonsillectomies is probably second only to that which is expected with incomplete abortions.

The method of abortion is determined by the age of the embryo or fetus, but the guidelines vary with the physician, hospital, or clinic. These guidelines have become more uniform in the past few years with increasing experience with suction currettage (see below). Early abortions, up to eight weeks conception age, carry less immediate and long-term risks than those done later, and even less risk than carrying the baby to term, though the complications of abortion often create sterility, which delivery risks seldom do. Early diagnosis of pregnancy is imperative. Statistics from many pregnancy testing facilities indicate that more and more pregnancies are being diagnosed early for just this reason. Also, early abortions are cheaper. Education has been effective, but there will always be women and girls who postpone confirmation of what they suspect is true; late abortions will always be requested.

Good inpatient or outpatient hospital and clinic care should include the following. 1) Preoperatively: some attention to the psyche, a discussion of available options, explanation of the procedure to be used, a chest X-ray, blood tests (to include Rh, hemoglobin, and blood typing), adequate anesthesia, and a good medical history. A positive pregnancy test and a pelvic examination to rule out the possibility of an ectopic pregnancy are also indicated; scraping out an empty uterus does not remove the ectopic pregnancy and subjects the pregnant woman to two anesthetics, if the ectopic is not diagnosed until the time of the currettage. 2) Postoperatively: at least an eight to ten hour "watch" and most physicians would prefer 18 hours, a discussion of possible complications which might require a return visit, a discussion of contraception, a two or six week return appointment, and treatment of the Rh negative patient.

In the first three or four days past an expected menstrual period, *menstrual extraction* (suction) will remove embryonic material before a pregnancy test can be done. Some physicians and clinics are now equipped to do menstrual extractions of the "unknown." Since it is an unknown pregnancy, the risk of infection, of missing an ectopic pregnancy, and of incomplete evacuation hardly seem worth using this method.

Up to 25 days past a missed period, some gynecologists will *"instrument"* the *uterine cavity* with a small currette which needs little or no dilatation of the cervix. There may or may not be a need for currettage later for a missed abortion, or an incomplete abortion (p. 222).

Up to three months, the time of the third missed period or a conception age of ten weeks, *suction currettage (vacuum extraction)* is usually done if the physician is experienced with it, or a *D and C,* if he prefers. Many physicians are now routinely following suction currettage with an "old-fashioned" curretting of the uterine cavity to insure complete removal of the contents. Local anesthesia is necessary for the dilatation of the cervix, but does little or nothing for the discomfort of the currettage. Suction is not as uncomfortable, but for a brief period feels like moderate to severe menstrual cramping. If you have seen any TV specials on early abortion, it is obvious that some girls can smile through five or six minutes of even severe cramping, if they know that is all there will be.

> . . . But it is dishonest and unjust to perpetuate the idea that there is nothing to it. For most women, the abortion is unpleasant and frightening. It can also be painful.
>
> The severity of the pain depends partially . . . on the woman's threshold of pain. . . . It has been my experience* that the more emotional conflicts a woman brings to the operation, the more pain she will feel. . . . If a woman is frightened and upset, she will brace herself to maintain control. It's normal and we all do it . . . but it also seems to make the uterine contractions more severe.[23]

* This writer spend three months working in a New York City abortion clinic.

Suction currettage is gradually becoming more effective with increasing experience; some of the early procedures were incomplete. There is also less risk of infection and perforation in inexperienced hands, though both can and do occur. It is also less unpleasant for the physician, since fetal parts are not clearly identifiable.

Between three and four months is a questionable period; the embryo is too large and the uterus too soft and thin for a safe D and C, or an adequate suction currettage, and there is not enough amnionic fluid around the fetus for a *salting out* procedure (see below). Girls and women are frequently surprised and puzzled when they have been hearing "come early for safety" and then are told to "wait two weeks and come back." They simply did not come early enough. Any of these three procedures may be done during this three to four month stage, but the risk of complications is much greater with all of them (see Laminaria).

Salting out means injecting saline (salt) solution, or at one time glucose solution (sugar), into the fluid-filled space around the embryo or fetus, either through the abdominal wall, or from below, vaginally. The fetus dies, and the uterus starts contracting sometime in the next 24 to 36 hours. A dead fetus is delivered from below, usually in the hospital bed.* Most nursing personnel do not like their almost total responsibility in this miniature labor and delivery. Some irresponsible clinics inject saline and send women home to go into labor and deliver there, or in some nearby hospital or emergency room. This should be a hospital procedure from start to finish. Even these saline abortions frequently need postdelivery currettage.

Saline injection is undoubtedly better for the uterus and the cervix than late currettages; there is seldom any manipulation of the cervix which might lead to complications with future pregnancies (p. 141). But there is some evidence of occasional increased bleeding at the time of delivery of this immature fetus, related to the effects of the saline on blood clotting, and there is always the possibility of saline (a stronger solution than that used routinely for intravenous use) being injected into areas other than the amnionic cavity, with possible fatal results. Occasionally, labor does not occur and has to be induced with pitocin (see below).

Hysterotomy, opening the uterus through an abdominal incision, and removing the live fetus corresponds to a miniature Caesarian section. Since the advent of saline abortions, there has been little indication for this procedure as a primary method of abortion. Occasionally it is necessary if the saline fails. It creates some of the same problems as a section in term pregnancies, namely, the possible need for a repeat section with future pregnancies because of a weakened area in the uterine wall.

---

* A series of 21 patients, ages 15 to 38, with pregnancies from 15 to 22 weeks, delivered in a time span ranging from 13 to 74 hours.

Some women who have gone out of the United States for abortion of very late pregnancies have encountered *packing*. This means insertion of some soft, sterile item through the cervical canal, and between the amnionic sac and the uterine wall. This stimulates the onset of contractions and the living fetus delivers from below, prematurely. There is greater risk of infection with this method, and it is seldom used in the United States except under special circumstances.

Rupture of the membranes, breaking the bag of fluid around the fetus and allowing the fluid to drain out, often stimulates labor within 24 to 36 hours, if the fetus is six or seven weeks from term. Labor may also be stimulated with pitocin (intravenously or intramuscularly) after the membranes are ruptured, or after saline has been injected. Infection is a risk with this type of intra-uterine interference also, unless the baby is at term and about to deliver spontaneously. In contrast to the presence of ruptured membranes prior to labor or in early labor, the primary concern with infections during attempted abortion is obviously not with the fetus, but with the mother and her future reproductive capacity, as well as her immediate well-being.

Prostaglandins, a group of naturally occurring hormones, have been shown to stimulate uterine contractions even in very early pregnancies. They have been used orally, on impregnated tampons, and by injection. They are still in the category of research methods, and have many unpleasant side effects on muscles other than the uterine muscle, and as yet appear to have no advantage over any of the methods described above. Many of the abortions stimulated in this way have to be finished with a currettage. The hoped-for advantage with this method was avoidance of mechanical dilatation of the cervix.

Summary

We feel that we have to emphasize that abortions are unpleasant for most doctors as well as most patients, though there are those patients who are so overwhelmed and relieved with being freed of their pregnancy that they may even be orgasmic with the genital manipulation required, regardless of the discomfort. No one can demand that an individual doctor do an abortion; she can only request. We feel strongly that the militant proabortion groups would have looked less militant and would have been better received if they had substituted "abortion on request" for "abortion on demand"; however, it sometimes takes noise, and banging on doors and tables to make any impression worthy of notice by the communications media.

When abortions are legal, patients who go to hospital clinics may "demand" abortion, but no private patient can force an individual doctor to do an abortion, if he does not wish to do one. But refusing a distraught patient, or a couple who has conceived out of ignorance or contraceptive failure, is extremely difficult, if the procedure is legal and the pregnancy is early. It is just as difficult and unpleasant for the physician to see young women or couples who have clearly been acting irresponsibly, coming in for their first, second, or third abortions, expecting the physician to "pick up the pieces" of their irresponsibility. Even physicians who have fought long and hard for abortion reform have difficulty comprehending this type of gross negligence. If they do the third abortion, their rationale is usually that the woman is obviously disturbed, and that no child deserves this kind of mother. But, they also know that their efforts in making abortion available to all income groups would inevitably include this kind of female as well. Women who have money can "afford" to be careless and unthinking.

It is difficult for antiabortion and many proabortion people to understand the motives of doctors who do abortions all day long, day in and day out; most physicians, if they do abortions in a clinic, do them only one or two days a week, or only half-days. For some, money is a solace, but there has always been room in every civilized society for hangmen and executioners and, of necessity, they have usually been paid well because they are in short supply.*

Larned, a nonprofessional (see p. 229), noted in an excellent article about her three months experience working in an abortion clinic that the staff workers were disturbed by the "doctors' notorious insensitivity" to the patient and their need, even in conference, to wear their white coats: "God forbid, that someone should forget who they were."[24] She, and others, fail to consider that a procedure with this much emotional overlay for the patient and the physician cannot be approached in anything but a mechanical fashion; to absorb the emotion of a new patient every 20 minutes, or to take off the uniform (the white coat) is to let down one's guard and become ineffective. Even if money is the primary motivation, or if physicians know they are doing an essential service with some expertise, in the larger sense it is often felt to be morally reprehensible. Even though legal, life and death are involved, the physicians, not the attending personnel, are the ones who are ultimately totally responsible.

The most frequent question one hears about these nonhospital clinics (free-standing clinics) is not about safety, but about the disparity in costs between a well-run clinic and an abortion done in a hospital clinic. The answer is simple, and the best of the free-standing clinics will tell you why. They usually have either a direct hospital affiliation, or are located on the "doorstep" of a good hospital. These clinics do not have to pay the overhead for bloodbanks, operating rooms, anesthetists, nursing care, beds, housekeepers, or the standby expertise needed to treat some of the complications of abortion. These essential

---

* We are acquainted with two physicians whose activities and abortion clinics were started primarily to force review of existing legislation; they were successful in forcing this review. Both of these men, whose concern was with the indigent who could not afford hospital procedures not covered by insurance or state aid, gave up their personal, direct patient involvement prior to the Supreme Court's surprise decision. "Enough is enough," one said.

facilities are furnished and paid for by the nearby hospital on a 24-hour basis, whether or not they are used. The better run clinics also do not incur the risks of aborting any pregnancies over the eight or ten weeks size. Physician costs (charges) are about the same in both situations, but represent a lower percentage of the total cost for the hospital patient, than for the free-standing clinic patient. However, at the present time, free-standing clinics are not eligible for state aid payments for the indigent, or for insurance payments; hospital patients can use their insurance or state aid.

A final note: The reader should not conclude from our oblique references to the relative emotional ease with which an early abortion can be done versus the unpleasantness of late abortions, that we think that life is any less precious at the 32-cell stage. We do not. We only wish to emphasize just exactly what the law is asking doctors to do; the patient does not see the aborted material.

VIEWPOINTS

We believe that the population crisis is so threatening to the quality of human life that for the sake of the individual, the family, and society, we must bring population and resources into balance by learning to control our fertility. Toward this end, we believe that contraception is far preferable to abortion. But we also believe that abortion, performed under proper conditions, is preferable to the birth of an unwanted child.

We believe that every child should be wanted by and born into a family that is able to feed, clothe, educate and, above all, love him; that the family is the basic unit of our society and that the married life of the parents should encompass sexual activity whether or not for purposes of procreation; that appropriate contraception, which spaces children and elminates the fear of unwanted pregnancies, strengthens family ties and establishes a sense of responsible parenthood; that in view of the problem of overpopulation, every couple has a responsibility to society, as well as to their own family, not to overburden the world with more lives than it can sustain.

We believe that responsible parenthood demands consideration not only of the number of children individual parents want but also of the effect of that number on society as a whole.

We believe that the necessary limitation of family size should be and can be achieved voluntarily by far more attention to the adequate availability of contraceptives, by the legalization of abortion, and by educational programs to motivate people to practice family planning. For the good of all, we should educate ourselves and others to the necessity of restricting family size as a prerequisite for a life of quality for our children's children and for the generations to follow.

We believe that no woman should be forced to bear an unwanted child. A woman should be able to have an abortion legally if she has decided that this is the only solution she can accept and if the physician agrees that it is in the best interests of mother and child. She should be encouraged to seek the best social and spiritual counseling available before reaching a decision; and the physician, for his own support, should have the opportunity to confer with colleagues of his choosing if he feels the need for such consultation.

Believing that abortion should be subject to the same regulations and safeguards as those governing other medical and surgical procedures, we urge the repeal of all laws limiting either the circumstances under which a woman may have an abortion or the physician's freedom to use his best professional judgment in performing it.

We believe that no physician should be forced to perform an abortion if this violates his conscience; but, if this is so, he has an obligation to refer his patient to another physician willing to serve her.

From *Who Shall Live?*
A Report Prepared by the American Friends Service Committee
(New York: Hill and Wang, 1970), pp. 62-65.

• • • • • • • • • •

New York—The press has not widely noticed an extraordinary appeal that has been lodged by the State of Connecticut asking the Supreme Court to review its decision of last January in respect of abortion. On that occasion the court ruled that no state can deny a woman the right to an abortion during the first few months of her pregnancy on the grounds that the fetus is not a "person" in any constitutional sense and is not therefore entitled to the protections given to a person.

The court was not itself anxious to rule just when in the embryonic process someone comes alive, satisfying itself to say that "We need not resolve the difficult question of when life begins."

Brookhart v. Janis

The State of Connecticut reminds the Supreme Court that in 1966, in *Brookhart v. Janis*, the court observed that "When constitutional rights turn on the resolution of a factual dispute, we are duty bound to make an independent examination of the evidence in the record." It is such an independent examination that the State of Connecticut has conducted. And 14 states of the union have joined Connecticut, as *amici curiae*. The court is considering the matter at this moment.

Connecticut has imposed upon itself rigorous scientific responsibilities, to which end it begins its 55-page brief with testimony from scientists.

Dr. Albert William Liley is professor in perinatal physiology in the postgraduate school of obstetrics and gynaecology at the University of Aukland.

"In 1963," says Dr. Liley, "I developed a technique for the transfusion of blood to the baby *in utero*. This work demonstrated conclusively that the unborn child, like any other person, could be ill and could have his disease diagnosed, his condition assessed, and his malady treated.

"In a number of genetic and biochemical problems, definite diagnosis can be established as early as the 14th week, and, in the Rh baby, therapy has been undertaken as early as the 18th week of intrauterine life. With advances in technology these limits will be moved back earlier in pregnancy. The unborn child is my patient, and I respect and protect his life as I would the life of any other patient."

Views of Mayo doctor

Dr. Hymie Gordon is chairman of the department of medical genetics at the Mayo Clinic. He introduces his testimony philosophically.

"The modern biological concept of human individuality is remarkably in harmony with that of some of the oldest theological concepts. The rabbis of the Talmudical period and the early Christian fathers taught that life entered the fetus at the moment of conception. Modern biology teaches the same thing. . . . True, environmental influences both during the intrauterine period and after birth modify the individual's constitution and continue to do so right until his death, but it is at the moment of conception that the individual's capacity to respond to these exogenous influences is established.

"It is an ignorant presumption to suggest that we are in a position to weigh its (the living cell's) life against that of another. A clear distinction must be made between the unquestionable right of the mother to decide whether or not she is to become pregnant, and the unquestionable right of the unborn baby to life."

'Conclusive proof'

Dr. Micheline Mathews-Roth, of the department of microbiology and molecular genetics at Harvard, deposes that "studies in embryology and genetics have conclusively proved that the embryo from conception to birth is a living human individual. . . ."

Dr. Paul Rockwell, director of anesthesiology at Leonard Hospital, Troy, New York, writes that "in 1958 or thereabouts, while giving an anesthetic for a ruptured ectopic pregnancy at eight weeks gestation, I observed what I believe was the smallest living human being ever seen. A tiny human male (approx. 1 cm.) was swimming vigorously in the amniotic fluid from the end of his umbilical cord within the intact, transparent embryo sac. This tiny male was perfectly developed with fingers and hands, toes and feet. . . . It is my opinion that if the lawmakers and people realize that very vigorous human life is present, even at this early stage of development, it is possible that abortion would be found much more objectionable than euthanasia."

From William F. Buckley, Jr.,
"Abortions and Embryology,"
Philadelphia Evening Bulletin, 1 April 1973.

• • • • • • • • • •

In panels and discussions on religion and abortion I frequently have cited my favorite set of statistics: one hundred percent of the bishops who oppose the repeal of anti-abortion laws are men and one hundred percent of the people who have abortions are women. These "statistics" have the double advantage of being both irrefutable and entertaining, thereby placing the speaker in an enviable situation vis-a-vis the audience. More important than this, however, is the fact that this simple juxtaposition of data suggests something of the context in which problems concerning the morality of abortion and the repeal of anti-abortion laws should be seen within the wide context of the oppression of women in sexually hierarchical society. . . .

Society as we know it is characterized by a sexual caste system in which men and women constitute birth-ascribed, hierarchically ordered groups, having unequal access to "goods, services, prestige, and well-being" (from Berreman's description of caste.) . . .

Since the condition of sexual caste has been camouflaged so successfully by sex role segregation, it has been difficult to perceive anti-abortion laws and anti-abortion ethical arguments within this context. Yet it is only by perceiving them within this total environment of patriarchal bias that it is possible to assess realistically how they function in society. If, for example, one-sided arguments using such loaded terminology as "the murder of the unborn child" are viewed as independent units of thought unrelated to the kind of society in which they were formulated, then they may well appear plausible and cogent. However, once the fact of sexual caste and its implications have been unveiled, such arguments and the laws they attempt to justify can be recognized as consistent with the rationalizations of a system that oppresses women but incongruous with the experience and needs of women. . . .

At this moment in history the abortion issue has become a focal point for dramatic conflict between the ethic of patriarchal authoritarianism and the ethic of courage to confront ambiguity. When concrete decisions have to be made concerning whether or not to have an abortion, a complex web of circumstances demands consideration. . . . Essentially women are saying that because there is ambiguity surrounding the whole question and because sexually hierarchical society is stacked against women, abortion is not appropriately a matter of criminal law. In our society as it is, no laws can cover the situation justly. Abortion "reform" generally works out in a discriminatory way and is not an effective deterrent to illegal abortions. Thousands of women who have felt desperate enough to resort to criminal abortions have been subjected to psychological and physical barbarities, and sometimes these have resulted in death. . . .

Women—many of them victims also of economic and racial oppression —have just begun to cry out publicly about their rights over their own bodies. . . . Women are making explicit the dimension that traditional morality and abortion legislation simply have not taken into account: the realities of their existence as an oppressed caste of human beings. For example, [the] claim that science has provided sufficient means for avoiding the beginning of the life process is out of touch with the realities of individual situations. [The] admonition that one should acknowledge the consequences of the sex act is of high moral tone, but it doesn't have much meaning when applied after the fact to the case of an economically and culturally deprived adolescent. As for the "rights of the putative father"—[one] really should speak to a few young women who would be willing to tell it to him like it is. . . .

From Mary Daly,
"Abortion and Sexual Caste," Commonweal,
4 February 1972, pp. 415-418.

References

1. Letter to the Editor, *Family Circle,* May 1973.

2. James Dickey, "Adultery," *Poems 1957-1967* (Middletown, Conn.: Wesleyan University Press, 1967).

3. Ernest Hemingway, *For Whom the Bell Tolls* (New York: Charles Scribner's Sons, 1940).

4. Ernest Hemingway, *Green Hills of Africa* (New York: Charles Scribner's Sons, 1935).

5. Ernest Hemingway, *To Have and Have Not* (New York: Charles Scribner's Sons, 1937).

6. Eustace Chesser, *The Human Aspects of Sexual Deviation* (New York: William Morrow & Co., 1971).

7. Personal Communication, Dean of Students, University of Pennsylvania, 1973.

8. Marya Mannes, *Out of My Time* (Garden City, New York: Doubleday and Company, 1971).

9. Karl Menninger, quoted in *Time,* 6 August 1973, p. 41.

10. Philip Sarrel, Oral presentation, U. S. Naval Hospital, Philadelphia, March 11, 1972.

11. Association for Voluntary Sterilization, *Newsletter,* Summer 1973. It is of interest to note that the Association for Voluntary Sterilization (AVS) has sold 20,000 male vasectomy lapel pins and only 2,000 female ligation pins or pendants. Each is the appropriate male or female symbol with a broken or separated circle.

12. Shirley Southwick, "The Psychological Side Effects of Vasectomy," The *New York Times,* 14 January 1972.

13. John Fried, "The Incision Decision," *Esquire,* June 1972.

14. W. H. W. Inman and M. P. Vessey, "Investigation of Deaths from Pulmonary, Coronary, and Cerebral Thrombosis and Embolism in Women of Childbearing Age," *British Medical Journal,* 2 (1968): 193.

15. Victor A. Drill, "Oral contraceptives and thromboembolic disease. I Prospective and retrospective studies," *Journal of the American Medical Association,* 219 (1972): 543.

16. S. J. Segal, "Contraceptive Research: A Male Chauvinist Plot?" *Family Planning Perspectives,* 4 (July 1972): 3.

17. *Ibid.*

18. *Ibid.*

19. Barbara Seaman, *Free and Female* (New York: Coward, McCann & Geoghegan, 1972).

20. Blair Sabol, "Harry the F. from Philly," *New York,* 14 August 1972.

21. S. Pantelakis, G. C. Papadimitriou, and S. Doxiadis, "Influence of induced and spontaneous abortions on the outcome of subsequent pregnancies," *American Journal of Obstetrics and Gynecology,* 116 (July 15, 1973): 6.

22. G. K. Stewart and P. Goldstein, "Medical and Surgical Complications of Therapeutic Abortions," *American Journal of Obstetrics and Gynecology,* 40 (October 1972): 4.

23. D. Larned, "Programmed for Pregnancy," UR (October 29, 1972).

24. *Ibid.*

8

· · · · · · · · · Adolescence · · · · · · · · ·

In this chapter we will examine the development of human sexuality during adolescence, that period in the life process during which an individual is no longer thought of as a child, but has not yet been accorded the status of adult. In many societies, adolescence is of very short duration, and may not in fact be seen as a significant period in the life cycle. Increasingly in the developed societies, however, we have come to delineate sharply this period, and to recognize, even as we help to create, some new problems for human living. Our focus, of course, will be on the problems of sexual development during this period.

Adolescence, as a physiological phenomenon, begins at an earlier age now than in former times, due largely to improved nutrition and health practices. And increasingly in Western societies, it is lengthened as a sociocultural phenomenon, long after young men and women have reached biological maturity, or at least long after they have reached the age when they are biologically able to procreate. The lengthening of adolescence seems to be related to changes which have taken place in the past century in the economic and familial systems. We no longer need the labor of young people to survive economically. And we no longer need to begin families early and to reproduce often to have sufficient numbers of people available to help in the economics of family life. In the past and still today in less developed societies, these activities have propelled young people to early maturity; that is, to begin in their teens to play the roles of work and marriage which are to be theirs through the remainder of their lives.

In the United States and elsewhere, an adolescent culture and social life have been emerging that are distinctive of both the periods that preceded them and those which are to follow. Among the most significant features of the adolescent life-style are those which define and redefine female and male sexuality. While most young people learn the basic differences between the sexes well before their tenth birthday, it appears that it is during the adolescent years that the sociocultural significance of sexuality develops. And in developed societies, the emerging sexuality is nurtured more and more in isolation from adult female and male roles, and in environments especially adapted to adolescent life ways (the high schools and colleges of America). Thus, the sexual revolution appears to be, in part at least, a function of this phenomenon of adolescence.

The primary purpose of colleges and universities may be the further intellectual development and occupational preparation of young people. Colleges have the latent function of keeping young people out of the labor market and off the streets where they might otherwise compete with older people for jobs and space. (We have not yet raised the question seriously of why we bother to give so much leisure time to young people, or to believe that it is more valuable to educate the young than the middle aged or even the old. We seem almost to be hooked on the belief that adolescence is the proper time for young people to discover themselves and that they will make this discovery better on a college campus than in a job.) At the same time and also in a latent manner until recently, high schools and colleges have served to encourage young people to question the traditional views of sexuality, and gradually to evolve their own. Nevertheless, this period is viewed with a great deal of ambivalence and anxiety by society at large. Heiss and Goldblatt state the matter well: "With the possible exception of old age, no other phase of individual development is so clearly marked by negative connotations and lack of positive sanctions."[1]

As a matter of fact, adolescence is like old age in that changes in economics and health have radically increased the numbers of people to be found in these social "groupings," as well as the length of time they may be expected to "be there," without meaningful roles to play in and for society. That is, since we value such things as work, achievement, and productivity, there is a concomitant tendency to devalue both adolescence and old age.

The logic of our system seems to be that when people enter the labor force on a full-time, fully committed basis, they are expected to know who they are, and so they are no longer adolescents. It is our thesis that working for a living on a full-time basis rather than the experience of full sexual interaction defines the end of adolescence in this and other societies. It is the roles people play, and occupational roles in particular rather than age and sex performance per se, that define and limit adolescence. A person becomes an adult in human society when he or she can perform economic roles, and take his or her place in the society's labor force.

We know from comparative anthropological studies that young people are permitted to engage in premarital sexual intercourse in some societies, while such behavior is proscribed in other societies. Necking, petting, and now sexual intercourse are increasingly common among the unmarried in industrial societies, but such behavior does not and has not bestowed adult status on the sexually active. Since contemporary society seems willing to allow the young an extended period of time during which to work out their sexual identities, and to provide them with a place to carry out their search for identity, we will want to give appropriate attention to the physiological and the psychosocial dimensions of adolescence as we now understand them.

The Complexity of Physiological Change

If all of the subtle and not so subtle changes which characterize adolescence and the onset of puberty in the female and the male (growth spurts, menstruation, breast development, pubic hair, axillary hair, leg hair, beards, spontaneous ejaculations, muscular development, acne, and increase in the size of the penis and testes, change in contour of the labia, plus the overall awareness of the opposite sex) were to occur on every child's thirteenth birthday, plus or minus a week or two, one might have reason to hope that everyone, parent, child, and physician, would be thoroughly instructed and aware. There might then be very few surprises. The psychology of the change would not only be simplified, but perhaps to some degree controlled. If there were a delay of more than one week in the appearance of the change, the child would be examined and reassured that if nothing happened in another week, some tests would be done, and nature would be encouraged to proceed on schedule. (After all, note how well we are managing pregnancies these days.) Thus, in the space of some two or three weeks, age peers would be psychological peers at age 13.

We would certainly have an easier time developing norms to govern behavior for teenagers. We might even be able to develop group structures which would foster relatively easy learning about sexuality and sex roles. (The latter two are related, but not the same phenomena. Sexuality refers to the experience of one's self as a fully sexed person, physiologically. Playing sex roles refers to the experience of playing roles which society has defined as appropriate to either female or male according to genital structure. It should be recognized that one's experience of self is strongly influenced by society's social role definitions, and is in no sense simply a response to biological stimuli. In fact, of course, in most societies sex roles and sexuality have been closely intertwined phenomena.)

But instead of simple growth to maturation, there is almost a ten-year range of normal development into sexual maturity, at least in a developed society like the United States. While this age span has come to be normal, it is difficult for teenagers and their parents to see it as such. Peer groups of teenagers are determined as much chronologically as they are physiologically, and the young cannot easily escape daily comparisons. They are often thrown together in somewhat artificial peer groups for several years or more before they can assert their sexual independence. Meanwhile, they are constantly observing and comparing, listening to a variety of advice about sex, and all too often not hearing any advice when they are troubled and don't know precisely what questions to ask.

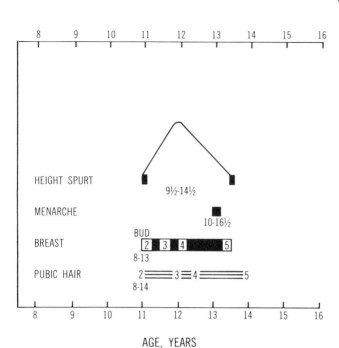

Figure 8-1. Diagram of sequence of events at adolescence in girls. An average girl is represented; the range of ages within which some of the events may occur is given by the figures placed directly below them.

Individual variations in sexual development are largely accompanied by parental tendencies to postpone communication in this area. This tendency may be due in part to parental reluctance to see their "babies" growing up. In larger measure, noncommunication reflects traditional sexual attitudes and behavior which are only now beginning to change. The interplay of physiological with sociocultural forces simply exacerbates the problem of maturation. The wonder is that most young people survive the experience. The following quotations from interviews on female sexuality, seem typical:

My parents never talked to me about sex. I did not even learn about menstruation from my mother. I was thirteen when I had my first period. I discovered it in the toilet at school. I must admit that I was a bit frightened, but I accepted it, as I knew that it had to happen to me. I never told anyone, not even my mother. I felt that it was something you just didn't talk about. I learned about sex through experience.[2]

My parents never talked about sex in front of me, and it wasn't until I had studied the human reproductive system in the biology

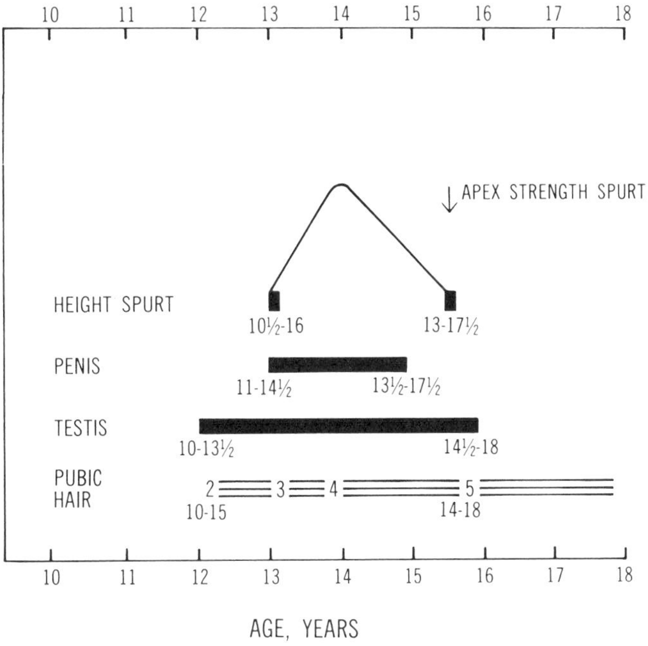

Figure 8-2. Diagram of sequence of events at adolescence in boys. An average boy is represented; the range of ages within which each event charted may begin and end is given by the figures placed directly below its start and finish

lessons at school that I felt that I could talk about sex to my mother. Until then I didn't understand what sex was all about. . . .

I began to become aware of my sexuality when I reached puberty. I was curious about all the changes that were going on in my body. . . .[3]

The Endocrinology of Puberty[4]

Figures 8-1 and 8-2 represent the four physical characteristics which define puberty for the majority of adolescents as they observe themselves and each other. The other changes of puberty which are closely related to these are not usually listed as sexual characteristics, but they are; that is, the muscular development of shoulders, thighs, and the extremities, the rearrangements of fatty deposits in girls which create waistlines and hips, the coarsening of the skin on the thighs, upper arms, and face, acne (even if it is only one bump), and changes in the shape of the nose, especially in males. These changes occur in both boys and girls, to varying degrees, and are probably better indices of maturing, at least to the onlooker who sees a total person (clothed), than to the individuals themselves, because they create an impression of "an almost adult" at first glance.

The adolescent growth spurt of the average girl usually occurs two years earlier than that of the boy.* During the year or so which includes the peak velocity of growth, a boy usually grows from 3 to 6 inches and a girl from $2\frac{1}{2}$ to 5 inches. This growing spurt is evidenced more in body length than in leg length. (Look at a group of fifth, sixth, and seventh grade girls, especially. They are all legs and arms, sometimes used gracefully and sometimes not, but by the eighth and ninth grades this gangliness is lost.) Practically every muscular and skeletal dimension takes part in this relatively brief acceleration of growth, even the dimensions of the head (the skull), which up to this time had been quite stable.

In Figures 8-1 and 8-2 you will note that, once begun, the "total" process of puberty in girls covers a period of about three years, and in boys, four years. But also note that the age of onset has the same variation, which means that some children will be "through" before others have started. This can give rise to many social, educational, and psychological problems which are not helped even by those school situations in which the population is quite homogeneous with regard to nutrition, economic class, or ethnic background.

The only real constants in growth and development at the time of puberty and slightly beyond are the sequence of events and the total time involved. Knowing this progression of events can be extremely helpful for parents of this age group. Predicting changes that are yet to come can be reassuring and introduces the language of sexuality into the family vocabulary; for example, on noting breast development in a girl, a mother can easily say that she will probably be menstruating in the next year, or eight months, "You probably should have some menstrual pads in your closet," or, "Take some pads to camp this summer, just in case." Such awareness can also help parents of boys to understand why their sons begin wearing their underwear under their pajamas, or no pajamas, to suggest jock straps if they seem uncomfortable in swim suits or in sports, and to keep relatively calm when boys grow out of their pants every three months for a year or two. The need for male underarm deodorants, which only a generation ago was vehemently denied by many adult males, seems to be communicated from boy to boy. Single parent families have even more problems in understanding these day-to-day idiosyncracies of opposite-sexed pubescent children; the most knowledgeable female or male parent is not

---

* This is the reason for the prevalence of tall girls and short boys at the sixth and seventh grade dances, and even later.

really equipped to handle these situations in the opposite-sexed child in the optimal manner they expect of themselves.*

Briefly, this sequence of events in girls is: development of the breast bud (2) and downy pubic hair over the pubic bone (the mons); the beginning of the growth spurt and its peak, menarche; continuing development to the adult stage (5) of breasts and pubic hair; and the characteristic widening of hips believed to be due to the influence of estrogen on growth centers in the pelvic bones.

The sequence of events in boys is, briefly: growth in the size of the testes (an increase in the size of the tubules in the testes) and changes in the scrotal skin, early pubic hair (2) over the mons, penis growth along with the peaking of the growth spurt. Less constant for boys and girls is the time of development of axillary (underarm) and perianal hair, though the latter is usually late. The facial hair becomes apparent around the corners of the mouth at about the same time as the axillary hair. Generally the ability to grow a full beard also defines the time of maturity of the penis, testes, and other sexual characteristics in the male. The beard, or mustache, as a symbol of virility has some basis in fact. With growth of the penis and testes occurs also the development of the internal glands (prostate, bulbo-urethral, seminal vesicles) which provide spermatic fluid. The ejaculation of fluid with penile erection may occur as soon as a year after the beginning of penis growth even though it is not yet of mature size. To the question, "Are there sperm in this first ejaculation?" there is no good answer. How do you carry out a scientific study, even carefully designed, on the sperm content of the first ejaculation?† The same uncertainty holds when trying to answer the question, "Are those first menstrual cycles associated with ovulation?" There is certainly evidence in the form of pregnancies that some early ejaculates have viable sperm and some early menstrual cycles are ovulatory. It is probably best to assume that ova are released from the beginning, or from early puberty, when rape or intercourse in this age group presents questions of pregnancy. If males in this age group are actively seeking physical sex by force or persuasion, it is best to assume that the ejaculate contains sperm until proven otherwise. (Sperm are not essential to sexual function or desire in any age group.)

---

* A family in our acquaintance was vacationing with their 9- and 10-year-old boys on an island in the Caribbean during a water shortage. The boys had their one soapy bath in two weeks in a tub outside, and their mother who was helping rinse by throwing pails of used water on them, was very surprised and disturbed to discover that they both had visible pubic hair growth at this young age. She hadn't seen them naked since they were 4½- or 5-years-old. Once home, her pediatrician reassured her after examination, and both boys experienced a normal, early puberty; by age 13 and 14 they looked like the average 15- or 16-year-old.

† Mature sperm may be found in the testes of 12-year-olds, but the question regarding transport still remains.

Not only do males have a slightly longer period of external pubertal changes than females, they also continue their absolute physical growth for a longer period, usually extending well into the period of the appearance of adult secondary sexual characteristics. Even voice changes are relatively late, though again variable, in this sequence of events, and are believed to be due to the effect of testosterone on the growth centers of the cartilages of the larynx (the sometimes prominent "Adam's apple" of adolescents).

This wide variation in the time of onset of pubertal changes, especially growth, can cause many problems for young people and their parents. Those who arrive at the physician's office, partly instigated by the discomfort of the young teenager and partly by the parents, are primarily oriented toward too much or too little height, and only secondarily toward the delay in onset of other changes. Again, it would appear that cultural norms rather than biology per se influence the course of behavior.

In girls who are otherwise normal, there is no treatment which will effectively speed up growth or the onset of other changes without compromising final adult height; in boys, testosterone can be used, but with a similar risk and the additional possible risk of inhibiting (by feedback mechanisms) the boy's own production of testosterone.

Much of vertical growth occurs by an increase in length in the long bones (arms and legs) of the body. This growth occurs at the ends, between two bony areas, one in the very ends of the long bone and the other in the central portion of the bone. Hormones (estrogens, androgens, and growth hormone) act on this area for a period of time which appears to be genetically determined in normal individuals, and then these bony areas fuse, join, or become continuous. This fusion marks the end of growing. The use of hormones to stimulate growth "ahead of time" has to be supervised carefully to avoid premature fusion.

Girls are usually brought to their doctor because they are too tall, too soon, and boys, because they are too short for too long a time. Gallagher feels that when the patient's anxiety and that of his parents reaches a level that cannot be assuaged except by medication (in the absence of other abnormalities except simple delay in growth in the case of the male), testosterone used in small doses for periods of four months is better than long-term continuous therapy.[5] Patients must be watched carefully for excessive masculinization as well as its accompanying increased libido (sexual desire). Human growth hormone has little or no masculinizing effect, but is in short supply and normally used only for severe disorders.

Girls who seem to be growing at a too rapid rate should be treated prior to the onset of menstruation and before the end of the growth spurt; sometimes this can mean starting therapy as early as eight or nine years of age. Treatment, though its effectiveness is still in some doubt, consists of estrogen in monthly, cyclic doses over a four- or five-year period. However, this may be feminizing, that is, producing uterine bleeding and some premature breast development.

The gross disorders of growth and development are generally visible early in childhood and are usually associated with decreased thyroid hormone or more often with some chronic systemic disease of the lungs, heart, kidney, or liver. Malfunction, or congenital and acquired abnormalities of the central nervous system, especially those which affect the hypothalamus and the pituitary gland, also result in growth disorders. Skull films (X-rays of the bony skull surrounding the pituitary gland) are one of the first procedures done in these early disorders of growth, or when recognized at a later age. The "master gland" label for the pituitary has much basis in fact.

For the previous discussion we have assumed that the reader knew some things and didn't need to know others; for example, what puberty is, and where the hormones come from. The brief discussion which follows may help to clarify some of the important questions.

Puberty is defined as that time when males and females become capable of reproduction (common law has established this as age 14 in males and age 12 in females). The word itself comes from "downy," or "fine hair." The pubescent girl or boy is at the "downy hair" stage of development, not yet quite capable of reproduction.

The external and visible changes and the internal (physiological) changes of adolescence are brought about by hormones which are either secreted for the first time or secreted in much higher amounts than previously. The exact relationships between a specific hormone and a specific change are not well documented for two reasons: 1) Only recently have tests for determining some hormone levels relatively easily become available, and some of these are still incomplete, involved, and expensive. 2) Even some of these tests require procedures which may be appropriate for the hospitalized child, or for the child with obvious deficiencies or an abnormality, but which are inappropriate for routine use in the normal child, and usually unacceptable to either the normal child or his parents. The normal child is not generally volunteered by his parents for any long-term study involving more than the external characteristics of growth. Also, long-term studies in this area are limited by the transient nature of our population. Tanner says that only about 2,000 children have been studied in this way in the past 50 years.[6]

The use of hormones for treatment of growth and development disorders is also limited by the supply of these hormones in pure form, with the exception of the hormones which have been synthesized; even some of these have enough known and unknown side effects on areas other than the particular problem involved to limit their usefulness in many minor disorders or disorders which seem to be simply a matter of delay in onset. The disadvantages and the unknowns often outweigh the apparent advantages, especially the psychological advantages of treatment, and their use in therapy is frequently a compromise.

Hormones which are known to be involved in varying and to some extent unknown degrees in growth and sexual development, originate in the anterior pituitary, the ovaries, the testes, the adrenal glands, and the thyroid.* The parathyroid glands are also involved in the calcium and phosphorus metabolism essential to bony growth. (The pineal gland in the *rat* brain has recently been found to exert some influence over the onset of puberty.)

The anterior pituitary gland at the base of the brain secretes hormones which stimulate the ovaries, testes, adrenals, and the thyroid; and if one goes a bit further back in the cycle, the pituitary is partly dependent on stimulation from the hypothalamus, other centers in the brain, and perhaps even the pineal gland (all of which are located above the pituitary in the brain proper). Pituitary activity is also turned off and on by secretions from the glands it stimulates, a feedback mechanism important in the menstrual cycle, as well as in the functions of other endocrine glands.

Pituitary. Two hormones from the pituitary, FSH (follicle-stimulating hormone) and LH (luteinizing hormone in the female) or ICSH (interstitial cell-stimulating hormone in the male) act upon the egg follicle cells in the ovary and on the tubules and Leydig cells of the testes. LH and ICSH are the same hormone.

ACTH (adrenocorticotrophic hormone) and TSH (thyrotropic hormone) act upon the adrenals and the thyroid, respectively. Growth hormone and prolactin (a hormone associated with milk production but not with breast development) appear to act directly on target areas involved with growth and lactation (milk production), respectively, or on the bones and muscles, and the secretory glands of the female breast.

Gonadotrophins (FSH, LH or ICSH) are both found in boys *and* girls and adolescents and adults, just as androgenic and estrogenic substances (see below) are found in both boys and girls in this age group and later, though in differing amounts. (see also LHRF, p. 70)

Ovaries. Estrogenic substances are produced by the ovary in response to stimulation by the gonadotrophins. The ovaries also produce other hormones related to the maintenance of menstrual cycles and pregnancy (p. 125).

Testes. Testosterone is produced from the Leydig cells of the testis which have been stimulated by ICSH.

Adrenals. Androgenic (masculinizing) and estrogenic (feminizing) substances are produced in both males and females in response to stimulation by ACTH.

Thyroid. Thyroid hormone is produced in response to stimulation by TSH, but the exact role of thyroid hormone in growth, development, and menstrual disorders is not clear. Amenorrhea (the absence of menstrual periods) is frequently associated with both increased and decreased thyroid activity, sometimes only minor degrees of either. Decreased thyroid activity or absolute lack is associated with marked disorders of growth and development, if present at birth or within the first few years of life. Thyroid hormone is an anabolic hormone (it facilitates *constructive* metabolism, or the synthesis of complex materials from simple materials, which is what growth is).

On Learning About Who We Are as Sexed Persons

In the above sections we have examined the physiological process of sexual maturation, of coming of age sexually in a physical sense, of reaching puberty and menarche. These facts are well established. We also know that their meaning varies with societies and cultures, and apparently within societies now as the adolescents and their parents form what are, in some ways, differing subsystems and subcultures. While it is not our purpose in this book to try to establish causal factors regarding how we come to perceive our sexuality, to establish our own sexual identity, and eventually to relate to others as sexed persons, it is important to remind the reader of the importance of this process, to offer some hints in the brief discussion which follows, and to urge the reader to look for fuller discussion in any of several texts on the subject.

What is it to be a female or a male? How do we obtain our ideas of selves as sexed persons? We learn of ourselves and of others through watching and listening and gradually taking the roles of others, both imaginatively and in action. The earliest others in our lives are mothers and fathers and siblings. We learn to take as our own their attitudes toward us, their values and beliefs. And we learn to take their attitudes toward themselves. We know who and what mothers are by the way they act toward us and our siblings. Through interaction, we assimilate their attitudes and behavioral norms toward both their own and the opposite sex. That is, we obtain our ideas of human sexuality, not simply by virtue of our own makeup, but more importantly, by virtue of what the people we interact with say about being male and female, and do about it in the way they behave. Thus, a child who sees her mother in the kitchen all day will have a different idea of mother from the child who is taken off to a nursery school all day where she sees and interacts with surrogate mothers, then goes home to a scene where both mother and father share kitchen activities, and share putting her to bed.

Over time, we come to assimilate into our own roles, and attitude and belief systems, aspects of the roles and accompanying attitude-belief patterns of others with whom we have interacted extensively.[7] Even though we do not yet know the exact nature of the role which various family members play in the formation of ourselves, we do know the following:

1. The strongest sexual identity and role-learning is between mother and daughter, and despite our changing patterns, this continues to hold true. What this means is that the daughter learns about being a mother, a housekeeper, but not a wife and lover.

2. Fathers who are warmly nurturant of their sons are more likely than fathers who are not, to have sons who identify with them and model themselves after them. This kind of nurturance on the one hand and modeling on the other produces males with strong masculine orientations. This pattern is much less common than the mother-daughter one and more restricted to middle-class

family life.[8] The focus of socialization appears to be on the role of father and breadwinner rather than on that of husband and lover. Neither the masculine nor the feminine identities being acquired deal overtly with sexuality itself. They deal more with the nonsexual activities in which females and males engage. Thus, children grow up observing that daddies go to work, mommies stay home, daddies are interested in sports, mommies are interested in soap operas. And these sex roles begin to define their sexuality, and may even dominate it.

3. In this situation, it becomes of interest to inquire about the impact of siblings on each other. Studies of two child families reveal that siblings have an increasing if complementary role to play in sex role learning. In a family with one boy and one girl, in which the girl is older, she assimilates masculine traits into her personality without loss of feminine traits. She merely adds to her behavioral repertoire.[9]

The boy with a sister has more feminine traits than a boy with another brother, and if the sister is older, the boy reveals substantially more femininity than the boy with another brother. The effect of assimilating opposite sex characteristics is most noted upon the younger of the two siblings.

In three and four child families, quite different patterns or combinations may emerge, depending on the sex split and on the ordinal arrangement (which sex comes when).

It should be emphasized that the sex characteristics being learned are primarily not overtly sexual, but have to do with male and female sex roles. Still, we may hypothesize that cross-sex siblings will be more effective in heterosexual relations outside the family than same-sex siblings because they are more sensitive to the opposite sex and have some understanding of the characteristics of the opposite sex in certain roles. As stated previously, females and males who have nurturant mothers and fathers, who also appear to be living harmoniously with each other, may be expected to establish sexual identities which make heterosexual activity a positive part of their lives. Indeed, findings consistently show that parents who are perceived to be happily married by their children, are the best single predictors of marital happiness in the children themselves.[10] Conversely, it has recently been suggested that young people are less and less impressed with the preachings of parents who are increasingly caught up in divorce, so that they do not see these parents as role models.[11] Still, these are rather limited and inadequate approaches to becoming sexually mature persons.

Dating in Early Adolescence

Dating as we know it is a peculiarly American phenomenon. Every major text on marriage and the family deals extensively with the subject.

We need only summarize some of the major features here and relate these to sexual development, and then to some of the findings in recent articles which show continuing change in adolescent sexual behavior and attitudes.

We note that dating serves several functions for the participants themselves and for the society at large. In the latter case, dating assures the support of such societal values as independence of the young from parental control, and supports the idea of the nuclear family, even as it fosters the basic value of egalitarianism. That is, it is the major way by which young people of both sexes express the value of equal choice in the selection of a marriage partner. In many ways, dating is a logical extension of American political ideology in the realm of marriage and the family, for it fosters in people a sense of freedom of choice, individualism, and equality which are hallmarks of the American dream.

At the individual level, dating serves as the process by which young people test their ideas about themselves and the opposite sex, and gradually learn to shape their own self-identity. Increasingly, our identities are not shaped by the mere fact of birth in a family, or by simply learning the appropriate roles from mother and father. And most assuredly, dating is the process by which young people come to learn about the pleasures of heterosexual sex.

In some ways, dating is, if not the core activity, at least the primary preoccupation of adolescence. It has evolved concurrently with the emergence of and elaboration of adolescence in society, and it has spread gradually throughout other developed societies. It is also the activity over which adults express the greatest amount of concern (drug usage is after all not so widespread a practice as is dating) and the least amount of direction, control, or instruction. What kind of instruction do young people get from adults about dating? If development of one's sexuality is so important to self-fulfillment, why do adults do so little to insure some direction and control, rewards and punishment? Primarily it would seem because they are no longer certain what these ought to be. Those who are certain of the validity of traditional ways narrowly restrict dating and are clear on the importance of virginity before marriage. Those who are totally permissive encourage their children to enjoy sexual pleasure as they mature, from masturbation to petting, to coitus. Most adults seem to be caught in between, to recall imperfectly their own sexual behavior and to make halfhearted efforts to preach the old restrictions, while giving the car keys to the children. We will review the results shortly, but first we should sum up the forces at work here.

1. Sex drives mature together with the most dramatic physiological changes that the individual will undergo for the next 30 years.

2. Both society and the family are more uncertain than ever how to handle these changes.

3. The adolescent is trying to learn her or his identity, what it means to be female, and what it means to be male.

4. Sex role learning regarding the traditional division of labor is increasingly changing and subject to redefinition. It is more and more acknowledged that females can do most things that males can.

5. The adolescent pattern is increasingly to confront physical growth and sex drive with sociocultural confusion and ambiguity.

6. Research has shown that the great revolution in heterosexual behavior took place during and after World War I, especially for women. But during the 1920s, 1930s, and 1940s, traditional sex role learning (especially relative to the division of labor) remained normative; traditional sexual morality was preached, but behavioral changes were taking, and had taken place. As has been true of so many other facets of human endeavor, society is slow to acknowledge these behavior changes. For a certain period of time, norms and attitudes tend to lag behind behavior.

7. Among the factors encouraging adolescent independence in sexual matters is the fact that until recently sexual behavior was a taboo subject at all age levels. Public displays of affection between parents which can be seen by children are rare; even rarer is the occasion when a child may see parents "making love"; among the preadolescents, the dominant tendency is to discourage any talk about sex. Sex jokes are dirty, sex organs are not to be displayed, physical beauty is to be admired at a distance. The message from adults and from society is at once clear and paradoxical: sexuality, sex around the house, is a very private matter, a personal thing; at the same time we foster public sex on television and in magazines and newspapers in every imaginable way. It has been left largely to adolescents themselves to establish the links between these two forces; that is, what they have done and are doing. They are increasingly tolerant and supportive of their peers. It is not too much to hypothesize that teenagers are becoming important sources of ideas about sexuality and sex identity for their confused parents. At the same time, it is the confused parents themselves who are responsible for much of the ambiguity and change. They were among the agents of change during the time since World War I; they were more and more influenced by Freud and the post-Freudian thinkers, by Dr. Spock and permissive training, and by Kinsey's research which dared remind them of what their behavior actually was like, and how much it diverged from the existing norms; and many of them participated, either directly as concerned Catholics, or indirectly as bemused onlookers, in the controversy over birth control in the Catholic Church. The controversy extended far beyond the simple question of whether and what kind of birth control was permissible. It opened up questions about sexual love and marriage which influenced a significant proportion of the American people. Once the questions extended to premarital sexual activity, the doors of change opened wide. Finally, came the great challenges to authority during the 1960s: the authority of the churches, the authority of the schools, the authority of the government, and the authority of the family. In every area, the rules which had seemed in so many cases to be of nearly divine origin were being tested and found wanting by most of the young and many adults. Some of the results as they affect

human sexuality are beginning to emerge now. We will briefly review some of the more salient ones here.

The Latest Survey of Teenagers

A recent survey of American teenagers included findings that were both expected and surprising. For example, Kinsey had reported that 3 percent of his white middle-class respondents were nonvirgins by age 15. The recent study by Kantner and Zelnik of a representative sample of whites showed that 11 percent were nonvirgins at age 15, and by age 20, some 40 percent acknowledged that they were nonvirgins.[12]

The most common teenage illness after the common cold is reported to be venereal disease, with 3,000 cases of syphilis and 150,000 cases of gonorrhea reported among America's 27 million teenagers in 1970.[13] At the same time illegitimate births increased from 8.3 per 1,000 teenagers in 1940 to 19.8 in 1972. Homosexuality itself, if not greater in percentage, is more openly acknowledged and tolerated and even accepted.

Kantner and Zelnik found that despite the relatively easy availability of contraceptives, young people seemed to be willing to run the risk of pregnancy. Some 75 percent of the girls admitted that they made little or no effort to achieve contraceptive protection.[14] The risk-taking itself is explained by several factors which reveal interesting aspects of sexual thinking: they don't like to admit that they are going to have intercourse; contraceptives are unromantic; abortion is more readily available; the sanctions against nonmarital pregnancy are not all that severe any more; the odds against conception are perceived to be high; they just don't care. These attitudes appear to be in keeping with the level of instruction which teenagers receive from their parents on the subject of sexuality.

Whatever the amount of risk involved, it is clear that sexuality is taking on new meanings with adolescents. And these meanings are demystifying sex, removing it both from the realm of the not proper and from the world of the mysteriously grand. It's not something to get hung up on; it gives you a good feeling; it is something you do to relieve the tensions for your guy—and your gal; it's a part of the fun of growing up. It's what everyone else in the group is doing—so what's new? As we will see in the next chapter, by late adolescence, the problem for male or female may well be how to justify still being a virgin.

VIEWPOINTS

Love and discipline are the foundation of all values. A successful home is a school for love. If children are not loved from infancy through their growing years, they cannot learn to love other persons and to become happy, affirmative adults.

But love is not enough. Children need discipline if they are to develop competent, self-confident personalities. . . . In the imposing of discipline, some uncertainty and some inner conflict are natural. Only a humorless martinet would fail to have occasional doubts about the right course. But doubt is one thing and abdication is another. Those parents who do not persevere in rearing their children according to their own convictions are not leaving them "free" to develop on their own. Instead, they are letting other children and the media, principally television and the movies, do the job.

Contemporary American children grow up to confront opportunities for moral risk-taking which were unknown until recently. The invention of birth control pills and the availability of abortion have weakened the taboos against premarital sex. If a safe "morning-after" pill is developed in the coming decade, as seems likely, any pragmatic sanction against sexual promiscuity will disappear, except for the continuing risk of venereal infection.

Some modern parents are already so defeatist on sexual issues that they are having their 14-year-old daughters fitted with diaphragms or given prescriptions for the pill. But the powerful emotions surrounding the sexual act cannot be screened out as easily as the sperm. It is these emotions which young people have to learn to manage.

Children of both sexes have to be taught what wise mothers have always told their daughters, which is that an intimate and important experience is cheapened and coarsened when it is divorced from love. If persons use one another like disposable plastic cartons, the emotional content of the experience becomes comparably trivial. There are those who argue that sex can be completely pleasurable even if one barely knows one's partner or loathes him or her. I would suggest that most young people are not so tough or neurotic. Whatever they may protest to the contrary, their feelings are engaged in the sexual act and their feelings are bruised when it leads nowhere.

In sexual relations as in other areas of life, Americans have to relearn the satisfactions of self-denial and anticipation. It would do no harm to 16- and 17-year-old boys and girls to know the facts about sex and yet not engage in intercourse. A certain amount of frustration and tension can be endured—and with good effect. Only modern Americans regard frustration as ranking higher than cholera in the scale of human afflictions. An older, wiser attitude regarded self-restraint as a necessary part of becoming mature and creative. But if our children are to learn how to wait and how to discipline themselves, they will have to acquire these habits long before adolescence.

From William V. Shannon, "What Code of Values
Can We Teach Our Children Now?"
The New York Times Magazine,
16 January 1972, pp. 51-52.

. . . .

"How do you think a parent should go about telling a boy what he needs to know about growing up?" a mother we know asked her 16-year-old son, Richard, who, she felt, had had a reasonably good briefing.

"What's there to know?" her son replied. "One day you start producing sperm, you have nocturnal emissions and there you are. You told me that."

Fortunate the boy like Richard who has been told, feels satisfied and secure about the information given, who feels no anxiety about the fact that he has come of age sexually. Not every boy knows what he needs to know, accepts the advance billing with equanimity, or feels secure with his own sexual maturity once he has matured.

In fact, there appears to be a big difference between the sexes in the matter of finding out about sex. When questioned, most teenage girls seem to feel that they have been adequately prepared for the onset of menstruation. Most of them are neither surprised nor particularly disconcerted when it arrives, seeming to feel reasonably free to discuss any problems which may arise with their mothers. And for those who don't, there are always those little booklets that mothers can provide.

Not so with boys. Psychiatric caseworker John J. Paonessa, in his rather thorough survey of teenage boys, found that it was the rare boy who had received adequate—or indeed any—preparation for his first nocturnal emission. Boys he talked to were unprepared for the occurrence in advance, felt anxious, unhappy and often guilty about it, and seemed reluctant to discuss the problem with their parents.

Why is it that we prepare our sons for sexual maturity so much less than our daughters?

It may be because most mothers, feeling quite secure about menstruation, find it reasonably easy to discuss the topic with their daughters. But, in many families, talking to the boy is left to the father. Fathers in general seem to find the necessary information harder to convey and perhaps, too, they are a little less comfortable about what it is they have to tell. And though certainly all that needs to be told is available in various books, so far as I know nobody has put out that companion pamphlet to What Every Young Girl Should Know.

What you tell is not as important as that you communicate: In telling any child about any aspect of sex, exactly what you tell is probably far less important than that you talk easily and comfortably and that you keep the lines of communication open. And in telling boys about sex and sexual maturing, there is often not only a lack of communication between parent and child, but also between parent and parent.

From Louise B. Ames and Joan Ames Chase,
"What Every Young Boy Should Know,"
Family Circle, March 1972, p. 68.

• • • • • • • • • •

. . . and the last thing I wanted was to sit through it with my mother, to let her know I knew, to see her seeing me. . . . I wasn't really shy, and not a blusher, certainly, but this seemed too sensitive an area for casualness. Telling dirty jokes was one thing, but taking sex seriously (and not as we usually did, giggling over its ickyness and groaning "Grossness, *plus*")—that was harder. Four letter words and slang I could pronounce with no trouble, but the official terms, the ones printed in the little pink booklet they gave us to take home, in preparation for the Now That You're a Woman film, words like that (and *woman* was one) caught in my throat.

It wasn't the facts I objected to—sex education I certainly applaud. It was words like "special" and "cherish" and "miracle" and "gift", the notion of Woman's Secret Burden, with connotations of brave, silent suffering (the boys would never know what we went through—for them; we'd let them think they were the tough ones)—that's what I detested, and why I entered adolescence with some amount of anguish. . . .

Even now, a couple of years removed from beer and bucket seats and gear shifts sticking up at awkward angles and late night radios glowing in the dark until, at last, the announcer would speak of "this morning," and not "tonight"—even now I feel uneasy, writing about what went on in those cars. It was a pretty important thing to do (I catch myself from saying *pastime*—it was more central than that. It's hard not slipping into anthropologist's talk, tribal life among the high school natives—there is a tendency to condescend). Observing seems like an intrusion, because it's easy to find comedy in zealous awkwardness, easy to smile (safe in one's composed delicacy and arranged grace—ankles crossed and hair brushed) at the clumsiness of others. The truth is that what went on in the seats of cars, on rec. room couches and summer cabin mattresses—stiff with December ice and warmed with no more than a blanket and a body—those things weren't meant to be watched.

From Joyce Maynard, Looking Back,
A Chronicle of Growing Up Old in the Sixties,
Garden City, New York, Doubleday and Company, 1973, pp. 25-28, 97.

References

1. Robert D. Heiss and Irene Goldblatt, "The Status of Adolescents in American Society: A Problem in Social Identity," in Jerold Heiss, ed., *Family Roles and Interaction* (Chicago: Rand McNally and Co., 1968), pp. 383-398.

2. Sandra McDermott, *Female Sexuality: Its Nature and Conflict* (New York: Simon & Schuster, Inc., 1970), p. 209.

3. *Ibid.,* p. 191.

4. The reader is referred to Lytt I. Gardner, *Endocrine and Genetic Diseases of Childhood* (Philadelphia: W. B. Saunders Co., 1969).

5. See P. R. Gallagher, in Gardner, *Endocrine and Genetic Diseases of Childhood.*

6. James M. Tanner, *Growth at Adolescence,* 2nd ed. (Oxford, England: Blackwell Science Publication, 1969).

7. Orville G. Brim, Jr., "Family Structure and Sex Role Learning by Children: A Further Analysis of Helen Koch's Data," in Heiss, *Family Roles and Interaction,* pp. 341-357.

8. See for example, Paul Mussen and Luther Distler, "Masculinity, Identification, and Father-Son Relationships," in Heiss, *Family Roles and Interaction,* pp. 358-373.

9. Brim, "Family Structure and Sex Role Learning," p. 353.

10. See for example, Gerald Leslie, *The Family in Social Context* (New York: Oxford University Press, 1967), pp. 481 ff.

11. *Time,* 21 August 1972, p. 36.

12. John Kantner and Melvin Zelnik, "The Probability of Premarital Intercourse," *Social Science Research,* 1:335, 1972.

13. "VD—The Epidemic," *Newsweek,* 24 January 1972, pp. 46-50.

14. John Kantner and Melvin Zelnik, "Contraception and Pregnancy: Experiences of Young Unmarried Women in the United States," *Family Planning Perspective,* 5, 1 (Winter, 1973): 21-35.

9

· · · · · · · · · · · Premarital · · · · · · · · · · ·
and Nonmarital Sex

Introduction

AMERICAN SOCIETY has been moving from an antisex to a prosex orientation, with prosex manifestations now evident in adolescence and teenage dating. The most notable feature of this "positive" discovery of sexuality in adolescence is not that it is a change from an era in which no sexual stimulation took place to the current scene of condoning premarital, full sexual pleasure. Rather the change appears to be a shift along a continuum, a shift both in the nature and extent of the sexual stimulation permitted and a shift in the way people perceive and feel about what they are doing.

All the evidence from history indicates that almost all males and a large percentage of females have masturbated before their twenty-first birthday. In the antisex days of our culture, we were made to feel guilt and shame about this habit, and worry about our mental health as a result. Since masturbation was for many males in the United States closely related to necking and petting experiences with females, it is no wonder that today's parents are still hung up and confused about their feelings concerning how their teenage children ought to feel and to behave.

Today the shift is away from autoerotic stimulation and uneasy feelings about the obviously pleasurable sensations, toward heterosexual stimulation as a healthy form of expression, manifested in petting to orgasm in early adolescence, and in full heterosexual intercourse involving penile-vaginal penetration by the time of young adulthood. The latter is rapidly becoming the norm for the older adolescent, in and out of college. In this chapter we will review the facts very briefly, examine the value-belief-attitude framework within which the new mode is developing, and consider some of the new life-styles and their possible consequences in terms of human sexuality.

A Cross-Cultural Perspective

There have been a number of national studies of premarital sexual behavior. Despite variations in methodology and in questions asked, the conclusions are similar: about half of the males and less than half of the females have had full coital experience by age 21.[1] There then follows much discussion about the extent of change during the past 30 years and about what may be expected during the 1970s. We would like to focus here on a study reported by Christensen and Gregg which is helpful because it is cross-cultural and cross-national, and includes a time perspective of ten years.[2] They studied changing sex norms and behavior in two regions of the United States and in Denmark, in 1958 and again in 1968. At the time of the 1958 study, the three sites were described as: "highly restrictive Mormon culture in the Intermountain region of western United States; moderately restrictive Midwestern culture in central United States; and highly permissive Danish culture which is a part of Scandinavia."[3]

The study is interesting in that it compares both attitudes toward important features of sexuality and actual sexual behavior of the respondents in both time periods. As we consider whether the data may be representative of today's youth, the reader should keep in mind that the samples themselves were not drawn to be representative, and that the students who volunteered were drawn largely from social science classes. There is much evidence that social scientists are more liberal than other scholars,[4] and it may well be that students taking social science courses are more liberal than students who don't. Nevertheless, the findings fall well within the range of all other studies.[5]

Table 9-1 shows the percentage of students who claimed premarital coital experience in 1958 and in 1968.

A clear-cut pattern emerges both by sex and by region and subcultures. In addition, there is a definite pattern of increasing coital activity among females that tends to have been downplayed or not found in earlier studies during the

Table 9-1

Percentage of Respondents in Three Samples with Premarital
Coital Experience, 1958-1968

Years	Intermountain		Midwestern		Danish	
	Males	Females	Males	Females	Males	Females
1968	37	32	50	34	95	97
1958	39	10	51	21	64	60
Difference	−2	22	−1	13	31	37

Adapted from Table 3 as presented in Bell and Gordon, p. 55.

1960s. Mormon culture is most restrictive of sexual behavior, Danish most permissive, and the Midwestern United States is in between. In the United States, males are still more likely than females to have had premarital coital experience by the time of the study. But in the United States, males reported no change in the ten year period while the percentage for females jumped notably, both in the Intermountain and the Midwestern samples. The largest jumps occurred in Denmark, from a significant majority in 1958 to almost universal experience in 1968, and total convergence between females and males.

Table 9-2

Percentage of Respondents Approving of Premarital Coitus, 1968 and 1958

Years	Intermountain		Midwestern		Danish	
	Males	Females	Males	Females	Males	Females
1968	38	24	55	38	100	100
1958	23	3	47	17	94	81
Difference	15	21	8	21	6	19

A number of attitudinal questions were also posed, and as expected, revealed general convergence with behavior. But there were some exceptions, with the most notable found in Table 9-2.

In all three samples during the ten-year period, more females than males became more approving of coitus. But this is hardly surprising, given the fact of the sexual revolution and of the women's liberation movement during this time. Nor is it so surprising that there is such close convergence between attitude and behavior in 1968. What is interesting is the way the cultural factor appears to be operating in the Mormon as compared with the other two regions. In both time periods in the Mormon region, a larger percentage reported coital experience than approved of it, reflecting the continued strength of religious proscriptions. The same proscriptions appear to have been operating in the Midwest in 1958 but to have disappeared by 1968. We would expect in the future that there would be close convergence between the attitude and the act, with a slightly larger percentage approving than actually performing. As Christensen and Gregg suggest, a larger percentage of adolescents today than ten years ago are living in conformity with the norms which they have internalized. Thus, presumably by reducing anxiety, tension, and guilt, they are able to confront their sexuality more openly and candidly.

Social Control Mechanisms in Change

All human social behavior is controlled by a combination of internal and external mechanisms. Many of these are visible to us as social sanctions. Thus, traditionally, a young woman who had "preserved her virginity" until marriage would wear a white gown to symbolize her virginity. This fact would be highly regarded by all concerned and would be positively sanctioned.

The major internal control mechanisms have centered about the human conscience and the teaching of the morality of right and wrong. In Western societies, organized religion has played a major role in setting the standards for right and wrong. Also involved in the development of the conscience is the social self and one's social identity. Or, to put it another way, one's conscience is the core of the social self, of one's identity. One may answer the question, "who am I?" in terms of one's standards of right and wrong. To violate these standards is to raise serious questions within one's own mind about who one is. In a way, one's conscience represents one's self-expectations in the core areas of social life. At least this would be the traditional view.

Sexual behavior could be and was circumscribed by the traditional ideas and beliefs which we have alluded to so often. But society has also relied on external mechanisms to help reinforce the internal. Thus, to the internal belief that virginity was a good, perhaps the supreme good which a woman could bring to her marriage, was always added the sanction threat that lack of virginity might mean no marriage at all, loss of family name, disgrace, and loss of dowry.

During this time, there were no sanctions against nonvirginity of males. It is true that fornication, whether committed by females or males, was a "sin," but males were more or less expected to "sin" as part of their natural inclinations. Thus, the prevalence of what we have come to think of as the double standard of sexual morality. Not surprisingly, females have traditionally felt more guilt about so-called sexual transgressions than males.

As the social control mechanisms governing sexual behavior have lost their force, so also have feelings of guilt and anxiety lessened. Bell reports from his own research that a longitudinal study of college students showed that the coeds in the 1968 study were more likely to have had sexual intercourse at all levels of the dating relationship, but to have felt less guilty about their behavior than had their coed counterparts ten years previously.[6]

Reiss elaborates on the process of change that has been taking place: The fact is that young people have never refrained from necking, petting, or coitus just because they had guilt feelings about their behavior. The long lines of Catholic teenagers and young adults waiting to go to Confession were testimony to the observation that it often appeared that for Catholics, "The sin of the flesh was the only sin just as obedience was the only virtue." Indeed, Reiss notes that both females and males reported some guilt feelings about their sexual activity, but that as they continued with the conduct, the guilt feelings diminished. As the guilt feelings diminished, they would move on to more advanced stages of sexual activity, repeating the process until they reached coitus.[7]

Another variation on the change, and perhaps one which many readers will find close to their own experience, is aptly illustrated by a case reported in a recent issue of *Time* magazine:

Sue Franklin, now 25, had a traditional middle-class Midwestern upbringing. In 1965, when she was 18 and a college freshman, her sorority sisters talked about their sexual feelings only with extremely close friends, and nearly all gossiped about girls they suspected of having affairs. "Virginity was all important," Sue remembers. Then her boy friend of five years' standing issued an ultimatum: "Either you go to bed with me or I'm leaving you." She gave in and was overcome with remorse. "My God," she thought, "what have I done? The more I learned about sex, the guiltier I felt, especially about enjoying it. I almost felt I had to deny myself any pleasure. My boy friend felt bad, too, because I was so hung up."

Sue's sister, Pat, on the other hand, was just 15 and in high school when she first went to bed with a boy. Only one thing bothered her: fear of getting pregnant. She appealed to Sue, who helped her to get contraceptive advice from a doctor. Since then, Pat has had one additional serious relationship that included sex. Observes Sue: "Pat had as healthy an attitude as could be imagined, as healthy as I wish mine could have been. She and her friends are more open. They're not blase; they don't talk about sex as they would about what they're going to have for dinner. But when they do discuss it, there's no hemming and hawing around. And boys don't exploit them. . . . It's not like the pressure that builds when sex is denied or you feel guilty about it. . . . They don't see sex as something you can do with everyone; they're not promiscuous."[8]

It would appear then that external negative-type sanctions to govern and control sexual behavior are disappearing and are being replaced by internal mechanisms which are highly permissive. Young people are increasingly free to decide for themselves the nature and extent of their sexual behavior, reflecting societal patterns of increasing egalitarianism and convergence on behavior between females and males. In this sense, at least, the sexual aspect of one's self is less and less guilt-ridden and more and more pleasure-oriented. The consequences of this on love, marriage, and the possibility of enduring human relationships will be examined in the following chapter.

A Cross-Class Perspective

It would greatly aid our understanding of human sexuality to have available as much information on working-class and noncollege older adolescents as we have on middle-class college students. The fact is that in the United States especially, college students have been the prime focus for sex research simply because students are more accessible, and perhaps more willing to discuss these questions openly. Some recent research on lower-class sexuality in West Germany helps to close the gaps and to enlarge our understanding of the way in which social and cultural factors impinge upon the biological to produce variations in sexual attitudes and behavior.

The Stable Working Class. Sexual Behavior in the Noncollege World.

It is well to remember that the majority of young people throughout the world do not go on to formal higher education. For most young people, their formal education ends with high school. With the rapid rise of the junior and community colleges in the United States, it would appear that we will soon be enrolling a majority of our young people, ages 18 to 21, in some form of higher education. Most studies show that college-age young people are more liberal in viewpoints than their noncollege confreres, whether the item under discussion be politics, use of marijuana, or religion. Does this liberation of the mind hold also for the matter of sexual behavior and attitudes?

Such studies as Whyte's *Street Corner Society,* Rainwater's *Family Design* and Liebow's *Tally's Corner* suggest a pattern of fairly universal early coital experience by lower-class men, a rather limited, or narrow, or rigid attitude about what should constitute proper sexual activity (male atop and female passive), and a considerable gap between the norm that a woman should be a virgin at marriage and the reality. Male-female sexual relations tend to be fraught with tension, uncertainty, somewhat mechanical, and characterized in general by little emotional communication between the partners. In short, what little research has been reported on lower-class sexual behavior in the United States suggests that the pattern has differed sharply from that of the middle class. Lower-class young people may experience coital activity sooner, but are also less likely to explore its depths and variations, and to relate it to "ideas of love," affection, and other aspects of interpersonal behavior.

On the other hand, Scandinavian scholars have not found the variations along class lines that Americans have reported. On the contrary, they report that the ideology of romantic love pervades all class levels, that both females and males report positive feelings about sexual behavior, and that regardless of social class, behavior is partner-centered and oriented toward mutual satisfaction.[9]

Sigusch and Schmidt carried out a study in West Germany on single, Protestant and Catholic, unskilled and semi-skilled urban workers, both female and male, age 20 and 21 at the time of the study (1968-69). By age 19, more than two-thirds of both males and females had experienced coitus, had engaged in coital activity at least occasionally during the year, and their primary orientation toward coital activity was one of permissiveness with affection; that is, it was permissible for people in love or who expressed affection for each other. There was little support for the double standard idea, while at the same time there was strong evidence that both females and males intended to marry the persons with whom they were carrying on their sexual activity. Especially for the women, love was cited as essential for approval for premarital sexual activity.

These young workers opposed the idea of having sexual intercourse with a person other than the one they were engaged to, had ambivalent attitudes toward casual sexual encounters, and strongly supported the idea of sexual fidelity in marriage. Where variations occurred in the findings, men were more likely than women to have had more different sexual partners, to consider the possibility of casual sexual intercourse, and to countenance the possibility of extramarital sexual behavior. But for the most part, these young workers were oriented toward monogamous marriage, and felt very strongly about helping their partner to achieve sexual satisfaction.

Despite the convergence in their actual behavior, there were some important differences noted in the way in which females and males thought about their sexuality. For example, a majority of females and males believed that males have more sexual desires than females, that women should be more reticent than males in the initiation of sexual relations, and that women are naturally more faithful than men.[10]

Emotional reactions to coital activity also varied somewhat. In keeping with Reiss's observation that early coital activity is accompanied by feelings of remorse, guilt, or shame, fully one-third of the females (and 25 percent of the males) reported this early feeling. A majority of the females (but only 12 percent of the males) found the first experience unpleasant. But, as Reiss has also observed, these feelings tend to give way to more positive emotional reactions over time. Feelings of shame and unpleasantness almost disappeared after a year or more of coital activity, while feelings of happiness, of "it was fun," and personal satisfaction were reported by a majority of both sexes, with males still more positive in all cases.

Despite these positive emotional responses, only a minority of the women reported achieving orgasm always (6 percent) or almost always (19 percent). A large majority of the women (67 percent) who did not achieve orgasm regularly reported varying degrees of frustration and disappointment, and tended to blame their partners rather than themselves for this failure. They felt strongly that mutual sexual satisfaction should be the goal of their activity, and were not about to be passive in the face of failure. If these data can be believed, it would appear that the new sexual norms which we discussed earlier are spreading generally throughout all social classes, at least in Europe, and may not depend on taking college courses on family and sexuality, or on reading the literature on what every woman should know. For whatever reasons, sexual expectations have been raised, premarital sexual intercourse seems to be accepted as normative, but sex with affection is the dominant theme, and at least among the working-class young of West Germany, ideas about sex and marriage remain rather traditional. What seems to have happened is that attitudes and behavior have converged among the working class also.

The West German working-class group studied was a stable one, and seems to vary sharply from the working-class and lower-class groups which have been studied in the United States. Thus, some of the differences in the findings (United States lower-class behavior has been found to be less love and person related) may be due to real class differences. The stable working class approximates middle-class norms while the unstable lower-class has divergent norms and behavior patterns.

A related study comparing these working-class young people with German female and male college students sheds further light on sexuality in this older adolescent age group.[11] Among the sexual experiences studied and compared were masturbation, coital experience, coital technique, and frequency of orgasm. The findings may be summarized as follows:

Masturbation. Students reported earlier masturbatory experience than did workers; males began earlier than did females, and at all age levels, more males than females reported masturbatory experience. By age 21, 90 percent of both male groups but only about half of the worker females and less than half of the college student females had masturbated at least once. It would appear that sex gender rather than social class was the more important variable in this aspect of sexual experience. Interestingly, the students reported much more active incidence of masturbation in the 12 months preceding the study. More than 80 percent of the male students but only 57 percent of the male workers reported such activity for the year preceding the study, and the students reported an average of some six occurrences per month, compared with only 2.5 for the male workers. The pattern was similar for the females, with 38 percent of the students and only 15 percent of the workers reporting masturbation during the previous year. In the latter cases, however, the frequency was so low that the authors could not develop reliable statistics. Again, regardless of social class, males are more likely to masturbate and to do so frequently in this older adolescent group.

Coital experience. Now the picture changes. Social class becomes more important than sex. At every age level up to 21, more workers than students reported first coital experience. The difference is striking by age 20: more than 80 percent of both female and male workers, but only 44 percent of the male and 33 percent of the female students, reported coital experience. (Note that the West German students closely resemble their United States counterparts in this regard, while the workers are closer to the experiences reported by Danish students.) Again, a larger percentage of workers than students reported coital activity during the year prior to the study (male 71 percent to 42 percent, and female 71 percent to 39 percent). One the other hand, students reported a higher monthly incidence of coitus (2.8 vs. 2.4 and 4.6 vs. 3.2). When the incidence rates for masturbation and coitus are combined, there seems to be little overall difference in total incidence of sexual activity within male and female groupings. But students are more active on a monthly basis; that is, they engage in more of both kinds of activity. And taken overall, it would appear that students are more sexually active than workers, even though a smaller percentage have had coital experience.

Coital technique. Students reported a greater variety of sexual techniques, with both males and females reporting higher levels of experience with manual-genital contact, woman as well as man active, cunnilingus and fellatio (oral-genital contact) during foreplay, and nudity in coitus. Differences between workers and students reached more than 20 percentage points in activities such as cunnilingus and fellatio. These findings support research in the United States which has consistently shown that working- and lower-class people tend to be more restrictive in their sexual behavior, limiting it pretty much to coitus proper. This is also consistent with many of their attitudes as revealed in an earlier section of this chapter.

Frequency of orgasm. At first glance, it would appear that female workers experience orgasm more frequently than do students, but this tendency seemed to be caused in part by the fact that students began their coital experiences at a later age than did workers. Given the evidence that it takes time for females to achieve orgasm adequacy, that large numbers, even a majority, find the first few experiences unpleasant, and that worry about pregnancy may also hamper ability to achieve orgasm, the data are less surprising. When students and workers who have experienced coitus during a one-to-three-year period are compared, the differences in orgasm frequency disappear. Still, a large percentage of both groups reported experiencing orgasm only sometimes, seldom, or never (52 percent of the workers and 40 percent of the students).

In the matter of attitudes toward sexuality, all four groups supported a permissive ethic, with the qualification that all four groups also supported the value of marital fidelity. Workers achieved financial independence earlier than did students, and this fact seems to relate directly to the earlier age at which they begin coital activity. But they also married earlier than did students, and engaged less often in masturbatory and other sexual practices than in coitus itself. It would be difficult to conclude from these data that workers were more permissive than students in their sexual activity and attitudes. It might be more accurate to say that social factors, such as whether one goes on to further education or goes quickly to a formal occupation around age 16 or 17, strongly condition one's sexual attitudes and behavior, and perhaps even the amount of time one will have available for premarital sexual activity. The subculture of the manual worker does not seem to provide as wide a variety of patterns of sexual behavior as does student subculture. This difference offers another example of the fact that sex is more in the mind than in the genitalia.

Alternate Life Styles in Later Adolescence

Traditional

Hidden in all of the above data is the fact that in the United States and in some other Western countries at least, a significant percentage of young people, both females and males remain virgin during most of their adolescence. The meaning of this virginity varies greatly, since it apparently includes all those people who have limited their sexual expression to holding hands, kissing, necking, and petting. And doubtless, there are some who have engaged in fellatio and cunnilingus who still consider themselves virgins because they have avoided coitus. But what of those females who have engaged in sexual intercourse without achieving orgasm? It might make more sense to say that a person is virgin who has not experienced orgasm in sexual intercourse with a partner of the opposite sex.*

There seem to be two somewhat divergent views about traditional virginity. One is that one's sexuality is such a prized possession that it should not be squandered loosely or even tampered with; it is a great gift to be given to one's chosen partner in life. In its highest form, it is assumed to be such an enriching, emotional, total expression of one's self in the most intimate form of communication that human beings can know, that too much is lost if one tries to develop this form of communication with more than one person in a lifetime.

Another traditional view is that sublimation of one's sexuality is a higher form of expression of self than is submission to one's sexuality. This view holds that sexuality is that which relates human beings back to the lower animals, and suppression of sexuality allows human spiritual values to grow and develop. It is this traditional view of sexuality which has lost so much ground in the Western world in recent years. No major Christian religious body even affirms it any more, although there are still visible strains among some of the major branches. What Reiss, Christensen, and others have found is that this traditional view has been widely rejected by all youth. If they do not engage in sexual intercourse during adolescence, it may be because they prize the value of their sexuality as something special for someone special.

---

* Traditionally, virginity means that there has been no penile-vaginal penetration. It may be that a new form of emotional virginity will emerge as physiological virginity recedes in importance. Clearly, the meaning and importance of virginity are undergoing change.

But other perspectives seem to be developing; one heard frequently is that it isn't worth it to get involved sexually, at least in early adolescence. Many young women, especially, don't feel the need for full sexual expression before marriage. They find their lives sufficiently full of activity that they don't need coitus to be able to get on well with their world. They find the pure physical pleasure of casual sex unnecessary, do not wish to establish sexual bonds which lock them in before they are ready for a serious relationship, and find that they are sufficiently secure about themselves to be able to wait until they feel ready, which may or may not be until marriage or at least until engagement.

The Coed Dorm Phenomenon

The 1960s saw the beginning of the end of a number of hallowed traditions on America's college campuses: the all-male and all-female college, signing in and signing out, parietal hours, and the refusal of college medical authorities to provide contraceptive services for their students. As Yale, Princeton, and Notre Dame welcomed women to their campuses as students rather than as weekend guests, new norms for personal conduct were already well in evidence throughout the country. The idea that the university administration stood *in loco parentis,* came under increasing scrutiny. By 1972 a significant proportion of American college and university administrators had come to the conclusion that the older adolescents who were living away from home were or ought to be capable of taking care of themselves, and that it was not the function of the administration to oversee their personal sex lives.

Indeed, the question now seems to be the limits, if any, which the administration will place on living patterns. A broad spectrum of living arrangements has emerged, some under official administration sponsorship and some strictly informal. In brief, coeducation has finally come to the dormitory, in both small and large, private and public universities from coast to coast: Beloit, Oberlin, Stanford, Michigan, Vassar, Michigan State, and the list goes on. It is estimated that 70 percent of residential campuses have coed dorms.*

The patterns vary, but increasingly, the students themselves are deciding the nature of the structures that are emerging. The most common pattern still seems to be females in one wing and males in another, or females on one floor and males on another, with visiting hours ranging from no limits to some arbitrary number ranging from 12 to 18 hours. In a few cases, coeducation means females and males living in adjoining rooms, and in the fall of 1972, a couple of schools permitted experimental patterns with female and male roommates on campus. In most cases, separate bathrooms are maintained, but some students have accepted a pattern of labelling toilet stalls "his" and "hers."

* As reported by Ann Blackman, Associated Press writer, in column "Saturday Night."

What does it all mean? The common remark heard from those of us who went to college in an earlier generation is that "it's a shame we were born 30 years too soon!"; or "And, to think, I almost got thrown out of college for doing this!" In our fancy, we imagine one huge sex orgy. Unfortunately, the data do not seem to support that imagery.

The new dorm patterns on campus fit well with changing patterns of dating. Saturday night parties, regular dances, and the fraternity-sorority thing have been losing ground. The coed dorm further encourages the decline of traditional dating arrangements. It must be admitted that much of traditional dating took place in an atmosphere of make-believe, fostered inequality and even subtle forms of sexual exploitation; for example, a male spent money to show a female a good time, but hoped for sexual favors in return. Young people saw each other out of sexual-social context, especially on the all male and all female campuses. With the increasing informality of dress and undress, less and less concern about hairdos and makeup, young people are seeing each other as people really are during the course of a normal day. Indeed, many college deans, and students talk glowingly about the brother-sister relationships which coed dorms seem to foster. It may be wondered if this is any more apt a description of the sexual patterns that are developing than the orgies envisioned by the older generation. In fact, what would it mean for human sexual development to say that coed dorms foster sibling relationships more than sex-specific relationships? Perhaps the coed dorm permits the development of sexual expression among young people in a way that doesn't push them into coital activity the way traditional dating does. It is an empirical question too early to be answered whether the daily experience of living together in easy familiarity will in any significant way alter the development of male and female sexuality in these later stages of adolescence. In any case, it seems clear that this new form of social organization of college residential life closely reflects the increasing tolerance of changes in sexual mores.*

The two sides of privacy. College students argue that their sexual behavior is a private matter, one concerning the individuals involved, and is no longer the proper concern either of their parents or of school authorities, especially as this behavior is not harmful to the well-being of society. And they make a case that there is simply no evidence that their more permissive sexual behavior has been harmful to society, or to themselves. For their part, university officials acknowledge that there is a certain consistency between the university goals of fostering intellectual autonomy, independence in thought, self-actualization, and the student desire for the right to autonomy in matters of sexual behavior. In this case, privacy means the freedom from parietal hours, essentially the removal of restrictions on visiting rights between females and males in resi-

---

* We have seen some evidence that coed dorms may foster their own kind of limited heterosexual contacts by creating their own kind of satisfying, self-sufficient "family."

dential campus buildings. The privacy they seek is one which fosters an atmosphere in which young people can develop meaningful relationships, "for a natural and relaxed atmosphere that allows intimate communication, and that may, but does not necessarily, bring physical intimacy. . . ."[12]

A second side of the privacy problem concerns the students themselves. It refers to the internal rather than the external control mechanisms that are employed to achieve conforming behavior. Fundamentally, it concerns the question of how much a given individual wants to share of herself with others, to be known by others. It is the degree of intimacy that one will permit others to share with one. *But this privacy may be as much threatened now by peer-group pressures as the other privacy by administrators trying to stand in loco parentis.* A college sophomore summed up the problem succinctly in discussing the embarrassment of being a virgin in today's permissive campus setting:

These days one's privacy is no longer one's own. Even the act of refusing to give it up is intruded upon. It's no longer just the non-virgin who subjects herself to intense scrutiny: now it's the virgin whose very refusal is scrutinized, maybe even more closely than her surrender would be. People don't talk much about who's on the pill or who's sleeping together, but there's endless speculation about who isn't. "What's the matter with her?" they ask. "Is she frigid?" "Lesbian?" . . . Her abstinence, in short, is fair game for everyone.[13]

Self-actualization may be as difficult to achieve in an atmosphere of strong peer-group pressure as it was under the careful eye of resident counselors, and cautious deans.

Homosexuality

Perhaps the most notable aspect of the changing attitudes toward human sexuality centers on homosexuality, both male and female. Our discussion here will consider only homosexuality between consenting adults. While this form of homosexuality is still labelled as criminal behavior in many states, there appears to be an emerging consensus that this form of sexual behavior is no more the law's business than is other sexual behavior among consenting adults.[14]

For purposes of this chapter, we accept Gebhard's definition of homosexuality: "physical contact between two individuals of the same gender which both recognize as being sexual in nature and which ordinarily results in sexual arousal. Psychological homosexual response may be defined as the desire for such physical contact and/or conscious sexual arousal from thinking of or seeing persons of the same gender."[15] In a more complete discussion of homosexuality, it might be important to differentiate between those persons who are aroused sexually by physical and psychological contact, and those who actually carry this arousal to contact leading to and causing orgasm of one or both partners. It is certainly important to differentiate between homosexuality involving only consenting adults and that which involves adults and adolescents or even preadolescent youth as is the case with pederasty.[16]

Technically, homosexuality refers to such sexual behavior whether the partners are both female or both male, but in usual parlance, the term homosexual is reserved for male sexual preference for another male while the term lesbian is used to refer to female sexual preference for another female rather than a male.

Causal factors. Homosexuality is as old as human sexuality. In some periods of history, it has been extolled (Plato) as a high form of love. And many of the world's famous have been overtly or by implication psychologically favorable to homosexuality (Plato, Julius Caesar, Michaelangelo, D. H. Lawrence, Gide, Joan Baez).

Hooker cites four major theoretical orientations toward homosexuality:

(1) Is the human organism psychosexually neutral at birth, so that learning processes determine homosexual object choice in adults, or are there "inherent sexual predispositions" which selectively influence the effects of learning? (2) What is the nature and content of the learning processes by which homosexual object choice develops? Is the appropriate developmental model a deviant role or a personality system with intrapersonal traits, motives, and gender identifications incompatible with the social-sexual capabilities and self-other expectancies of adult relations with the opposite sex? Does positive conditioning of sexual responses to persons of the same sex, or negative conditioning to persons of the opposite sex, or a combination of both, account for homosexuality? (3) Are particular periods in the development process, such as early childhood or adolescence, critical for homosexual object choice? (4) Are parent-child relationships in the nuclear family crucial in determining whether an individual becomes homosexual, or are peer relationships in childhood and adolescence, and deviant subcultures in adolescence and early adult life, of equal or possibly greater importance?[17]

Research to date has not been able to do more than suggest that some or all four orientations may be involved in every case of homosexuality.

Perhaps the most widely accepted idea is that pathogenic relations between child and parents are a crucial determinant. But then why don't all such relations lead to homosexuality?

And why is it that large numbers of individuals who engage in homosexual activity in adolescence neither define themselves as homosexuals nor continue this activity in adulthood? Or why is homosexuality considered to be without social stigma among some small societies in other parts of the world?

Hooker concludes:

From the limited evidence currently available, it is clear that the diverse forms of adult homosexuality are produced by many combinations of variables, including biological, cultural, psychodynamic, structural, and situational. No single class of determinants, whether psychodynamic, cultural, or biological, accounts for all or even one of these diverse forms.[18]

Research has failed to reveal personality characteristics which would differentiate homosexuals from heterosexuals.

As for sex role preference in sexual behavior, current studies show that "male homosexuals indicate that a large proportion of them habitually perform either role, according to their own or their partners' momentary preference."[19]

But in prisons and other correctional institutions, it has been found that the male who plays the male role of inserting the penis is not considered homosexual, but the male who receives the penis (either anally or orally) is considered homosexual and stereotyped with feminine and homosexual attributes. An aggressive male in a prison or related institution may perceive this as the only way he can continue to assert a male form of behavior.

Fragmentary studies from female prisons suggest a similar pattern, namely that the person who assumes the "masculine" role is defined and defines herself more frequently as the homosexual partner than the female who plays the traditional female role.

Incidence.   Despite the fact that homosexuality is as old as sex itself, information on its incidence is sketchy at best, if for no other reason than it has for so long been condemned in Western societies. The evidence itself centers mostly on college-educated and middle-upper income persons. Most overt homosexuality among males occurs between puberty and age 16; most of the rest occurs before age 25. That is, the incidence itself of one or more acts occurs pretty much between the ages of 12 to 13 and 25. But the great majority of these acts do not lead either partner to become steady homosexuals. The evidence does indicate that between one-quarter and one-third of adult males of college background have had at least one overt homosexual experience.[20] Gebhard goes on to say that "about 4 percent of the white college-educated adult males are predominantly homosexual."[21] And he notes that this figure corresponds closely with those obtained from studies in Europe.

Among females, the incidence is not nearly so confined to early adolescence, but is spread rather evenly until age 30. Gebhard estimates the ultimate incidence at between 15 and 30 percent for the unmarried college educated female. And for the adult female population as a whole, Gebhard estimates the accumulative incidence at between 10 and 12 percent.[22] One important reason for the lower incidence is that females have homosexual encounters over a more extended period, and usually get married before age 25, with little incidence after that time period. Whether the lower incidence in adolescence is related to socialization, or to physiological or other factors can only be hypothesized at this time. Finally, Gebhard states that for the adult female population as a whole "the incidence of predominantly homosexual individuals is between 1 and 2 percent, probably nearer 1."[23]

Again, the European findings are consistent with those of the United States.

Social control and homosexuality. Homosexuality is outlawed in all of the United States except two—Illinois (which modified its laws in 1962) and Connecticut (which changed its laws in 1971). Punishment varies for the crime, but in actual fact punishment is variable and haphazard at best, and in some places like New York City, the police punishment is more and more in the form of harassment and mental annoyance. Of course for many years, homosexuals lived more under the fear of simply being found out, and blackmail has probably been the most feared form of punishment.

Perhaps the great break in social and legal attitudes about homosexuality occurred with the publication and lengthy discussion of the Wolfenden Report in Great Britain.[24] The key phrase in the report that became law is that homosexuality between consenting adults (over age 21) is no longer against the law. Important in the decision was the increasing support which the Report received from religious leaders across denominational lines. The influence of this Report on thinking in the United States and elsewhere has been increasing in recent years.

An important sign of the changing posture on homosexuality is found in the fact that the American Psychiatric Association has agreed to hear arguments on whether homosexuality should continue to be labelled as a form of mental disorder. Dr. J. Marmor, Vice President of the APA and Professor of Psychiatry at the University of Southern California, is quoted by The *New York Times* as saying "homosexuality in itself . . . merely represents a variant sexual preference which our society disapproves of but which does not constitute a mental illness."[25] And the article quotes several other psychiatrists who acknowledge that many homosexuals are well adjusted and cannot be distinguished from heterosexuals in their nonsexual behavior.

The increasing willingness of people to identify themselves as homosexuals, either as members of the Mattachine Society (begun in 1950) or as Daughters of Bilitis (1955) suggests that the sanctions and social control mechanisms against homosexuality are rapidly breaking down, just as they are breaking down or have broken down in other areas of sexual behavior. But more than that, the openness and frankness, not to say bluntness, of these movements causes us to reevaluate the place of human sexuality in human life, and especially in marriage. As Tom Driver says:

> *The rise of homosexuality and bisexuality in society exerts a pressure on marriage that causes us to reappropriate its meaning. If this is done, we are freed to recognize that the forms of sexual love do not matter when compared to the dignity of persons and their capacity for trust.*
>
> *The gay liberation movement raises homosexuality to political consciousness. It prevents our regarding the topic as merely a "psychological problem" or a matter of "private morality." It forces us to consider policy. The movement should have our thanks if it causes us to reconsider the policies of marriage, and most of all if it helps us to see that sexual plurality is the very scene and stage upon which are played the dramas of love.*[26]

> *Males (and females) do not represent two discrete populations, heterosexual and homosexual. The world is not to be divided into sheep and goats. Not all things are black nor all things white. It is a fundamental of taxonomy that nature rarely deals with discrete categories. Only the human mind invents categories and tries to force facts into separated pigeon-holes. The living world is a continuum in each and every one of its aspects. The sooner we learn this concerning human sexual behavior the sooner we shall reach a sound understanding of the realities of sex.*
>
> Alfred C. Kinsey

The relatively recent use of the word "homophile" to describe homosexual organizations represents an attempt to remove the "sexual" from "homosexual," and for a good reason. There is a tendency for the uninformed, "straight" population to think of homosexuals, male and female, primarily in a sexual context, forgetting that homosexuals are, first of all, people with the same wide diversity of talents, needs, and conflicts that one finds in all human beings. Homosexuals may be politically and sexually conservative or liberal, promiscuous or chaste. They may be blue-collar or white-collar, male or female. They have the same wide variation in ambitions, drives, and the need for "making a living," the same mixed feelings about whether they should simply exist in the best possible manner, or perpetuate themselves in their children, or their work. They also have many of the same problems with physical sexuality—impotence, frigidity, and the inability to relate in a physical way to individuals with whom they are clearly infatuated or whom they admire or love. Their sexuality is also learned and evolves over a period of time, with experience. They, too, were born into heterosexual households and have grown up with many of the same taboos about physical sexuality that are common to the straight population.

There is no need to describe "what they do with each other" because the erotic areas of the body and the mind are common to us all and have previously been discussed at length. However, the sexual liberation of women has given rise to at least one change among the liberated lesbians, just as it has among the liberated heterosexual women; namely, there is less need to emphasize the masculine-feminine, aggressive-passive, butch-femme roles in relationships at either the physical or emotional level. This change even extends into the every-day details of two people living together. Jill Johnston, a very vocal and articulate lesbian, noted on a TV program that she never goes to bed with a woman with a specific role in mind: ". . . it can be the whole kaleidoscope."[27] With this liberation, there is less emphasis on vaginal stimulation as a primary source of sexual pleasure and release, and upon the use of artificial penises (dildoes), a practice which has never been as prevalent among lesbian females as imagined by the straight, vaginally-oriented world. Vaginal stimulation does not need to be considered as the primary stimulation by either lesbians or heterosexual females, though it usually does add an extra dimension to physical sexuality.

This aggressive-passive role-playing is also disappearing, or not deemed essential, in liberated male homosexual relationships, just as it is disappearing among liberated heterosexual male-female relationships.

Homosexuals are individuals whose sexual attraction is to members of the same sex and whose pleasures in the everyday aspects of living are enhanced by sharing them with a member of the same sex. They still remain either female and regard their partners as female, or male and regard their partners as male.

Bisexual individuals enjoy close emotional relationships with either sex, with crushes, infatuations, and love, which may or may not lead to pleasurable physical sexuality, depending on the mutuality of the feeling. There are a number of individuals who, over the years, grow into or out of a period of bisexuality or who, because of societal pressures and a desire for personal, emotional stability, discard bisexuality for either homosexuality or heterosexuality as a permanent life style. This decision making may come at that point in a bisexual's life when it is time to "settle" into one's vocation. This may mean moving into the limited environment of a small town or a city with a wife or husband, thereby limiting contacts with the homosexual population or making any possible relationship more conspicuous and therefore undesirable; or it may mean "disappearing" into the relative anonymity of a large city where societal pressures on homosexuality are not quite so intense, and there is a wider range of acceptable partners.

With the increasing understanding that homosexuality is a reality for many people and not simply evidence of neurotic behavior, it has gradually become more acceptable for homosexuals to "come out" of heterosexual marriages and adopt their preferred life-style. A few courts are beginning to allow lesbians to keep their children, and granting wider visitation privileges, and sometimes even custody, to homosexual fathers.

Transsexuals are individuals who, for environmental and physiological reasons, are basically either males caught up in female bodies, or females caught up in male bodies. As transsexuals are recognized as a separate category, we are beginning to understand that one of their problems is that they are often perceived to be homosexuals when, in fact, they are not. The stigma of homosexuality may make it difficult for them to relate to anyone. Some may require surgical and medical treatment of their physiological disorder in order to function well in any aspect of living (see Bibliography).

Transvestites, individuals who wear clothing of the opposite sex, make up a grouping, male and to a lesser extent female, which is often assumed to be homosexual or has homosexual "tendencies." Generally speaking, they are not. Transvestism has many variations. There are males who like to wear articles of female clothing while making love with their understanding or tolerant wives. There are males, not necessarily transsexuals or homosexuals, who enjoy wearing female clothing as professional entertainers. There are males who wear female clothing in public to attract other males, though their own maleness may be perfectly apparent. There are female homosexuals who adopt totally male dress and hair styles to identify themselves in the masculine-feminine role though this is discouraged by the more liberated group of lesbians.

Kinsey's discussion of transvestism[28] should be read by those who are interested and may just lead the reader to the following conclusion: Repetitive or habitual transvestism (not associated with transsexualism) for overt sexual gratification may represent one real sexual dysfunction which does not *quite* fit into any normal continuum involving male and female sexual behavior; it is, perhaps, closer to an emotional disorder than a physiological reality.

In a clinical situation, it is impossible to make quick, "spot" diagnoses of homosexuality among women or men, especially among the student population. But routine questioning, such as, "Do you have a need for contraception?" sometimes will bring the answer, "No, I'm a lesbian or homosexual," or "No, not recently, I'm a bisexual." We are hearing this more frequently now than in the past—it seems to be easier to say aloud. However, this information is seldom essential to gynecological or any medical examination or diagnosis, but anything which aids a doctor in knowing the patient better will result in more understanding and better emotional and physical care.

It is our hope that this brief discussion of other dimensions of sexuality has answered some basic and common questions and will give the reader a baseline for further reading and understanding of themselves and others.

The Commune

We will have more to say about the commune as an alternate form of marriage in the following chapter. Nevertheless, it is appropriate to introduce the topic here because to a significant degree, the communal experiments in the United States seem to involve the more highly educated rather than the less educated, the college graduate or dropout rather than the high school dropout, the more liberal rather than the less liberal. It is an experiment of the affluent, well-educated middle class who continue to seek a new life-style. Indeed, the new coed dorm styles may or may not lead to continued experimentation with communal arrangements during the 1970s. And finally, we should note that the commune is for many young people the last stage of sexual growth and experimentation in later adolescence. It bridges the period between late adolescence and young adulthood, as its members who are sexually active generally range in age from 17 to 30 and over.

There seem to be two major types of communes, those found in cities and those found in rural areas. And their orientations seem to be different. Typically, the city commune houses college graduates and dropouts who are leading more or less conventional lives in pursuit of occupational careers including graduate school, but who have found communal life more enjoyable than life isolated in a single room or a small apartment. They generally share the cooking and housekeeping, but not the sexual activity. In the majority of 18 communes studied, it was found that "some" sexual license was permitted, but only three permitted "much" such free expression.[29] The public image of the communes as places where sexual orgies take place much as they do in coed dorms is simply not supported by the facts. The monogamous pair-bond unit of traditional middle-class life continues to manifest its strength in communal life.

The question may be raised whether the reason for such relatively limited amount of free sexual expression (sexual union with a multiplicity of partners during any week or month) is due to the fact that those experimenting now with communal life are, after all, first generation practitioners who, as Roberts suggests, have been socialized to traditional monogamous patterns, and are encountering difficulties in trying to free themselves from traditions. Or is the problem related to the degree to which sexual expression can be divorced from other emotional expressions, from commitment of one person to another, from some degree of possessiveness that gives sexual expression more meaning and pleasure than can be obtained from the physical pleasure experienced in isolation from these feelings? And is this second possibility not also part and parcel of our traditional ways of thinking about human relationships?

The point is that many people in and out of communes find the pair-bond relationship richly rewarding and do not wish to abandon it, even if they are not interested in traditional marriage patterns. The point is also that for a variety of reasons* which we don't fully understand, communes seem to be short-lived, even when pressures from the outside community do not hasten their disintegration. It may be another generation yet before we can have a clearer picture of the part that communes may be expected to play in the sexual development of females and males.

This is not to suggest that there are no advocates of sexual freedom; far from it. As one female member of the Sexual Freedom League puts it: ". . . I really enjoy sharing my bed with another warm critter . . . and if that critter cares to initiate any sex play, I'm generally agreeable. . . . Sex is fun. It's also a very enjoyable—and effective way to tell a friend, I love you."[30]

Nevertheless, membership in the Sexual Freedom League has not grown very much in recent years. It is another option for those who find in it a way to express themselves. But it hardly seems a threat to traditional sexual patterns. Indeed, some recent interviews with older adolescents indicate that group sex and group marriage have little appeal. Young people are relieved to be increasingly free of the old guilt feelings and dirty feelings about sex. If anything, the trend in their behavior is toward a relaxed view of sex "as a natural, beautiful thing." Casual sex, devoid of other social commitments, seems to be a prize of little value to this new generation of young people. Many young people are also aware of and comfortable with the idea that one can care about another in the short space of one or two hours. Sexual activity in this situation may be seen as a rational expression of this activity. Increasingly it appears that sexuality is less and less centered in the pelvis and more dependent on attitudes of mind. Respect for the rights and for the personal growth problems of others is also a part of the new scene, and this respect may be a more important mechanism of social control than the old fear of pregnancy or the thought that sexual expression outside of marriage was sinful.

Some Problems of Premarital Sex

She, however, while not able to stand the crowd's scorn for her virginity, could not go to bed with just anybody. So she carefully decided which guy in her circle was going to be the first (one always has a special feeling for the first).   Sidney Callahan   1970

* These reasons include such simple matters as: adapting to a variety of modes and norms about housekeeping, division of labor and finances, which tend after a time to affect the emotional rather than physical aspects of the relationship. In a larger sense, the attempt to practice democracy in decision making leads to decisions which are not made in order to avoid conflicts, but which eventually lead to conflicts. The reader can readily recognize the difficulties encountered by a multiplicity of persons trying to adapt to each other.

Womanlike they did not want to get tough with their men, and so, womanlike, they got screwed.

Germaine Greer   1972

For a Sad Lady

And let her loves, when she is dead
Write this above her bones:
"No more she lives to give us bread
Who asked her only stones."

Dorothy Parker   1940

A SENSE OF HUMOR is almost a prerequisite for the adequate handling of some of the problems *females and males* encounter in dating relationships which include intercourse. And it is sometimes difficult to have a sense of humor about what is happening in a onesided, intense infatuation in the late teens, twenties or thirties, or any premarital age; this usually comes with experience, and often only in retrospect. Males frequently feel just as "used" within a relationship, or after a relationship has terminated, as females, but only gradually and recently have they been able to verbalize this in a similar style; for example, examine the real content of numerous articles about premature ejaculation, impotence, demanding women, and parts of Mailer's *The Prisoner of Sex.*

It is also difficult to accept that many of the problems which arise are, realistically, not related to sexual activity per se but to the fact of sexual activity outside of marriage. This does not make them less soluble or insoluble, but simply means that it often requires a little more maturity to establish and maintain relationships outside of marriage than it does to enter into a marriage relationship without previous sexual experience. The marriage license often shields one from the risks of pregnancy, VD, and even from the emotional impact of sexual dysfunctions for a while, though it does make it necessary to face up to those problems of living together which emerge in the marital setting and which have little to do with sexual function. But marriage may be a safe haven established by law which reduces the threat of being left.

A premarital relationship may be threatened by VD, pregnancy, abortion questions, and ego problems related to sexual performance and dysfunction, but the everyday details of living together are much easier to handle. The problems of dirty laundry, socks strewn about, how one squeezes the toothpaste tube, and the budget (if there is one) are solved either by ignoring them because they are not important in a "temporary" situation, or by being very candid about them, since being candid will not threaten a "temporary" situation; there is always someone or someplace else.

The special privilege of the unmarried relationship is the privilege of leaving, but leaving often takes courage and maturity. This may account, in part, for the apparent inability of many "steady" couples who are sexually involved, but no longer emotionally involved, to go their separate ways. It is often easier and more comfortable to stay together, postponing the need for getting out in the world alone, and competing once again. There are an increasing number of such couples seeking sexual counseling during a premarital relationship, encouraged by psychiatric and religious services who provide and encourage such counseling, that is, marriage counseling outside of marriage. Each member of a couple may need some psychiatric help in learning how to relate to others and about herself or himself; it is another question whether this counseling service itself encourages dating couples to remain together. Again, the privilege of the young and unmarried is the privilege of leaving, and the existence of sexual intercourse in a relationship need not be the major criterion which determines staying.

However, intercourse in a relationship often seems to represent a certain amount of commitment and to demand an equal amount of loyalty. This may be a way of acknowledging a subconscious belief in the long prevalent attitude that sexual intercourse is automatically endowed with some profound human value. Leaving may create some guilt about having enjoyed sex at a very personal level without finding that profound human value, at least in the form they were led to expect. Leaving may also create doubts about oneself: how can bed be so good and we cannot get along at any other level? Am I at fault? What is it I lack, or want, or need? The feeling that intercourse represents commitment may be one of the biggest hurdles that participants in the recent evolution of sexuality have to face. But this, like all other information concerning sexuality, is difficult to communicate before the fact, since many relationships are still entered into, initially, as possible marriage relationships. When disillusionment sets in, the problems of leaving become real.

This problem of leaving may begin to fade when it is gradually accepted that intercourse represents only a single facet of any relationship and that it can serve a number of functions within that relationship. Males have always been "allowed" to know this and to use sex in many ways if they desired. There are an increasing number of females who are enjoying the same sexual freedom, but society-at-large and, also, many females are not yet comfortable with this newly acquired female freedom.

Of the three, sometimes militant, feminists quoted at the beginning of this section, two, Dorothy Parker and Germaine Greer, candidly admit to a wide variety of experiences, and have often described in poetry and prose common, recognizable patterns of "dating" with uncommon candor and wit. The increasing prevalence of *almost* casual sex demands a similar kind of understanding from an increasingly large number of individuals; but many are still preoccupied by the desire to master the physical aspects of the sexual revolution with some degree of emotional comfort, which is only the first step for those who are interested in going in this direction.

However, a variety of sexual experiences does not insure growth, if these experiences are not utilized and incorporated into one's thinking about the next. No one need be sexually active to grow and mature, to absorb, and to sort out information she or he reads and hears. Even the vicarious experiences which we have presented, or the *apparent* and real experiences of friends, can be of value, if the sources are carefully considered.

A variety of sexual experiences entered into with a clear understanding that this sexual activity is only fun-oriented for both, and without commitment, often yields a higher percentage of success if measured, as most measure it, by absence of sexual dysfunction. However, sex is used in many ways, which may or may not be dysfunctional for one or both partners:

> . . . an easy solution for every problem. While it is not a bad tranquilizer, it really shouldn't be used to calm you down, or to send you to sleep, or to put some distance between you and your problems. It should also not be used to make you feel beautiful and lovable and needed . . . to give you control over another person . . . to fill in time . . . to make you feel you're good at something . . . because you can't bear to be alone . . . because you secretly like to suffer . . . because you don't want to have to think.[31]

Sex is used in all of these ways and many more, inside and outside of marriage, by females and males. If there is no recognition by either partner of the basic motivation in any given occasion, this kind of usage may almost automatically carry with it dysfunctions or create problems.

But the fun approach to intercourse on the casual level often postpones thinking about oneself in relation to others—a kind of instant relationship, instant gratification, that requires little thought and perhaps only some preliminary rationalization. However, experiences of all types can be utilized.

There is always difficulty in applying the principles of science to human behavior; the results are almost always a compromise because of the many variables. The case history below, though unfinished, illustrates some common, but subtle, situations in contemporary dating with some vital variables removed.

A 26-year-old female graduate student in a health field with a social and psychiatric orientation came in with a complaint of mild dyspareunia associated with lack of lubrication. Her primary concern was her decrease in interest in sexual activity. When we asked about contraceptive methods which might be related to the dyspareunia, she told us that one ovary had been removed at age 18 and a year later her other ovary and her uterus had been removed. She had been on hormone replacement therapy for seven years without any problems. She had been sexually active for all of these years, successfully and orgasmically. She enjoyed sex. There had been a number of three and four month relationships as well as some one-night-stands. We asked her what she told her partners when or if they asked about contraception. She said, very simply, that they never asked. She had never had to tell a sexual partner that she was sterile.

Her current lack of interest in sexual activity was in contrast to her very real interest, now, in getting married. She had found someone whom she was interested in and who was interested in her. There had been no intercourse, and he was agreeable to this, though she was not pretending that she was a virgin. But she could not understand what had happened to herself: "Can you become frigid?"

The above illustrates: the male assumption that "she" is taking care of herself in regard to possible pregnancy; her awareness of the fact that sex can be fun; her acceptance that males are not expected or required to be concerned about females to be good sexual partners; interest in sex need not be tied to the risk of pregnancy; the training and ability to assist others in similar situations does not carry over to analysis of oneself, though it aided her in quick recognition of a possible source of her problem. It would appear that the problem which she had postponed and eventually buried, had surfaced, not in its real form, but almost unrecognized, as a lack of interest in sex. She did not want to put herself in the position of having to answer questions about contraception with the truth, nor did she wish to risk losing a good, caring male.

Virginity vs. Chastity

Dictionary definitions of these two terms might be of value to those who are considering their present state of sexual activity:

> *virgin:* a., a girl or woman who has never had sexual intercourse;...b...c... d...e...f., a boy or man who has never had sexual intercourse.
>
> *chaste:* not having engaged in *unlawful* sexual intercourse; pure in style; subdued, simple. *Obs.: unmarried.*
>
> *fornication:* voluntary sexual intercourse between two unmarried persons or two persons not married to each other.*

So, if one's background allows, it is quite possible to have had sexual intercourse, be nonvirginal, and still be chaste. Fornication is included because in

* *Random House Dictionary.* Unabridged, 1966.

some states it still represents the "unlawful" portion of the definition if it is part of the criminal code. A revision of the Pennsylvania code omits fornication, though it continues to include homosexuality and unnatural sexual acts.

These differences may seem like very fine points, but many young and older individuals choose even subtler differences to justify whatever they are doing, or not doing.

We don't use anything (for contraception), we really don't have intercourse.

This is the comment of a girl with a delayed menstrual period who admitted that there had been intravaginal ejaculation on two or three occasions. Intercourse, for her, apparently meant something more than this. Her definition did seem to be related more to elapsed time and her responsiveness than to the physical act itself.

For some, virginity has become basically a mechanical question, as in the strict definition:

You just get to that point and you're curious and wonder what the next step is like—so you do it.

Well, I've done that. I don't have to pretend anymore. Now I can wait for someone I really like.

The problem, after the first time, regardless of the reasons is that intercourse becomes easier and easier, with or without emotional involvement, except the emotion of the moment.

The most interesting development, and it was predicted by some, since sexual defiance and militancy peaked a few years ago and has given way to permissiveness, is the decreasing need for many females to apologize for their virginity to their gynecologists and to a certain extent, to their peers. Virgin males and females may still be viewed as "queers," strange, or "having a problem" in some circles, but the definition of sexual sophistication and freedom now allows the options of openly expressed and desired virginity. Males are still at some disadvantage with their peers in this area, but often much less so with their women. However, the sexual pressures in the environment still exist, and create self-imposed pressures which cause young men to weep in the chaplain's office, or in their local sexual counseling service because they have never *learned* how to kiss a girl.

The factor of commitment, even of a temporary nature, is clearly intimately involved with a feeling of being "chaste," though that may not be the exact word which is used. Everyone has his or her own definition of what is right, what is emotionally comfortable—an unconscious reference to "pure, undefiled." Everyone eventually, or quickly, also, has a fairly clear idea of what is *un*comfortable at any point in time. And the limits of what is emotionally comfortable and uncomfortable also change with time and experience, even within marriage. But, in general, if viewed from the outside, the double standard still favors males. They only become suspect when they appear to make commitments and then break them, though this is still easier for males than for most females. Someone may call these males bastards, but few are surprised.

Females are still suspect in both situations (which can be very confining) whether they are casual, or make commitments in a three or four month relationship with a view toward marriage. They may feel quite comfortable in the latter situation, but getting out of it with one's reputation still intact, is often quite another matter. The world is still set up so that it profits some females to create a situation in which "he" leaves, when and if leaving becomes the only alternative. This creates a better self-image and public image for her, if this is an important consideration, and is, emotionally, much easier to handle.

The new sexuality has reduced, if not eliminated, the status importance of physically attractive partners in dating situations. Dating used to be a public event and points were scored with one's friends and others according to the physical attractiveness of one's date. The slightly older generation physicians working in contraceptive clinics in recent years are sometimes nonplussed by the kinds of girls who arrive for contraceptives, certainly not the kinds they were *dating* in the recent past, though they may have married the same types.

The mechanics of this development are easy to understand and the "phenomenon," as the one or two articles on the subject term it, is logical. Coeducational living in college dorms allows a closeness and contact at a casual intellectual level never possible before, an appreciation of the "head." This kind of closeness and inevitable touching can proceed into sexual contact, also with an ease never before possible. Sexual contact, and finding that they are able to function sexually as females and males, and are desirable as females and males, can be very reassuring to those who are insecure about their physical appearance, especially in situations which are usually preceded by some mutual admiration in other areas of living. Thus, no one is, in fact, being used, and the experiences can be very useful in helping a human being to mature—to feel like a "whole" human being.

The new sexuality, with its options for young people, and its problems, seems certain to alter the structure of marriage, but as we shall see in the following chapter, seems unlikely to threaten it as a social institution. But if there has been an active premarital sexual life followed by marriage, there are at least five possible directions that sexual behavior may take within marriage:

1) We have mentioned elsewhere that if the pleasures of sex are dependent to some degree on the risk (or defiance) involved, then these pleasures may be lost when sex is legalized with a license, and there may be temporary problems if the source is not recognized. One such may be the attempt to create excitement with extramarital sex.

2) If there has been a wide variety of experiences prior to marriage, one or both partners may realize that looking someplace else for more than they are getting out of marriage is a rather futile gesture. In this case they may decide to direct their energies toward making this one work—the pastures are simply not greener or better elsewhere.

3) A wide variety of premarital experiences can make intermittent sexual dysfunctions within marriage easier to handle, since both have some experience and knowledge about themselves, their needs, and the needs of others.

4) If sex has been very casual without the establishment of even short-term relationships, there is the possibility that the nonsexual aspects of marriage and physical sex may be considered as separate entities—extramarital sex will mean nothing more than the emotion of the moment—with unpredictable consequences.

5) A casual attitude about physical sexuality and serial relationships may postpone children because they would hamper this potential of freedom, or it may be extended into a casual attitude about the responsibilities inherent in the marriage license, and also create some emotional ease with the idea of divorce.

Sexual permissiveness does allow postponement of marriage until that time when women and men have done their traveling, their schooling, or worked as long as they care to. Both can enter marriage for reasons other than sex, and there may be fewer females and males in their late thirties and forties feeling unfulfilled because they missed some of the increasing pleasures and options of being single. This need not postpone maturing or prolong adolescence; but it does provide the opportunity, experiences, and basis for continued growth throughout one's life and can prevent a marriage from growing dull, or one or both partners being full of secret regrets about what might have been.

None of the above discussion, however, is meant to suggest that the 30 percent to 50 percent of couples who apparently still enter marriage as virgins, are, by that fact alone, less likely to achieve sexual satisfaction in marriage, or generally satisfying marriages. Perhaps the key question is whether people are marrying chiefly to satisfy sexual drives frustrated premaritally by the belief that virginity was vital, and thus tending to gloss over other aspects of their relationship. Too often, they have let themselves believe that they would "live happily ever after" once they could relate to each other in full sexual expression. Virgin couples with a healthy understanding of themselves and awareness of the strengths and weaknesses of the other may expect to do at least as well as their more sexually experienced peers. For if the data on postmarital adjustments of the sexually experienced reveal little or no reason to believe that premarital sexuality necessarily lessens the chances for marital success, neither do the data suggest that lack of such experience is necessarily harmful to marital success. Perhaps the most that can be said is that marital success is dependent more on attitudes of mind than amount and quality of premarital sexual experience.

Summary

It is very difficult to achieve a balanced perspective in a chapter, or even in a book like this. In the foregoing pages we have attempted to present an accurate portrayal of sexual development in adolescence in American and to some extent Western society. But there is still a fairybook quality in the data which requires that we remind the reader that the elimination of the old fears hasn't solved all problems. Among other things, we are now able to begin to focus on the interpersonal problems that have emerged with the new sexual morality. Several college campuses have opened sex counseling clinics for students. Many students come to these clinics concerned because they are not sexually active. Premature ejaculation among males seems to be a common problem; and females fed on the literature that orgasms are heavenly events, are frustrated either at not achieving orgasm, or at finding themselves still very much in this world in the midst of orgasm. The message is clear: young people are expecting too much too soon from sexual union.

VIEWPOINTS

As a general principle, I favor premarital sex. If premarital sex were taboo, we would leave ourselves open to all the neurotic conflicts that were prevalent in Victorian days. I see no danger in premarital sex when it is undertaken by emotionally responsible young people. There are dangers when immature and irresponsible young people enter into sexual relationships. The main danger is that sexual indulgence at too early an age can weaken the developing ego and undermine the sense of self.

Sexual activity—specifically coitus—should be an expression of physical and emotional maturity. Unfortunately, one cannot set an arbitrary age as the criterion of maturity, and so the problem is complicated. In any event, the issue is not one that can be regulated by society since, today, most young people assume that they have the right to govern their own lives. And they are sufficiently free from parental control to act upon this assumption.

If young people are raised with a sense of personal responsibility, they will naturally avoid intercourse until they feel that they can handle themselves responsibly. Removing external restraints pushes the problem back into the early years of childhood, for it is during these years that the ability to take personal responsibility for one's behavior is engendered. The individual who hasn't gained this ability will encounter many difficulties and suffer much pain as he embarks upon adult sexuality. It may be that through this pain the person will find himself and develop responsibility. I have known many young people who went through a stage of sexual promiscuity and emerged with a higher degree of personal integrity. I do not believe the dangers are great. Those who fail to make it and become lost in the subcultures are the seriously disturbed who would inevitably flounder in the turbulent seas of modern living.

Premarital sex poses no threat to the stability of the marital relationship. The fact that a man or a woman has intimately known others of the opposite sex does not mean that he or she will find difficulty in forming more permanent relationships. In fact, premarital sexual experience may promote the stability of the marital relationship, if both partners know that they have chosen each other with some knowledge of what sex should offer.

The same thing, however, cannot be said of extramarital sex. If extramarital sex is accepted as normal, then there can be no real faith in a marriage. If a person wants to be free to know other partners, then why marry?

It is my experience that people who engage in extramarital sex do so because they are not satisfied in their marital relationship. This may be a fault of the marriage, or it may be due to the inability of such individuals to find any meaningful satisfaction in their own lives. Whatever the reason, one should not condemn them. However, in neither case is extramarital sex a solution to their problem. Inevitably, such behavior leads to a crisis which may sometimes improve the marital situation; though in most cases, the crisis ends in the destruction of that relationship.

From Alexander Lowen,
Sexual Latitude: For and Against
(New York: Hart Publishing Co.), pp. 61-63.

• • • • • • • • • •

Christians gratefully acknowledge that sex is one of God's gifts and that it has been given to us richly to enjoy. Sexual intercourse is an experience of the most intimate and intense kind. In the act of sexual intercourse two persons become, in a profound and mysterious sense, "one flesh." Intercourse, in relation to two persons who truly love one another, symbolizes and also seals an underlying unity of heart and mind. It is love which gives to intercourse its sanctity and significance; and within marriage, it is through repeated acts of intercourse that love is strengthened and renewed. Sexual intercourse, apart from love, is in Shakespeare's graphic words "lust in action."

Sex finds its proper fulfillment in marriage. . . .

There are some who argue that since sex is a personal matter, there are no limits to what an individual may do, except those limits the individual imposes on himself. This presupposes an individualistic, atomic view of society. We do not, in other areas of life, accept the view that a man may do what he likes; we insist that there are limits.

In this life, pleasure is always the by-product of something else; like the pot of gold at the rainbow's end, it eludes those who make it their goal. It is not by indiscriminate and inordinate indulgence, nor by desperate strategies of experimentation, that we heighten and intensify sexual feeling. It is by accepting the fact that there are limits, not only to what is possible but to what is permissible, that we enjoy Eros's elusive rewards.

What is possible is physiologically determined—there is, after all, a mathematical limit to the number of positions available for coitus. What is permissible is determined by our understanding of the place of sex in the life of man.

The normal avenue for the expression of sexual desire is marriage. There are a few who achieve the difficult art of self-control through sublimation: witness the life of Jesus. For the religious man, the goal is continence before marriage, and fidelity within marriage. For those who reject these traditional standards as normative, the alternatives, apart from self-control, are promiscuity and perversion.

Shakespeare aptly described the life of promiscuity as "a waste of spirit in a desert of shame." Norman Mailer speaks satirically of those who are forever seeking an orgasm more apocalyptic than the one that went before. They are set on a fool's quest. In this realm, as in all others, the law of diminishing returns applies.

From Dr. Stuart Babbage,
Sexual Latitude: For and Against
(New York: Hart Publishing Co.), pp. 28-35.

• • • • • • • • • •

You mention the changing of the sexual mores. I wonder how you feel about the so-called new morality, and its reflection in literature and film. Is this progress, in your view?

There are days when I feel that nothing has been more liberating to men and women than getting all this stuff out from under the carpet. It was, so to speak, like going from the cesspool to a proper plumbing system. But having done that, I think a lot of it ought to be flushed. I think it was

Rebecca West who was asked to read "Naked Lunch" and said, "I do not wish to spend my time with my nose trapped in somebody else's toilet." I agree.

Isn't the inference that sex is dirty?

It can be smelly. Perhaps there was some reason that nature chose to put the genital regions so close to the anal. Sex is a very private act. The minute it is made commonplace, it loses a great deal of its mystery and power. I saw in the paper this morning, which amused me to no end, that Mae West walked out of "Last Tango in Paris." What she walked out on was, of course, the destruction of the *mystique* of sex. I think the destruction of that *mystique* is a great, great loss.

Quotes by Clair Booth Luce from M. W. Lear, "On Harry, and Henry and Ike and Mr. Shaw," *New York Times* magazine, 22 April 1973, p. 10.

References

1. See Robert Bell, "Premarital Sex," *Social Deviance* (Homewood, Ill.: Dorsey Press, 1971), Chap. 2; see also *Sex and the College Student*, Report 60, Group for the Advancement of Psychiatry, 104 East 25th Street, New York, New York, 1965.

2. Harold T. Christensen and Christine F. Gregg, "Changing Sex Norms in America and Scandinavia," *Journal of Marriage and the Family* (November 1970): 616-627. Reprinted in R. Bell and M. Gordon, eds., *The Social Dimension of Human Sexuality* (Boston: Little, Brown and Co., 1972), pp. 47-65.

3. Bell and Gordon, *Social Dimension of Human Sexuality,* p. 50.

4. See Everett C. Ladd, "Professors and Political Positions," *Science,* 163, 28 (March, 1969): 1425-1429.

5. For example, they compare closely with the results of a national study carried out by Ira Reiss as reported in his article, "How and Why America's Sex Standards are Changing," *Transaction* (March 1968): 26ff.

6. Bell, *Social Deviance,* p. 58.

7. Reiss, *Transaction,* pp. 27-28.

8. "Teen-Age Sex: Letting the Pendulum Swing," *Time,* 21 August 1972, pp. 34-40.

9. Volkmar Sigusch and Gunter Schmidt, "Lower Class Sexuality," *Archives of Sexual Behavior,* 1, 1 (1971): 30.

10. *Ibid.,* pp. 38-39.

11. Gunter Schmidt and Volkmar Sigusch, "Patterns of Sexual Behavior in West German Workers and Students," *The Journal of Sex Research,* 7, 2 (May 1971): 89-106.

12. *Sex and the College Student,* p. 82.

13. Joyce Maynard, "The Embarrassment of Virginity," *Mademoiselle,* August 1972, p. 411.

14. The interested reader should consider among others the following recent publications on homosexuality: "Homosexuality: Final Report and Background Papers," National Institute of Mental Health Task Force, Publ. No. (HSM) 72-9116 (Washington, D. C.: U. S. Government Printing Office, 1972); Tom F. Driver, "Homosexuality: The Contemporary and Christian Contexts," and Peter E. Fink, "Homosexuality, A Pastoral Hypothesis," *Commonweal* XCVIII, 5 (April 1, 1973).

15. Paul Gebhard, "Incidence of Homosexuality in the United States and Western Europe," in "Final Report and Background Papers," p. 26.

16. For a recent study on pederasty, see Parker Rossman, "The Pederasts," *Society* (March-April 1973): 29-35.

17. Evelyn Hooker, "Homosexuality," in "Final Report and Background Papers," pp. 11-12.

18. *Ibid.,* p. 14.

19. *Ibid.,* p. 16.

20. Gebhard, "Final Report and Background Papers," p. 27.

21. *Ibid.,* p. 27.

22. *Ibid.,* p. 28.

23. *Ibid.,* p. 28.

24. *The Wolfenden Report,* Report of the Committee on Homosexual Offenses and Prostitution, American ed. (New York: Stein and Day, 1963). Sir John Wolfenden and his committee presented the report to the British Parliament in 1957, and after almost nine years of debate and discussion, the key recommendations on homosexuality were passed into law in 1966.

25. Dr. J. Marmor as quoted in Boyce Rensberger, "Psychiatry Reconsiders Stand on Homosexuals," The *New York Times,* 9 February 1973, p. 24c.

26. Driver, "Homosexuality: The Contemporary and Christian Contexts," p. 106.

27. See also Jill Johnston, *Lesbian Nation: The Feminist Solution* (New York: Dutton, 1971).

28. Alfred C. Kinsey, et al., *Sexual Behavior in the Human Male* (Philadelphia: W. B. Saunders Company, 1948).

29. See Ron E. Roberts, *The New Communes* (New York: Prentice-Hall Spectrum Book, 1971), p. 38.

30. *Ibid.,* p. 45.

31. Lillian Roxon, "The Intelligent Woman's Guide to Sex," *Mademoiselle,* August 1973.

10

Introduction

WE GREW UP with the conventional wisdom that if we followed the rules on dating and courtship, sooner or later we would get married. And that was a state much to be desired. In fact, it used to be said with due pride some few years back that U.S. Americans were about the most married people in the world, staunch defenders and even proponents of monogamous marriage, and of sexual union confined within marriage. But, as we have seen in the preceding chapters, today the assumptions and assertions regarding marriage are under fire in the United States, as are the traditional patterns of dating and courtship. In this chapter, we will examine marriage as a social institution in the United States, the forces threatening traditional patterns of behavior, and also emerging new patterns and their implications.

Contracts, Old and New*

Sociologists have often remarked that one of the significant changes in human social behavior during the past two centuries has been the movement away from behavior based on ascribed social characteristics, such as race, ethnicity, religion, lineage, social class, prestige—that is, those characteristics about which the individual could do little or nothing, but which largely determined his life history—and toward behavior based on characteristics which the individual and groups he could join could have influence over, often through the formation of contracts spelling out and thus limiting the control which others might have over his life. With regard to marriage, this has meant the shift away from marriages arranged by families for their children, and in the process allowing young people increasing amounts of freedom in dating and courtship. Nevertheless, the freedom still ended with choice of partner in a contract that was distinctly unmodern in its structure of rights and obligations.

---

* It should be recognized that for many couples traditional contracts were taken for granted. Their requirements were part of the cultural milieu. On the other hand, contracts that are written by the couples themselves derive their value from the fact of mutual agreement on wording prior to marriage and may or may not be referred to consciously after marriage.

A contract is an agreement between two or more persons which is binding in law, and which binds them to do certain things for each other. Throughout history, the marriage contract in almost all societies has focused on at least two areas of social life, the sexual and the economic. Husbands and wives agree to exchange sexual favors, and also to work out a division of labor in order to assure their survival. It is noteworthy also that throughout history, despite the appearance of some variety in forms, the most dominant form of marriage has been the monogamous, the pair-bond relationship binding one man with one woman, presumably for the duration of their lifetime. Polygynous (a husband having two or more wives simultaneously) and polyandrous (a wife having two or more husbands simultaneously) forms of marriage have enjoyed varying degrees of popularity and success, but have reflected the economic, political, and social success of the male (polygyny) on the one hand, and the economic plight of the society (polyandry) on the other. In either case, the forms guaranteed sexual pleasure for the male and limited social status for the female. Indeed, the close relationship between the economic and the sexual may be seen in the fact that adultery of the wife was subject to severe punishments, and in ancient society was seen almost as a violation of male property rights. Thus over time, the marriage contract became a highly generalized series of obligations binding couples, and while other aspects of social life were undergoing rapid social change, there was no effort made to change this contract to meet the changing times.

The Traditional Contract

The formal marriage contract which probably binds most married couples in the United States is some variant on this version from *The Book of Common Prayer*:

> *I take thee to be my wedded spouse, to have and to hold from this day forward, for better, for worse, for richer, for poorer, in sickness and in health, to love and to cherish (and for the female, to obey), till death do us part.*

This is in reality a highly restrictive contract, as it is understood that each member of the couple expects to focus his or her sexual activity on the other, and the husband promises to support the wife economically even as she is expected to provide him with an orderly home. The contract implies a permanency, "Till death do us part," which continues to have force for the great majority of married couples. Remember, three out of four couples in the United States are still married to their first marriage partner, which may or may not reflect the seriousness with which this contract is still held, despite easing of the divorce laws in recent years.

Herbert Otto has succinctly summarized some of the most important assumptions that have built up around the traditional marriage contract over the years:

1. Marriage furnishes a means for the giving and taking of love, understanding, and for sexual fulfillment.
2. Sexual relations should take place only (or largely) between the two partners.
3. Marriage offers a measure of security, comfort, and stability, so that both partners soon learn to know what they can expect. Boundaries are set by husband and wife and it is their expectation that these will be respected.
4. Marriage involves a set of responsibilities and duties. It also involves certain roles—"what a husband is and should be" and "what a wife is and should be."
5. Marriage is for the raising and rearing of children and "having a family."
6. Marriage is a means of "weathering life's storms and ups-and-downs."
7. Marriage means companionship, someone to talk to.
8. Marriage is an insurance against a lonely old age.[1]

It seems fair to say that for many younger couples, as well as most older couples, these are the assumptions which guide their marriage. An increasing number of scholars and professionals working in the marriage counseling field have begun to question these assumptions and the actual behavioral patterns which have been manifested by couples observing more or less traditional marriages. For example, the O'Neill's call this a closed type of contract which tends to stultify a marriage and the development of the partners as individual persons. Specifically, they point to the following:

1. The contract tends to place the partners in bondage to each other. That is, more often than not, a sense of possessiveness takes over, and people feel that they belong to each other. But this is not a freely-held feeling and cannot be, in the traditional context.

2. The contract tends to diminish the identity of the individual and to emphasize self-sacrifice; usually the wife is the one who sacrifices herself for husband and children, although it is not uncommon for husbands to feel that they are getting little in return for their economic efforts.*

---

* Jessie Bernard makes a strong case that marriage is in fact much more beneficial to the mental well-being of men than that of women. See *The Future of Marriage*, by Jessie Bernard (New York: The World Publishing Co., 1972), especially Chaps. 1, 2, and 3.

3. At the same time the contract creates a couple-image; a person is seen in terms of the partner; invitations are couple-oriented, and people are always on guard to protect the image of the happy couple.

4. In the most traditional cases, role behavior is sex linked, and duties and obligations, as well as rights, are understood as deriving from the "natural order of things;" for example, "the woman's place is in the home."

5. Sexual fidelity, physical and even psychological, is required. So strongly held has been this assumption, that until recently, adultery was the only cause for divorce in some states.

6. Finally, they assert that the traditional contract enforces togetherness under the mistaken belief that only thus can the marriage be preserved.[2]

The reader should keep in mind that while these consequences have been real for many couples, they have not by that fact been disastrous for their marriages. Women have found much comfort in the self-sacrifice role, and sometimes have received important public support and satisfaction thereby. But increasingly this role orientation has been demeaned, and even the women themselves seem apologetic about being "just a housewife." And many husbands and wives still live by traditional views of what a husband is and what a wife is, and are happy with their division of labor. The point to be made is that the traditional contract worked within a particular historical context; but even if it still works, it may be less satisfactory than some alternatives, especially given our changing understanding of the nature of females and males.

Perhaps more than any other area of behavior, the traditional contract has affected the sexual behavior of spouses. For until recently, the de facto reality of marriage was that it provided a regular outlet for male sexual tension, and at the same time provided a regular and legitimate means of procreation—indeed, for most wives marriage was for the begetting and rearing of children. Research on married couples who were at least 50 years old at the time of the study reveals the following patterns:

1. *Sex was not of equal importance to husband and wife, but was of much greater importance to the husband. Women did without sex for extended periods while their husbands were absent, or during widowhood, and generally did not report this as sexually frustrating.*

2. *Sex had quite a different meaning for husbands than for wives. Men showed much greater appreciation than women of the visual aspect of sexual encounters. Men showed much greater interest in experimentation with different sexual techniques and positions than women. Women far more than men viewed sex as an expression of love. Men were more drawn to a variety of partners, while women reported this much less frequently.*

3. *Husbands generally preferred intercourse with greater frequency than their wives. Three times as many men as women reported higher preferred frequency of intercourse than their spouses reported.*

4. *The most common complaint about their sex lives made by husbands was that their wives were not interested enough in sex, and were not sexually responsive enough. The most common complaint by wives was that their husbands were oversexed.*

5. *Female orgasm was of problematic occurrence. Its absence or infrequency was one of the best predictors of marital maladjustment in every study which included data on this issue. The sex lives of many couples were organized around the problem of bringing the wife to orgasm.*

6. *Unless the wife was unusually interested sexually, she generally set the upper limit on sexual frequency, and the husband generally set the lower limit.*[3]

These general patterns should not be construed to suggest that the differences between females and males in married sexuality are biologically determined. We have reflected on that theme thoroughly in Chapter 1. Rather, these differences may reflect traditional socialization patterns. And this would include the male's failure to appreciate female sexuality. In this sense, there may well be biological differences in sexual nature and response. But marital sexuality will be a function of the degree to which the couple understands and relates to these differences. The differences themselves do not determine what the couple's sex life will be like.

Finally, the importance and emphasis on sexual union in the traditional marriage may be seen by the strictures of the Roman Catholic Church; one of the few causes for annulment of a marriage performed in the Catholic Church was that it was not consummated sexually; a related cause was that one of the partners refused to have children.

The Liberated Contract

Traditional expectations about marriage have gradually given way to progressive ideas among ever increasing numbers of people. They still see monogamous marriage as a viable institution, but they see the need for new modes of thinking about sexuality and sex roles in marriage. They see marriage as a liberated social institution, and if they still think in contractual terms, the contract is now an open and flexible one, as opposed to the traditional, closed and restrictive one.

More important, marriage is seen as a voluntary social relationship in which both partners expect to share, in which work and sex roles are not foreordained by the fact of birth or tradition, but are selected on the basis of free choice. Thus, the freedom of sexual love in marriage implies that a wife does not give herself to her husband, nor does he see himself as deserving of sexual gratification because of some contractual obligation on the part of the wife. Both partners choose to give themselves freely to the other and to seek and expect a full measure of gratification for themselves, as well as for their partner.[4] In fact, many couples feel that in a truly equal and voluntary relationship there is no need for carefully constructed contracts.

Apparently several patterns are emerging, with some couples finding value in developing written contracts which specify role expectations, while others simply understand that theirs is a voluntary relationship built on love and affection, reciprocity and sharing. Whatever the precise nature of the relationship, there is agreement that:

The spouse earning the larger salary is not necessarily doing the more important work;

spouses may choose any of several divisions of labor without implying that the choices are more or less valuable;

responsibility for taking care of the children should be shared, and not left to "mother";

household duties should be shared, but again spouses may freely choose to take on certain activities. The emphasis must be on freedom of choice.[5]

Again, in a liberated marriage the couple is concerned to develop means of communication which will make it possible for them to work out a design for living that is mutually rewarding.[6] The couple strives to be honest and open, to trust each other, and to be flexible. In a word, the liberated, or open, contract is a "natural" outcome of the relationships developed in the new world of premarriage, and reflects the changes taking place in the economic and political sectors of society.

The Communal and Group Marriage Contracts

Just as an increasing number of couples are liberating themselves from what they considered to be an unduly restrictive traditional marriage contract, so are many young people turning at least temporarily away from monogamous marriage. Communal and group marriage forms have become sufficiently prevalent as to come under the scrutiny of news analysts and scholars alike. There is less likelihood of a formal or written contract in either case, although there is much evidence that the chances of this type of marriage, if it can be so called, of enduring, are related to the degree to which clear expectations are developed among the participants. Where chaos and promiscuity exist, the group or commune seems to be very short-lived.

A major difference between group and communal marriage is that in group marriage it is expected that the members will have more or less promiscuous sexual relations with the other members, while in communal marriage, there is no such necessary expectation. Thus, Ellis defines a group marriage as one in which a relatively small number of adults—say, from four to fifteen—live together, ". . . sharing labor, goods and services, bearing and raising their children in common, and engaging in promiscuous sex relations, so that every male in the group has intercourse, at one time or another, with every female in the group."[7]

Whether the marriage is of group or communal structure, it seems that the chances for survival are increased if sexual interests are not the primary reason for the formation of the unit. In any case, it has become clear also that the communal and group marriage forms, while they may free people from the old constraints posed by traditional marriage, require a complex and fairly explicit set of arrangements. Ramey states the problem in this way:

Since society has not prescribed norms, standards, and activities for group marriages or communes, a great deal more preplanning and exploration must be undertaken to work through expectations and structure behavior for these largely uncharted waters than is the case upon entering into dyadic marriage.[8]

These arrangements need not be made in any formal, contractual sense, but if a communal family hopes to survive, some arrangements must be made. For example, one communal family of 11 persons, holds regular house meetings to try to iron out differences. Despite their high idealism and desire for deep personal relationships, their meetings "often bog down over small differences, such as noise in the house at night, deciding who 'claims' the refrigerator, who waxes the floors, and who handles the bookkeeping."[9]

Perhaps one of the more important aspects of this unwritten contract is the implication of its impermanence: "no one is bound to remain if he decides to go, and anyone can be turned out by a democratic vote of the group."[10]

The major objectives of communal-group marriages are: personal growth, economic and emotional security, a variety of sex partners, diffusion of classic sex roles, and less child-rearing responsibilities for any single individual, coupled with greater concern for the emotional development of the child. What kinds of people may then be expected to contract a plural marriage? The Constantines describe them as follows:

Individuals must be reasonably suited in certain obvious ways: absence of or only limited jealousy, ability to cope with complexity, sharing, generous, mature, in touch with motivations and emotions. We might say a best bet would be a truly self-actualizing person. Unfortunately, the near ideal psychological makeup is rare. Quite possibly few individuals, and that may include few among those currently trying, are really suited for multilateral marriage. We do not predict it will ever be a structure practiced meaningfully on a large scale.[11]

The above description suggests that group or communal marriages depend for their success much more on psychological characteristics of the individual than on the structural features of the group or commune. In fact, of course, such marriage experiments are not new in the United States, going back as they do to the early 1800s; but still there are no institutionalized norms which could provide workable models for those interested in this form. Thus, the impermanence is not at all surprising. But, where sexual activity is narrowly proscribed, many communal marriages are beginning to look like extended families.

Monogamous Marriage: Problems and Possibilities

What are the ongoing marital consequences of the traditional and open-marriage contracts? Some information can be gleaned from research carried out during the past few years.[12] At the same time it is not too farfetched to say that the popular television show "All in the Family" provides archtypes of these two contracts. Archie and Edith are blue-collar people with traditional orientations toward all aspects of marriage. They have clearly defined and separated sex roles, overt sexual and emotional expression is narrowly restricted, Archie has a tavern to which he retreats on occasion, and a TV set to which he retreats when at home. Their personalities seem fixed, and such interaction as there is seems merely to reinforce traditional sex role definitions.

On the other hand, Gloria and Mike are overtly sexual in their behavior, talk about liberation from traditional roles, and their interaction is patterned to suggest that they are concerned about mutual development and gratification. Where Archie emphasizes duty, Mike emphasizes spontaneity; Archie sees Edith as a good housekeeper and cook, and wishes she would keep quiet; Mike sees Gloria as a helpmate and lover and encourages her to share experiences with him (albeit Mike often slips back into traditional patterns. But when he does Gloria challenges him; Edith does not challenge Archie).

These contrasting patterns have been organized into two opposing types which we may conceptualize as the end points on a continuum. At one end, representing the behavioral consequences of traditional marriage contracts, is the segregated conjugal role type, in which the husband and wife largely perform their roles independent of each other, or in an interaction pattern typified by Archie and Edith. At the other end of the continuum is the pattern emerging from the open-marriage or liberated contract; it is a pattern of joint conjugal role activity, that is, one in which husband and wife work together on their problems, invest a great amount of their self in the interaction, in the expectation that both self and other personality needs will be met in the process. Dutiful role performance is at best a minimum expectation of this pattern, and more often than not, may be seen as an impediment to marital adjustment, as the couple seeks personal development through intense interpersonal involvement but within and outside the home. To a considerable degree Mike and Gloria exemplify this type.[13]

Problems

Role differentiation and sexuality in marriage. It should come as no surprise to the reader that sexual behavior in marriage seems to be affected by these differing marital role patterns, which in turn seem to be related to social class differences. We have already documented much evidence for this in the attitudes and behavior of teenagers and young adults, in the United States and elsewhere. Perhaps a word is in order about why social class may affect how a person views herself or himself sexually, and accepts or rejects certain kinds of sexual behavior. In general, the higher the level of income and education (common indicators of social class) which a person has acquired, the more likely is s(he) to express a broad rather than a narrow interest in sexuality, sexual technique, concern for mutual satisfaction, a liberated marriage contract, and joint conjugal relationships. The lower the level of income and education the less likely is the above pattern to manifest itself and the more likely is the traditional, segregated role relationship to manifest itself. Education especially seems to be a manifestation of the cultural milieu in which an individual grows up and develops her/his personality and sense of selfhood. The middle class as compared with the lower class has access to a broader range of ideas through literature, conversation, and other media about the possibilities for human behavior, and even if brought up on traditional ideas about marriage and marital sex roles, middle-class persons are more likely through the interactions which take place to question these ideas and thus to change. That is, there is in the middle-class milieu, a greater conduciveness to change than is to be found in the lower-class milieu. Over time, we would expect that new ideas and practices accepted by the middle class will trickle down into the lower classes (it should be noted that the reverse has also taken place, e.g., the wearing of blue jeans).

Specifically, some of the important research findings include the following:

For women the Kinsey study reports that erotic arousal from any source is less common at the lower educational levels, that fewer of these women have ever reached orgasm and that the frequency for those who do is lower. For men the pattern is less clear-cut as far as frequency goes, but it is apparent that fore-play techniques are less elaborate at the lower educational levels, most strikingly so with respect to oral techniques. In positional variations in intercourse, the lower educational levels show somewhat less versatility, but more interesting is the fact that the difference between lower and higher educational levels increases with age, because positional variations among lower status men drop away rapidly, while the decline among more educated men is much less. This same pattern characterizes nudity in marital coitus.[14]

When Rainwater separated his data according to whether couples could be classified as having segregated or joint conjugal relations, he found as expected that wives in segregated relationships were much more likely (40 percent to only 7 percent) to complain that their husbands were inconsiderate of their needs for sexual gratification. Or again, some 36 percent of wives in segregated role relationships saw sex primarily as a duty, but only 14 percent of wives who enjoyed joint role relations saw sex in this way.

Several points need to be kept in mind: Not all working- and lower-class couples live lives marked by segregated role relations; and not all who live out segregated role patterns complain about their sexual relations. But whatever the class standing of the couple, it seems clear that the psychosocial consequences of one's definition of marriage will be very different. The difference lies in the fact that in joint conjugal relationships sexual relations are both more extensive in nature and more likely to be assimilated into the larger context of the marital relationship. Where husbands and wives play out traditional roles in a highly segregated manner, sexual relations are less extensive, and are seen as discrete acts which get rid of tensions, and provide relief—and pleasure, primarily for the male.[15]

Our examination has to this point considered how different definitions of sex role behavior in marriage relate to sexuality in marriage. The economic dimension cannot and should not be left out of this examination, that is, the degree to which the husband is successful in the economic sphere. It is still too early to be able to draw any conclusions about married couples both of whom work in a liberated marriage. The fact is that most joint conjugal and segregated conjugal patterns are constructed with the husband as the expected breadwinner. Scanzoni offers the following explanation of the way in which economic success of the husband fosters successful adjustment in modern marriages:

> *If we accept as given that expressive satisfactions (companionship, physical affection, empathy) are the obvious goals of modern marriage, and that the major latent goal is status and economic well-being, then we may say that the latent goal influences the attainment of the manifest goal. Specifically, the greater the degree of the husband's integration into the opportunity system (the more his education, the higher his job status, the greater his income), the more fully and extensively is the interlocking network of marital rights and duties performed in reciprocal fashion. The economic rewards he provides motivate the wife to respond positively to him, and her response to him in turn gives rise to a continuing cycle of rectitude and gratitude.*[16]

If Scanzoni is right, we can say that the reason why joint conjugal relations and extensive sexual behavior are more characteristic of the middle class is largely due to the security which economic success brings to the couple. It facilitates a broad range of social and sexual relations. Interestingly, Scanzoni's explanation is based on the model of male dominance of the marketplace; companionship and equality are achieved within the social and sexual sphere of marriage, and do not appear to be dependent on female achievement of economic liberation through a work career outside the home.

But the fact is that the percentage of "working" wives has risen steadily during the past 75 years, probably both as a spur to and a derivative of the companionship ethic. Probably the more appropriate explanation is that companionship, as well as traditional marriage, are fostered to the degree that husbands and wives live up to each other's expectations.

Liebow made similar observations from his study of black streetcorner life. The ability of a husband to support a wife and child provides him with a use value easily recognized by all; he has met an important obligation of his sex role. But, in addition, the act of steady provision of support establishes the husband's identity as a man, in his own and other's eyes. But it is precisely this ability which is denied to the streetcorner man. The structure of slum life and of the way the slum relates to the larger society seem to doom him. As Liebow puts it, for the streetcorner man, ". . . marriage is an occasion of failure. To stay married is to live with your failure, to be confronted by it, day in and day out. It is to live in a world whose standards of manliness are forever beyond one's reach."[17]

The following should be noted: A poor socioeconomic environment dims prospects of marital success, fosters segregation of conjugal relations and traditional ideas; on the other hand, a rewarding environment is conducive to marital success, fosters joint conjugal relations, and varying degrees of liberationist views. Most married couples of whatever social class live out their lives within these parameters.

Sexual maladjustments and marital dissatisfaction. Sexual and marital disharmony are by no means the problem only of the poor, or of the working class. Indeed, the very nature of the intimacy and commitment which an open or modern marriage fosters, can be a source of strain, tension, and eventual failure for the couple, as expectations rise and performance falls short. Nowhere is this a greater problem than in the area of sexual union.

Long before couples openly discussed sexual matters, and sex manuals were easily available which fostered a positive attitude toward sexual union, research showed that at least one-quarter of married women seldom or never achieved orgasm, and that one of the major causes of marital unhappiness (but by no means the only or principal one) was related to sexual disharmony. Specifically, it has been found that in addition to the ability of the wife to achieve orgasm with some degree of regularity, sexual harmony and thus marital harmony were also influenced by the degree to which couples agreed on the desired frequency of sexual intercourse. As indicated elsewhere, women generally expressed less interest in intercourse and desired sexual relations less frequently than did men. This may well have been related to the cultural definitions of the times.* And as we have noted throughout this book, these definitions are changing, and with them, the patterns of satisfaction and dissatisfaction.

As women gradually come to recognize that their capacity for sexual response is at least equal to and may even surpass that of men, they are beginning to state openly their desire for increased sexual activity. Masters and Johnson report findings showing that fully one-fourth of the wives in their study reported that sexual relations were "too infrequent." This seems an ironical switch from the past, and the not so distant past at that, and Bell warns that the problem is not merely a switch, but a complicated one, since the uninterested woman could at least satisfy her husband's physical need by passive reception of his penis into her vagina. An uninterested male does not provide even that minimal satisfaction to a female seeking pleasure through intercourse. Bell notes, "The results may be far more serious for the inadequate or uninterested male than they were for the restricted female in the past."[18]

This problem seems mitigated in part because more and more men are interested in and sensitive to their wives' sexual needs, and are aware of female sexual response and its dimensions. And they are learning that ability to share sexual experience can enrich both lives. Still, technical knowledge is one thing, and achievement is another. And for middle-class couples in an achievement-

---

* As well as to the degree to which women feared pregnancy, or had mates who did not know how to help their wives achieve sexual satisfactions.

oriented society, sexual union can become another test with specific performance goals.[19]

The issue is complex; couples take sex and intimacy seriously in modern marriage. They work hard at developing an intimate and meaningful relationship. They are trying to liberate each other from traditional sex patterns, and often they are doing this from a socialization base that is fairly traditional. There is no easy way out, for sexual and marital disharmony seem just this side of happiness in marriage.

Sex and aging. A brief word may be in order on the problems of sexual adjustment throughout the life cycle. There is general acknowledgement of the fact that sexual intercourse takes place most frequently during the early years of marriage and that there is a gradual decline with advancing years. An all too simple explanation is to state that male sexual response reaches its peak during late adolescence and then gradually tapers off. Thus, it is male decline in sex drive with advancing age that explains the phenomenon.

More recently, it has been suggested that habituation and accommodation may be more important factors than age itself in explaining the decline in sexual activity. With regard to habituation, the argument runs that it is difficult to maintain the same level of gratification with long-term repetition of the same act. The excitement and thrills which are part of the development of a sexual relationship may be expected to wear off with habituation. Udry puts it bluntly that "marital sex with the same partner 100 times a year for ten years is likely to lack novelty."[20]

With habituation comes also an accommodation to changing needs and interests. Unless husbands and wives make an effort, there is much in their daily lives to divert them from sexual response, and to offer them satisfactions in place of the sexual.

Again, middle-class couples, with their greater general ability to rely on symbolic sexual stimuli, through movies, literature, music, or simply erotic conversation, seem to evidence a slower rate of decline than do working- and lower-class couples. And, of course, for many and an increasing number of couples, decline in frequency of coitus does not imply a decline in sexual satisfaction at all; the partner may not be new or novel; and the variety of positions may not approach infinity, but we can assure the young who are wondering about the long range, that sex in marriage can continue to provide great pleasure, especially when it is joined with other psychosocial pleasures which a couple has learned to share.[21]

Possibilities

Happiness in marriage: possibility or probability. When all is said and done, whether people are living via traditional or open-marriage patterns, whether their relations are more segregated or cooperative, the question arises, are they happy in marriage? For many couples throughout history, the question about happiness in marriage might seem silly or even ludicrous. What does marriage have to do with happiness? The perplexed Italian father in "Lovers and Other Strangers" could not understand his son's desire for a divorce on the grounds that he and his wife weren't happy together: "So what's happiness got to do with marriage?" he asked his son in honest exasperation.

But that is just the point. Whatever happiness is, it is more and more a primary goal of contemporary marriage. People expect marriage to bring them happiness, and if they don't find happiness in marriage, they expect to be able to dissolve the marriage and try again. Sociologists of the family have become increasingly interested in happiness as it has become more and more of a problem for modern marriage. And they have developed measures to differentiate between marital success as an objective reality, and marital happiness as subjective reality. That is, we can define a marriage as successful if a couple never divorces, or if it fulfills the commonly accepted expectations about married life, and appears to support marriage as an institution through the image it projects of a couple which gets along.

Happiness is seen as a more subjective phenomenon, not how a couple appears to others, but how each member evaluates his or her marriage. A happy marriage would be one in which both members defined their situation as a happy one, for whatever reasons. Clearly it is no easy task to measure either marital success or marriage happiness. And there has been a wealth of criticism of the methods used to date. The interested reader should consult the literature on the subject.[22]

Most of the findings here are extensions of the materials presented earlier in this chapter; namely, that marital success and happiness are positively correlated with education, occupation, and income, such that the higher the levels and the more prestige attached, the more stable and successful the marriage.

An interesting new facet of the attempts to measure marital happiness is found in the study by Orden and Bradburn. They developed independent measures of psychological well-being and marriage happiness, and found a high correlation. They also found a high percentage of happily married couples in their national sample (60 percent very happy, and only 3 percent not too happy).* They suggest that given the increasing ease of divorce, their study shows that people who are married are fairly happy, and that those not happy move toward divorce. Thus, the data suggest a high degree of happiness of

---

*A *Life* magazine survey, based on a questionnaire published in the April 28, 1972 issue which was focused on Marriage, reveals that 80 percent of the respondents rated their marriages as "happy" or "very happy." There were 62,000 respondents, and 45 percent of them were under 30 years of age, and 70 percent had attended college (as published in *Hartford Courant,* 14 November 1972, p. 11, by UPI). We may expect that there was a notable sampling bias in reader response. Still, the results are supportive of other findings.

married couples today. And their findings hold also for working wives, when the wives are working not only out of necessity, but also because they want to and are in the labor force out of choice.[23]

Finally, it should be noted that Alice Rossi reports evidence that greater freedom of choice for women has positive implications for marital sexual relationships:

> *Men and women who participate as equals in their parental and occupational and social roles will complement each other sexually in the same way, as essentially equal partners, and not as ascendant male and submissive female. This does not mean however, that equality in nonsexual roles necessarily de-eroticizes the sexual one. The enlarged base of shared experience can, if anything, heighten the salience of sex qua sex. . . .[24]*

In summary, it may be said that the trend toward equality, companionship, and shared life experiences in contemporary marriage reveals no evidence that marriages are less happy today than in earlier times, nor that marriage is declining in favor. Marriage seems to be more and more, a love relationship in which each partner is concerned for the optimal development of both of them.[25]

Sexual Behavior of Married Couples Outside the Marital Bond

Traditional Forms of Extramarital Affairs

Not all marriages are happy; not all happy marriages apparently depend on sexual fidelity for their continuance, nor does unhappiness over sexual matters necessarily mean that one or both partners will become involved in extramarital affairs. The reader might ponder the fact that the phrase "extramarital affair" always implies a sexual affair. Couples have long since accepted the fact that contemporary life throws members of the opposite sex together in such a variety of ways that there can be no thought of maintaining exclusivity of relations in the nonsexual sphere. But wait, "extramarital affair" always has meant what it still means today. And it has the same meaning for those in segregated as well as in joint shared relations. Is there something about this form of social interaction, that gives it a special place?

Ever since the Kinsey reports, we have been aware that even in U.S. American society, there is a fairly high rate of sexual infidelity among married couples, that is, that at least half the husbands, and more than one-fourth of the wives, admit that they have broken their marriage vow of sexual fidelity. There is no evidence that the rate has gone down in the past 25 years, and some that it has gone up at least for females.[26]

In Latin America, sexual infidelity for the husband has been almost institutionalized; that is, it has been part of the expectation about male behavior. Not so in the United States, where strong Puritan and Catholic Jansenist teachings have long opposed such behavior. Yet its prevalence precedes the so-called sexual revolution.

No easy explanations are available. Extramarital coitus is low in the early years of marriage, higher in the middle years, and lower for the male after age 40, but not necessarily for the female. With regard to social class, among the least affluent the incidence is higher in the early years and gradually declines, while middle-class couples increase their extramarital behavior in the middle years. But overall, there seems to be more extramarital activity among the working and lower than among the middle classes. From the point of view of the individual, explanations range over the following factors: a desire for a variety of sex partners; a way of asserting independence from one's spouse, a reflection of a poor sexual relationship with one's spouse, an opportunity to experiment with sexual techniques which are not available within the marriage. Overriding these factors is the realization that the opportunity structure of modern society provides both spouses, but especially husbands, with interaction situations which make extramarital encounters more probable than ever before. Conventions, meetings, business engagements, secretaries, travel, all help account for the fact that opportunity itself has become the largest single factor in extramarital coitus.[27] The continual stimulation of the two sexes in social and on-the-job contacts appears to be a more important aspect of the opportunity structure than does the availability of partners to be found in the cocktail lounge, although the latter is not unimportant as a source of sexual companionship. In the latter case, the reference is not so much to a traditional house of prostitution, but to a public lounge where people come looking for sexual companionship.[28]

Poor marital sexual adjustment per se does not seem to be a major cause of extramarital coitus. Rather, married couples more often point to a general dissatisfaction with the overall emotional aspects of their marriages, which suggests that those who succeed in developing a companionship type of shared joint conjugal relations are much less prone to extramarital affairs. And finally, it must be noted that not all spouses condemn their partners for these affairs. There is a range of acceptance from simple refusal to be outwardly bothered, to passive acceptance, to relief or even active support which may provide some indirect kind of gratification through empathy to the other partner.[29]

The Tearoom Trade

A little-known area of extramarital affairs involves the homosexual. A pioneering study by Humphreys provides a picture of sexual behavior that suggests that many men make a sexual adaptation to an unsatisfactory marital situation which has minimal impact on the marriage-family itself. Humphreys' study was comprised of less than 30 cases, and involved verified incidents of homosexual fellatio encounters in public restrooms (called "tearooms" by the participants). Subsequent interviews were carried out in such a way that the respondents were not aware of the relationship between the interview and their homosexual activity. Humphreys termed these involvements "instant sex" for they were highly impersonal (there was little if any verbal contact between the participants), fairly quick (the entire encounter generally lasted for no more than 15 minutes), and easily available (most of the tearooms were located in public parks readily accessible to the roadways).

Humphreys describes the subjects of his research as follows:

The majority of my research subjects are married and living with their wives. From the data at hand, there is no evidence that these unions are particularly unstable; nor does it appear that any of the wives are aware of their husband's secret sexual activity. Indeed, the husbands choose public restrooms as sexual settings partly to avoid just such exposure. I see no reason to dispute the claim of a number of tearoom respondents that their preference for a form of concerted action that is fast and impersonal is largely predicated on a desire to protect their family relationships.[30]

Finally, Humphreys found that 11 respondents (40 percent) could be characterized as clearly manifesting segregated role relationships in their marriage.

Swinging or Mate-Swapping

Apparently more common to contemporary marriage, and certainly more widely winked at by society is the phenomenon called swinging or more descriptively, mate-swapping. In fact, the phenomenon is so common today that it became the subject of an Archie and Edith episode in "All in the Family," in October, 1972. Edith innocently answered a "friendship" letter in a mod magazine, and before she knew it she and Archie were being visited by a couple fully expecting to change partners for the evening. In conformity with the sociological evidence on the subject, the couple was portrayed as typical middle class; and when Archie accused them of being Communists, the husband's wounded reply was that on the contrary, he had been a delegate at the Republican National Convention.

Swinging is a relationship involving two or more married couples who mutually decide to switch sexual partners or to engage in group sex. It is estimated that there are between one million and three million couples who exchange partners on a somewhat regular basis in the United States, that is, at least three times a year.[31]

Swingers are very much like middle America in most other external social categories, with only a small percentage forming a category which might be said to emphasize a total new life style of which swinging is a part. On the contrary, swingers are very much committed to conventional monogamous marriage. In swinging, apparently they are seeking ways to bolster a sagging partnership. Denfeld and Gordon have delineated four aspects of swinging which they believe supports this proposition:

1. *Swingers have developed rules that serve to define the sexual relationship of marriage as one of love, of emotion.*
2. *Recreational swingers are occasionally known to drop out of swinging, at least temporarily, while the wife gets pregnant. By not swinging, the couple can be assured that the husband is the father of the child; unknown or other parentage is considered taboo. This reflects a traditional, middle-class view about the conception and rearing of children.*
3. *A common word in the swinger's vocabulary is discretion. Swingers desire to keep their sexual play a secret from their non-swinging or "square" friends. They want to protect their position in the community, and an effort is made to limit participation to couples of similar status or "respectability."*
4. *Some of the controls on jealousy are: 1) that the marriage commands paramount loyalty, 2) that there is physical but not emotional interest in other partners, 3) that single persons are avoided, and 4) that there be no concealment of sexual activities.*[32]

If we accept the Kinsey data from an earlier generation, we may be able to interpret the data on swinging as indicating that it is if anything supportive of rather than disruptive of monogamous marriage as practiced in the United States. It seems a modification of rather than a break from earlier patterns. The modification is that the double standard is lowered as both partners participate; extramarital sex is no longer condoned only for the male.* More than

---

* In an exploratory study, Henshel found evidence that the decision to "swing" is still controlled pretty much by the husband and is not a decision mutually discussed and arrived at. She concludes: "In the context of decision making, swinging can be viewed as a male institution, and confirmations of the advent of a 'sexual revolution' and of the abolition of the double standard should be reconsidered." See Anne-Marie Henshel, "Swinging: A Study of Decision Making in Marriage," *American Journal of Sociology*, 78, 4 (January 1973): 885-891. Quotation from 890.

that, couples actually use this means to romanticize and enliven their dull, routine married life. As for the future, some scholars expect that from 15 to 25 percent of married couples may adopt swinging at some time in their married life. However, a married couple, both members of which are anthropologists and both of whom studied swinging as participant observers perceive a more limited future:

Given economic prosperity as a necessary condition for increasing sexual freedom, it is quite possible that with the economic difficulties this country is now facing the number of available acceptable sexual alternatives will decline and swinging may all but disappear from the American scene.[33]

Divorce: The Dissolution of Marriage and the Contract

Just as economic factors enter into the question of happy vs. maladjusted marriages, and into traditional and new patterns of extramarital sexual activity, so do economic factors seem to be important to an understanding of divorce in

TABLE 10.1
AVERAGE ANNUAL PROBABILITY OF DIVORCE BY SELECTED CHARACTERISTICS*

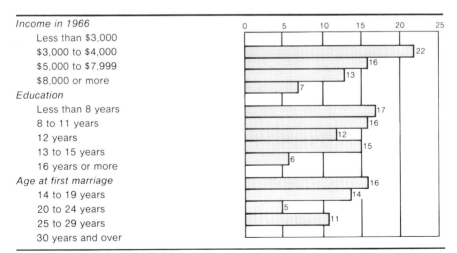

	0	5	10	15	20	25
Income in 1966						
Less than $3,000						
$3,000 to $4,000						22
$5,000 to $7,999				16		
$8,000 or more			13			
Education		7				
Less than 8 years					17	
8 to 11 years				16		
12 years			12			
13 to 15 years				15		
16 years or more		6				
Age at first marriage				16		
14 to 19 years				14		
20 to 24 years	5					
25 to 29 years			11			
30 years and over						

*Per 1,000 white men in their first marriage less than five years.
Source: Paul C. Glick and Arthur J. Norton, "Frequency, Duration, and Probability of Marriage and Divorce," *Journal of Marriage and the Family*, 1971, 33, 307–320 (p. 314 cited).

society. For the fact is that the single most important factor in predicting divorce is husband's level of income (see Table 10-1). Consistently, throughout the years, it has been shown that the lower the level of income, the higher the probability of divorce. Just as higher income fosters joint conjugal relations, so does low income make any kind of stable marriage less probable. Lower income of course is associated with lower levels of education and with early age at first marriage (see Table 10-1). The marital cards seem stacked against those of low income, for the fact also is that early marriage more often occurs among those of lower than those of higher income levels.

These facts suggest that those who would like to see divorce rates reduced might do well to concentrate on why such factors as education level, income, and occupation so strongly influence the probability of divorce.[34]

Are divorce rates high or low? We not only need to focus on the way in which forces outside the family affect the stability of family life; we need also to take a more careful look at some historical developments. It is much too simple to say that our ancestors had low divorce rates, less than two per thousand married couples as late as 1890. Does this mean they were happier than today's married couples who have divorce rates hovering around ten or eleven per thousand? How do we interpret the fact that in 1890 the death rate per year for married couples was thirty per thousand, while today it is about twenty per thousand? If we add death rates and divorce rates for both time periods we discover that the overall rate for the dissolution of marriages, that is marriages broken either by death or divorce, is about the same, some thirty to thirty-two per thousand.[35]

Another way of looking at the meaning of divorce is to recognize that at least three out of every four first marriages never end in divorce in the United States. And among these, a high proportion express themselves as subjectively happy or very happy in their marriage. A higher proportion than ever before of those who find their marriages unsatisfactory, are seeking divorce, and remarrying. As religious, social, and economic strictures against divorce break down, and as new ideas about sexuality and sex role behavior are adopted, the question of whether or not divorce is a threat to marriage must be rethought carefully. It certainly seems less and less related to sexual and individual idiosyncratic problems, and more related to societal and economic questions.

The Future of Marriage

A review of the foregoing pages leads to the conclusion that marriage continues to be a viable social institution, a satisfying form of social interaction and a human group with a future. Indeed, a good indicator of this may be the optimism with which the home builders of America and their mortgage investors contemplated the year 1973. They anticipated that some 2.2 million couples would marry in 1973, and that some 446,000 of these would move into their own homes. Despite the turmoil of the recent years, and the changes in attitudes and behavior regarding human sexuality, the number of marriages in the 1970s has been up about 25 percent over the 1960s. Admittedly, much of the percentage increase can be attributed to the fact that such large numbers of young people who formed the early part of the post World War II baby boom are now entering marriage age. But the point is that they are getting married, and pursuing the conventional goal of a house in the suburbs. And armed as they are with the information on the "population crisis," they are planning on owning a home first as a necessary prerequisite for the begetting and rearing of 2.3 children.[36]

American businessmen are not the only ones who have not given up on marriage. Having survived almost 40 combined years of marriage ourselves, and some nine living children, we are prepared to give testimony to the fact that the struggle to create our own roles and to learn to share in the marriage enterprise provides benefits that outweigh the tribulations. We would accept as our own the words of Dr. Laura Singer of the American Association of Marriage and Family Counselors who states the case for marriage in this way:

I think if I came back in a hundred years I'd still find marriage here in some form or other, whatever they may be calling it. . . . The one-to-one commitment is hard as hell, but no viable alternative presents itself that is as rewarding, as intimate and as significant.[37]

If we want to increase the probability that marriage will be rewarding, intimate, and significant, it would seem necessary that the society embark on programs which will enhance the educational, occupational, and income opportunities for those segments of the population which on every indicator are now in a weak position to realize this potential human relationship.

VIEWPOINTS

During this year, I will be among 1,848,000 Americans who will be divorced.

I don't want to be, I am horrified by the prospect, I think it is the most devastating thing that could happen to my family, but it is going to take place.

My wife wants it.

We would seem to have everything to live together for. We have four wonderful sons who need us both; they range in age from 6 to 16. We have a large, comfortable house in Connecticut.

The house is on two acres which have been perfect for raising the boys these last eight years: woods in back where they have played and made camp sites and slept out; a ballfield where they have grown from being able to dribble underhand pitches a few feet from home plate to socking them over a distant stone wall; a little slope where they go sleigh-riding and tobogganing.

We live across the street from a lake where the whole family goes swimming and boating and the boys catch bass that we cook for meals and where we play hockey with the neighborhood kids when the lake is frozen.

A special joy is the big fireplace in our livingroom where we are snug in the winter, occasionally roasting marshmallows but usually just letting the wood we collect in our fields pop away as a pleasant companion.

I thought we were a perfectly happy family until my wife told me, without any advance warning, that she didn't love me anymore and wanted a divorce. Not a matter of infidelity or alcoholism or beating or arguments or desertion, but that it didn't mean anything to her anymore and she wanted out.

I have been waking about 5 o'clock each morning for the last year, hoping that this nightmare had gone away. I have wept more than I ever thought I could, hoped, prayed; but the reality remains and it won't change. It seems to me impossible that so much happiness and so much sadness could be happening in the same lifetime. But we go grinding slowly, torturously and inevitably toward a divorce.

My wife and I really were married in a different world. We are both 44; we were married twenty years ago. Those were the times when you looked for "togetherness." You found someone who was the "other half," who had qualities that complemented yours and filled you out, and you put them together and marched in lockstep through marital happiness. And we did. I enjoyed fully my role as husband and father; my wife appeared to be enjoying hers as wife and mother: she does not feel the same today in hindsight.

After my wife told me she wanted a divorce, we went to marital counseling for about a year. We learned many things about destructive patterns which we were not aware of before: things like dominance and dependence and imposing of wills and acquiescence and blocked and thwarted growth. We learned probably as much, too, about the way outlooks have changed concerning roles, marriages and divorce.

And I guess that is where my problem really lies. The world, or at least that part of it concerned with psychological counseling, has changed in ways I seem unwilling to accept. Not that I want to cling to negative, destructive patterns, or "the old way." But we are now in a time which says that you get in touch with yourself, find out what your needs are, and then fill them. That is paramount.

My wife accepts this completely. She needs freedom, independence, out from under what she felt was a smothering relationship; her whole outlook on life has changed, I don't fit into it any longer: so, divorce.

I don't feel this way but I am left with a crumbled view of a marital world which doesn't have much popularity anymore. I feel that relationships aren't disposable; that you just don't throw them away after more than two decades. That married life and parenthood are a whole spectrum: of being a good father, of being a decent and dedicated and loving husband, of recognizing—above all—that everyone has problems and that you work at them together for the happiness of all. I guess what I am really saying is that the "I" becomes "we," a six-fold "we" in this particular case, and that this is the life reality which has to be faced and answered.

Nobody is saying I can't hold these views. They are just saying that they are a little old-fashioned, a little quaint, a little square, and a little unreal in our present-day world. And that, most of all, they aren't very relevant anymore to what is actually happening to me.

I ask myself: at some point, doesn't a counter-revolution have to take place? Don't the excesses in favor of the liberation of the individual have to be met by a consideration of the needs of families, of the other party? Doesn't a psychology which hands a license to a wife to do what she wants in these times fueled by the themes of women's lib have to be called to some accounting of responsibility? Doesn't someone in the new psychological movement have to come forward and say: "My God, wait a minute, what are we doing to ourselves?"

I think of what it is like to be a child today—one of my own children—and what a dreadful experience that must be. Who speaks for them? While the adults are fulfilling themselves, finding their identities, liberating themselves from restrictive life situations, who is taking into account the welfare and well-being of the children? What happened to notions like commitment, responsibility and, an even more discredited concept, suffering?

Am I just feeling sorry for myself? Am I just full of self-pity? I don't think so. I also don't think that I am unique. I am one man, hurt, groping. I do not have answers to the most important questions of my life. But I think that for the good of all of us, as a people and as a society, we had better start coming up with better ones than we have now.

> From Albert Martin, "I Am One Man, Hurt,"
> *The New York Times,*
> 25 June 1973.

• • • • • • • • • •

I believe we should work toward a standard that would contribute to individual dignity and well-being, would contribute to the strength and stability of our society, and would promote enduring companionships.

Such a standard seems to call for three elements:

1. Premarital intercourse should be considered only where the couple have a time-tested relationship of trust, loyalty, devotion and love.
2. Premarital intercourse should be considered only when the couple are mature enough to understand the consequences to themselves, their families, and any children that may result from the act. It is just as reasonable to expect a young person to reach a certain age before he copulates as it is to expect him to reach a certain age before he is granted a driver's license. Certainly, intercourse is not for a high school-age youngster—and I would also add a female college freshman, since such a girl has just emerged from family scrutiny, is eager for popularity in her new setting, and is most likely to be exploited by upperclassmen. Several psychiatrists have also made the point that adolescence is a difficult period in personality formation, and that adolescents are simply not ready for the meaning of intercourse and, in fact, may be hurt by it.
3. Sexual intercourse should be considered only when the couple are so devoted to each other and so mature that they have begun making long-term plans that will include each other. This devotion would be known and be recognized by their close friends and parents.

As for a code regarding extramarital affairs, society should continue to regard infidelity as a serious and unhealthy development, since children and the stability of society are involved.

In view of the percent of marital breakdowns from divorce, annulment, separation and desertion—about 50%—it is obvious that marriage bonds have become unprecedentedly brittle. Some suggest that the answer is to loosen the bonds through serial mating, through communal living, and through single-parent marriages. All these ideas have some plausibility, but I don't see any of them as the answer. I believe that, instead, marriage should be strengthened by taking two steps: (1) The couple wanting to marry should be made to wait for a full month after they file their application during which time they can reflect before the ceremony actually takes place. This procedure would wash out millions of unions that wind up as disasters. (2) The first two years of marriage should be considered a confirmation period. If after two years either partner thinks the marriage was a mistake, he or she can withdraw without a court proceeding that would leave the partners scarred. If the couple have given birth to a child, that in itself would act as confirmation that they want to continue the marriage. With the great advances in contraception and with the legalization of abortion, there should not be any unwanted children.

From Vance Packard, *Sexual Latitudes: For and Against* (New York: Hart Publishing Co.), pp. 100-102.

. . . .

I do not think we are being asked by either the gay or the women's movement to give up marriage. I think we are being asked to do three things, one compatible with tradition and two not:

1. We are being asked to think of marriage as a special vocation, thus not a natural, a religious, nor a social fate. This means that marriage should be chosen, not stumbled into, nor contracted because it is the expected thing. There are also other ways to live. This is what marriage has, in principle, meant all along. It is the sense behind the venerable doctrine (which the church took over from ancient Roman law) that the essence of marriage is the willing consent of the partners. We ought not to grumble at having to relearn this basic principle from radicals.
2. Life outside marriage is not necessarily or even normally virginal. I doubt if it ever has been for most people, but there would have to have been a Kinsey in every age to prove it. In any case, to prove the opposite—that marriage means the moral right to have intercourse—is no easier. Here again we are being asked to consider marriage as the choice of a life together, not primarily or exclusively as a sexual arrangement.
3. Life inside marriage is not to be construed as forbidding sexual relations with other persons. If this seems to strike at the very foundation of marriage, that is because we have insisted on viewing marriage as a sexual contract, with the result that we do not care what sacrifices of personhood it requires, or else (more often) wink at the "indiscretions" that accompany it.

I do not call into question the teaching that marriage is a lifetime commitment, that its nature is exclusive, and that it is based upon fidelity. I wish only to question whether these concepts are righly understood when they are taken to refer primarily and necessarily to sexual congress. Is it not instead the case, both in theory and in practice, that the validity of a marriage is judged by the intent and consent of the partners? What counselor, when hearing a case of adultery, would judge by the act committed rather than by the agent's testimony of love, concern and willingness to preserve the married relation? In these matters, to be sure, there is an important aspect known as "injury"; but this is not an absolute standard unless the "injured party" is of an absolutist persuasion. Wise counselors learn that the greatest threat to marriage is, in fact, absolutism.

From Tom Driver,
"Homosexuality: The Contemporary and Christian Contexts,"
Commonweal, 6 April 1973, p. 106.

References

1. Herbert Otto, "The New Marriage," in Herbert Otto, ed., *The Family in Search of a Future* (New York: Appleton-Century-Crofts, 1970), pp. 117-118.

2. Nena and George O'Neill, *Open Marriage* (New York: M. Evans and Co., 1972), p. 55.

3. J. Richard Udry, *The Social Context of Marriage,* 2nd ed. (Philadelphia: J. B. Lippincott Company, 1971), p. 364.

4. See Joseph and Lois Bird, *The Freedom of Sexual Love* (New York: Doubleday and Company, 1970).

5. See *Life,* 28 April 1972, p. 43; and *Time,* 20 March 1972.

6. O'Neill, *Open Marriage,* p. 74.

7. Albert Ellis, "Group Marriage: A Possible Alternative?" in Otto, ed., *The Family in Search of a Future,* p. 85.

8. James Ramey, "Emerging Patterns of Behavior in Marriage: Deviations or Innovations," *The Journal of Sex Research,* 8, 1 (February 1972): 25.

9. *Life,* 28 April 1972, p. 72.

10. *Ibid.,* p. 72.

11. Larry Constantine and Joan Constantine, "Multilateral Marriage: Alternate Family Structure in Practice," mimeographed. 1970, pp. 11-12.

12. See, for example, Jessie Bernard, "The Adjustments of Married Mates," in Harold T. Christensen, ed., *Handbook of Marriage and the Family* (Chicago: Rand, McNally and Co., 1964), p. 687.

13. See the following for variations on the above theme: Elizabeth Bott, *Family and Social Network* (London, England: Tavistock Publications, 1957); Lee Rainwater, *Family Design* (Chicago: Aldine Publishing Co. 1964).

14. Rainwater, *Family Design,* p. 99.

15. *Ibid.,* pp. 101-102.

16. John Scanzoni, *Sexual Bargaining* (Englewood Cliffs, N. J.: Prentice-Hall, Inc., 1972), p. 65.

17. Elliot Liebow, *Tally's Corner* (Boston: Little, Brown and Co., 1967), p. 136.

18. Robert Bell, *Marriage and Family Interaction* (Homewood, Ill.: Dorsey Press, 1963), p. 314.

19. William H. Masters and Virginia Johnson, "Sex and Equality," *Redbook,* March 1972, p. 212.

20. Udry, *Social Context of Marriage,* p. 377.

21. See William Simon and John Gagnon, "Psychosexual Development," *Transaction,* 6,3 (March 1969): 17.

22. See, for example, Ernest W. Burgess and Harvey T. Locke, *The Family from Institution to Companionship,* 2nd ed. (New York: A.B.C., 1953), pp. 378-391; Willard Waller, *The Family: A Dynamic Interpretation* (New York: Holt, Rinehart and Co., 1951); pp. 368-369; and Clifford Kirkpatrick, *The Family: As Process and Institution* (N.Y.: The Ronald Press, 1955), pp. 340-346. For a trenchant critique of

the marriage adjustment studies, in addition to the reflections of Bernard referred to earlier, see Judith Long Laws, "A Feminist Review of the Marital Adjustment Literature: The Rape of the Locke," *Journal of Marriage and the Family,* 33, 3 (August 1971): 483-516.

23. Susan R. Orden and Norman Bradburn," Working Wives and Marriage Happiness," *American Journal of Sociology,* 74, 4 (January 1969): 392-407.

24. Alice Rossi, "Equality Between the Sexes: An Immodest Proposal," *Daedalus,* 93, 2 (Spring 1964): 648.

25. For an elaboration of this idea of love, see Nelson Foote, "Love," *Psychiatry,* 16 (1953): 245-251.

26. See Alfred Kinsey, et al, *Sexual Behavior in the Human Male* (Philadelphia: W. B. Saunders Company, 1948), p. 382; *Sexual Behavior in the Human Female* (Philadelphia: W. B. Saunders Company, 1953), pp. 421, 431-436; and Udry, *Social Context of Marriage,* p. 380.

27. See Ralph Johnson, "Some Correlates of Extramarital Coitus," *Journal of Marriage and the Family,* 32 (1970): 449-456.

28. See Julian Roebuck and S. Lee Spray, "The Cocktail Lounge: A Study of Heterosexual Relations in a Public Organization," *American Journal of Sociology,* 72 (1967): 388-395.

29. See especially John F. Cuber and Peggy B. Haroff, *The Significant Americans: A Study of Sexual Behavior Among the Affluent* (New York: Appleton-Century-Crofts, 1965).

30. Laud Humphreys, *Tearoom Trade* (Chicago: Aldine Publishing Co. 1970), pp. 105-106.

31. See the following for studies on swinging: Gilbert Bartell, *Group Sex: A Scientist's Eye Witness Report of the American Way of Swinging* (New York: Peter H. Wyden, 1971); W. and J. Breedlove, *Swap Clubs* (Los Angeles: Sherbourne Press, 1964); and D. Denfeld and M. Gordon, "The Sociology of Mate Swapping or The Family that Swings Together Clings Together," *Journal of Sex Research,* 6, 2 (May 1971): 85-100.

32. Denfeld and Gordon, "The Sociology of Mate Swapping," pp. 9-11.

33. Charles and Rebecca Palson, "Swinging in Wedlock," *Society,* 9, 4 (February 1972): 37.

34. Scanzoni, *Sexual Bargaining,* pp. 20-43.

35. See M. DeFleur, W. D'Antonio, and L. DeFleur, *Sociology: Human Society,* Diamond Printing (Glenview, Ill.: Scott, Foresman and Company, 1973), p. 532.

36. See "2,226,000 Marriages Are Predicted," *Hartford Courant,* 21 January 1973, p. 6E.

37. As quoted by Martha Weinman Lear, in "Save the Spouses, Rather than the Marriage," *New York Times Magazine,* 13 August 1972, p. 28.

Glossary

We are including this discussion of some common medical and surgical terms and procedures because almost everyone will hear them at some time in her or his life, and frequently they are not well understood by either the patients, their families, or their friends.

Endocrinology A medical and surgical subspecialty in disorders of the endocrine organs, for example, thyroid, pancreas (diabetes), adrenals, pituitary. Endocrinologists may be found in pediatrics, obstetrics and gynecology, and general medicine.

Obstetrics and Gynecology Obstetrics is a medical and surgical specialty in all aspects of pregnancy.

Gynecology* is a medical and surgical specialty in diseases of the reproductive tract of females, with some overlapping into urology in females (e.g., urethral disorders), and infertility in males.

Urology A medical and surgical specialty in disorders of the urinary and reproductive tract of males, and the urinary tract of females (the kidneys, the bladder, and the urethra).

There are a growing number of doctors interested in adolescent medicine as a specialty; they have emerged primarily from pediatrics and general medicine. Each of the medical and surgical specialties has always had its pediatric counterpart, but adolescence has only recently been identified as a unique area requiring a special approach for specific problems, though the actual medical and surgical treatment is essentially the same as that used in the adult population.

Some Common Suffixes, Procedures, and Vocabulary

-ectomy Surgical removal: hyster*ectomy,* removal of the uterus.

-oma A localized abnormal growth; a tumor, benign or malignant.

-oscopy Viewing of internal organs, with or without magnification: cyst*oscopy,* viewing the inside of the urinary bladder.

-otomy Surgical opening of an area of the body or a specific hollow organ: hyster*otomy,* opening the uterus.

Atrophy Loss of original size, shape, or physiology; a decrease; for example, the atrophic lining of the vagina due to a loss of estrogen, postmenopause.

Benign Refers to noncancerous growth.

---

* Gynecology may be pronounced with a soft or a hard "G"; this varies with geographical and academic areas.

Biopsy Removal of small samples of living tissue for microscopic examination; for example, a cervical biopsy.

Breast Examination Any nodule or lump in the breast or in the underarm area should be examined and followed at intervals by a physician experienced in breast examination. Many gynecologists include breast examination and thyroid examination in their routine gynecological checkup, since women see gynecologists more often than any other physician. In some areas of the United States, gynecologists also do breast surgery. However, in most areas, general surgeons are usually those who have the most experience in breast surgery and in following breast lumps, pre- and postsurgery.

Self-examination of the breasts at postmenstrual, monthly intervals after some annual reassurance that they are normal will acquaint a female with what is normal for her, and therefore any change from normal will present fewer questions in her mind. The procedure is simple: While lying down flat, palpate each quadrant of the breast carefully, from the nipple outward. While standing in front of a mirror, lean slightly forward so the breasts hang down and look for areas of skin which seem to be wrinkled or attached to something beneath the skin. The deep underarm area should also be felt for nodes or lumps.

Early malignant lesions of the breast are seldom painful. Girls with a history of chronic, cystic breasts have a difficult problem because the breasts appear to be full of small and large "lumps" which are intermittently uncomfortable, sometimes in a cyclic fashion. Use of the birth control pill often accentuates this discomfort to a point where the pill has to be discontinued.

Any discharge from the nipple, clear or bloody, especially if onesided should be investigated immediately. Clear discharge from "pregnant" breasts is not unusual at any stage of pregnancy, but should be noted and mentioned on the next prenatal visit.

Cancer of the breast in the male is rare, but any lump in the male breast should be investigated.

Surgical removal of breast cancer may be followed with irradiation therapy. The amount of tissue removed and the use of irradiation depends on the size of the cancer, the presence or absence of metastases to the underarm, and the surgeon's experience and training. Consultation is always in order, if there are questions in the patient's mind.

Carcinoma Cancer or a malignant growth; for example, carcinoma of the ovary, vulva, prostate, or thyroid.

Catheterization Draining the urinary bladder by inserting a tube through the urethra into the bladder.

Douching (dooshing) Vaginal douching is a four-minute procedure done while sitting on the toilet. It may be done every four or five days (no oftener) for general hygiene, but it is seldom essential for good health in the vaginal area. The healthy vaginal lining is normally slightly acid and has its own secretions. Excessive douching, unless indicated, destroys the normal acidity and secretions, and can give rise to uncomfortable symptoms and signs of dryness, i.e. burning and decreased lubrication. *Procedure:* Block the opening to the vagina with the hand that is holding the douche tip, allowing the fluid (water with vinegar or commercial douche powders added) to flow in and balloon the vagina slightly until there is a feeling of fullness. Expel the fluid with the same muscles which are used to urinate. Do this three or four times (see p. 84).

Hypertrophy Localized overgrowth of an area or organ which exceeds the normal; for example, hypertrophy of the clitoris or the labia minora, or a callous on the hand.

Hysterosalpingogram An X-ray of the pelvic area after dye has been introduced into the uterus (hystero-) and the tubes (salpingo-); a procedure to demonstrate the patency of the Fallopian tubes or distortions of the uterine cavity.

Infantile Describes an organ which is, or remains at, prepubertal size; for example, the uterus, the penis.

Malignant Refers to cancerous growth.

Metastases Cancer which has spread beyond its original site; for example, metastases to the lung from an ovarian cancer.

*Pap Smear (test)** Superficial cells from the cervix are removed with a cotton swab or tongue blade and placed on a slide for microscopic examination. Experienced cytologists (cell specialists) examine them and look for typical cancer cells, or cells which appear precancerous. Depending on the laboratory, they are read as Class I through IV or V. Class I is normal in all laboratories. Class II may or may not require an immediate repeat test. Classes III through IV or V will require an immediate repeat test or biopsy or conization. Gynecologists always ask for an immediate reading of the slide if the cervix appears abnormal, but routine Pap tests from asymptomatic, normal appearing cervices usually take two to three weeks for reporting, and these "routine" tests show early precancerous or cancerous changes just often enough to make Pap tests important even when there are no symptoms.

Any sexually active female should have a Pap test every six months; any female over age 25 should do the same. Any female with intermenstrual bleeding or with postmenopausal bleeding should have a Pap test immediately, or a uterine biopsy or D and C to diagnose the presence or absence of uterine cancer. Menopausal or postmenopausal females who are on estrogen therapy for any one of several reasons should not assume that their uterine bleeding is necessarily related to their estrogen intake.

Pelvic Examination An adequate pelvic examination can usually be done in females of any age. Obesity and patient anxiety are the only factors which may prevent adequate examination of the internal organs (uterus, tubes, and ovaries).

The pelvic examination includes the following: visual and manual examination of the external genital area, insertion of the speculum (see below) into the vagina which allows visualization of the cervix and the walls of the vagina; a Pap smear; a culture of the cervical excretions, if indicated (see Gonorrhea); withdrawal of the speculum; insertion of one or two gloved fingers into the vagina and placement of the other hand on the lower abdominal wall; palpation (feeling) of the position of the uterus and its size and contours between the abdominal and vaginal hand; palpation on the right and left of the uterus to determine the size, location, and tenderness of the ovaries and the Fallopian tubes.

---

* Named for Dr. George Papanicolaou.

The "mechanics" of the entire pelvic examination should seldom take more than a few minutes. The time consuming aspects of pelvic examinations for the patient and the physician depend on the amount of time it takes the patient to get up on the examining table, to arrange herself in the optimal position for adequate examination, to arrange the sheet drape (see below), and to relax so that the introitus is not tight and the abdominal wall is soft and not tense with breathholding, and the time necessary for the physician to do some initial touching of the knee and thigh to desensitize the patient to genital touching and to allow slow insertion of the speculum and slow opening of the speculum for the comfort of the patient.* Of necessity, the preliminaries should take time, which presents opportunities for questions and answers.

No sharp instruments are used in routine pelvic examinations. There is some brief, deep palpation which can produce mild aching, and palpation of normal ovaries can sometimes create briefly uncomfortable feelings which are often coupled with fears that they might become more uncomfortable. If a patient complains of discomfort in the pelvis or a history of intermittent discomfort, the physician, for obvious reasons, leaves this area or region to be examined last.

Examination of the internal pelvic organs through the anterior rectal wall (a rectal examination) is necessary in very young girls or those of any age with a hymeneal ring which is too narrow to admit one gloved finger. Rectal examinations are essential in obese patients when the palpating hand on the abdomen feels nothing. Rectal examinations should be done in all females (and males) over age 30 or 35 to rule out rectal abnormalities. Some gynecologists routinely check their pelvic "findings" with a rectal examination.

The speculum is a duckbill-shaped instrument which comes in several widths and lengths. It opens like a "duckbill" and expands the vaginal walls, but the portion of the speculum at the introitus opens only slightly. A nasal speculum (such as doctors use to inspect the inside of the nose) can often be used, without discomfort, for vaginal examination in infants and older children. This is usually indicated only when there is some question about congenital abnormalities of the reproductive tract or a history of trauma, for example, criminal manipulation or insertion of some foreign object into the vagina.

The desire to avoid routine pelvic examinations is the normal reaction for most females, whether it is their first or fifteenth, and whether or not they are in or out of the health professions, and whether or not they are comfortable with sexual activity at the personal level. It is an emotionally uncomfortable position to be in, no matter how brief or even physically comfortable it may be. Assuming that some discomfort in the pelvis will go away of its own accord, as it often does, and will not require examination is also a normal behavior pattern. Fear of what the pelvic pain or abnormal bleeding might mean often delays the pelvic examination in young and old.

It is difficult for many women, and often their husbands, too, to feel that a male gynecologist can view and manipulate female genitals without arousal of some sexual feelings. It is equally difficult for some women to believe that the

---

* The speculum may be warmed quickly in warm water from a nearby faucet; this is not an unreasonable request for a patient to make.

genital area can be manipulated without arousal of some unpredictable feelings in the patient, herself. The white coat, the uniformed nurse, the bright lights, and the drapes (sheets) serve a very useful function in removing all sexuality from the atmosphere. The drapes are not used, as some claim, to "hide" a forbidden area.* The attraction which some women feel for their doctors, especially obstetricians and gynecologists, is based on the doctor's sensitivity and listening ability, not on the physical aspects of their "relationship." Many women find that their doctor is the only person they know on whom they can unload all of their personal feelings and questions about their own sexuality. To find a sympathetic, understanding ear in this area of one's life is always a good experience. Sensitivity and nonjudgmental understanding of female concerns is not confined to either sex among gynecologists. The personal and patient experiences of a gynecologist, male or female, are the primary determinants in creating empathy and understanding, and, most important, these allow adaptation to the wide variety of female "types" which come into a busy office every day. Every female is different, with different needs in this area of her life, even though there are some basic similarities. If she finds that a specific doctor does not fit her emotional needs, even though very competent, she should look elsewhere until she finds someone who fills her specific need for a father, mother, sister figure, or simply someone who treats her like an understanding peer.

Plastic Procedure   Surgical repair of a defect; for example, plastic surgery of the face, the vagina, the perineum.

Postcoital Test   Examination of spermatic fluid removed from the vagina shortly (one to four hours) after ejaculation; an infertility procedure to determine numbers and motility of sperm in the natural environment.

Surgical Procedures in the Female

A-P Repair   A plastic procedure which repairs weakened anterior and posterior walls of the vagina.

Colpotomy   Opening the vaginal wall just behind the cervix; depending upon the size of the incision, the opened space may be checked for free blood from a suspected rupture of a tubal pregnancy, or the space may be used to do tubal ligations "from below," or simply to view the position and appearance of the tubes and ovaries, i.e. *colposcopy.*

Conization   Removal of a cone-shaped portion of the cervix surrounding the opening, or the cervical os. This is usually a diagnostic procedure which may also remove a precancerous area of the cervix (see Pap Smear).

Cystoscopy   Viewing the inside of the urinary bladder through the urethra, but occasionally via an opening in the lower abdominal wall.

D and C   Dilatation (D) of the cervical opening to the uterine cavity and currettage (C) (scraping) of the uterine cavity; there are several indications for this procedure: abortion, spontaneous or induced, diagnosis of unexplained uterine

---

* Ellen Frankfort, *Vaginal Politics* (New York: Quadrangle Books, 1972).

bleeding at any age (the removed tissue is examined microscopically), and often a therapeutic (curative) procedure for excessive uterine bleeding of known or unknown cause.

Episiotomy   An incision made in the stretched, posterior perineum early in the second stage of labor, running from the introitus posteriorly, and creating a V-shaped enlargement of the lower end of the posterior vaginal wall and the perineum. This incision shortens the second stage of labor, enables use of forceps when needed, prevents tearing of the perineum during delivery, and is believed to decrease the effects which prolonged stretching might have on the lower vaginal wall and introitus (see Rectocoele, Cystocoele). A "gaping" introitus, without muscular control, is poor sexually, but can be repaired at the time of the next pregnancy, or if no further pregnancies are planned, surgical repair of this area is often combined with an A-P repair (see above), since the two areas are often involved simultaneously.

Female Circumcision   This is not practiced in modern societies and is gradually disappearing, from the upper class on down, in emerging countries. Female circumcision includes many different procedures in different cultures and societies: removal of the foreskin or prepuce over the clitoris, removal of the clitoris, removal of the clitoris and labia majora, removal of the labia majora only, removal of the labia minora only, or any combination of the above.

Hymenotomy   Surgical enlargement of a rigid hymeneal opening, usually followed by two to three weeks of dilatation by the patient. Mechanical dilatation, or repeated stretching, of the nonrigid hymeneal ring may be accomplished in several ways *without* pain or bleeding: the manual manipulation occurring during genital stimulation may be effective over a period of time; stretching the opening with the cardboard tube of some tampons for 30 seconds each time a tampon is used will be effective in two or three menstrual cycles; or, the tampon may be used as a dilator over a two or three week period on a once- or twice-a-day basis; gynecologists have graduated dilators which may be used if the opening is too small to admit a tampon initially. An introitus which admits two fingers is usually dilated enough to allow intercourse. Repeated gentle pressure of the erect penis against the introitus over a period of weeks also acts as a dilating force without discomfort or bleeding (see Fig. 2-4).

Hysterectomy   Removal of the uterus; *total hysterectomy* means removal of the cervix and body (fundus) of the uterus. At one time, "total" was misinterpreted as meaning uterus *and* ovaries. *Panhysterectomy* is an old term for total hysterectomy and was also thought to imply uterus and ovaries. *Subtotal hysterectomy* means removal of fundus only, leaving the cervix at the upper end of the vagina. This is seldom done now. "From above" means removal through an abdominal incision. "From below" means removal through the vagina, a *vaginal hysterectomy*. Removal of the uterus does not affect hormones in any known way, but it does remove the source of the menstrual flow and is a sterilizing procedure. The vagina remains functional whether the procedure is done from above or below.

Laparoscopy   Viewing the organs of the abdominal or pelvic cavity via an instrument inserted in a small incision in the abdominal wall, usually a small incision in the umbilicus.

Laparotomy   A surgical opening of the abdominal cavity (literally "flank") for surgical procedures, or examination of internal organs.

Myomectomy   Removal of myomas or fibroids (see below) from the uterus, leaving the uterus as a functional organ. Usually done if the fibroids are symptomatic and reproductive function is still desired.

Oophorectomy   Removal of the ovary; removal of both ovaries prior to menopause results in sterility and absence of the menstrual (ovulatory) cycle. Estrogen may be replaced with daily oral estrogen.

Salpingectomy   Removal (partial or total) of the Fallopian tube; bilateral total removal results in sterility, and is done only if they are chronically diseased and contribute to chronic pelvic discomfort. If diseased, they are usually nonfunctional.

Uterine Biopsy   Removal of small pieces of the uterine lining with a small currette which requires no anesthesia; this is a diagnostic procedure when there is a question about hormonal dysfunction; the tissue is examined microscopically.

Vaginectomy   Removal of the vagina; this is rare, but increasingly in the public awareness, and associated with vaginal lesions of a known precancerous, or cancerous origin (see p. 225).

Vaginoplasty   Construction of a vagina in males or females, where none existed previously. Three methods are currently used, all of which require dissection of the space and the introduction of a temporary dilator to allow tubular healing and prevent adhesion of the walls during healing. The space may simply be dissected and allowed to heal around the dilator. The space may be lined with skin from the inner thigh. The space may be lined with peritoneum (lining of the abdominal cavity which lies just above the dissected space and can be pulled down into the space) and allowed to heal. With adequate estrogen stimulation, all of these vaginas look like vaginas and act like vaginas, physiologically, within a few months.

Vulvectomy   Surgical removal of the vulva (labia majora); the primary indication is almost always a malignant lesion of the vulva.

Wedge Resection   Removal of a wedge of ovary, usually bilaterally; sometimes done to induce ovulation when absence of ovulation is associated with ovaries which have very thick capsules or coverings.

Medical Conditions in the Female

Bartholinitis   Acute or chronic inflammation of Bartholin's glands (see p. 121).

Cervicitis   Inflammation of the cervix, with or without vaginal discharge, bleeding, or discomfort; treatment may be local antibiotics, cauterization (electrocoagulation), or cryosurgery (freezing).

"Cyst on the Ovary"   Eggs develop in follicles or cysts which enlarge gradually to the time of ovulation and then decrease in size and disappear. Occasionally a cyst remains or enlarges to more than normal size, and the ovary will be tender or uncomfortable, or simply be enlarged to slightly more than usual size when felt during a pelvic examination. Repeat pelvic examinations should be done at two or three month intervals to check whether or not the ovary has increased or decreased in size, or remained the same. An increase in size might indicate that the

enlargement is due to something other than a follicular cyst. If it decreases in size or remains the same over a four or five month period, this would indicate that it was, or is, a follicular cyst.

Cystitis Inflammation of the urinary bladder with symptoms of pain prior to urination, burning with urination, frequency and urgency of urination.

Cystocoele Bulging of the bladder into the weakened anterior wall of the vagina with symptoms of incontinence and difficult urination.

Fibroids Benign growths in the wall of the uterus which may or may not be symptomatic with excessive or irregular bleeding, or a "heavy feeling" depending on their location and their size. These are usually present only in older, premenopausal women and will decrease in size, postmenopause. They can enlarge the uterus to the size of a four month or larger pregnancy, or they can be located on the surface of the uterus with a long or short stalk containing blood vessels. This latter type frequently creates acute emergencies with abdominal pain and bleeding into the abdominal cavity.

Prolapse "The fallen womb"; the ligaments which suspend the uterus in the pelvic cavity stretch and allow the uterus to descend into the vagina, occasionally as far as the introitus, with urinary and bowel symptoms and problems with intercourse (see A-P Repair, Cystocoele, Rectocoele, Vaginal Hysterectomy).

Rectocoele Bulging of the anterior rectal wall and its contents into the posterior wall of the vagina with symptoms of constipation and difficulty with bowel movements.

Salpingitis Acute or chronic disease of the Fallopian tubes (see PID).

Urethritis Inflammation of the urethra with symptoms similar to those of cystitis.

Vaginitis Inflammation of the vagina.

Surgical Procedures in the Male

Castration Removal of both testes. If done before puberty, there will be no development of secondary sexual characteristics (see Pubertal Changes). Traumatic castration (war injuries, accidents) will prevent further sperm production, but if the testes are retrieved in time, they can be implanted in the remains of the scrotum or in the thigh so that hormone production will be maintained. Self-mutilation is occasionally seen in mentally disturbed males. Criminal castration is almost always associated with murder of the victim, the mutilation occurring after death, or sometimes before. Bleeding with castration can be profuse, but seldom exceeds a pint of blood (the amount of a blood donation). The blood vessels along the spermatic cord and in the scrotum retract and narrow rather quickly, stopping the flow (see orchidectomy).

Circumcision Removal of the foreskin or prepuce covering the glans. Usually done, if desired, by the obstetrician at birth, or on the third day after birth (see balanitis, phimosis).

Hernia Repair (also herniorrhaphy) The canal through which the vas deferens passes from the scrotum to the pelvic cavity is occasionally weakened at the outer or inner opening, or the openings are enlarged so that a portion of the abdominal contents will protrude into them, creating a bulge when standing, which usually disappears when lying down. This can be uncomfortable, depending on the extent of the weakened area, and can be dangerous if the bowel gets caught (incarcerated) in the ring at either end of the canal, or in the canal itself. Repair of this weakness obliterates the rings except for a very small area for the vas deferens. Hernias may be congenital defects (a child is born with one or both sides defective) and these quickly show themselves in the first few months of life with straining or crying, or after the child starts walking. They are rarely seen in adolescents or in the twenties and thirties age group. The incidence increases in the older male population when tissues begin to weaken. "Rupture" is another word for hernia. The "truss," a belt with a large pad which is placed over the hernia area to keep it from bulging, is of very little value and simply postpones inevitable repair or may, if the hernia is small, postpone surgical repair until emergency surgery is necessary because the herniated abdominal contents are caught.*

Orchidectomy   Surgical removal of testis or testes. Surgical removal is done if there is a malignant tumor of the testis, or if there is a hormone dependent tumor of the prostate gland (see Castration).

Orchidopexy   Attaching the undescended testis or, rarely, testes to the bottom of the scrotal sac. This is usually done, for aesthetic reasons, prior to school age or at least prior to age eight. If not done prior to the onset of pubertal changes, the testis will not produce sperm.

Penectomy   Surgical removal of the penis; a procedure associated with transsexual surgery, males to females, or with cancer of the foreskin or glans of the penis. Cancer of the penis is extremely rare; some urologists say that they would have to remove "five miles of foreskin to prevent one penile cancer." This comment casts some doubt on the common feeling that circumcision prevents cancer of the penis.

Prostatectomy   Removal of all or a portion of the prostate gland because of benign or malignant growth. A "t-u-r" or *transurethral resection* of the prostate is common in elderly males. A benign hypertrophy of a portion of the prostate may compress the urethra, giving rise to symptoms of dribbling, difficulty in urination, and occasionally cystitis. This portion of the prostate gland is removed via the urethra, using a urethroscope. The entire prostate gland may be removed for malignant disease either from "above" via an incision in the lower abdominal wall or from "below" through the perineum, the area between the base of the scrotum and the rectum. Examination of the prostate gland is done by palpation through the anterior rectal wall.

Vasectomy   Removal of a portion of the vas deferens on both sides for the purpose of sterilization (see Vas Ligation).

---

* Hernias are rare in females. Their area of weakness which allows bulging and/or pain is located just below the inguinal ligament in the upper part of the thigh. In the male, the bulge and discomfort are just above the inguinal ligament.

Medical Conditions in the Male

In general, any portion of the male reproductive tract, (testes, epididymis, seminal vesicles, prostate, urethra) may become involved in infections of any adjacent reproductive structure or even with generalized bacterial or viral infections in the body, for example, gonorrhea, influenza, mumps. These are labeled according to the primary source of discomfort as urethritis, vesiculitis, epididymitis, and so forth.

Balanitis   Inflammation of the glans of the penis; this is associated with phimosis (see below), and retraction of the foreskin is extremely painful, restricting erection and intercourse. This is frequently seen in adult, uncircumcised, diabetic males and is one of the few indications for circumcision in adults.

Hematocoele (he-mah-toe-seal)   Blood (hema-) in the confined cavity (-coele) lying near the testis; usually due to trauma and causes some scrotal swelling; needs definitive diagnosis.

Hematuria   Blood in the urine; seen occasionally with gonorrhea but should always be investigated.

Hydrocoele   A scrotal swelling caused by clear fluid accumulated in the confined space near the testis; sometimes congenital.

Orchitis   Inflammation of the testis or testes, for example, mumps orchitis*; there are symptoms of pain, but very little external swelling because the capsule of the testis is very tight. The primary fear with orchitis is subsequent sterility. Early surgical treatment is often necessary to relieve the pain and decrease the possibility of sterility. The testicular pain associated with excessive sexual stimulation without ejaculation may be relieved by ejaculation, or by taking a deep breath, holding it, and bearing down as if to have a bowel movement.

Peyronie's Disease   Localized thickenings of connective tissue between or around the erectile tissue spaces of the penis; this results in deformed and sometimes painful erections; usually seen in middle-aged and older males; relatively rare.

Phimosis   Adherence of the foreskin to the glans of the penis; not limited to those who are uncircumcised, since circumcision leaves variable lengths of foreskin which should also be retracted daily with cleansing of the base of the glans.

Pyuria   Pus (white blood cells) in the urine indicating infection.

Spermatocoele   A scrotal swelling near the epididymis with fluid containing spermatozoa; needs definitive diagnosis.

Urethritis   Inflammation of the urethra (see VD); this irritation may, as may all other irritations of the genital tract in males, give rise to painful, unpredictable, spontaneous erections.

Varicocoele   A dilated vein (a varix) in the scrotum, along the spermatic cord, usually on the left side, but it may be present on both sides; it may or may not be symptomatic with feelings of pressure and heaviness after standing for a period of time. It usually disappears when lying down. It can be removed, surgically, and some feel that there is a relationship between the presence of a varicocoele and lowered male fertility. This has not been clearly established.

---

* Females may have ovarian pain (oophoritis) with mumps infection.

Bibliography

Chapter 1. Female and Male: *He* Created Them.

D'Antonio, William V. "The Problem of Population Growth in Latin America." In Pike, F. B., ed., *Latin American History: Select Problems.* New York: Harcourt Brace Jovanovich, 1969.

Ehrlich, Carol. "The Male Sociologist's Burden: The Place of Women in Marriage and Family Texts." *The Journal of Marriage and the Family* (August 1971).

Gadpaille, Warren J. "Biological Fallacies of Women's Lib." *Hospital Physician* (1971).

Gilder, George. "On Rediscovering the Difference." *National Review,* 3 August 1973. Excerpted from Gilder, George. *Sexual Suicide.* New York: Quadrangle Books, 1973.

Gornick, Vivian. "Why Radcliffe Women are Afraid of Success." *New York Times Magazine,* 14 January 1973, p. 10.

Kinsey, Alfred C., et al. *Sexual Behavior in the Human Female.* Philadelphia: W. B. Saunders Company, 1953.

————. *Sexual Behavior in the Human Male.* Philadelphia: W. B. Saunders Company, 1948.

McDermott, Sandra. *Female Sexuality.* New York: Simon & Schuster, Inc., 1971.

Mannes, Marya. *Out of My Time.* Garden City, New York: Doubleday and Company, 1971.

Masters, William H. and Johnson, Virginia. *Human Sexual Response.* Boston: Little, Brown and Co., 1966.

Mead, Margaret. *Male and Female: A Study of Sexes in the Changing World.* New York: Dell Publishing Co., Inc., Laurel Edition, 1967.

Money, John and Ehrhardt, Anke A. *Man and Woman, Boy and Girl: Differentiation and Dimorphism of Gender Identity.* Baltimore and London: Johns Hopkins University Press, 1972.

Sherfey, Mary Jane. *The Nature and Evolution of Female Sexuality.* New York: Random House, 1972.

Toffler, Alvin. *Future Shock.* New York: Random House, 1970.

Chapter 2. Intercourse: Anatomy and Physiology, Function and Dysfunction.

Brady, J. P. "Frigidity." *Medical Aspects of Human Sexuality* (November 1967).

————. "Roundtable: Frigidity." *Medical Aspects of Human Sexuality* (February 1968).

Comarr, A. Estin. "Sexual Function Among Patients with Spinal Cord Injury." Long Beach. *Urologica Internationalis* 25 (1970).

Dickenson, R. L. *Human Sex Anatomy.* Baltimore: The Williams & Wilkins Co., 1933.

Mailer, Norman. *The Prisoner of Sex.* Boston: Little, Brown and Co., 1971.

Mann, Thaddeus. "Drugs and Male Sexual Function." *Research in Reproduction,* Planned Parenthood Federation, 4 March 1972.

Masters, William H. and Johnson, Virginia. *Human Sexual Inadequacy.* Boston: Little, Brown and Co., 1970.

————. "Plain Talk for Women Who Lie About Sex." *Redbook,* September 1972.

Seaman, Barbara. *Free and Female: The Sex Life of the Contemporary Woman.* New York: Coward, McCann & Geoghegan, Inc., 1972.

Storr, C. "The Bugaboo of Male Impotence." *Cosmopolitan,* October 1972.

Chapter 3. Intercourse: Reproduction and Pleasure

Berkey, B. R. "Too Tired for Sex: Fighting the Fatigue Factor in Sexual Disharmony." *Medical Aspects of Human Sexuality* (September 1972).

Davids, Ron. "Talking Without Words (Pheromones)." *Science Digest* (February 1973).

"Female Sexuality: What It Is—and Isn't." *Mademoiselle,* July 1971.

Michael, R. P. and Keverne, E. B. "Pheromones in the Communication of Sexual Status in Primates." *Nature,* 25 May 1968.

Wilson, Edward O. "Animal Communication." *Scientific American* (September 1972).

Chapter 4. Intercourse: Violence, Business, Disease

Amir, Menachem. *Patterns in Forceable Rape.* Chicago: University of Chicago Press, 1971.

Barclay, S. *Bondage: The Slave Traffic in Women Today.* New York: Funk and Wagnalls, 1968.

Bell, Robert R. and Gordon, Michael. *The Social Dimension of Human Sexuality.* Boston: Little, Brown and Co., 1972.

Bryan, James H. "Apprenticeships in Prostitution." *Social Problems* 12 (Winter 1965).

Davis, A. J. "Sexual Assaults in the Philadelphia Prison System and Sheriff's Vans." *Transaction,* December 1968.

Fiumara, N. J. "Gonococcal Pharyngitis." *Medical Aspects of Human Sexuality* (May 1971).

————. "Oral Syphilis." *Medical Aspects of Human Sexuality* (September 1972).

Gagnon, John H. and Simon, William. "Sexual Encounters Between Adults and Children." *Siecus* Study Guide No. 11, 1970.

Geis, Gilbert. "Group Sexual Assaults." *Medical Aspects of Human Sexuality* 5 (May 1971).

Hayman, C. R., et al. "Rape and Its Consequences." *Medical Aspects of Human Sexuality* 6 (1972).

———— and Lanza, C. "Sexual Assault on Women and Girls." *American Journal of Obstetrics and Gynecology* 109 (February 1, 1971).

Hirschi, Travis. "The Professional Prostitute." *Berkeley Journal of Sociology,* VII, 1.

Hollander, Xaviera. *The Happy Hooker.* New York: Dell Publishing Co., 1972.

Knee, Steven T. "Complexities of Gonococcal Infection." *Medical Aspects of Human Sexuality* (April 1972).

Millet, Kate. "Quartet for Female Voices." In Gornick, Vivian and Moran, Barbara K. eds., *Women in Sexist Society*. New York: New American Library, 1972.

Owen, R. L. and Hill, L. J. "Rectal and Pharyngeal Gonorrhea in Homosexual Men." *Journal of the American Medical Association* (June 5, 1972).

Pierson, Elaine C. *Sex Is Never An Emergency*. 3rd ed. Philadelphia: J. B. Lippincott Company, 1973.

Pittman, David J. and Rainwater, Lee. *Deviant Behavior: Social Process and Identity*. New York: Holt, Rinehart and Winston, 1972.

Schiff, A. F. "Rape." *Medical Aspects of Human Sexuality* 6 (May 1972).

Schwimmer, W., Ustay, K. and Behrman, S. "Sperm-agglutinating Antibodies and Decreased Fertility in Prostitutes." *American Journal of Obstetrics and Gynecology* 30 (1967).

Shearer, Lloyd. "What Every Woman Should Know—About Self-Defense." *Parade*, 26 August 1973.

Sheehy, Gail. *Hustling*. New York: Delacorte Press, 1973.

The Report of the Commission on Obscenity and Pornography. Washington, D. C.: Superintendent of Documents, U. S. Government Printing Office. Note: The paperback edition (Bantam Books, 1970) does not include reports of studies.

Winick, Charles and Kinsie, Paul M. *The Lively Commerce: Prostitution in the United States*. New York: Quadrangle Books, 1971.

Chapter 5. Reproduction: Endocrinology, Menstruation, Infertility

Behrman, S. J. and Kistner, R. W., eds. *Progress in Infertility*. Boston: Little, Brown and Co., 1968.

McClintock, Martha K. "Menstrual Synchrony and Suppression." *Nature* 229 (January 22, 1971).

Chapter 6. Reproduction: Pregnancy, Labor, Delivery

Berg, Alan. "The Economics of Breast-Feeding." *Saturday Review of The Sciences*, May 1973.

Bing, Elizabeth D. *Adventure of Childbirth*. New York: Simon & Schuster, 1970.

Broadribb, Violet and Lee, Henry. *The Modern Parents' Guide to Baby and Child Care*. Philadelphia: J. B. Lippincott Company, 1973.

Dick-Read, Grantley. *Childbirth Without Fear: The Original Approach to Natural Childbirth*. 4th rev. ed. New York: Har/Row Books, Harper & Row, 1972.

Elger, Marvin S. and Olds, Sally W. *The Complete Book of Breast Feeding*. New York: Workman Publishing Co., Inc., 1972.

Fitzpatrick, Elise, Reeder, Sharon and Mastroianni, Luigi, Jr. *Maternity Nursing*. 12th ed. Philadelphia: J. B. Lippincott Company, 1971.

Guttmacher, Alan F. *Pregnancy and Birth*. New York: New American Library, 1971.

Osofsky, Howard J. *The Pregnant Teenager: A Medical, Educational, and Social Analysis*. Springfield, Ill.: Charles C Thomas, 1972.

Parsons, Talcott. "Definitions of Health and Illness in the Light of American Values and Social Structures." *Social Structure and Personality.* Glencoe, Ill.: The Free Press, 1964.

Salk, Lee. *What Every Child Would Like His Parents to Know.* New York: David McKay Company, Inc., 1972.

Spock, Benjamin. *Baby and Child Care.* Rev. ed. New York: Hawthorne Books, 1968.

Chapter 7. Reproduction: Contraception and Abortion

Abortion Laws: A Survey of Current World Legislation. International Digest of Health Legislation 21 (1970):437-512.

Chessar, Eustace. *The Human Aspects of Sexual Deviation.* New York: William Morrow & Co., 1971.

Drill, Victor A. "Oral Contraceptives and Thromboembolic Disease. Prospective and Retrospective Studies." *Journal of the American Medical Association* 219 (1972).

————. *Oral Contraceptives.* New York: McGraw-Hill Book Company, 1966.

Fried, John. "The Incision Decision." *Esquire,* June 1972.

Greer, Germaine. *The Female Eunuch.* New York: McGraw-Hill Book Company, 1971.

Hafez, E. S. and Evans, T. N. *Human Reproduction: Conception and Contraception.* Hagerstown, Md.: Harper & Row, 1973.

Inman, W. H. and Vessey, M. P. "Investigation of Deaths from Pulmonary, Coronary, and Cerebral Thrombosis and Embolism in Women of Childbearing Age." *British Medical Journal* 2 (1968).

Korda, Michael. *Male Chauvinism! How It Works.* New York: Random House, 1973.

Larned, D. "Programmed for Pregnancy." *UR* (October 29, 1972).

Moyer, Dean L. *Progress in Conception Control.* Philadelphia: J. B. Lippincott Company, 1968.

Osofsky, Howard J. and Osofsky, Joy. *The Abortion Experience: Psychological and Emotional Impact.* Hagerstown, Md.: Harper & Row, 1973.

Pantelakis, S., Papadinitriov, G. C. and Doxiodis, S. "Influence of Induced and Spontaneous Abortions on the Outcome of Subsequent Pregnancies." *American Journal of Obstetrics and Gynecology* (July 15, 1973).

Peck, Ellen. *The Baby Trap.* New York: Bernard Geis Associates, 1971.

Segal, S. J. "Contraceptive Research: A Male Chauvinist Plot?" *Family Planning Perspective* 4 (July 1972).

Stewart, G. K. and Goldstein, P. "Medical and Surgical Complications of Therapeutic Abortions." *American Journal of Obstetrics and Gynecology* 40 (October 1972).

Tunnadine, L. P. *Contraception and Sexual Life: A Therapeutic Approach.* Philadelphia: J. B. Lippincott Company, 1970.

Westoff, C. F. and Bumpass, L. "The Revolution in Birth Control Practices of U.S. Roman Catholics." *Science,* 179, 4068 (January 1973).

Chapter 8. Adolescence

Callahan, Sidney. "For Parents: When Chastity Doesn't Make It." *National Catholic Reporter,* 4 September 1970.

Gardner, Lytt I. *Endocrine and Genetic Diseases of Childhood.* Philadelphia: W. B. Saunders Company, 1969.

Heiss, Jerold, ed. *Family Roles and Interaction.* Chicago: Rand McNally and Co., 1968.

Johnson, Eric W. *Sex: Telling It Straight.* Philadelphia: J. B. Lippincott Company, 1970.

————— and Johnson, Corrine B. *Love and Sex and Growing Up.* Philadelphia: J. B. Lippincott Company, 1970.

Josselyn, Irene M. *Adolescence.* New York: Harper & Row, 1971.

Kantner, John and Zelnick, Melvin. "The Probability of Premarital Intercourse." *Social Science Research* 1 (1972).

—————. "Contraception and Pregnancy: Experiences of Young Unmarried Women in the United States." *Family Planning Perspective* 5 (Winter 1973).

Leslie, Gerald. *The Family in Social Context.* New York: Oxford University Press, 1967.

Maynard, Joyce. *Looking Back: A Chronicle of Growing Up Old in the Sixties.* Garden City, New York: Doubleday and Company, 1973.

Mead, Margaret. *Twelve to Sixteen: Early Adolescence. Daedalus,* Fall 1971.

Tanner, James M. *Growth at Adolescence.* 2nd ed. Oxford, England: Blackwell Science Publication, 1969.

"Teenage Sex: Letting the Pendulum Swing." *Time,* 21 August 1972.

Chapter 9. Premarital and Nonmarital Sex

Anonymous. "My Daughter Changed Sex." *Good Housekeeping,* May 1973.

Bell, Robert R. "Premarital Sex." *Social Deviance.* Homewood, Ill.: Dorsey Press, 1971.

Bieber, Irving, et al. *Homosexuality.* New York: Random House, Vintage Books, 1973.

Christensen, Harold T. and Gregg, Christine E. "Changing Sexual Norms in America and Scandinavia." *Journal of Marriage and the Family* (November 1970).

Driver, Tom F. "Homosexuality: The Contemporary and Christian Contexts." *Commonweal* XCVIII, 5, 1 April 1973.

Erikson Education Foundation. *An Outline of Medical Management of the Transsexual.* September 1971. For this and other publications on this subject write to 4047 Hundred Oaks Avenue, Baton Rouge, La. 70808.

Fink, Peter E. "Homosexuality, A Pastoral Hypothesis." *Commonweal* XCVIII, 5, 1 April 1973.

Horwitz, Elinor Lander. *Communes in America: The Place Just Right.* Philadelphia: J. B. Lippincott Company, 1972.

Johnston, Jill. *Lesbian Nation: The Feminist Solution.* New York: Dutton, 1971.

Ladd, Everett C. "Professors and Political Positions." *Science* 163 (March 1969).

McCaffrey, Joseph A., ed. *The Homosexual Dialectic*. Englewood Cliffs, N. J.: Prentice-Hall, Inc., 1972.

Martin, Del and Lyon, Phyllis. *Lesbian Women*. San Francisco: Glide Publications, 1973. New York: Bantam Books, 1973.

Maynard, Joyce. "The Embarrassment of Virginity." *Mademoiselle,* August 1972.

National Institute of Mental Health Task Force. "Homosexuality: Final Report and Background Papers." Publ. No. (HSM) 72-9116. Washington, D. C.: U. S. Government Printing Office, 1972.

Reiss, Ira. "How and Why America's Sex Standards Are Changing." *Transaction* (March 1968).

Roberts, Ron E. *New Communes: Coming Together in America*. Englewood Cliffs, N. J.: Prentice-Hall Spectrum Book, 1971.

Rossman, Parker. "The Pederasts." *Society* (March-April 1973).

Roxon, Lillian. "The Intelligent Woman's Guide to Sex." *Mademoiselle,* August 1973.

Schmidt, Gunter and Sigusch, Volkmar. "Patterns of Sexual Behavior in West Germany Workers and Students." *The Journal of Sex Research* 7, 2 (May 1971).

Sigusch, Volkmar and Schmidt, Gunter. "Lower-Class Sexuality." *Archives of Sexual Behavior* 1, 1 (1971).

Socarides, Charles. *The Overt Homosexual*. New York: Curtis Books, 1972.

The Wolfenden Report. *Report of the Committee on Homosexual Offenses and Prostitution*. American Ed. New York: Stein and Day, 1963.

Wolff, Charlotte. *Love Between Women*. New York: St. Martin's Press, Inc., 1972.

Chapter 10. Marriage

Bartell, Albert. *Group Sex: A Scientist's Eye Witness Report of the American Way of Swinging*. New York: Peter H. Wyden, 1971.

Bell, Robert R. *Marriage and Family Interaction*. Homewood, Ill.: Dorsey Press, 1963.

Bird, Joseph and Bird, Lois. *The Freedom of Sexual Love*. Garden City, New York: Doubleday and Company, 1970.

Bott, Elizabeth. *Family and Social Network*. London, England: Tavistock Publications, 1957.

Breedlove, W. and Breedlove J. *Swap Clubs*. Los Angeles: Sherbourne Press, 1964.

Burgess, Ernest W. and Locke, Harvey T. *The Family from Institution to Companionship*. 2nd ed. New York: A.B.C., 1953.

Christensen, Harold T., ed. *Handbook of Marriage and the Family*. Chicago: Rand McNally and Co., 1964.

Courtenay, Michael. *Sexual Discord in Marriage: A Field for Brief Psychotherapy*. Philadelphia: J. B. Lippincott Company, 1968.

Cuber, John F. and Haroff, Peggy B. *Significant Americans: A Study of Sexual Behavior Among the Affluent*. New York: Appleton-Century-Crofts, 1965.

De Fleur, M., D'Antonio, W. V. and De Fleur, L. *Sociology: Human Society*. Glenview, Ill.: Scott, Foresman and Company, 1973.

Denfeld, D. and Gordon, M. "The Sociology of Mate Swapping, or the Family that Swings Together Clings Together." *Journal of Sex Research* 6 (May 1971).

Duvall, Evelyn Millis. *Family Development*. 4th ed. Philadelphia: J. B. Lippincott Company, 1971.

Foote, Nelson. "Love." *Psychiatry* 16 (1953).

Humphreys, Laud. *Tearoom Trade*. Chicago: Aldine Publishing Co., 1970.

Johnson, Ralph. "Some Correlates of Extramarital Coitus." *Journal of Marriage and the Family* 32 (1970).

Kirkpatrick, Clifford. *The Family as Process and Institution*. New York: The Ronald Press, 1955.

Laws, Judith Long. "A Feminist Review of the Marital Adjustment Literature: The Rape of the Locke." *Journal of Marriage and the Family* 33, 3 (August 1971).

Liebow, Elliot. *Tally's Corner*. Boston: Little, Brown and Co., 1967.

Masters, William H. and Johnson, Virginia. "Sex and Equality." *Redbook*, March 1972.

O'Neill, George and O'Neill, Nena. *Open Marriage*. New York: M. Evans and Co., 1972.

Orden, Susan R. and Bradburn, Norman. "Working Wives and Marital Happiness." *American Journal of Sociology* 74 (January 1969).

Otto, Herbert, ed. *The Family in Search of a Future*. New York: Appleton-Century-Crofts, 1970.

Palson, Charles and Palson, Rebecca. "Swinging in Wedlock." *Society* 9 (February 1972).

Rainwater, Lee. *Family Design*. Chicago: Aldine Publishing Co., 1964.

Ramey, James. "Emerging Patterns of Behavior in Marriage: Deviations or Innovations." *The Journal of Sex Research* 8 (February 1972).

Roebuck, Julian and Spray, S. Lee. "The Cocktail Lounge: A Study of Heterosexual Relations in a Public Organization." *American Journal of Sociology* 72 (1967).

Rossi, Alice. "Equality Between the Sexes: An Immodest Proposal." *Daedalus* 93 (Spring 1964).

Scanzoni, John. *Sexual Bargaining*. Englewood Cliffs, N. J.: Prentice-Hall, Inc., 1972.

Simon, William and Gagnon, John. "Psychosexual Development." *Transaction* 6, March 1969.

Udry, J. Richard. *The Social Context of Marriage*. 2nd ed. Philadelphia: J. B. Lippincott Company, 1970.

Waller, Willard. *The Family: A Dynamic Interpretation*. New York: Holt, Rinehart and Winston, 1951.

Index

abnormalities, fetal, 223, 224-225, 247
abortion
  causes of, 223-225
  vs. contraception, 186, 207
  criminal, 226-228
  doctors and, 231-233
  induced, 225-231
  spontaneous, 155, 222-225
  and sterility, 105, 138
  therapeutic, 228-231
  types of, 222-223
  viewpoints on, 233-237
abstinence, for contraception, 196-198
adolescence, 239-256
  in the female, 245
  as life-style, 239-241
  in the male, 245-246
  physiology of, 241-248
  psychological aspects of, 249-256
  studies of, 253
  venereal disease in, 111-112, 253
  viewpoints on, 253-256
adrenals, 248
adrenocorticotrophic hormone (ACTH), 248
adultery, *see* extramarital sex
affection, *see* love
aging, 50, 303
amenorrhea, 134, 248
American Friends Service Committee, 234
Ames, Louise B., 255
Amir, Menachem, 123
amniocentesis, 155-156
amnionic fluid, 180-181
anal intercourse, 35, 83, 91, 197
analgesia, in labor, 168-171
androgenic substances, 248
anesthesia, in labor, 168, 178-179
Antosh, L., 124
anus, 35
A-P repair, 322
aphrodisiacs, 69-70
arcflex diaphragm, 205

areola, 35
artificial insemination, 140-141
Association for Voluntary Sterilization, 237
atrophy, 318

Babbage, Stuart, 288
balanitis, 327
Barclay, S., 108, 124
Bartell, Gilbert, 317
bartholinitis, 324
Bartholin's glands, 40, 121
basal body temperature (BBT), 127, 138, 198-199
Batterberry, A., 88
Batterberry, M., 88
beds, 74-75
Behrman, S. J., 124, 142
Bell, Robert, 261, 289, 302, 316
"benign," 318
Berkey, B. R., 88
Bernard, Jessie, 293, 316
Bing, Elizabeth, 165
biopsy, 319
Bird, Joseph, 316
Bird, Lois, 316
birth control pill
  advice about, 212-214
  effects of, 211-215
  endocrinology of, 125, 126
  and the fetus, 224-225
  and menstruation, 133-134, 211-212
  reasons for using, 215, 218
birthchairs, 178
bisexuals, 275
Blackman, Ann, 268
bleeding
  in abortion, 222
  birth control pill and, 211-213
  in menstruation, 130, 134-135, 211-212
  placental bleeding, 160
  withdrawal bleeding, 211-212
"blighted ova," 223